The Mulatta
and the Politics of Race

Teresa C. Zackodnik

D1471392

UNIVERSITY PRESS OF MISSISSIPPI

JACKSON

www.upress.state.ms.us

The University Press of Mississippi is a member
of the Association of American University Presses.

Paperback Edition 2010

Library of Congress Cataloging-in-Publication Data

Zackodnik, Teresa C.
  The Mulatta and the politics of race / Teresa C. Zackodnik.
    p. cm.
  Includes bibliographical references and index.
  ISBN 1-57806-676-X (cloth : alk. paper)
    1. American fiction—African American authors—History and criticism. 2. Race
in literature. 3. American fiction—Women authors—History and criticism.
4. Political fiction, American—History and criticism. 5. Politics and literature—
United States. 6. Women and literature—United States. 7. Racially mixed people
in literature. 8. Race relations in literature. 9. Racism in literature. 10. Women in
literature. I. Title.

PS374.R32Z33 2004
813.009'3552—dc22   2003027611

British Library Cataloging-in-Publication Data available

The Mulatta and the Politics of Race

Contents

Acknowledgments

This project was supported by the Social Sciences and Humanities Research Council of Canada. I am indebted to the staff of several libraries and archives for their assistance: the Bienecke Collection of Yale University, the Rare Books and Manuscripts Division of the Boston Public Library, the British Library Newspaper Library at Colindale, the New York Public Library Main Branch, the Schomburg Center for Research in Black Culture, and the interlibrary loan departments of both McMaster University and the University of Alberta. I wish also to thank research assistants whose work has been invaluable in the development of this book: Jacqueline Baker, Michael Borshuk, and Karen Engle.

Both this project and I, myself, benefited in countless ways from the mentoring, support, and incisive criticism of Donald Goellnicht, Mary O'Connor, Joan Caldwell, and Lorraine York. The chairs of the English department at the University of Alberta since my hiring have supported this work's development, and my thanks go to Patricia Demers, Jo-Ann Wallace, and Jim Mulvihill. Time and again the English department at Alberta has proven to be a dynamic place to work, where I've been lucky to find both friends and a home. Here my students have kept me thinking about the mulatta and future directions for my work in unexpected and always rewarding ways. Susan Hamilton, Daphne Read, and the students of "Public Feminisms" helped to give Chapter 2 its start, and our evening conversations were enlivening.

I count myself very fortunate to have worked with two writing groups while completing this project. Their suggestions and critique, as well as their friendship, have been offered in a truly generous spirit; thanks to Glenn Burger, Lesley Cormack, Judy Garber, Susan Hamilton, Lois Harder, Susan Smith, Mark Simpson, and Heather Zwicker. I am also grateful to Cheryl Suzack for stimulating conversations about race, the law, and critical race theory. To Daphne Read, for talks about African American literature, race in the classroom, and her example as a teacher and scholar, I say a special thanks.

This project has also benefited from the editorial suggestions of Martin Hewitt, Teresa Hubel, Neil Brooks, and the anonymous readers at *American Quarterly* and *Nineteenth-Century Feminisms*. Earlier versions and portions of Chapters 1, 2, 3, and 5 appeared, respectively, as: "Fixing the Color Line: The Mulatto, Southern Courts and Racial Identity," *American Quarterly* 53.3 (September 2001): 420–51; "The Enslaved as Spectacle: Sarah Parker Remond, Ellen Craft, and American Slavery in England," *Nineteenth-Century Prose* 29.1 (2002): 78–102; "Little Romances, the Value of Fiction, and Noble Black Women: Frances Harper's *Iola Leroy* and Pauline Hopkins's *Contending Forces*," *Nineteenth-Century Feminisms* 2 (2000): 103–24; and "Transgressions and Excess: Passing as Parodic Performance in Jessie Fauset's *Plum Bun* and Nella Larsen's *Passing*," in *The Literature of Racial Ambiguity*, ed. Neil Brooks and Teresa Hubel (New York and Amsterdam: Rodopi Press, 2002), 45–69. At the University Press of Mississippi, I thank Craig Gill for his interest in my work, piloting it through the review and publication process and finding a generous reader whose suggestions were insightful. Thanks also to Robert Burchfield at Doghouse Editing and Research Services.

For their unfailing friendship and interest in whether this book would have a life beyond my desk, I am grateful to Katherine Binhammer, Glenn Burger, Gail Corning, Sandra Hagan, Susan Hamilton, Steven Kruger, Carol-Ann Sabean, and Aaron Supryka. Steven Kruger's remarkable friendship, support, and sound judgment continue to be a gift. Finding a dear friend and supportive colleague in Susan Hamilton has been more important than I can say. She offers an understanding I have come to count on.

Lastly, my family has supported both my work and the choices that have led to it, and for this I have been grateful. To Robert Brazeau, whose confidence in me is unstinting and whose support and love I have depended upon time and again, go feelings I can never fully express. But I hope to spend many days trying. Finally, this and everything still to come go to Ailsa, who has made so much possible since she arrived.

Introduction

Let's face it. I am a marked woman, but not everybody knows my name. "Peaches" and "Brown Sugar," "Sapphire" and "Earth Mother," "Aunty," "Granny," God's "Holy Fool," a "Miss Ebony First," or "Black Woman at the Podium": I describe a locus of confounded identities, a meeting ground of investments and privations in the national treasury of rhetorical wealth. My country needs me, and if I were not here, I would have to be invented.

—Hortense J. Spillers, "Mama's Baby, Papa's Maybe: An American Grammar Book"

I think: my raciality is socially constructed, and I experience it as such. I feel my black-self as an eddy of conflicted meanings—and meaninglessness—in which my self can get lost, in which agency and consent are tumbled in constant motion. This sense of motion, the constant windy sound of manipulation whistling in my ears, is a reminder of society's constant construction of my blackness.

Somewhere at the center, my heart gets lost. I transfigure the undesirability of my racial ambiguity into the necessity of deference, the accommodation of condescension. It is very painful when I permit myself to see all this. I shield myself from it wherever possible.

—Patricia J. Williams, *The Alchemy of Race and Rights*

In her 1995 study, *The Politics of Color in the Fiction of Jessie Fauset and Nella Larsen*, Jacquelyn McLendon posed a provocative question that has gone unanswered: "Is it possible, through theorizing, to situate these texts within a specific set of black intertextual relations even though the tragic mulatto is a figure of white creation?" (12). While a critical focus on the mulatta in African American texts has been lacking, both before and since McLendon raised the possibility of this figure's importance to black women writers, the study of passing saw a virtual explosion in the mid-1990s. With conference panels, special journal issues, and essay collections as well as single-author studies, passing and its politics have piqued our interest like never before.[1] It is here that we see the mulatta both granted the most power and most sharply condemned as engaged in an individualist politics that keeps firmly in place that which it questions. Trading on her "whiteness," the passing mulatta is said at once to "interrogate," if not subvert, "the ontology of identity categories and their construction" (Ginsberg 4) and to be wholly dependent upon them, since "[t]he limited subversion of the pass always requires that the terms of the system be intact. It is precisely the presence of rigid and artificial institutional binaries that not only produces the pass but also solicits the social practice of passing" (Robinson, "It Takes One" 735).

To set these views alongside one another suggests that passing is currently being considered in all its complex ambivalence, yet this is often not the case.[2] Rather, criticism on passing tends to position it as subversive, and thus successful, or as complicit, and subsequently failed, as it pursues the larger debate of whether "race" can be read as a performative. This split is the result, Gayle Wald argues, of ignoring or downplaying the "discontinuities" between "the moral, political, and theoretical dimensions of all passing narratives" that mean the "cultural and political implications of . . . 'becoming' black [may] complicat[e] the theoretical questions of racial fluidity and performativity that . . . [passing] brings to light" (15). Consequently, passing is considered as either "the sign of the victim, the practice of one already complicit with the order of things, prey to its oppressive hierarchies" (Tyler 212), or an act that "calls into question the very notion of authenticity . . . [and] threatens to call attention to the performative and contingent nature of all seemingly 'natural' or 'obvious' identities" (Scholssberg 2). Passing narratives are either seen as "concern[ed with] the American mechanism for the cultural and genetic reproduction of whiteness . . . stress[ing] the politics of race espoused by authors who insist on an ethics of racial authenticity as a component of identity" (Mullen 73) or are said to be "about the failure of blackness or whiteness to provide the grounds for a stable, coherent identity" (Kawash 63). Such readings leave the study of passing locked in a dualism that "echoes the binary logic of race" (Wald 15), thereby replicating what such scholarship saw passing itself as potentially interrogating. Moreover, when studies of passing go beyond racial passing to consider gender as an identitarian category that can be staged, thereby "subvert[ing] the cultural logic of gender categories" (Ginsberg 2), they consider "cross-dressing," "transvestism," or "transgendering" and tend to isolate gender from that "complex set of racial injunctions" that, as much as a "heterosexualizing symbolic" (Butler, *BM* 167), form the masculine and feminine imperative in U.S. culture.[3] In other words, while studies of passing acknowledge the imbrications of race, sexuality, gender, and class, most tend to isolate one form of passing for consideration. Yet, since gender, sexuality, and class are strongly racialized, one may be said to "pass" or to perform a gender identity without necessarily crossing from female to male or vice versa, or to stage the perceived sexuality of another race or class without necessarily crossing from straight to queer.

African American women's work with the mulatta figure intervenes in these critical blind spots of passing studies—the binary logic of successful or failed passing, and the tendency to elide the interimplications of identitarian categories in favor of exploring the challenge an act of passing poses to a single category. The mulatta's ambiguous racial identity has made her an ideal figure through which African American women have explored the racialization of gender, sexuality, and class in American society, as well as the ambivalence of passing in ways that go beyond the simple duality of subversive versus complicit acts. While the "tragic mulatta" was the creation of white female abolitionists and functioned in post–Civil War American fiction as a sensationalized figure of ruined womanhood, African American women put the mulatta to diverse political use in antislavery oratory and in fiction from the late 1840s through the 1950s. They used the mulatta figure to invoke and manage both American and British abolitionist empathy and identification; to contest racialized notions of womanhood in the postbellum United States; to critique the politics and proclivities of the "New Negro Renaissance"; to play on the taxonomic fever of early-twentieth-century American culture; and to question postwar optimism at midcentury. Though called to function in critically different ways at these different historical moments, the mulatta figure was used by African American women to rhetorically transgress and contest a color line that attempted to police and secure racial identities as they were interimplicated with class, gender, and sexuality. In order to consider black feminist uses of the mulatta figure, *The Mulatta and the Politics of Race* sets dominant American cultural constructions of the mulatta, particularly juridical and "scientific," against the rhetorical and textual strategies of African American women who used this figure for political purposes from the mid-nineteenth century to the mid-twentieth. The mulatta's politicized play on the color line is more fully understood in the context of judicial decisions and scientific theories that gave voice to competing cultural beliefs in the larger American society. Indeed, as Gabrielle Foreman has recently noted, "[m]ulatto/a-ness as a representational trope often designates a discursive mobility and simultaneity that can raise questions of racial epistemology, while it also functions as a juridical term that constrains citizenship by ante- and postbellum law and force" ("Mama?" 506). Far from fixing the color line, juridical and sociocultural modes of policing and securing racial difference were often anxious about the mulatta, but they also made possible the crossings and transgressions we see occurring in the culture at large and represented in African American women's oratorical and fictional texts.

Frances Harper's *Iola Leroy* (1892), Pauline Hopkins's *Contending Forces* (1899), Jessie Redmon Fauset's *Plum Bun* (1929) and *The Chinaberry Tree* (1931), and Nella Larsen's *Quicksand* (1928) and *Passing* (1929), focusing on mulatta heroines, are frequently read as adopting white values and a bourgeois ethos.[4] However, these writers arguably "talk out both sides of their mouths," signifying on the very values they have been accused of colluding with, and accessing narrative strategies used by both "mainstream" and African American writers in order to challenge constructions of race and racialized womanhood.[5] Such textual strategies are all the more evident when we place these writers in the larger context of African American women's political culture that included the abolitionist work of Ellen Craft and Sarah Parker Remond, who embodied and invoked the figures of the "white slave" and the tragic mulatta. In perhaps more recognizably political uses of the mulatta through double-voiced appeals on the abolitionist platform, we see the roots of textual strategies employed by African American women writers in the late nineteenth through the mid-twentieth centuries. Thus, in African American women's rhetorical and textual strategies, we can trace a development or genealogy of the mulatta as a figure of hybridity who reaches across, challenges, and confounds the color line. Far from being a "whitened" ideal, the mulatta becomes a liminal figure who transgresses racial distinctions and racialized notions of womanhood in order to challenge dominant cultural understandings of such identity categories. The mulatta is a highly ambivalent figure who enables a double-voiced address and a black feminist use of parodic performance or "passing."

Through the 1850s, Ellen Craft and Sarah Parker Remond played on their white reform audiences' interest in and identification with the mulatta and redirected their attention to the material conditions of American slavery they were being called to oppose. Frances Harper and Pauline Hopkins created mulatta heroines who "pass" for "true women" yet also embody a noble black womanhood in texts that openly contested late-nineteenth-century American notions of racial difference. Finally, Jessie Fauset's and Nella Larsen's mulattas critique both sides of the Jazz Age color line and pass across it in various ways. While Craft and Remond must be understood in the context of a developing transatlantic feminist abolitionist network and its tropes, they also engaged in a degree of passing themselves. Craft passed for a white man in order to escape slavery, an escape that, along with her promotion as "The White Slave," became drawing cards for her appearances on the antislavery lecture circuit with her husband, William, and fellow abolitionist William Wells Brown. Remond, though free-born, never mentioned her status in her lectures and seems to have "passed" with her white British audiences as another "sable visitor" or fugitive slave lecturer. Consequently, she was able to use the Victorian fad for black Americana to her advantage. The mulattas in the works of Harper, Hopkins, Fauset, and Larsen also undertake acts of passing of various natures that confound the color line and should be read in the context of both an American racial imaginary and an African American cultural practice of dissemblance that challenged racial hegemony. Be it the way in which African American minstrel performers gained control of their blackface performances and what they signaled, or the carnivalesque practices of Election Day, an African American tradition of subversive performance that confuses authentic with counterfeit is longstanding. The mulatta in the appearances, oratorical texts, and fiction of African American women can be said to participate in what Joseph Roach has called "genealogies of performance." These mulattas function as "manifest[ations]," "transmi[ssions]," and "reinvent[ions]" (Roach xi) of a fetishistic figure, originally the product of white American imagination, to become figures engaged in parodic performances that should be read as part of an ongoing "historical transmission and dissemination of [African American] cultural practices through collective representations" (Roach 25) like the parodies of white power enacted on Election Day.

The Mulatta

The mulatta's challenge, it is important to note, is not limited to a color line white Americans have historically policed. As Stuart Hall argues, naturalizing and fixing categories of identity like "blackness" also entail a policing of the color line from the "other" side: "[A]s always happens when we naturalize historical categories, we fix that signifier ["black"] outside of history, outside of change, outside of political intervention. . . . We are tempted to display that signifier as a device which can purify the impure, bring the straying brothers and sisters . . . into line, and police the boundaries—which are of course political, symbolic, and positional boundaries—as if they were genetic" (30). Such policing, then, takes place on both sides of the color line, underscoring that the mulatta and passing challenge both "blackness" and "whiteness." Historically, whites have worked to blacken biracial individuals in order to ensure white "purity" by assigning everything "other" to "blackness," but African Americans also have a history of regarding people of white American and African American descent as "not black enough" at times. Michael Awkward has noted that policing what is black and what might not be black enough entails both "border disputes" with the "adversarial racial other" and "intraterritorial responses to the adoption of behaviors, world views, and methods of interrogation which those who seek to determine racial meaning assume are not endemic to their specific cultural place" (3).

It should come as little surprise, then, that the mulatta has been a vexed figure for African American studies.[6] The creation of white female abolitionist Lydia Maria Child, the mulatta became popular in American fiction as the "tragic mulatta" in antislavery tracts published from 1845 to 1865 (Berzon 54).[7] These tracts, and particularly Child's work, "encoded the oppression of race, gender and condition in . . . a series of plots centering on the sexual abuse of female slaves," thereby risking "feeding our national obsession with interracial sex" more than drawing the reader's attention to the peculiar institution and its abolition (Yellin 54, 74). Moreover, the tragic mulatta in the hands of white female abolitionists became a vehicle or "proxy" for articulating the oppression of free white women, as the trope of "woman as slave" grew in currency from the 1820s through the mid-1860s.[8] Critics have characterized tragic mulatta plots as conceiving of "blackness . . . as taint" (Gillman 229), plots in which the "almostwhite character['s] . . . beauty, intelligence, and purity are forever in conflict with the 'savage primitivism' inherited from . . . her Negro ancestors" (Berzon 99). Consequently, we have understood the early history of this figure to be that of a doomed "whitened ideal" who communicates white notions of racial difference to a largely white audience or who expresses white women's concerns about their material condition. Despite this early history, however, the mulatta, and even the "tragic mulatta," has been variously characterized by both white and black American writers. In fact, Werner Sollers argues that the "tragic mulatta is less stereotypical than we have been led to believe" (238) making "the insistence on naming or otherwise invoking [her] . . . itself . . . a stereotype that could profit from some fresh investigation" (228).

This need for fresh investigation is particularly true of African American writers' use of the mulatta figure, given that scholarship in this area frequently invokes elements of much earlier criticism without interrogating its reading protocols and subsequent demands for particular representations. Sterling Brown's 1937 definition of the "tragic mulatta," revised by critics who followed him, contains elements that arguably resurface in more recent criticism, thereby continuing to determine our readings of the mulatta figure and our assessments of the writers who employed her.[9] Unacknowledged, and perhaps largely unknown, is Brown's derivation of this definition from John Herbert Nelson, a Southern apologist and racial conservative (Sollers 233), and frequently unrecognized is the way in which Brown's reading, and so too the subsequent criticism that is indebted to it, is based on a realist aesthetics. It is worth summarizing Brown's elements of the "tragic mulatta" in order for us to recognize these critical echoes. Brown tended to homogenize narratives that focused on mulatta characters as "tragic mulatta" narratives, which he pronounced abstract, clichéd, unrealistic, and unoriginal; he argued such fiction avoided serious issues and more "representative" black characters in favor of depicting mulattos as intelligent and mulattas as beautiful but "doomed." For Brown, this fiction supported racist beliefs because it represented inherited traits as divided by blood, with whiteness credited with positive traits and blackness with negative ones. Consequently, he concluded that whites were the sole readers interested in these narratives because the characters were nearly white and reaffirmed their racial prejudice. Finally, Brown contended that even though white writers were more apt to use the tragic mulatta "stereotype," it remained just that, a consistent stereotype across the work of both black and white writers.[10]

Brown's reliance on the criteria of a realist aesthetics was not limited to critical and reading protocols of the late 1930s. Rather, as Claudia Tate points out, the Black Arts or Black Aesthetic movement of the late 1960s and early 1970s continued to judge the mulatta figure harshly on similar grounds decades later. The Black Arts movement did not ask "whether, for example, the preponderance of light-skinned characters in the late-nineteenth-century domestic novels signaled a meaning other than racial ambivalence and/or intraracial privilege of light skin color" (Tate 80). Both of these possibilities, of course, stem from realist readings and demands, allowing little in the way of a politicized use for the mulatta figure in the work of African American women. Full-length studies focused on the mulatta in American literature are few, and, with the exception of Werner Sollers, their authors quote Sterling Brown as informing their reading of this figure and assert that "in black-authored fiction, the mulatto functions in much the same way" she or he does in "the white literary tradition," as a tragic figure because she or he "wants to be white . . . [and] is physically like the white author" and reader

(Dearborn 140).[11] Following Gabrielle Foreman's definition, we might call these readings of the mulatta figure "white mulatto/a genealogies," given their "over-emphasis on patrilineal descent and an identification with and projection of white desire that continually revisits the paternal and the patriarchal, the phallic and juridical Law of the (white) Father" ("Mama?" 506).

In addition to this critical trend dismissing the mulatta figure as a racist white creation who cannot escape her (white) origins circulates the rather entrenched, but more recent, reading of the mulatta as enabling cultural mediation or dia-logue across the color line. Again, in such readings the possibility that the mulatta may be a figure for challenging the color line, an American racial imag-inary, and interimplicated identitarian categories is not considered. In her land-mark 1987 study, *Reconstructing Womanhood*, Hazel Carby argued that "the figure of the mulatto should be understood and analyzed as a narrative device of mediation" (89). Critics continued to follow Carby's lead through the 1990s and beyond. For example, Susan Gillman sees the mulatta as central to a tradition of "race melodrama," which she sees as "[f]undamentally a literature of *race rela-tions*" (224). Siobhan Somerville not only affirms Carby's assertion but also cites Judith Berzon and Mary Dearborn, whose work on the mulatta derives from Brown's, as she argues that the mulatta is a "vehicle for narrative conflict and ten-sion" because she "symbolizes both psychic and social dilemmas" (79–80, 84). Despite the developments in the field since Carby's study, we have not pressed on this reading of the mulatta as a passive device that "has two primary func-tions: as a vehicle for an exploration of the relationship between the races and, at the same time, an expression of the relationship between the races" (Carby, *Reconstructing* 89).

The Mulatta and the Politics of Race proposes that African American women speakers and writers quite consciously used the mulatta as a highly political figure to enter developing debates regarding identity and the position of black women at distinct moments in the nineteenth and twentieth centuries. I use the term "mulatta figure" in this study in a deliberately nonrealist way, but rather to name the trope recurring in the texts, both oratorical and fictional, on which this study focuses. Characters who we might argue are not phenotypically mulatta—that is, having one "black" and one "white" parent—function as mulatta figures in the texts under consideration. To continue to pursue or invoke terminology at one time operative within a virulent system of racial categorization that might strike us as more "accurate" risks reinscribing race as biological reality rather than social construct, but it also risks eliding this figure's work in and development

across these texts.[12] Rather than naively participating in an obsessive racial classification that terms like "mulatta," "octoroon," and "quadroon" upheld, African
American women mobilize the mulatta figure to interrogate and challenge
notions of racial difference and the hierarchies they furthered. Finally, the
"mulatta figure," with mulatta/mulatto's connotation of "twoness"—the *Oxford
English Dictionary* notes its derivation from the Spanish for *mule*, the usually
sterile offspring of an ass and a mare—signals the double-voiced appeal these
African American women most frequently employed to address their audiences and
signify on existing cultural beliefs, texts, and representations.[13] Joseph Roach's
notion of performance proves quite useful in understanding the mulatta in
African American women's texts, in its doubleness, as more than a simple reinscription of that "tragic" figure of white imagination. As Roach conceives of it,
performance is " 'restored behavior' or 'twice-behaved behavior,' . . . behavior
that 'is always subject to revision' " (3). More than repetition, "the restoration of
behavior . . . [necessitates] reinvent[ion] or recreat[ion]. . . . [R]estored behavior
[is] not merely . . . the recapitulation but . . . the transformation of experience
through the displacement of its cultural forms" (Roach 29). At the hands of
African American women writers and orators, the mulatta of tragic mulatta fame
is restored rather than reinscribed, and in the process she is transformed and the
racial work she performed displaced so that she becomes not a figure through
which white fantasies of racial difference are played out but rather one through
which the color line is tested and transgressed.

Double Voice and Black Women's Texts

African American women speakers and writers like Craft, Remond, Harper,
Hopkins, Fauset, and Larsen "talked out both sides of their mouths," using the
mulatta to offer a double-voiced address to the audiences of their appearances
and lectures or to signify on the very values they have been accused of colluding
with in fiction that accesses both "mainstream" and African American narrative
strategies to challenge their era's constructions of womanhood and race. These
black women engaged in complex forms of address that at times evoked certain
audience responses only to challenge, redirect, or parody them. A technique of
appeal that seems to have been quite central to the oratorical efforts of antebellum African American women and, as Carla Peterson argues, a discourse used
"to write racial uplift" in nineteenth-century African American literary texts,

"African-American writers [and speakers] constructed a productive discourse generated from within the [African American] community that borrows the vocabulary and categories of the dominant discourse only to dislocate them from their privileged position of authority" (14). The seemingly straightforward "borrowing" of existing "vocabulary," "categories," representations, and rhetorical or narrative techniques from "the dominant discourse" is key to double-voicedness: "Indeed, while this African-American discourse appears merely to reiterate the dominant discourse, it in fact disrupts it and 'challenges its boundaries.' . . . [I]t introduces what [Homi] Bhabha has called 'denied knowledges' from the native culture into the dominant discourse so as to 'estrange' that latter's 'basis of authority' " (Peterson 14).

In their abolition work, African American women orators often found themselves speaking to predominantly white audiences and working within reform movements that attended little to the needs of African American women. Consequently, double-voiced addresses enabled them to appear to offer well-worn appeals to the empathy of their white listeners, encourage their identification with the bondsmen and -women who were the subjects of their lectures, yet also critique that very empathy and identification as eliding the differences in material condition between free white and enslaved blacks to which they were calling attention. In their fiction, black women used a double-voiced discourse to address the concerns of an African American audience while appearing to appease or appeal to a white audience. Double voice was also used to invoke certain stereotypes and cultural conventions circulating on both sides of the color line in order to play on them in ways that have often gone unnoticed. In other words, these speakers and writers negotiated audiences and readerships in ways that were ambivalent and multivalent, but they also negotiated dual "traditions," signifying on existing tropes or motifs within contemporary genres for alternative purposes.

While Henry Louis Gates has argued that "the black tradition is double-voiced," and that "Signifyin(g) . . . as formal revision . . . is at all points double-voiced" (*Signifying* xxv, 22), African American women's rhetorical and literary texts are arguably distinctive within this "tradition" given their racial "otherness" to the dominant culture and their gendered "otherness" within their own communities.[14] In other words, black women speak across the charged lines of race and gender, making it imperative that we focus our attention on both interracial and intraracial dynamics and concerns as they impinge upon and are addressed by black women. Using the dialogic theory of Mikhail Bakhtin, as does Gates in elaborating his theory of "Signifyin(g)," Mae Henderson reminds us that "black women speak from a multiple and complex social, historical, and cultural position-ality" ("Speaking" 119). This positionality, argues Henderson, necessitates that black women "enter simultaneously into familial, or *testimonial* and public, or *competitive* discourses," speaking "a discourse of racial and gendered difference in the dominant or hegemonic discursive order . . . [and] a discourse of racial and gender identity and difference in the subdominant discursive order" ("Speaking" 121). Consequently, what Henderson calls "the interlocutory charac-ter of black women's writings," to which I would add black women's oratory, bespeaks "a relationship of difference and identification with the 'other(s)' " both across the color line and intramurally ("Speaking" 118).

To say that black women negotiate their complex positionality through double-voiced discourse is not to suggest, however, that they take up a mediating role between black and white, between male and female. We must remember that Henderson cites "competitive discourses" as operative within black women's double-voiced address. Unlike the prevailing critical consensus on the mulatta as a narrative device of mediation, I read these texts, both oratorical and literary, as contesting rather than mediating the bounds of racial and racialized gender identities. These women trespass on territory that was fiercely protected and policed in their day and continues to be in our own, a trespassing that can be produc-tive, as Henderson has argued elsewhere: "[A]lthough 'to transgress' literally translates as 'to step across,' it also carries with it legal and moral connotations—as in 'trespass'—which are essentially negative. Therefore, breaking down structures of resistance not only speaks to breaching the ramparts that bolster the systems of containment and categorization . . . it also concerns the modifying of limits in order to transform the unknown or forbidden (metaphorical borderlands) into habitable, productive spaces for living" ("Introduction" 2).

Signifyin(g) and Performativity

Henderson's transformation of the forbidden into the habitable strongly echoes Henry Louis Gates Jr.'s theorization of "Signifyin(g)," that African American trope of tropes that turns on indirection, repetition, and reversal. Quoting Bakhtin, Gates calls signifying "black double-voicedness" or "a black double-voiced word," in the Bakhtinian sense "a word or utterance . . . decolonized for the black's pur-poses 'by inserting a new semantic orientation into a word which already has—and retains—its own orientation' " (*Signifying* 51, 50).[15] Importantly, Gates differentiates between what he terms unmotivated and motivated signifying. Gates likens unmotivated signifying to pastiche and calls it "literary history naming itself" by referencing, in a nonadversarial way, texts in the black tradition that have come before. Motivated signifying, however, is like parody but specifically functions in the black literary tradition "to redress an imbalance of power, to clear a space, rhetorically [and to] . . . achieve occupancy in this desired space" (*Signifying* 124). Most important, perhaps, is an understanding of signifying not only as a trope that produces meaning through indirection or reversal but also as a trope of "repetition and revision, or repetition with a signal difference" (*Signifying* xxiv).

Whether one recognizes that "signal difference" is at the heart of signifying itself. Citing the Signifying Monkey Tales, an African American oral form, Gates underscores that "the Monkey dethrones the Lion only because the Lion cannot read the nature of his discourse. . . . In other words, the Monkey speaks figuratively, while the Lion reads his discourse literally" (*Signifying* 85). This means that we must bear in mind that signifying gestures can go unnoticed, that "the inherent irony" of signifying or a double-voiced discourse may "not be understood" by those not "possessing the mastery of reading" that a speaker or writer may be invoking in her or his act of signifying (Gates, *Signifying* 77). After all, this rhetorical strategy turns on indirection. Moreover, the possibility that a discourse can be misread or read rather differently depending upon one's mastery or knowledge further necessitates we consider that texts can be read quite differently by readerships in different cultural locations and with different cultural knowledges. A characteristic common to the texts considered in *The Mulatta and the Politics of Race* is their double-voicedness, their signifying, which produces dual messages and enables multiple readings. This complexity has made for frequent and rather long-lived misreadings, the most common being these texts' wholesale complicity in what they are, in fact, interrogating. In a sense, these texts can be said to "pass" with readers who are unable to notice or comprehend "the inherent irony" or site and mode of their critiques. To consider the importance of the reader to signifying presses on Gates's theory, for as William Spurlin has noted, "the view of reading presupposed in [Gates's] theory of African-American literary criticism still seems very much predicated on . . . internal feature[s] of the text, signifying in themselves, prior to and unmediated by the act of reading" (735). Rather than limiting our understanding of signifying to that which is inherent to the black text, *The Mulatta and the Politics of Race* argues that texts may signify in rather different ways, and signify on different expectations, given the readerships they address. And it is possible, indeed it is a common feature in the texts considered in this study, for that signifying to be multiple, so that texts can be read very differently by readerships that come to them with different values, different understandings of "racial difference," or different expectations of genre.

The Mulatta and the Politics of Race, then, reads these texts through Gates's theories of signifying, adding Mikhail Bakhtin's, Linda Hutcheon's, and Margaret Rose's theories of parody as an ambivalent narrative strategy that is a double-voiced and multileveled hybrid composed of two orders or voices that are both opposed to, and mutually reinforce, one another. Enabling us to consider the ambivalence of the mulatta, they argue that the parody resembles the parodied text, thereby reinscribing its value at the same time it contests that value or hegemony but also paradoxically gaining a certain currency it would otherwise lack. Parody is both destructive and reconstructive, opposes what it resembles, is both critical of and sympathetic to its target. Throughout, The Mulatta and the Politics of Race explores the performances in which African American women orators or the mulatta heroines of African American women's fiction were engaged as frequently parodic. While Gates would confine the African American trope of "Signifyin(g)" to a largely rhetorical strategy, The Mulatta and the Politics of Race seeks to expand that theory to include acts as modes of signifying. While Gates does consider jazz as well as the "play of language—both spoken and body language," or the performance of signifying and not only its content, I would like to press on his unelaborated assertion that "Signifyin(g) [is] a structure of performance" that applies to more than "verbal and musical texts" (Signifying 69). Ellen Craft's performances as "the white slave" and Sarah Remond's as that oddity of "the sable visitor" and lecturer also signify on their audiences' expectations and sensational interests. The mulatta heroines of Harper's, Hopkins's, Fauset's, and Larsen's novels enact a form of signifying that I call a parodic performance of racialized womanhood, and when she passes, the mulatta often signifies on interimbricated notions of gender, race, and sexuality. These women speakers and writers also employ signifying as a rhetorical strategy that plays on, contests, and works to revise notions of "blackness" and "whiteness," existing narrative forms and rhetorical tropes, and the reception of their texts. In order to fully apprehend the signifying strategies of African American women as they mobilize the mulatta as politicized figure, we need to read signifying as rhetorical or textual strategy, as interplay between text and reader, and as act. The Mulatta and the Politics of Race works, then, to bring together theories of signifying and parody with theories of performance and performativity. These connections are suggested by Gates's contention that "Signifyin(g) [is] a structure of performance," and by the echoes between his theory and definitions of performativity like that of John Kronik in his "Editor's Note" to the 1992 special issue of *PMLA* on performance: "The performative . . . is a cultural act, a critical perspective, a political intervention" (45).[16]

Performativity, however, has been the subject of debate within both studies of racial passing and African American studies, as critics have considered whether race can be said to be a performative and, if so, what its political or critical possibilities might be. As Andrew Parker and Eve Kosofsky Sedgwick succinctly define it, "performativity has enabled a powerful appreciation of the ways that identities are constructed iteratively through complex citational processes" (2). Yet the ethics of readings enabled by theories of performativity are called into question by African Americanists like Valerie Smith, who finds that such theories risk eliding the historical and lived experience of racialization and gendering in the United States: "I find discussions of the performativity of race and gender . . . of limited usefulness precisely because . . . I resist the evacuation of historical experience from the construction of raced and gendered bodies" (51). Moreover, the question of whether performativity permits of a "choosing" or agential subject is a significant one, both to critics interested in resistant literary or cultural productions of historically oppressed peoples and to those who argue that performativity theorizes the subject as constructed, thereby calling its "political promise" (Rothenberg and Valente 295) or resistant potential into question. Those critical of Judith Butler's theories of performativity have faulted her for "rel[ying] on a volitional politics even as she disavows volitionality in her model of subjectivity," of "asserting a willed citationality that she claims can reliably control and subvert the very conventions on which it depends" (Rothenberg and Valente 295). Butler has answered such criticism in *Bodies that Matter* by arguing against a "choosing subject . . . at the center of [her] project" and for an understanding of "construction as constitutive constraint," which "does not foreclose the possibility of agency, [though] it does locate agency as a reiterative or rearticulatory practice, immanent to power, and not a relation of external opposition to power" (x, 15). This understanding of agency as "located within the possibility of a variation on that repetition" or reiteration (Butler, *Gender Trouble* 145) and Butler's contention that "if subversion is possible, it will be a subversion from within the terms of the law, through the possibilities that emerge when the law turns against itself" (Butler, *GT* 93), are highly suggestive for reading the mulatta figure as engaged in parodic performatives, acts of signifying, that in their ambivalence interrogate the construction of identities and the possibilities of their subversion. I say "possibilities," for questions about whether conceiving of race as a performative undoes it "as a strategy of social power" (Wald 95) and whether "the logic of performativity" can " 'solve' the problem of institutional subversion or recuperation" (Robinson, "Forms" 237) are not confined to current criticism. Rather, as we will see, those African American women speakers and writers for whom the mulatta was a useful politicized figure with which to challenge notions of race and racialized womanhood were not always convinced that the mulatta's "passing" undid the hierarchies they sought to interrogate and redress. Instead, the mulatta was, they seem to have acknowledged, a figure that came with certain risks, one in which they were not always fully invested, and one that, importantly, did not neatly resolve questions of identity and power but enabled a more complex exploration of their workings on both sides of the color line.

Performing "Blackness," Performing "Whiteness"

If the mulatta's various acts of "passing" are arguably acts of signifying and parodic performatives, they are also part of an African American cultural tradition of subversive performance and should be considered in that context. However much African American studies has seemed unwilling to consider passing, or the performance of "whiteness," as part of a tradition that includes the performance of stereotyped "blackness," the connections between the two are potentially fruitful and offer us another way to reconsider "passing" in its various forms in African American women's texts.

Thanks to criticism on minstrelsy by scholars like Eric Lott, Michael Rogin, and W. T. Lhamon Jr., we have come to a more complex understanding of blackface performance. Lott's study was groundbreaking in its call to recognize that even while performing a stereotype, African American minstrel and vaudeville entertainers exercised a degree of control over, and distanced themselves from, caricatures of blackness.[17] Yet we seem to be more hesitant to read the performance of whiteness or passing in a similar register. Rather than reading African Americans playing "the darky" as assimilating to a white racist notion of "the Negro," Lott carefully distinguished between "a structured set of white responses" to African American culture and African American culture and expressivity itself, as well as between levels or layers of imitation in such performances. "[I]t was possible for a black man in blackface, without a great deal of effort, to offer credible imitations of white men imitating him," argued Lott (101). "The primary purpose of the mask, then, may have been as much to maintain control over a potentially subversive act as to ridicule" (Lott 113). Despite this work on minstrelsy, African American studies remains largely resistant to reading racial passing as a potentially subversive act. Yet perhaps minstrelsy and the mulatta are more intimately connected than we have yet considered. For Lhamon, minstrelsy "respon[ded] to 'amalgamation'. . . by enacting miscegenation. Blackface performers worked out ways to flash white skin beneath a layer of burnt cork, stage the pastiche grammar of a creole dialect, and recast traditional Irish melodies with fantasy images of fieldhand fun shadowed by violence and dislocation. . . . Blackface minstrelsy was a . . . complex attempt to understand racial mixing and accommodate audiences to it" (42).

Minstrelsy was complex and mixed; it spoke to a variety of social anxieties, including class and racial differences, as well as the fear that these distinctions were not always maintained. It could be both coercive for African Americans and profoundly unsettling to those whites who paid to see its images, as Ralph Ellison observed in his 1958 essay "Change the Joke and Slip the Yoke." Ellison notes that while the image of blackness generated by minstrelsy was initially *performed* by white showmen and later by African American vaudeville entertainers, the stereotype was often thrust upon African Americans, generally, who were expected to *embody* it. "These entertainers . . . in order to enact a symbolic role basic to the underlying drama of American society assumed a ritual mask and role taken on by white minstrel men when *they* depicted comic Negroes. Social changes . . . have made for certain modifications (Rochester operates in a different climate of rhetoric, say, than did Stepin Fetchit)," writes Ellison, "but the mask, stylized and iconic, was once required of anyone who would act the role. . . . [I]t was our Negro 'misfortune' to be caught up associatively in the negative side of this basic dualism of the white folk mind, and to be shackled to almost everything it would repress from conscience and consciousness"(47–48). Ellison goes on to point out that while white Americans may live "unmarked" by race, white identity is inextricably bound up in constructions of the "other": "Here another ironic facet of the old American problem of identity crops up. For out of the counterfeiting of the black American's identity there arises a profound doubt in the white man's mind as to the authenticity of his own image of himself" (53). If minstrel caricatures of blackness could cause an uncertainty in white Americans regarding the stability of their identity, what effect might an increasing awareness that whiteness was performable have had? Certainly, anyone who read the numerous articles on passing in newspapers and journals, as well as novels of passing written by white and black Americans alike, was aware that passing for white was not only the subject of narrative but an American reality. And while readings of passing as subversive are often undercut by the assertion that it is an ambivalent act that partakes of and depends upon the very power structure we would like to see it challenging, the ambivalence of minstrel masking has not, likewise, kept us from inquiring into its complexity and the threat to white identity it may have presented.

We know that minstrelsy and its performances of stereotyped blackness reached their greatest popularity from the 1840s through the 1850s. But by the turn of the century, with minstrelsy's development into vaudeville, the parodies of minstrel blackface that African American performers had engaged in all along became decidedly more pronounced and pointed challenges to white power and authority. Through the popular success of vaudeville shows from the 1890s into the twentieth century, African Americans moved from controlling their individual performances and collaborating with whites in the creation of shows to writing, producing, and staging their own shows. Bert Williams and George Walker, who initially performed in blackface in minstrel productions, became instrumental in the development of black musical comedies like their own *Bandana Land, Sons of Ham,* and *In Abyssinia.* In the 1890s Williams and Walker were performing their parody of minstrel shows in New York, advertising themselves as "Two Real Coons," and by 1903 their *In Dahomey* was one of the first black comedy revues to play on Broadway (Anderson 36–38). Bob Cole and Billy Johnson staged *A Trip to Coontown* in 1897—"the first musical farce written, produced, and owned by Afro-Americans" (Krasner 318). David Krasner argues that these early black comedies facilitated both the presence of African Americans in American theater and the development of an African American dramatic tradition: "Black theatre emerged in a state of opposition, creating a form of 'hidden transcripts.' . . . Parody surfaced as a performative subversion of white authority, undermining and destabilizing racist stereotypes" (318). For example, Cole and Johnson's *A Trip to Coontown* ended with a finale entitled "No Coons Allowed," parodying American racism while dramatizing African American lived experience under its effects:

No coons allowed
No coons allowed

This place is meant for white folks that's all
We don't want no kinky-head kind
So move on darky down the line
No coons allow'd in here at all. (qtd. in Krasner 318)

While African Americans performed and parodied white notions of blackness in minstrel and vaudeville shows and later in black musical comedies, African Americans also undertook performances of whiteness. Ralph Ellison asserts that survival strategies rather than self-denigration formed the foundation of the " 'darky' act": "Very often, however, the Negro's masking is motivated . . . by a profound rejection of the image created to usurp his identity. Sometimes it is for the sheer joy of the joke; sometimes to challenge those who presume, across the psychological distance created by race manners, to know his identity" (55). Literal survival also motivated African Americans who masked their identities or performed alternative identities during slavery. A number of African American women escaped from slavery by performing whiteness and/or masculinity so well that they were never suspected of being runaways. William Still's *The Underground Railroad* (1879) tells of Maria Weems's decision to disguise herself as a boy and successfully escape from her master. And there is, of course, William and Ellen Craft's famous escape in which Ellen posed as an ailing white Southern gentleman, as well as Harriet Jacobs's two performances in blackface as a sailor, performances so successful that "the father of my own children came so near that I brushed against his arm; but he had no idea who it was" (Jacobs 172).

These strategies of performing identities to gain physical freedom, or donning the mask of blackness to earn a living, can arguably be seen as part of a tradition of African American performance that undermines white authority and works to redress an imbalance of power. Indeed, there is an established African American tradition of engaging in performances that ridiculed or played whites for fools and worked to subvert hierarchies and social divisions. Perhaps the most well known example of such performances is Election Day, in effect a communal parody of whiteness. Dating from the 1750s, Election Day was an annual carnivalesque celebration. "On this day blacks chose their own government officials, who had real power among themselves and, for the space of the celebration at least, symbolic power over whites. Part appropriation of similar ceremonies, part African survival, this political ritual openly burlesqued the dominant culture," documents Eric Lott. "Amid the usual celebratory excess, culminating in the election of black kings, governors, and judges, blacks enacted rituals of reversal in which they lampooned their masters, wore their masters' clothes, and mounted their masters' horses" (46–47).

Election Day can be read through Bakhtin's notion of the carnivalesque: dualistic and ambivalent; reveling in the unseating of power or "the *joyful relativity of all structure and order, of all authority and all* (hierarchical) position" (Bakhtin, *Problems* 124); indulging in a temporary shift in power that will inevitably be returned to those in authority. And while Election Day took place on a sanctioned and prescribed day, and the positions of power blacks occupied reverted to whites at day's end, Lott details both the sanctioned or "usual celebratory excess" and the parodic acts in which blacks engaged. In dressing and behaving like their masters, slaves went beyond the authorized and ritualistic to parody whiteness and white power. Ambivalently partaking of the very hierarchy it would otherwise seek to subvert, Election Day operated as a "*decrowning double*; it is that same 'world turned inside out' [and] for this reason . . . is ambivalent" (Bakhtin, *Problems* 127, emphasis added). Slaves temporarily taking on positions reserved for whites would implicitly affirm the power and desirability of such positions. Moreover, since the shift in power was temporary, with the "usurped" positions always reverting to whites, Election Day also served as an annual reassertion of the white "right" to power and control. However, for slaves to "lampoon" and "burlesque" whites through imitation suggests that subversion rather than affirmation of white authority was a distinct part of those unsanctioned activities of celebration. A master might be entertained by the incongruence of his slaves taking on the roles of political power beyond his plantation, but he would quite likely find it unsettling to see himself the subject of ridicule; slaves playing at king or governor would be one thing, having slaves wear his clothes and mimic his behavior would be another.[18] And while Joseph Roach does not cite Election Day as precedent in the "performance genealogy" of the Zulu Social Aid and Pleasure Club's Mardi Gras float parade, its performance of " 'King Zulu' . . . 'The Big Shot of Africa,' 'The Witch Doctor,' 'Governor,' 'Province Prince,' and 'Ambassador' " (19) echoes and extends that much earlier tradition. As Roach points out, King Zulu parodies "Rex, King of Carnival," who "[s]ince 1872 . . . has reigned annually over Mardi Gras" and is "[t]raditionally chosen from the ranks of [New Orleans's] business elite" (18). While King Rex asserts "[m]ore than a century of white supremacist entitlement," King Zulu "deconstruct[s] . . . that white genealogy and [offers] the veiled assertion of a clandestine countermemory in its stead" (Roach 20). Performing "whiteface minstrelsy," King Zulu's "white greasepaint under his blackface discloses an acute reflexivity ... [as] Zulu ... mock[s] absurd Eurocentric stereotypes of divine kingship" (Roach 21). Like those governors of Election Days, King Zulu and his crew parody white power and extend that parody to a whiteface minstrel performance mocking white notions of blackness. The layers of King Zulu's performance—black performing as white performing stereotyped blackness—contest white constructions of race and so, too, the power that depends upon them.

It is this tradition of African American subversive performance that I ask readers to keep in mind as *The Mulatta and the Politics of Race* considers the politics and political uses of the mulatta, the ambivalence of both this figure and the act of passing, and the possibilities for reading the mulatta as engaged in parodic performances of racialized womanhood and whiteness that signify on power structures African American women sought to redress. *The Mulatta and the Politics of Race* begins by examining juridical, popular, and scientific notions of the mulatta and race as central to contextualizing the very different politics of African American women speakers and writers examined in this study. Chapter 1 reads selected legal decisions regarding racial identity, from colonial antimiscegenation laws to mid-twentieth-century segregation cases, through Pierre Bourdieu's notion of "the force of law." Critical race theory has focused on miscegenation statutes to argue that "mixed-race" individuals have threatened, yet ultimately come to be contained by, racial definitions designed to secure whiteness as an untainted and inviolable identity. Race in American courts and the popular imagination was a far more complex and shifting concept than these studies suggest, however. While courts were recognizing whiteness as privilege and property, they were far from uniformly concerned to regulate its "transfer" and "enjoyment" only among those biologically determined to be white. Rather, judges and juries determined racial identities by appealing both to the corporeal or biological and to the social. The legal system was reinforced by the nineteenth-century mania for classification, and this chapter also considers that mania and the consequent development of a number of sciences and their theories of race. Legal and scientific pronouncements on race interacted to enable each other such that scientific "evidence" affirmed the courts' decisions, and the codification of ever-more refined distinctions between blackness and whiteness validated the development of new scientific schools, theories, and studies aimed at proving inherent racial difference. This focus on the law and science together shows us how tenuous was the identification Craft and Remond solicited and managed in their audiences and how strategically Harper, Hopkins, Fauset, and Larsen played on stereotypes of the mulatta to undermine the investment of both race and gender in a politics of visibility.

Focusing on the American appearances of Ellen Craft in 1849 before she left for England following the passage of the Fugitive Slave Law in 1850 and on her British lecture tour (1851) and that of Sarah Parker Remond (1859), Chapter 2 argues that their appearances and appeals on the antislavery platform capitalized on a fascination with the "tragic mulatta" figure or "white slave" and on the currency of the "woman as slave" trope. Craft's "whiteness" clearly affected both her American and British audiences, who saw her as a living exhibit of the lowest to which American slavery would sink. Remond's lectures, in turn, invoked the figure of the "whitened" slave in order to stress slavery's horrors and facilitate an empathic appeal. Remond carefully managed that empathy by moving between embodied and rational appeals and by standing as a figure her audiences could imagine would be enslaved in America. Craft's and Remond's ability to "pass" with their audiences was also central to their success. While Craft passed as that fictional character come to life, the tragic mulatta, Remond effectively passed for a former or fugitive slave, thereby capitalizing upon the fad of "sable visitors" recently escaped from American slavery. In fact, Remond may well have been read not only as fugitive slave but also as "whitened" slave, given that reports frequently stressed her femininity as equal to that of her British sisters, marking a certain "whiteness" through that attention to refinement and propriety.

In Chapters 3 through 5, *The Mulatta and the Politics of Race* proceeds in two distinct and connected movements from the mulatta figure "passing" as a "true woman" to the mulatta passing for white. Late-nineteenth-century America increasingly regarded identity as an accretion of behaviors. The cult of domesticity, part of a larger regimentation of the social that included an explosion of etiquette manuals during the late 1880s and 1890s, regarded appearance and conduct as more than mere indications of character. They were identity itself. Chapter 3 outlines the dictates of true womanhood as it sought to define white womanhood in a dialectical and exclusionary relationship to black womanhood largely through constructions of the black female body. Consequently, early black feminists sought to reclaim the body, promoting a noble black womanhood that acknowledged the realities of black women's lived experience. Within this climate of contested notions of black womanhood, Frances Harper and Pauline Hopkins wrote *Iola Leroy* and *Contending Forces*, novels that unseated identity from the body and its biology, thereby challenging existing notions of racial difference. Through political strategies of parodic imitation, Harper and Hopkins wrote their mulatta heroines as effectively "passing" for "true women." This chapter examines these novels as "double voiced," a strategy earlier pursued by Craft and Remond and continued in the work of Fauset and Larsen. While our knowledge of how *Iola Leroy* and *Contending Forces* were read is necessarily limited, contemporary reviews and the writers' prefaces build a sense of how the ambivalence of the mulatta figure might facilitate very different readings of these novels.

Depicting the overdetermination of things black in Harlem as empowering and limiting, profitable and exploitative, for African Americans in general and black women in particular, Jessie Fauset and Nella Larsen represent the mulatta figure in their novels as a hybrid of stereotyped womanhood. Chapter 4 argues that the result is a powerful critique of the belief that empowerment would follow from representations of African Americans like those offered by Harper and Hopkins. The mulatta may "pass" for a "true woman," but is this ultimately liberating for her, or does it simply render her an icon of black respectability much like primitivism rendered her an icon of exotic sexuality? Fauset and Larsen parody their audiences' expectations based on packaged "blackness" and stereotypes of the mulatta. The represented communities of these novels construct the mulatta as a corporealized boundary separating white from black, "good" society from "disreputable," in a manner that serves to consolidate racial and class identities from both sides of the color line. However, if the stereotype's power, as well as the power of race as a discursive formation, lies in the ambivalence of overdetermined identities, that very ambivalence is also the site of a potential subversion. Fauset and Larsen use the mulatta figure to explore womanhood and race as constructs whose fixity is threatened by characters who cross those lines separating class, racial, and gender identities. Both of these novels confront white and African American readers with essentialist notions of the mulatta, often holding in tension a resistance to, and acceptance of, ideals of white womanhood and the mulatta as a polysemic model of black women's lived experience.

Chapter 5 reads Fauset's *Plum Bun* and Larsen's *Passing* as points around which the debate over what race means has been pursued, as well as engagements with that debate in narrative form. Within African American studies, the resistance to conceiving of race as performative, as an accretion of behaviors and stylizations on the body's surface, has arguably stalled a further pressing on existing readings of passing. Rather than mediating between whiteness and blackness, thereby consolidating racial hegemony and defining racial boundaries, Fauset's and Larsen's mulatta characters pass selectively as white and black, engaging in a performative that challenges American notions of race as a natural closed category. Moreover, Fauset and Larsen explore the interimplications of race, gender, class, and sexuality through their characters' acts of passing. Yet figuring race as performative is not the sole thrust of their politics, despite the popularity of this reading in late-twentieth-century criticism. Rather, this chapter argues that Fauset and Larsen were engaged with debates over "authentic blackness," as Martin Favor calls it, that peaked during the Harlem Renaissance. By passing in convincing yet at times excessive performances, Larsen's and Fauset's mulattas move beyond passing in order to be "mistaken" for white and challenge readers to see the fundamental error in understanding passing as masquerading for the racial "other." This inscription of excess is also characteristic of mimicry as an ambivalent political strategy, as Homi Bhabha argues, and has been a central aspect of African American expressivity, as critics since Zora Neale Hurston have documented. Those moments at which Fauset and Larsen invite us to read their heroines as stereotypically "black" rather than "white" are highly unstable, and their identities are represented as so ambiguous and ambivalent that it is difficult to determine what is performance and what is authentic, what is constructed and what is natural. In this way, these writers participated in the ongoing debate of "authentic" blackness within the Harlem Renaissance and played on the larger taxonomic fever it was a part of within the national culture.

The Mulatta and the Politics of Race concludes by considering the question of when passing ends, or "passes out," and when the mulatta figure's use by African American women writers might ebb. Studies of passing frequently contend that passing and passing narratives end roughly by the 1930s. Recently, Gayle Wald has argued not only that the passing narrative disappears from African American literature but that the "postpassing narrative" deploying the "trope of the *refusal to pass*" emerges in its stead. Such confessional narratives were published in periodicals like *Jet* and *Ebony* through the 1950s alongside articles citing the return of passers to "the race" given the progress to end racial discrimination in employment. However, the end of passing is not as monolithic or complete as the postwar optimism of postpassing narratives would suggest; rather, the mulatta continues to function as a trope through which African American women writers critique and trespass on the boundaries of race, class, and gender. Dorothy Lee Dickens's *Black on the Rainbow* (1952) and Reba Lee's *I Passed for White* (1955) continue and notably revise some of the textual strategies of their predecessors, together contesting the trend of 1950s postpassing narratives, which failed "to represent class" or "to interrogate classed and gendered constructions of racial passing" in favor of depicting their characters' renewed "race loyalty" (Wald 121).

While reading these platform appearances and oratorical and fictional texts as exploring a politics of positionality and the imbrication of race, gender, class, and sexuality, we must also keep in sight the overdetermination and myriad constructions of blackness in America that Hortense Spillers and Patricia Williams speak to in the two epigraphs that open this introduction. Regardless of the overdetermination or "invention" of blackness and however much these texts confront and challenge such stereotypes, there remains a significant difference between what Karla Holloway calls "publicly constructed" and "privately authored" identities—between the manipulations, condescension, and deference Patricia Williams speaks of as so painful to acknowledge and the will to self-definition that encompasses both communal African American traditions and individual determinations of self. Holloway maintains that "in American culture, and in the imaginative representations of that culture in literature, our compromised environments valorize publicly constructed racial and sexual identities, but they do not support privately authored identities that may be at odds with public representations" (60). The opposition to "privately authored" identities never results in their absence; rather, self-determined identities have been built on a rich history of confronting and manipulating constructions of blackness, as well as preserving both individual and communal identity in African-inflected cultural forms and their New World adaptations.

This study, then, works to attend to the ways in which these African American writers interrogate constructed identities and notions of identity that defy categories serving the interests of a racialized imbalance of power. Toward that end, questioning who reads, or makes meaning, and from what position; interrogating constructions of whiteness as racially unmarked and blackness as marked; and investigating the ways in which these authors may have negotiated the different audiences they necessarily addressed become quite significant. Crossing borders to present a double-voiced address in order to speak to both black and white audiences may mean these texts risk metaphorizing race. As Ann duCille puts it, "black culture is more easily intellectualized when transferred from the danger of lived black experience to the safety of white metaphor, when you can have that 'signifying black difference' without the difference of significant blackness" ("Occult" 600). However, these texts work to keep the material conditions of both "publicly constructed" and "privately authored" identities in sight as they interrogate and reconceive racialized identities forged in both inter- and intramural contexts.

The Mulatta and the Politics of Race

Chapter 1

Fixing the Color Line

The Mulatta, American Courts, and the Racial Imaginary

In "Racial Histories and Their Regimes of Truth," Ann Laura Stoler argues that contemporary studies of race tend to read retrospectively, "flattening" what is often a more vexed terrain in order to "distinguish between racisms of past and present." The consequence is the implication that "racisms once existed in more overt and pristine form. . . . [A] biologized, physiological and somatic racism of the past [is] held up as fundamentally distinct from a more nuanced, culturally coded, and complex racism of the present" (183). Indeed, examinations of race in American culture tend to follow what we might call a progressivist narrative in which "race becomes increasingly defined as an inherent corporeal difference in the nineteenth century" (Wiegman 30), as a focus on skin and morphology gave way to a focus on blood and its fractional admixture as traceable through both genealogy and how that blood would "tell" on the body's surface. This development, according to such narratives, is grounded in a focus on "the emergence of the human sciences . . . [and] comparative anatomy['s] . . . break with the assurance of the visible to craft interior space, to open the body to the possibilities of subterranean and invisible truths and meanings . . . [so that] race was situated as potentially more than skin deep" (Wiegman 30).

To be sure, a focus on blood and its so-called admixture seems to become more prevalent in the racialist sciences from the 1850s onward, yet American notions of race and racial difference in the culture at large hardly conform to a turn from a less than reliably read exterior to blood as truth. Rather, taking white justices and juries as indicative of wider white American cultural beliefs regarding race and racial difference, we see that physically inspecting "tell-tale" characteristics of blackness continued well into the 1920s in cases deciding racial identity. Moreover, for over a century, from the early nineteenth through the mid-twentieth, American courts and their juries were considering reputation or association—the social, or

what we might call one's performance of whiteness or blackness—as more definitive of an individual's race than the biological, whether read on the body's surface
or mapped in its interiors as fractions of blackness. Not only was race in America
less "pristine" than many accounts have led us to believe, but what race meant was
not monolithically the determination of white Americans and a powerful tool of
white supremacy. African American intellectuals, and particularly those espousing
black nationalist politics, pursued their own notions of what defined both races
generally and "the" black race specifically. Often, their work invoked the very
racialist rhetoric we might expect them to have opposed, particularly a romantic
racialism and understandings of race as an "essence." In order to see that more
vexed terrain in which African American women rhetors and writers were intervening as they both manipulated and challenged American understandings of
race, this chapter examines select cases and particular trends in judicial decisions
determining the racial identity of both plaintiffs and defendants. These cases are
set alongside the contentions of key, emerging schools of human science rooted in
racialism so that we might see how the law and science were mutually constitutive,
though by no means in consensus, as they informed and were informed by a larger
American racial imaginary that included black intellectual thought. This chapter
will work to throw into relief the challenges to existing conceptions of race offered
by African American women in public appearances, lectures, and fiction that will
become the focus of the chapters that follow.

Abby Guy's Suit for Freedom

As Ariela Gross documents, Abby Guy and her children were listed as "the only
free negroes . . . of Ashley County," Arkansas, in the 1850 census. However, a
William Daniel, who claimed Guy as his slave, began treating her and her children
as such, leading "Guy to bring suit in the circuit court" (Gross 124). In July 1857
Abby Guy sued for her freedom and that of her four children. Testimony on Guy's
behalf noted that she had been supporting herself and her children by farming and
selling her own crops. The Guy family "passed as free persons": Abby's oldest
daughter "boarded out" so that she could attend school, and the family "visited
among white folks, and went to church, parties, etc., [such that one] should suppose they were white" (Catterall 5:252). Following these accounts of where and
how the Guys lived, the court required that the family be presented for physical
inspection by the jury, which was to base its decision of whether Abby Guy and her

children were black or white, slave or free, on their appearance as well as any testimony offered: "Here the plaintiffs were personally presented in Court, and the judge informed the jury that they . . . should treat their . . . inspection of plaintiffs' persons as evidence" (Catterall 5:252). Following their evidentiary "inspection" of the Guy family, the jury was told that the Guys had lived as "free persons" in Arkansas since 1844. In 1855 they moved to Louisiana, where a Mr. Daniel "took possession of them as slaves" roughly two years later, claiming that Abby Guy "came with . . . [him] from Alabama to Arkansas" as his slave (Catterall 5:253). Witnesses for Daniel testified that Abby's mother, Polly, was said to have been "a shade darker than Abby," such that they "could not say whether Polly was of African or Indian extraction" (Catterall 5:253).

Determining Abby Guy's status and race solely according to her complexion and that of her mother was complicated by the fact that neither woman's complexion was considered white, nor could they be said to be of either African or Native American descent. Consequently, the nature and degree of Abby Guy's "otherness" as focused through the lens of "blackness" became the issue in this case; investigating how black Guy was, not how white or "Indian," became the first step in containing the threat she posed. A Dr. Newton was then called to testify on Guy's behalf and, in an attempt to clarify racial distinctions, he cited additional bodily evidence: "[T]he hair never becomes straight until after the third descent from the negro. . . . The flat nose also remains observable for several descents." Daniel countered this testimony by introducing his father's will, which "devised Abby as a 'negro girl slave' to his daughter . . . bill of sale . . . 1825, conveying to him, for . . . $400, . . . 'one negro girl named Abby, thirteen years old'" (Catterall 5:253). Testimony apparently ended here, and Judge Sorrels then gave the jury the following instructions:

> If the jury find . . . that the plaintiffs had less than one-fourth of negro blood in their veins, the jury should find them to be free persons upon that fact alone—it being *prima facie* evidence of freedom—unless defendant . . . had proven them to be slaves. . . . If . . . less than one-fourth negro, . . . defendant can only prove them to be slaves, by proving . . . that . . . plaintiffs are descended from a slave on the mother's side, who was one-fourth negro or more. (Catterall 5:253)

The jury found in Abby Guy's favor, and the judge ordered that she and her children "be liberated."

Abby Guy's freedom did not go uncontested by Daniel, however; he appealed the verdict and "succeeded in having the case retried in neighboring Drew County, where he thought he would find a more sympathetic jury." The original verdict was upheld, and Daniel again appealed, citing the "improper exhibition of Guy's feet" (Gross 136). The Arkansas Supreme Court then reversed the initial decision. Chief Justice C. J. English based his reversal on the legislature's interpretation of the term "mulatto" in the Arkansas act regulating suits for freedom. He argued that rather than adhering to the act's definition of a mulatto as "a person . . . not full negro, but one who is *one-fourth* or more negro," the legislature had "manifestly used the word in a more latitudinous sense. . . . [T]hey meant to embrace . . . persons belonging to the *negro* race . . . of an intermixture of white and negro blood, without regard to grades" (Catterall 5:253).

In January 1861 Abby Guy again sued Daniel for her freedom, and again the court required that she and her children be physically examined in order to decide their race. Abby and her children were "permitted" to remove their shoes and stockings and to "exhibit their feet to the jury" (Catterall 5:262). Apparently, this evidence satisfied the jury, who ruled in Abby Guy's favor; Daniel's subsequent motion for a new trial was overruled. When Daniel filed for appeal, the 1861 judgment was affirmed by the court of appeals on the following grounds: "Physicians, whose testimony was introduced . . . state that the color, hair, feet, nose and form of the scull [*sic*] and bones, furnish means of distinguishing negro . . . descent. . . . No one, who is familiar with the peculiar formation of the *negro foot*, can doubt that an inspection of that member would ordinarily afford some indication of the race" (Catterall 5:262).

The mid-nineteenth-century court records that chronicle Abby Guy's tenuous liberty also reveal competing notions of race that hinge on a tension between appeals to the corporeal as the site of verifiable "quantities" and "expressions" of blood indicating one's racial identity and to notions of race appealing to the social. Far from securing an unwavering and strict color line, as we might expect in a racially stratified South whose economic and social order we understand as historically dependent upon a clear distinction between white and black, Southern conceptions of race were at best varied and, more often than not, contradictory in ways that were not, in fact, unique to the South. Rather, we see such a tension between race as biological and race as social or performable throughout the nation from the early nineteenth through the early twentieth century. In Abby Guy's suit for freedom, race was biological, transmitted by blood, diluted by its mixture to quantifiable fractions, and expressed by such physical characteristics as kinky hair, flat noses, and the distinctive *"negro foot."* However, this same case illustrates that race was also social, or what Ariela Gross calls "race as ascriptive identity" (133), a matter of reputation, personal conduct, and association. In effect, testimony on Abby Guy's behalf centered on both her lack of "negro" characteristics and on her sustained performance of "whiteness" as an industrious mother who, along with her children, was received by her community—its social circles and schools—as though she "were white."[1] Moreover, in this case race was simultaneously a matter of fractional degree as legislated by the state and interpreted by Justice English as an absolute distinction between "pure" whiteness and the one drop of "negro blood" that signified blackness. For years, amid these contradictions and interpretations, both literal and latitudinous, the Guys' liberty was never secure.

Abby Guy's suit for liberty and similar cases heard in American courts in which racial identities and commensurate social status were decided are instructive in tracing the contest over, and contradictions embedded in, notions of race operative across the nation. Although the Guy family lived in their community in a manner that caused their white neighbors and acquaintances to "suppose they were white," a single man's claim that they were his property immediately altered their status and identity from white to black, free to enslaved. And while Abby Guy was clearly neither white nor black, the corporeal challenge she and other "mulattas" posed to a social system built upon this racial binary caused the courts to marshal contradictory notions of race in order to silence and subsume such threats. Contained within these deliberations of the mulatta's racial identity was a reaffirmation of whiteness as an "original," "natural" state of being against which difference was repeatedly asserted as degrees of deviance.

Critical race theory has tended to focus on miscegenation law in its examination of how "mixed-race" individuals have threatened, yet ultimately come to be contained by, racial definitions designed to secure whiteness as an untainted and inviolable identity. As a result, much critical race theory that considers the mulatta is also part of a larger trend interrogating whiteness as regulated property and privilege.[2] Cheryl Harris's "Whiteness as Property" is one such example and a key contribution to the field, in which she argues:

> The state's official recognition of a racial identity that subordinated Blacks and of privileged rights in property based on race elevated whiteness from a passive attribute to an object of law and a resource deployable at the social, political, and institutional level to maintain control. . . . Whiteness as the embodiment

of white privilege transcended mere belief or preference; it became usable property, the subject of the law's regard and protection. (1734)[3]

However, a focus on miscegenation statutes and suits for divorce or annulment that appealed to them has produced misleading assertions regarding the ways in which race was conceived and deployed, and in what contexts. Race in American courts and the popular imagination was a far more complex and shifting concept than these studies suggest. While courts were recognizing whiteness as privilege and property, they were far from uniformly concerned to regulate its "transfer" and "enjoyment" only among those biologically determined to be white. Moreover, our inquiry into whiteness and blackness as constructed in and through judicial decisions should not be largely confined to cases concerning the marriage contract and miscegenation, as though "miscegenation laws" alone "formed a virtual road map to American legal conceptions of race" (Pascoe 49). Rather, judges and juries determined racial identities by appealing both to the corporeal or biological and to the social in contexts ranging from one's ability to testify in court or to attend a particular school, to the taxes one was assessed and one's freedom from enslavement.

A focus on the mulatta complicates and extends our understanding of race and its attendant distinctions between whiteness and blackness beyond the statutory regulation of miscegenous relationships and their threat to whiteness as property, to individual nineteenth-century cases that were much more uneven in the allocation of whiteness as privilege. This uneven or shifting understanding of whiteness turns on a significant tension between race as essentially biological and race as contingent upon the social as marked by reputation, social associations, and status. While we might be invested in an understanding of the judicial as the rule of law or the rational expression of objective and just determinations that rise above the social that it governs, these cases chronicle decisions that neither simply reflect "objective" determinations of race nor their subsequent public consumption as such. Rather, they show us a judiciary mired in notions of race circulating in the popular imaginary of its present and actively constructing "whiteness" and "blackness" in ways that ensured their circulation as "the real," however contradictory or unstable those constructions might be. By focusing on these tensions between race as biological and social, between the public's view of the judiciary as rational or objective and its deep implication in what it ostensibly "observed," I will work to suggest *how* the law is able to "create and maintain" racial identities rather than simply remarking that it does so. I aim, then, with a focus on the mulatta in

American courts, to take up Ian Haney López's call in *White by Law*. "Despite the spreading recognition [in critical race theory] that law is a prime suspect in the formation of races, however," writes López, "to date there has been no attempt to evaluate systematically just *how* the law creates and maintains races" (13, emphasis added).

Of particular concern is the way in which the "margins" of race become bodily manifest in the figure of the mulatta, who is repeatedly called to function as a racial borderland that delimits both whiteness and blackness. Though social relationships in America were everywhere miscegenated since the arrival of the first Dutch slaver and enslaved Africans in the colonies, courts of law have attempted to clarify and regiment those relationships in order to establish and preserve a distinction between white and black. As I will document, these distinctions were initially a matter of spirit; in other words, colonists originally evoked distinctions between "heathens" and "Christians" in order both to mark themselves off from Native and African Americans and to invest those distinctions with a divine authority that worked to naturalize race. That initial focus on spirit recurs in a later focus on morality and moral legitimacy as the mulatta's "predisposed" acts and behaviors become a focus not only for the law but also for science and open the door to race as contingent upon the social. Turning to specific cases that cluster at the turn into the twentieth century, we then see cases reading racial identity in and through social reputation and association. Repeatedly, however, legal decisions that fixed the mulatta's identity as black also appealed to a notion of race as naturalized by invoking bodily differences like complexion, fractional quantities of black "blood," and, thereby, the biological as "fact." While the corporeal is a familiar racial text in the emerging human sciences at this time and one regarded as "fact," in American courts judges and juries frequently confronted an "illegible" body that would not "tell" with any reliability, be it in acts or appearance. David Theo Goldberg has argued that appeals to the body as "unproblematically observable" have established an "underlying . . . unity for the discourse of race" (53–54). Such notions of race as figured bodily are based, for Goldberg, on the equation of the body as "a 'bounded system,' a system the boundaries of which are formed by skin," with the body politic that "is constituted always in terms of the bordered criteria of inclusion and exclusion, identities and separateness, (potential) members and inevitable nonmembers" (54). When the body politic is no longer assured of an "unproblematically observable" body in which to read race, we see a tension emerging in conceptualizations of race as discernible in the body's hidden interiors and their external expression, or as evident in the social reputation and associations of individuals whose racial identity has come under question. While the courts persisted in attempting to consider both the biological and the social from the mid-nineteenth century onward, the variable rulings they produced resulted in larger contradictions that voice that emerging tension between two very different understandings of race within American culture at large. The mulatta's threat is perhaps most evident in the court's inability to address questions of racial identity with any consistency and in the schism that develops in conceptualizations of whiteness and blackness. We see a judiciary attempting to naturalize racial differences through appeals to the body even while it simultaneously acknowledges the social construction of race by subsequent appeals to common knowledge and reputation.

Denials and Deferrals

Varied judicial decisions and the contradictory notions of race legitimated through them are neither accidental nor benign but rather the result of attempts to manipulate what Pierre Bourdieu calls "the law's elasticity":

> To varying degrees, jurists and judges have at their disposal the power to exploit the polysemy or the ambiguity of legal formulas by appealing to such rhetorical devices as *restrictio* (narrowing), a procedure necessary to avoid applying a law which, literally understood, ought to be applied; *extensio* (broadening), a procedure which allows application of a law which, taken literally, ought not to be applied; and a whole series of techniques like analogy and the distinction of letter and spirit, which tend to maximize the law's elasticity, and even its contradictions, ambiguities, and lacunae. (827)

Bourdieu reminds us of what we seem to take as less than obvious, that juridical sites and texts—laws, judgments, trials, briefs—reveal a larger social struggle for knowledge as power however much we might invest them with an ability to rise above such interests. "Thus the trial represents a paradigmatic staging of the symbolic struggle inherent in the social world," he writes. "What is at stake in this struggle is monopoly of the power to impose a universally recognized principle of knowledge of the social world—a principle of legitimized *distribution*" (Bourdieu 837). Or, as Patricia Williams puts it, "[t]he word of law, whether statutory or judge-made, is a sub-category of the underlying social motives and beliefs from which it is born. It is the technical embodiment of attempts to order society according to a consensus of ideals" (138–39). However, Bourdieu argues, a key aspect of "the force of law" is our investment of the judicial system with an objectivity and impartiality that masks the very power struggles acted out and contained within it: "[T]he system of juridical norms seems (both to those who impose them and even to those upon whom they are imposed) *totally independent* of the power relations which such a system sustains and legitimizes. . . . It thus legitimizes victories over the dominated, which are thereby converted into accepted facts" (817). For my purposes, what is most important about this ethical, logical, and objective quality acquired by juridical acts is that it enables the law not only to render local decisions regarding personal liberty, status, or tax exemption but also to construct and legislate identities as though courts were simply "observing" them in the "evidence" presented.

The kind of deferral or denial of the judicial system's constitutive acts that Bourdieu speaks to is present in the first colonial statutes designed to regulate miscegenous relationships. The first American legal records that specifically deal with race are the colonial laws and court decisions in which the term "mulatto," so open to contestation in Abby Guy's suit, first appears, beginning with a Virginian ruling of 1644 decreeing that " 'A Mulatto named Manuel' was to be a slave" (Williamson 8). While this ruling indicates that people of biracial descent were living in the colonies by at least the mid-seventeenth century, there was no attempt to legally determine the status of so-called mulatta children until 1662.[4] In the same year, Virginia enacted its first antimiscegenation law and repealed the long-standing English law of descent: " 'Whereas some doubts have arisen whether a child got by an Englishman upon a negro should be free or slave, be it therefore enacted by this present grand assembly, that all children born in the country shall be bound or free according to the condition of the mother' " (qtd. in Johnston 167). It would rapidly become clear to white Virginians, however, that this proclamation required revision in order to exclude all mulattas from whiteness and its attendant freedoms and privileges, since this act did not take into account the status of children of white mothers and black fathers. Maryland recognized earlier than Virginia the "threat" to established order involved in allowing mulatta children of white mothers to be free and moved in its antimiscegenation act of 1663 to enslave these children: " 'And forasmuch as divers freeborn *English* women . . . do intermarry with negro slaves . . . all the issue of such free-born women, so married, shall be slaves as their fathers were. . . . And be it further enacted, that all issues of *English*, or other freeborn women, that have already married negroes, shall serve the master of their parents, till they be thirty years of age and no longer' " (qtd. in G. Williams, 240). In 1664 Maryland became more punitive, ruling that white women bearing the children of slaves must serve "the masters of their husbands during the lifetime of the husband, and that the 'Issue of such freeborne wommen soe marryed shall be Slaues as their fathers were' " (Williamson 10).

Nearly thirty years later, Virginian colonists believed it necessary to publicly denounce these children, who were already deemed the illegitimate offspring of an illegal union and bound out as punishment for their parents' transgressions, declaring them " 'that abominable mixture and spurious issue' " (qtd. in Jordan 44), and "banish[ing] . . . from the dominion forever" (Johnston 172–73) any white man or woman who violated the antimiscegenation statute.[5] Virginia developed by far the harshest punitive laws regarding miscegenation, enslaving the biracial children of white women for thirty years and also providing for the control and discipline of future generations: "Where any female mulatto, or Indian, by law obliged to serve til the age of thirty or thirty-one years, shall during the time of her servitude, have any child born of her body, every such child shall serve the master . . . until it shall attain the same age the mother of such child was obliged by law to serve unto" (Catterall 1:70).[6] The colonists, then, were not only drawing a color bar that assigned "deviance" to the other side but were also defining blackness as the site of an abjection that could "contaminate" whites who entered into interracial relationships and result in their exile from the colonial family. With its stress on "abominable mixture and spurious issue," the Virginia Assembly sought to represent this guarding of racial borders as motivated by neither political, economic, nor psychical concerns. Rather, couched as it was in religious rhetoric, the protection of white "purity" was represented as divinely ordained. In messianic form, the deity—not the Virginia Assembly—called for the weeding out and punishment of all that was "abominable" and "spurious" in order that the colonists' errand in the wilderness be realized.[7]

The colonies established freedom as a privilege attendant solely upon whiteness, and by the early eighteenth century Virginia and Maryland had enforced a racial distinction that would be upheld in most of America. These early acts established a binary opposition of black to white through a corresponding relegation of status—only whites were free, all "others" were bond.[8] And since in 1667 Virginia had passed an act deeming "black or graduated shades thereof" as the mark of slavery (Catterall 1:57), all subsequently enslaved mulattas were effectively black by virtue of their status and complexion. Any middle ground between white and black was legislated out of existence. However, as James Johnston documents, by the late 1700s African Americans so light-skinned they appeared white proved the failure of these antimiscegenation controls: "A traveller in 1788 reports, 'I saw in this school a mulatto; one eighth a negro; it is impossible to distinguish him from a white boy.' . . . In 1783 another observer reports that in Maryland, 'there were female slaves, who are now become white by their mixture'" (191). The mulatta as tabooed figure on the American racial scene names not only the failed control of "illegitimate" racial mixing but, more important, threatens to expose the tenuous nature of whiteness. Despite repeated and complicated attempts to codify the mulatta's identity as black, individuals who were neither white nor black, but both, continued to threaten "cultural equilibrium" by unsettling the authority and stability of whiteness. Silencing this disruption by codifying the mulatta as black moves to define borders and secure a color line, even while it acknowledges the impossibility of conceiving of race as a natural, closed, black-white binary. This silencing speaks volumes, then, about the production of racial identities through juridical acts that were ostensibly observing the "natural."

Moral Legitimacy as Normative Logic: Silencing the Mulatta's Whiteness

Whites rather quickly sought to shift responsibility for all "transgressions" resulting in this "spurious issue," the mulatta, to the servant class. Not only were African Americans "savages" obeying what were believed to be the instinctual forces that white Americans attempted to deny in themselves, but to the servant class was also imputed a life of "uncontrolled desire." In a 1717 South Carolina statute entitled "An Act for the better Governing and Regulating White Servants [sic]," children of interracial relationships were "condemned to servitude for the 'indiscretions' of [their] parents" (Higginbotham 159). It continued to be popular among white Americans "theorizing" about the character and characteristics of the mulatta to argue, as Edward Reuter did in *The Mulatto in the United States* (1918), that mulattas were the result of relationships between "the outcast classes" of "the advanced race" and "the women of the inferior race" (88–90). If the "outcast classes" could not be blamed, whites could always appeal to a veritable lore detailing the "lascivious" sexuality of black women who, it was said, "everywhere seek sex relations with the men of the superior race . . . [and] feel honored by the attention of the higher class of men" (Reuter 93).

In part, bourgeois white sexuality came to be defined over and against images of the oversexualized African American woman, but "bastardizing" the mulatta further served to criminalize black sexuality and reify white sexuality.[9] The disruption posed by the mulatta's racial illegitimacy as neither white nor black, then, was neutralized to a certain extent by this concentration on issues of moral legitimacy. Hortense Spillers has argued that both the asexed black bondswoman, whose labor served to masculinize her, and the oversexualized black female, whose sexuality white men were supposedly powerless to resist, marked the boundaries of sexuality in antebellum American culture. "Those outside the circle of culture . . . were robbed of legitimate sexual being and, to that degree, defined the point of passage between inner and outer," writes Spillers. "The black American female, whether whore or asexed, serves an analogous function for the symbolically empowered on the American scene in fixing the frontier of 'woman' with her own being . . . [as] the imagined site of an illegitimate sexuality" ("Interstices" 86). For the black woman, the consequence of embodying a sexual borderland between sanctioned and illegitimate sexuality is the enduring legacy of an absence of sexuality. "[T]he black female is, if anything, a creature of sex, but *sexuality* touches her nowhere," argues Spillers. "[T]he black woman disappears as a legitimate subject of female sexuality" ("Interstices" 76). The mulatta, however, functions as a sort of zero limit of sexuality and morality. If the black woman is called to delineate a borderland in which legitimate sexuality is an impossibility for her, the mulatta as the product of interracial relationships under interdict proves doubly outlawed in American culture.

Dorothy Sterling's account of the system of *plaçage* and its relationships brokered via New Orleans's antebellum "fancy girl" markets illustrates the way in which the mulatta acquired a different sort of sexuality in the South than Spillers ascribes to black women generally:

> Slaves selected for their grace, beauty and light skins were shipped to the "fancy-girl markets" of New Orleans and other cities. . . . A *plaçee*, light skinned, well educated, chaste, was introduced to society at one of the famed quadroon balls, where attendance was limited to white gentlemen and free women of color. When her charms attracted a "protector," a period of courtship followed. The *maman* and protector signed a formal contract stipulating the support she and her future children could expect. . . . Her sons were taught a trade, while her daughters were trained to be the belles of future quadroon balls. (27)

Monique Guillory notes that many of the unions resulting from the *plaçage* system "were as exclusive and lasting as legitimate marriages," with children "often recognized and named for their European fathers" (81). However, the white male's recognition of his *plaçee* as "wife" had its limits, significantly, when it came to admitting his biracial children into the full rights and privileges of the Louisiana aristocratic family. "[N]umerous cases were heard in the New Orleans courts in which whites contested and blacks demanded inheritance rights," notes Guillory. "[F]ew free people of color won any of these cases" (81–82). Higher prices for mulatta slaves and the *plaçage* system were the consequences of a white male belief that mulattas sought their attentions whether enslaved or free: "It was thought that a rather large proportion of the free colored females, particularly free mulattos, were unchaste" (Reuter 150).[10] Paradoxically, the mulatta's chastity was a commodity that held good only long enough to attract a buyer. In such cases, we see the mulatta's body at once marking the limits of both lascivious sexuality and moral purity. Karen Sànchez-Eppler argues that "traditional notions of female purity attach . . . to the body—in its vulnerability to rape or enforced concubinage" (42). Since those "traditional notions" of vulnerability were race specific and "attached" to a white skin, the mulatta's body has been read in two directions simultaneously: her fair skin signals notions of chastity, purity, and delicacy, but within that same body is believed to flow a "tainted" blood that carries the so-called traits of a wanton sexuality. These conflictual readings cohere in the mulatta as a figure of womanhood rendered sexually available, of chastity as a commodity that is valued precisely because it is presumed impossible to violate. The very qualities that might guarantee her the protection of respect as a morally chaste woman would have attracted a Southern aristocrat excited by the paradox of an enslaved courtship. Even as she fixes the frontier of legitimate sexuality, arguably the mulatta's signal difference is that she has also been believed to contain the border between sanctioned and outlawed sexuality within her very person, readable if not on her body's surface then in its "tainted" interiors.

We might also read such an attention to morality in the construction of the mulatta operating in similar ways to fix the borders of sexuality and those of race itself, so that whatever disruption to a racialized social order this figure threatens is contained through a repeated silencing and exile. We would be mistaken to believe that these notions of moral illegitimacy circulated only within a popular imaginary and not courts of law or the developing human sciences. As the illegitimate offspring resulting from immoral and unsanctioned relationships, the mulatta was relegated to the periphery of the "normative." While the mulatta was figured as an outcast and some sort of moral limit case, this figure was also called to occupy a mediating position through which the boundaries of race were obsessively marked and delimited. Significantly, as the immorality surrounding the mulatta figure was voiced, the mulatta's whiteness was denied and silenced through a socially sanctioned racial designation as black. Consequently, even though the mulatta represented a corporeal manifestation of the constructedness of race revealing, as Henry Louis Gates Jr. asserts, that "the concepts of 'black' and 'white' . . . are mutually constitutive and socially produced" ("Criticism" 21), white Americans worked to foreclose such a challenge by labeling the mulatta a "bastard."[11] Any suggestion that race was not a stable and uniform entity was thereby silenced and exiled to the borders of civilized or moral society. These appeals to morality, then, were designed to outlaw the mulatta and make this figure one through which boundaries between white and black are repeatedly, though silently, secured. Such moral appeals are, for Bourdieu, integral to the power of the law though they often go unacknowledged as such: "It appears to partake both of the positive logic of science and the normative logic of morality and thus to be capable of compelling universal acceptance through an inevitability which is simultaneously logical and ethical" (818).

Evidence of the power of "blackness" in white minds is clearly operative in the late-nineteenth-century human sciences' racialization of morality. Far from limited to colonial statutes, the racial imaginary backed by the "objective" power of science constructed an image of blacks as the repository of immorality and vice. White Americans sexualized mulattas to an even greater degree than they did "pure Africans." In *Anthropology for the People* (1891), William H. Campbell referred to mulattas as " 'notoriously sensual, treacherous and brutal' " (qtd. in Mencke 125). Similarly, Frederick Hoffman, in *Race Traits and Tendencies of the American Negro* (1896), characterized mulattas as immoral: "Morally, the mulatto cannot be said to be superior to the pure black . . . most of the illicit intercourse between whites and colored is with mulatto women and seldom with those of the pure type" (184).[12] And Robert Bennett Bean, an anatomist at Johns Hopkins Hospital, wrote in 1906 that mulattas " 'have the sensuality of the aboriginal African, and all the savage nature of the primitives from the wilds of Europe, without the self-control of the Caucasian or the amiability of the negro' " (qtd. in Mencke 59).

The stereotype of the corrupt mulatta seems to have been a resilient one among both white and black scholars. In an article published in the *Journal of Negro History* (1918), Carter G. Woodson subscribed to the belief that miscegenation was largely confined " 'to the weaker types of both races' " (qtd. in Williamson 117). And E. Franklin Frazier, in *The Negro Family in Chicago* (1932), concluded that the mulatto community in 1920s Chicago had concentrated itself around the "sin street" of Chicago's South Side: "It was the headquarters of the famous 'policy king'; the rendezvous of the 'pretty' brown-skinned boys, many of whom ... 'worked' white and colored girls in hotels and on the streets; here the mulatto queen of the underworld ran the biggest poker game on the South Side. . . . To this area were attracted the Bohemian, the disorganized, and the vicious elements in the Negro world" (103). Indeed, the historical insistence within black middle-class communities that its biracial members be able to prove a respectable parentage attests to the power of this stereotype. Access to class-inflected social institutions like churches and clubs is popularly believed to have been determined by color; however, as John G. Mencke documents, "without qualities of education, wealth, proper family background, acceptable behavior patterns, etc., color itself counted for little" (26). If one could not supply "proper" ancestors or did not behave decorously, one would be denied a place in middle-class black social life.[13]

Such speculations on the character of the mulatta were not simply popular beliefs held by a nineteenth-century white public, as we have already seen, but they fueled racialist sciences like anthropology, anatomy, and sociology. Indeed, as late as the 1920s psychologists began devising scales to test the "personalities" of races. Measuring "integrity, kindliness, courage, unselfishness, reasonableness, refinement, cheerfulness and optimism . . . non-compliance, and finality of judgement," these tests "proved" that African Americans, Native Americans, and Mexicans possessed inferior personalities when compared with white Americans (Gossett 376). And mulattas, because they resulted from the intermixture of what were believed to be two very different races, were "assumed to show restlessness, instability, and all sorts of deviations from a harmonious and well-balanced personality type" (Myrdal 699).

The Body as Readable Text: The Mulatta's Blackness

Specifically, in the case of judicial decisions regarding the mulatta's racial identity, the dual logic of morality as a register of the social and science as "objective" or factual is repeatedly grounded in the body, so that two rather different understandings of race appeal to the same ostensibly readable text. This construction of the mulatta as a corporeal text of racial and sexual frontiers is part of a long-lived attempt to define who is black and who is white through appeals to the body that rely upon an individual's acts, physical appearance, and "blood." Significantly, what seems to be the first colonial law decreeing that one's color is evidence of one's status as free or bond arises from the contradiction baptized African American slaves embodied for colonists who believed bondage was an appropriate condition for "heathen" and "savage" races. Helen Catterall notes that upon the passage of the Virginia act in 1667, "baptism ceased to be the test of freedom and color became the 'sign' of slavery: black or graduated shades thereof. A negro was presumed to be a slave" (Catterall 1:57). This act documents the colonists' desire to define themselves through opposition to growing numbers of people of color in the colonies during the seventeenth century. Winthrop Jordan locates key changes in the colonists' terminology in the late 1600s: "From the initially most common term *Christian*, at mid-century there was a marked shift toward the terms *English* and *free*. After about 1680, taking the colonies as a whole, a new term of self-identification appeared—*white*" (52). The rationale for skin color as proof of freedom or enslavement became entrenched rather quickly. By 1709, "Samuel Sewall noted in his diary that a 'Spaniard' had petitioned the Massachusetts Council for freedom but . . . 'Capt. Teat alledg'd that all of that Color were Slaves'" (Jordan 52–53).

The move by white colonists to devise color as "the sign of slavery" *after* slavery had been instituted foregrounds a retrospective imagining that race is "natural" through what Colette Guillaumin calls "the system of marks." Guillaumin notes that such a "system of marks" accompanies the "social cleavages" for which it is only later called to function as cause: "[T]he mark *followed* slavery . . . and [was] advanced as if 'being black' existed in itself, outside of any social reason to construct such a form, as if the symbolic fact asserted itself and could be a cause" (33). While color seems to have been the focus in the seventeenth and eighteenth centuries, the legal system came to be reinforced by a mania for classification by the nineteenth century. This interest in classification and its application to differences between human beings supported the development of a number of human sciences and their theories of race. Moreover, legal and scientific pronouncements on race interacted to enable each other such that scientific "evidence" affirmed the courts' decisions, and the codification of ever-more refined distinctions between blackness and whiteness validated the development of new theories and studies aimed at "proving" inherent racial difference, lending credence to early sciences like phrenology and the later schools of sociology, anthropology, and psychology. These sciences were both supported by and furthered notions of race as a biologizing of character and culture grounded in the body and its blood.

This symbiotic relationship between science and the law as tools of a white supremacist ideology was a nineteenth-century American phenomenon. Racial typology divided human beings into at least four races according to their differing physical appearance; racial determinism held that "the species *Homo sapiens* was composed of distinctive varieties and that the behavior of individuals and groups was determined by their place in this natural order" (Banton and Harwood 30). Nineteenth-century racialism split along the lines dividing monogenists from polygenists, the former arguing for a single creation of human beings who might be physically different as a result of their environment but similar in all other respects, while the latter held that differences in culture and appearance between groups of peoples inhabiting various parts of the world were evidence of separate creations of distinct species. While these schools parted company on the question of "difference," they agreed that biracial individuals were inherently weak. Though they answered the "threat" of the mulatta differently, each school of thought reassured whites that a middle ground between black and white could not hold. The monogenist climatic theory of racial difference designated hotter climates more suitable for "the Negro" and argued that Africa was "the Negro's" "natural" home: " 'Instead of its being too hot in the South for white men, it is too cold for negroes, and we long to see the day arrive when the latter shall have entirely receded from their uncongenial homes in America, and given full and undivided place to the former' " (qtd. in Fredrickson 145–46). The climatic theory also provided a convenient answer to the dilemma of miscegenation, maintaining that mulattas "cannot stand the heat of a summer sun" (Williamson 94). Many white Americans in turn believed that the mulatta's "black blood" would find the cold as intolerable as her "white blood" found the heat. Polygenists also characterized biracial individuals as "unnatural" hybrids with "weaker constitutions" who were unable to "reproduce" and inevitably fated to die out in America.[14] If mulattas managed to survive, they would atavistically " 'revert' to the characteristics of the lower of their two progenitors," and they were "mentally, morally, and physically inferior to either parent group" in the first place (Mencke 43–44). Finally, some in this school believed that the mulatta could survive, but only in an environment suited to her black blood. Louis Agassiz, the reputable Swiss biologist who had emigrated to America in 1846 and became a converted polygenist, advised Dr. Samuel Gridley Howe, then president of the American Freedmen's Inquiry Commission, in the summer of 1863 of the mulatta's future in the United States as he saw it: " '[T]he colored people in whom the negro nature prevails will tend toward the South, while the weaker and lighter ones will remain and die out among us [in the North]' " (qtd. in Fredrickson 161).[15]

White Americans were, however, fascinated with the possibility that African Americans could become "white" even as they repeatedly "proved" that some vestige of "blackness" would always remain to secure the color line. In addition to speculating upon the mulatta's viability, they were also taken with the idea that blackness could be whitened artificially. Dr. Benjamin Rush, a close friend of Jefferson's, developed a "cure for blackness" in 1797 involving the pressure of garments that would absorb " 'the coloring matter,' friction, depletion through 'bleeding, purging, or abstinence,' fear, 'oxygenated muriatic acid,' and 'the juice of unripe peaches' " (Stanton 13). Rush's "diagnosis" was neither an isolated incident, a bizarre "solution" to the American "race problem," nor popular only in the eighteenth century. P. T. Barnum, knowing a profitable pursuit when he saw it, capitalized on the broad appeal of an agent that would "whiten" African Americans: "In 1850 he hired a black man who claimed to have discovered a weed that would turn Negroes white. . . . Barnum . . . trumpeted this discovery as the solution to the slavery problem, while the newspapers daily reported any changes in the black man's hue" (Lott 77). Despite its popularity as an oddity, the "whitening" of African Americans was also a possibility white Americans desired to see refuted. In 1906 Robert Bennet Bean published his findings on the correlation between complexion and one's abilities and character. Bennet Bean's study concluded, much as earlier polygenist studies had, that mulattas inherited " 'all the bad of both black and white' " in personality and tendency (qtd. in Mencke 59–60). White Americans might seem fascinated with the possibility of racial transmutation, but when they were confronted with it in the form of the mulatta, they consistently redrew the line keeping whiteness "pure" and all else "other."

For white Americans, physical differences like complexion quickly became only the external signs of a myriad of more subtle racial differences, ranging widely through individual abilities, intellect, character, and behavior to the collective characteristics of races. A proliferation of racial classifications based on comparative morphology resulted from the political climate of the mid-nineteenth century. The only agreement scientists seemed able to reach was that the white and black races were inherently different in ways that affirmed white racial supremacy. Polygenesis had become the racial theory of choice by the mid-nineteenth century with the establishment of the American school of ethnology. Dr. Samuel Morton, president of the Academy of Natural Sciences in Philadelphia and considered the founder of the school of ethnology with his publication *Crania Americana* (1839), was largely responsible for a keen American interest in phrenology that imputed intellectual ability to skull size and shape.[16] Phrenology grew out of the assumption that the brain is the seat of the mind; the size of each region, determined by the contours and size of the skull, was believed to be directly proportional to the level of its function (Stanton 35). Morton predictably "discovered" that whites possessed the largest skulls, Africans the smallest, and concluded that not only were people of African descent far less intelligent than whites, they were also " 'joyous, flexible, and indolent' " individuals (qtd. in Gossett 59).

The residue of polygenist notions like those forwarded by phrenology prolif- erated throughout the nineteenth century and into the early twentieth century, as theories connecting physical differences with innate and unchanging qualities of character, temperament, and intellect abounded. Disciplines such as physical anthropology, for example, heavily influenced popular conceptions of "race" and firmly upheld polygenism, or separate creations of distinct races, as John Mencke observes:

> [T]he idea that cultural differences among men were the direct product of dif- ferences in their racial physical structure; the assumption that these distin- guishing physical differences were virtually primordial in nature; the idea that the most important of these differences involved the human skull and brain; and the notion that out of the heterogeneity of modern populations one could reconstruct "types" which were representative of the "pure races" from whose mixture these modern populations derived—all indicated the impact of poly- genist elements. (45)

This type of thinking also persisted in sociology into the early twentieth century. In an article published in the *American Journal of Sociology* (1901), Charles A. Ellwood, president of the American Sociological Society, stressed "race instincts" and "innate tendencies" in the process of natural selection. In this article, Ellwood argues that black children develop the "mental and moral characteristics" of their race independently of social forces, environment, and education: " 'The negro child, even when reared in a white family under the most favorable conditions, fails to take on the mental and moral characteristics of the Caucasian race' " (qtd. in Mencke 68). Theories devoted to racial difference frequently relied upon or extended existing theories, often stifling challenges to established ways of thinking.

When color was recognized to be an unreliable racial "mark" with growing numbers of "fair-skinned" African Americans, blood was evoked as a further natural division between white and black. We do see a development, then, from relying on the body as a text of visible difference to reading the unseen in that body's genealogy or "blood kin" that "verified" fractional quantities of blackness. However, this development does not mark a clean break with earlier investments in comparative morphology as many studies of race in America would have it, nor was this focus on blood a new development of the nineteenth century and its developing human sciences. Rather, as the end of the eighteenth century approached, the distance between white and black in America widened with an increasing focus on genealogy and blood. In 1785 Virginia legally defined "a Negro as a person with a black parent or grandparent, a definition generally adopted at that time in the upper South" (F. J. Davis, 34). Until 1785, a mulatta could possess up to one-half "African blood," but with this law's enactment all persons possessing one-quarter African blood or more were considered "Negroes" and presumed to be slaves. The statutes that defined one's "blackness" and caused one to be presumed a slave became the "observation" of the color line "nature" had created.

Presumption of slavery "arising from color" or "color as *prima facie* evidence of slavery," as this rationale appeared in legal records, held sway into the nineteenth century, indicating that the white American mind was long occupied with what W.E.B. DuBois has called "grosser physical differences." The white American belief that "blood will tell" in some way or another was fed by the rapid development of "scientific" racial theories through the nineteenth century and upheld by so-called experts, to create an atmosphere in which individuals like Abby Guy and her children could be physically inspected in order to discover telltale signs of African blood. Statutes like Virginia's in 1785 and subsequent rulings through the nineteenth century show a judiciary informed by and working in concert with the emerging racialist sciences and illustrate what Robyn Wiegman calls the "begin[ning of a] . . . break with the assurance of the visible" (30). The practice of determining racial identity by means of physical inspection of "externals," however, continued in some states into the 1920s, as Charles Mangum documents in *The Legal Status of the Negro*:

> Where . . . the racial identity of a child is in question, that child may be exhibited to the jury (California 1923; Nebraska 1919). Furthermore, photographs of any one of the kinsmen of the person involved whose relationship is sufficiently close are admissible (Alabama 1928; Virginia 1914), and the same is true of a crayon portrait . . . (Federal Court case 1917). Evidence that such persons have kinky hair or some other peculiar characteristic of the Negro is also competent (Alabama 1928). (14)

Not only were externals invoked as the way blood "tells" and simultaneously regarded as unreliable with preference given to those unseen interiors, but the turn to "experts" in the course of appealing to race as biologically registered opened up further contradictions. The definition of an "expert" on racial identity was rather loose, to say the least, as this North Carolina case illustrates. In *State v. Jacobs*, a man named Jacobs was indicted in June 1859 "as a free negro, for carrying fire-arms." Jacobs was convicted, and the judgment affirmed upon appeal, based on "the testimony of an expert." This "expert" was a man named Pritchett, who by virtue of his occupation as "a planter, an owner and manager of slaves . . . more than twelve years . . . was well satisfied that he could distinguish between the descendants of a negro and a white person, and the descendants of a negro and Indian . . . [and could] also say whether a person was full African . . . or had more or less than half . . . African blood in him. . . . [Pritchett] stated his opinion that the defendant was . . . a mulatto" (Catterall 2:226). Peggy Pascoe situates this preference for "the opinion of the 'common man'" as a distinctly early-twentieth-century phenomena that resulted when judges sought to avoid the "heated" debates over biological or scientific determinations of racial identity growing with the rise of a culturalist challenge led by figures like Franz Boas (52–55). However, we see in *State v. Jacobs* that a man's social position and "vocation"—planter and manager of slaves—qualify him to become an "expert" offering determinations of blood, its quantity and expression, based solely on his daily "experience" with slaves rather than on any "scientific" knowledge. As early as the mid-nineteenth century, the distinction between expert or "common man" was becoming as muddied as that between race as visibly manifest in the body's externals or hidden in its interiors.

Race as Blood and Culture

White American beliefs about racial differences, be they physical, mental, cultural, or behavioral, began to be expressed as beliefs in race as blood itself that spanned the nineteenth and twentieth centuries.[17] While "blood" proves to be the omnipotent image associated with theories of race throughout the history of the construction of race in America, it became particularly insidious from the 1850s onward. George Fredrickson argues that the mid-nineteenth century saw a rise in "Anglo-Saxon racial pride" and a "concern for continued 'homogeneity'" that was enabled by the so-called scientific race theory it had created (132). Unsurprisingly, then, atavism was a popular fear associated with miscegenation. White Americans took care to reassure themselves that white blood was, as many white Americans thought, "genius-bearing."[18] A variety of nineteenth- and twentieth-century scientific studies and popular understandings of the effects of "blood admixture" attributed ostensibly greater intelligence in mulattas to their white blood, while less significant "traits" or "detriments" were traced to their black blood. Antislavery writings of the 1850s, such as C. G. Parsons's *Inside Slavery, or a Tour Among the Planters* (1855), occasionally praised the mulatta as superior to both blacks and whites: " 'The mulattoes . . . are the best specimens of manhood found in the South. The African mothers have given them a good physical system, and the Anglo-Saxon fathers a good mental constitution' " (qtd. in Fredrickson 121). Notably, blackness was figured bodily as responsible for "a good physical system," while whiteness was credited with reason and the intellect of "a good mental constitution." Such was the case when white Americans wrote on the subject. Civil War craniometric studies of soldiers were frequently cited as "proof" of the effects of blood intermixture upon the size of the skull and brain. A significant degree of white blood was said to " 'determine a positive increase in the negro brain which in the quadroon is only three ounces below the white standard' " (qtd. in Mencke 40). Craniometry was used in an attempt to claim that while white blood was responsible for increased intelligence among biracial individuals, no African American would ever be the equal of a white American.

Such claims had not abated by the early twentieth century.[19] Early psychological tests were devised and interpreted in the interest of supporting the popular belief among white Americans that the presence of various degrees of white blood resulted in corresponding degrees of intelligence. G. O. Ferguson's widely quoted 1916 study claimed that " 'the pure negroes . . . scored 73.3 percent as high; the mulattas scored 81.6 per cent as high; the quadroons scored 87.9 per cent as high as whites' " (qtd. in Wirth and Goldhamer 333). The "findings" of such tests went on to influence stereotypes of African American intellectual ability. From 1929 to 1959, the *Encyclopaedia Britannica*'s section on differential psychology described African Americans as intellectually inferior to whites with this caveat: " 'the greater the admixture of white blood, the closer does the Negro approach the white in performance' " (qtd. in Hirsch 39). Perhaps the most bizarre claim to arise in what became a veritable lore about mulattas was made by the new school of neurology, which traced the "mental confusion" of mulattas to the "strains of blood," both white and black, "running" within them: "Neurologists decided that the electrical signals that control the body run in one direction in white people and in the opposite direction in black people. Mulattoes, obviously, were bound to be a highly confused people. . . . [T]he slightest mixture—even one drop—was enough to upset the system and jangle the nerves . . . [making them] a shallow, flighty, and fluttering people" (Williamson 95–96). Race configured as blood represents, as Anthony Appiah argues, "the biological fleshing out of the metaphysical doctrine of the necessity of origins" ("But" 493).[20] Yet we see that white Americans were concerned with such a fleshing out as early as the mid-nineteenth century, if we take romantic racialism as a register of such concerns.

Mid-nineteenth-century white American minds were fertile ground for the contention that biology dictated character and behavior. This biologizing of character was a cornerstone of the ideology of fundamental racial difference, and the rhetoric white Americans found most appealing was a sentimental, or romantic, racialism. Developing its black stereotypes from the plantation romances of the 1820s and 1830s, romantic racialism often held that African Americans were children who required the protection of whites.[21] These views cut across the political spectrum of white America: proslavery forces used romantic racialism to argue that paternalistic slavery "protected" African Americans; abolitionists maintained that slavery "took unfair advantage of the Negro's innocence and good nature" (Fredrickson 102); a number of colonizationists called for the return of African Americans to their "native country" to prevent their further corruption in an "alien" culture. Alexander Kinmont achieved international attention in the early 1840s for his *Twelve Lectures on Man*, which theorized the inherent Christian nature of "the Negro." Kinmont argued that blacks possessed characteristics that would be desirable for whites to acquire: " 'light-heartedness,' a 'natural talent for music,' and, above all, 'willingness to *serve*.' " In fact, though he contended that the white race was currently more developed than "the Negro race," Kinmont believed it was imminently probable that people of African descent would develop a " 'later but far nobler civilization . . . return[ing] the splendor of the Divine attributes of mercy and benevolence in the practice and exhibition of the milder and gentler virtues' " (qtd. in Fredrickson 105). His assertions were immediately taken up by white clergy and the antislavery movement in the 1840s, and his contention that Africa would be the future home of "a peculiarly Christian and 'feminine' civilization" was capitalized upon by colonizationists in the 1850s (Fredrickson 115). Of course, this image of blacks as innately "feminine" also made its way into popular mid-nineteenth-century antislavery novels like Harriet Beecher Stowe's *Uncle Tom's Cabin* (1852) and Metta V. Victor's *Maum Guinea, and Her Plantation Children* (1861). Agencies designed to aid the freedmen in postbellum America were composed of white men who also believed in such rhetoric. Reverend Horace James, superintendent of Negro Affairs in North Carolina in

1864, argued against granting African Americans "equality of social condition," citing their inherently "servile" characters and dispositions: " '[Negroes] always make the most faithful, pliable, obedient, devoted servants that can enter our dwellings' " (qtd. in Fredrickson 180).

While it might seem that white Americans dominated theories of racial difference, recent work like Mia Bay's *The White Image in the Black Mind* documents the ways in which African Americans contributed to a growing "black ethnology" during the nineteenth century that "survived in black popular thought" well into the twentieth (202). Black nationalists agitating for social change in America during the mid to late nineteenth century accessed existing rhetoric on "racial character." Undoubtedly intending to counter the white construction of African Americans as "corrupt," black nationalists invoked a number of romantic racialism's tenets, including the idea that races had specific "contributions" to make to American society through "missions" fuelled by racial "instinct." Alexander Crummell, a principal spokesperson for Pan-Africanism in nineteenth-century America, believed that each race was essentially unique: " '[R]aces have their individuality. That individuality is subject at all times to all laws of race-life. That race-life, all over the globe, shows an invariable proclivity, and in every instance, to integration of blood and permanence of essence' " (qtd. in Appiah, *Father's House* 10). Crummell was committed to a "Christian civilization" of African Americans and viewed races as divinely ordained: "Races, like families, are the organisms and the ordinance of God, and race feeling, like family feeling, is of divine origin" (Crummell 46). W.E.B. DuBois also extolled collective goals toward which he urged African Americans to work, and in doing so he used a spiritualistic rhetoric. In his essay "The Conservation of Races" (1897), DuBois both defined "race" and invoked the then powerful rhetorical trope of a divine racial mission in the form of each race's "particular message, its particular ideal" (819). DuBois called on "the Negro people" to take up their mission, one that "*must* be inspired with the Divine faith of our black mothers, that out of the blood and dust of battle will march a victorious host, a mighty nation, a peculiar people, to speak to the nations of earth a Divine truth that shall make them free" ("Conservation" 823). Statements such as these at certain points in the development of his thoughts on race have caused scholars to place him in this tradition of "classic black nationalism" with its elements of "mysticism, authoritarianism, civilizationism and collectivism" (Moses, *Golden Age* 35). Mia Bay notes that such elements were part of politics within the Harlem Renaissance a decade later: "[T]he rise of a variety of messianic black nationalist movements such as the

Garvey movement, the Black Muslim sect, black Judaism . . . the African Orthodox Church . . . [and] the emergence of new religious sects led by charismatic black leaders such as Daddy Grace and Father Divine [made] race . . . a central concern . . . [and] all drew on the religious racialism of nineteenth-century black ethnology" (200–201). Such movements could claim the popular support of African Americans like never before.

While whites were defining and legislating racial identities according to blood, they were not the only Americans pursuing notions of racial purity as a guarantor of a group's identity and survival; rather, "blood" and its purity were also key concepts of nineteenth-century black nationalism. Martin Delany's was one of the earliest black nationalist expressions of the importance of racial purity for the past and future success of African Americans: "[A]mong those who have stood the most conspicuous and shone the brightest in the earliest period of our history, there are those of pure and unmixed African blood," he wrote in 1852. "The elevation of the colored man can only be completed by the elevation of the pure descendants of Africa" (Delany 87). Delany reasoned that if "pure Africans" were accorded equality with whites in America, African Americans of biracial descent could not reasonably be denied equal status and rights. Delany knew that biracial Americans could demand equality by claiming "consanguinity" with their ancestors of "unmixed African blood," but white Americans would never recognize "blood" ties between African Americans and their white ancestors, as well as the rights, privileges, and property that would then accompany such a heritage.

While Delany was clear about the goal he hoped to achieve with his appeal to racial purity, other black nationalists were not. Edward Blyden's "insistence on 'pure blood' " stemmed from his belief that African Americans had been accorded subordinate status in America not only because of white oppression but, more important, because of racial intermixture (Echeruo 676). Blyden, who argued through the 1860s that a biracial heritage was detrimental, was openly contemptuous of mulattas, whom he called " 'the mixed classes', 'the miscegens', 'the half and three-fourths white *protégés*', and (in several instances) the 'mongrel' breed" (Echeruo 677). Alexander Crummell also developed a reputation for "championing blacks against mulattoes" (Toll 42) and defined race in 1860 as a homogeneity of blood: " 'a RACE, i.e. a compact, homogeneous population of one blood ancestry and lineage' " (qtd. in Appiah, *Father's House* 10). However much Crummell may have argued that he did not disapprove of mulattas but only of the "Afro-American oligarchy," he would not have included individuals of biracial descent in "the African race" as he defined it.

DuBois seems also to have used the nineteenth-century preoccupation with blood for his own ends, but to argue for its less than central role in determining race and racial identity. In "The Conservation of Races," he proffers a definition of race that evokes blood as a commonly held criteria of a racial group, but not a requirement; more important to DuBois is a shared history of lived experience. "What, then, is a race?" he asks. "It is a vast family of human beings, generally of common blood and language, always of common history, traditions and impulses, who are both voluntarily and involuntarily striving together for the accomplishment of certain more or less vividly conceived ideals of life" ("Conservation" 817). In this definition, DuBois both evokes and refutes race as it was thought of at the turn of the century, making race less a matter of blood and more a matter of consent to common ideals and goals that result from the shared experience of oppression. He would go on to ironize the notion of race as solely a matter of blood in *Dusk of Dawn* (1940). In his chapter entitled "The Concept of Race," DuBois outlines the progression of his thought on " 'race' and race problems," and when he comes to tell of his experience as a student at Fisk from 1885 to 1888, he characterizes race as a composite. "[W]hen I went South to Fisk," he writes, "I became a member of a closed racial group with rites and loyalties, with a history and a corporate future, with an art and philosophy. I received these eagerly and expanded them so that when I came to Harvard the theory of race separation was quite in *my blood*" (*Dusk* 627–28, emphasis added).[22] For DuBois, blood becomes a metaphor for political commitment, not the carrier of inherent racial traits; racial groups are not natural formations along heritable blood lines but a group of individuals sharing certain loyalties and a degree of common experience while pursuing shared economic, political, and philosophical goals.

What Text Will Tell?: Growing Tensions between the Corporeal and the Social

Cheryl Harris asserts that the law's "allocation of race and rights . . . relied on bounded, objective and scientific definitions of race," especially blood, through the nineteenth and into the mid-twentieth century (1737–38). Harris goes on to argue that social reputation was uniformly regarded as secondary to rules of hypodescent:

> In adjudicating who was "white," courts sometimes noted that, by physical characteristics, the individual whose racial identity was at issue appeared to be

white and, in fact, had been regarded as white in the community. Yet if an individual's blood was tainted, she could not claim to be "white" as the law understood, regardless of the fact that . . . she may have . . . lived as a white person. . . . Although socially accepted as white, she could not *legally* be white. Blood as "objective fact" dominated over appearance and social acceptance, which were socially fluid and subjective measures. (1739–40)

However, despite the rhetoric that linked blood to inherent racial characters used by white Americans and certain black intellectuals from the early nineteenth century until as late the 1930s, we repeatedly find legal decisions in which blood does not override the social performance of a racial identity as judges and juries recognized it. During the first half of the nineteenth century, courts increasingly questioned whether "the African color" alone was sufficient proof of one's race in what could be conflicting rulings on racial identity. While in North Carolina, *Gobu v. E. Gobu* (1802), a case centering on the contested liberty of a free person of color, had reaffirmed the long-held assumption that a black complexion was a sign of slavery and a complexion indicating admixture was not (Catterall 2:18–19), four years later in the District of Columbia public conduct and reputation were said to outweigh color in *Minchin v. Docker* (1806): "Charles Cavender, a black man, was admitted to testify . . . after witnesses had testified that Charles had acted publicly for eleven years as a free man and was generally reputed as such. Duckett, Circuit Judge, said that . . . although color is *prima facie* evidence of slavery, yet the fact that the witness had, for a long time, publicly acted as free, turned the presumption the other way" (Catterall 4:159). However, the District of Columbia was by no means in agreement on this point, for in 1811—just five years later—color was evoked as the sole deciding factor in an African American man's suit for "assault, battery and false imprisonment." The decision in *Bell v. Hogan* held that "if a colored man was born a slave, his being permitted to go at large . . . and to act as a free man, was no evidence of his being free. . . . The plaintiff's color . . . justified his being taken up under suspicion of being a runaway" (Catterall 4:164).

From 1819 through the 1840s, New Jersey, Ohio, South Carolina, Delaware, and the District of Columbia held that "color was sufficient" to decide an individual's race and status. Yet in May 1835 a judge hearing *State v. Cantey* in South Carolina was required to rule on the race of several men who were presented as witnesses, since only whites could testify against whites in an American court of law. The genealogy of these men was submitted to the court "proving" that they had "one-sixteenth part of African blood"; however, they were also said to be "respectable . . . received into society, and recognized as white men" (Catterall 2:358). Their testimony was deemed admissible, and the presiding judge ruled that "if . . . the person has been received . . . as white, although there may be proof of some admixture . . . yet such a person is to be accounted white" (Catterall 2:358). The case was appealed on the grounds that, as men of color, their testimony was inadmissible. The court of appeals unanimously dismissed the motion for a new trial, with Justice William Harper arguing that the witnesses in this case must be regarded as white men:

> We cannot say what admixture . . . will make a colored person. . . . The condition . . . is not to be determined solely by . . . visible mixture . . . but by reputation . . . and it may be . . . proper, that a man of worth . . . should have the rank of a white man, while a vagabond of the same degree of blood should be confined to the inferior caste. . . . It is hardly necessary to say that a slave cannot be a white man. (Catterall 2:359)

In this case, performing as white—being regarded by whites as respectable and being received and recognized socially by them as white—outweighed any "proof" of blackness in the body. Eight years later in South Carolina, a case deciding the race of Thomas, John, and Harry Johnson for taxation purposes evoked a similar type of reasoning. Although the Johnsons' great grandfather was "a colored man," the judge in *Johnson v. Boon* (1843) instructed the jury to give reputation at least as much weight as they would genealogy: " 'Color . . . ought to be compared with all the circumstances . . . and if the jury were satisfied that the color, blood, and reception in society, would justify them in rating the relators as free white men, they had a right to do so. . . . [W]hen men had been acknowledged as white men, and allowed all their privileges, it was bad policy to degrade them to the condition of free negroes' " (Catterall 2:385–86). The jury "very properly" found the Johnsons to be white men and exempt from the taxes to which free persons of color were subject.

These rulings reveal that considering reputation alongside genealogy in the same case could result in a legal definition of race as reputation overriding "scientific" notions of race (degree of blood) and its expression (visible mixture). In a sense, then, despite the obvious fear of the passing mulatta that such cases registered and were charged to contain, judges and juries repeatedly considered the performance of whiteness at least as if not more important than the verification of whiteness through genealogy. The practice of deciding racial identity by considering a person's reputation continued through the 1840s in the District of Columbia and the state of Delaware; in fact, in all cases, reputation was said to override complexion and other physical features, and at times reputation even outweighed genealogy.[23] In other words, during the height of "blood as racial character" rhetoric, a rhetoric that continued into the twentieth century as we have seen, an equally and at times more powerful belief in race as read in the social and not in the body prevailed. If one had performed and had been taken as "white," one might well be deemed legally white despite evidence to the contrary.

Ian Haney López observes that in racial prerequisite cases deciding naturalization, citizenship, and, by extension, "whiteness at law," late-nineteenth-century courts "initially relied on both rationales [common knowledge and scientific evidence] to justify their decisions. However, beginning in 1909 a schism appeared among the courts over whether common knowledge or scientific evidence was the appropriate standard. Thereafter, the lower courts divided almost evenly on the proper test for whiteness. . . . No court used both rationales" (6). While López's focus on naturalization and citizenship produces his assertion that the schism between these conceptions of race emerged only in the twentieth century, we in fact find it much earlier. Whether a court chose "color" and complexion or genealogy and fractional quantities of blood as the evidence of race as biological, it set that rationale against the performance of whiteness or social reputation in those cases I have cited. López argues that "by 1909 changes in immigrant demographics and in anthropological thinking combined to create contradictions between science and common knowledge," whereas prior to this time "science and popular beliefs jibed in the construction of racial categories" (7). However, if we turn to other phenomena like a growing slave population, slave revolts, white supremacy campaigns, and African American migrations from the rural South to urban centers in the North and South, we see a growing anxiety about whiteness that instead made "knowledge" or evidence of an individual's racial identity rather fraught and unstable.

Especially in the South, the additional consideration of an individual's reputation in determining race was the result of a growing concern that, in fact, the body might be fallible "evidence" given the increasing numbers of mulattas, slave and free. In Louisiana and South Carolina, states with an established tradition of valuing their "free colored" population and maintaining good relations between whites and free persons of color, whites agitated against "social and legal definitions of blackness that bred a class of persons visibly black but legally white" (Williamson 65). Newspapers frequently called for the exile of all free people of color from these states.[24] The complication of racial definition with further qualifications during the 1830s and 1840s registers an increasing fear of slave revolt and a growing slave population that in many places outnumbered whites, but it also reflects a white Southern emphasis on "purity of blood" that underpinned a threatened social order.[25] White Southerners wanted to preserve their blood's so-called purity, but they also believed that white blood would be ultimately responsible for any mulatto-led slave insurrection, as a Virginia minister wrote in 1833:

> "That the high notions of liberty, the ardent feeling, and proud unbending spirit of the South should be imparted with their [white] blood to the mixed race . . . is what must be expected. Many mulattos know that the best blood of the South runs in their veins, they feel its proud, impatient and spirit-stirring pulsations; and see themselves cast off and oppressed by those that gave them being. Such a state of things must produce characters fit for treason, stratagem, and spoil." (qtd. in Johnston 298–99)

Frequently, this white fear was expressed in contradictory ways during the 1850s and early 1860s. During this period, white Southerners attempted to enlist the loyalties of a large "free colored" population that they hoped would intercede in, and diffuse, any slave uprisings. Yet at the same time that white Southerners sought an alliance with, and appeared to trust, free people of color, they also clearly felt threatened by the "other" among them: "[B]etween 1856 and 1859 no less than seventeen grand juries saw fit to call attention to the danger from free persons of color" (Williamson 66).

The heightened polarization of racial identities that resulted from this anxiety continued into the late nineteenth century. Grace Hale has argued that this was a particularly volatile period in the South:

> The Civil War . . . ma[de] whiteness a more important category, a way to assert a new collectivity, the Confederacy, across lines of class and gender that divided free southerners. . . . But by the 1880s . . . political conflicts, as well as the economic trends toward centralization, standardization, urbanization, and mechanization, accelerated and permanently institutionalized by the war, meant that American collective identity itself was now anything but clear. . . . The question of what structure of social ordering would replace the familiar hierarchies . . .

made this a period of volatility and uncertainty. Hierarchical structures founded
in the personalized social relations of specific localities lost their authority in an
increasingly mobile and rapidly changing society. (6)

While old social orders were threatened during this period, attempts to reassert
them continued nonetheless. Virginia Dominguez, in her study of Creole identity and racial classification in Louisiana, observes that "a near obsession with
metasemantics ruled much of the 1880s and 1890s," as the state became "engulfed
in the reclassification process intent on salvaging white Creole status" (143). Prior
to this period, both whites and blacks freely acknowledged that the Creole identity was claimed by members of both races. But during the late nineteenth century, white Creoles, under pressure of suspicions regarding "impure blood,"
rejected black Louisianans who claimed a Creole identity. In order to secure their
threatened social status, white Creoles insisted upon "the exclusive Caucasian
composition of the category," established "a number of white Creole organizations . . . to protect the status of the 'true' Creole," and "actively fought the publication of any book or article that referred to, or even implied," the existence of
Creoles of color (Dominguez 146–48). Dominguez's account of the extremes
white Creoles went to in order to "purify" their identity is a telling example of
how whiteness was being constructed through exclusions that were dependent
upon refining absolute distinctions between black and white.

Southern whites not only feared African Americans so "white as to easily pass
for a white man," but they also feared those whites who appeared to sympathize or
associate with African Americans (Johnston 192). Consequently, they applied the
notion of race as reputation and behavior to call into question the racial identity
and social position of certain whites as well. This practice reached a peak in North
Carolina's white supremacy campaigns of 1898 and 1900; the result, Joel
Williamson contends, was that "by about 1900 it was possible in the South for one
who was biologically purely white to become behaviorally black. Blackness . . . had
passed on to become a matter of inner morality and outward behavior" (108). In
Following the Color Line, Ray Stannard Baker relates a report carried by the *Atlanta
Georgian*, March 6, 1907, detailing the expulsion of a newcomer from South
Carolina who was suspected of being a mulatto attempting to pass for white. The
man returned with "a number of reputable white Carolinians" who attested to his
identity as a "white man" (R. S. Baker, 52). Neither reputation nor association, but
rather this man's status as unknown, aroused the suspicion of white Georgians.
The threat of the "white nigger," then, was used as a justification for effectively

controlling those whites whose commitment to white Southern economic, political, and social interests was questionable.

Yet however much the racial identity of white Southerners may have been disputed in rumors and popular accusations like these, "blackness" and degrees of black blood remained the focus of legal disputes of the mulatta's racial identity. Historically, the degree and definition of blackness, not whiteness, have been at issue in such cases across the nation, a focus that has actively worked to obscure the historical and cultural contingency of whiteness. If whites are marked, it is not by race but, as Guillaumin argues of all dominant groups, "by a convenient lack of interdiction" (41). Cases in which reputation or association decided the racial identity of plaintiffs said to be "black" span the years 1811 to 1938 but cluster around the 1890s through the early 1900s, those decades Hale calls particularly volatile for the South but ones in which other parts of the nation were clearly unsettled as well. Again, it is the performance of whiteness and its recognizability by other whites—friends, associates, spouses, parents, schoolmates, teachers— that became the focus of such cases. North Carolina considered an individual's association with "one race or the other" admissible in determining that person's race in 1892 (Mangum 15).[26] And in 1894 a Texas court admitted as evidence "tending to show that she is a white woman" testimony proving "a woman's first husband was a white man" (Stephenson 17). The state of Alabama also used the race of spouses as a "criterion" to decide race in 1903 and added as admissible evidence proving an individual is a "Negro" testimony "that the person has been treated by a Negro couple as their offspring" (Mangum 263). Significantly, here, it is not traceable genealogy but the "treatment" of the child as the offspring of one race or another, his or her socialization as white or black, that was decisive. Kentucky and Oklahoma ruled in 1905 and 1912, respectively, that an individual's attendance at "white schools in their home state or in the state from which they had emigrated" could be considered proof of her or his race (Mangum 15).

This clustering of legal decisions that read reputation as a marker of race is arguably part of a larger move to racialize class differences in response to greater social mobility in American society. The rapid change caused by increasing industrialization and urbanization, as well as an influx of immigrants and a migration of southern African Americans from rural areas to urban centers in the North and South, created a fluid and highly mobile society at the turn into the twentieth century. These shiftings of place were not only a matter of populations relocating but also of individuals attaining class positions that had previously been inaccessible. Hale has isolated just such changes as the impetus for the South's "culture of segregation" beginning in 1890: "A black middle class was rising, with its unhinging of black race and class identities, and hierarchies of personalized power were being subverted in the move to a more urban, less locally grounded, mass society. These threats made the ritualistic enactment of racial difference vital to the maintenance of white supremacy" (284). However, we see attempts to secure social divisions outside the South as well. Middle- and upper-class white Americans responded to this greater social mobility with an increased attention to, and regimentation of, the social. The increased publication and popularity of etiquette manuals are just such markers of this anxiety, which John Kasson argues "intensified in reaction to pressure from various directions, including the influx of new immigrant populations and the presence of a self-assertive new plutocracy" (60). Citing what he acknowledges is an incomplete enumeration, Kasson notes that "twenty-eight different manuals appeared in the 1830s, thirty-six in the 1840s and thirty-eight more in the 1850s. . . . In the period from 1870 to World War I . . . the flow of volume rose to a rate of five or six a year. . . . Etiquette books clearly constituted a major popular literary genre at this time as never before" (44). Robert Young also observes that bourgeois whites used rigid standards of behavior in an attempt to consolidate their power and position. "As the defining feature of whiteness, civilization merged with its quasi-synonym 'cultivation,' and thus the scale of difference which separated the . . . races was quickly extended so that culture became the defining feature of the upper and middle classes," Young documents. "These racialized class differentiations offered some consolation and fantasized intrinsic qualities of class during a period when it was patently evident that you could simply buy your way into the middle and upper classes" (95–96). By racializing class differences, American society—built upon individualism and equality "for all"—again attempted to mask through naturalization its social divisions of power so that white Americans could believe that their society was ordered around the natural divisions of race, not the artificial distinctions of class.

The (In)visible Body and Internal Contradictions

Commensurate with the development of an increasingly narrow definition of whiteness from the mid-nineteenth through the first half of the twentieth century was an expansion of "otherness." This period saw the emphasis shift from a focus on external expressions of race like complexion, "grosser physical differences," reputation, and association to the question of whether "one drop" would make a person black. Such a shift to increasingly finer distinctions between white and black in this focus on fractions of blood is a clear example of what Bourdieu has identified as the workings of the law to make the social reassuringly predictable during periods of flux: "By eliminating exceptions and the vagueness of uncertain groupings, and by imposing clear discontinuities and strict borders in the continuum of statistical limits, juridical formalization introduces into social relations a clarity and predictability" (849). The intent may have been to clarify racial distinctions and render racial identities less vague; however, the result was a nation unable to achieve a stable racial classification in this period. Both North Carolina and Louisiana vacillated between a fractional and a one-drop definition of race in the early twentieth century. North Carolina had, in 1901, adopted the "third generation inclusive" definition of blackness and extended it in 1908; yet in 1903 a statute regarding school attendance held that "no child with Negro blood in his veins, 'however remote the strain,' shall attend a school for the white race" (Stephenson 174). Kentucky, after having adopted Virginia's classification of one-quarter in 1835, narrowed its definition of blackness to "one drop" in 1911. But in 1932 a Kentucky court ruled that "a person who looks white, has straight hair, is of copper color, and has other characteristics of the white man is not a mulatto within the statute prohibiting the marriage of whites and Negroes or mulattos" (Stephenson 12). And in 1910 Louisiana used the one-drop rule to define members of "the colored race within the meaning of the Jim Crow Law" but also decided that an "octoroon" was not a "colored" person when deciding antimiscegenation cases: "[T]he term 'Negro' does not necessarily include persons in whose veins there is only an admixture of Negro blood, and . . . it clearly would not be applicable to a person in whom the admixture is as slight that even a scientific expert could not be positive of its presence" (Mangum 5). Yet Louisiana does seem to have had confidence in the ability of its "scientific experts" to discern traces of African blood, for it had already adopted a fractional definition of blackness—one-eighth—in 1908 and 1910 and refined that definition to more than one-thirty-second in 1970.[27]

Texas also failed to establish a consensus on its definition of racial identity as late as the 1920s and 1930s. In 1856 a Texas court had already expressed its trepidation of contradictory race and status designations that could result in an individual being considered "white enough" (removed from any African ancestor to the fourth generation) to "be a competent witness against a white person, but following the status of its mother, it would be a slave [sic]" (Catterall 5:295). By 1925, contradictory racial definitions remained a matter of legal record in this state. Both the school law and the antimiscegenation statute of 1925 define as black an individual with any African ancestry; however, the penal statute of 1925, in effect to enforce the antimiscegenation statute, lists as black those of "Negro blood to the third generation inclusive" (Mangum 8–9). It would have been possible for a Texas court to find a defendant guilty of violating the antimiscegenation statute but then be unable to impose any fine or jail term upon that same individual. While many states moved toward a "one drop" definition of blackness and a "pure blood" definition of whiteness over time, a significant number vacillated in their designations of race. Moreover, while nineteenth- and twentieth-century white Americans generally adopted notions of race as "blood" traceable through genealogy to fractional amounts, there remained states more concerned with that blood's "expression."

Perhaps one of the best examples of conflicting notions of what made an individual white or black is a 1910 case deciding the race of a child and her right to attend "the Brookland School, a white institution" in Washington, D.C. (Gatewood 166). Isabel Wall was the daughter of Stephen Wall, a man "'of extraordinarily light complexion,' and his white wife" (Gatewood 166). The Washington, D.C., Board of Education ordered Isabel to "attend a Negro school," but her father petitioned the court of appeals to allow her to attend a white school. In order to argue that his daughter was white, Stephen Wall "denied that he himself was 'a colored man' or that he was so recognized by neighbors and friends." The court countered with "proof" that Stephen Wall was "colored": he had operated "'a pool room in a colored neighborhood, that was frequented by colored people,'" and his grandmother was "'a very light mulatto woman.'" They further "estimated" that Isabel possessed "'Negro blood of one-eighth to one-sixteenth,' even though she had blue eyes, blond hair, and an 'unusually fair' complexion." Consequently, the court decided that Isabel Wall was "colored" and should attend a "colored school" because "complexion and physical appearance had little to do with determining one's racial status. . . . '[P]ersons of whatever complexion, who bear Negro blood in whatever degree, and who abide in the racial status of the Negro, are colored in the common estimation of the people'" (Gatewood 167). The Wall case evoked a number of contradictory notions of race: reputation may decide race, but only when the individual in question is deemed to be "colored" because he or she "abides in the racial status of the Negro"; an "estimation" of the fractional admixture of one's "blood" based on a thorough account of one's genealogy is a more reliable determinant of race than one's appearance, yet it is effectively a moot point since one drop of "black blood" makes one "colored"; and an attempt to evoke the "objectivity" of science by quantifying the racial components of one's blood is given great weight, but ultimately the deciding factor is popular opinion or "the common estimation of the people."

We might wonder why such contradictory notions of race evoked in individual cases, and the failure to establish consistent race and status designations across a variety of laws and statutes within states, did not undermine people's faith in the judicial system to the extent that they might begin to doubt its decisions. Bourdieu proves quite helpful on this point. He argues that as a "legitimized discourse" the law's power lays in its "constitutive tendency to *formalize* and to *codify* everything which enters its field of vision" (809). Perhaps more important, however, is the attention Bourdieu draws to the need for, and the ability of, the law to repeatedly ensure that its arbitrariness goes unnoticed by a public whose belief in the "truth" of the law must be continually reproduced by the law itself. "As the quintessential form of legitimized discourse, the law can exercise its specific power only to the extent that it attains recognition, that is, to the extent that the element of arbitrariness at the heart of its functioning (which may vary from case to case) remains unrecognized," he writes. "The tacit grant of *faith* in the juridical order must be ceaselessly reproduced. Thus, one of the functions of the specifically juridical labor of formalizing and systematizing ethical representations and practices is to contribute to binding laypeople to the fundamental principle of the jurists' professional ideology—belief in the neutrality and autonomy of the law and of jurists themselves" (844).

These very cases, then, in which the juridical power to produce and legislate racial identities is challenged also provide the necessary opportunities for juridical acts to claim, and through those claims maintain, the status of "truth." "In granting the status of *judgement* to a legal decision . . . the rationalization process provides the decision with the *symbolic effectiveness* possessed by any action which, assuming one ignores its arbitrariness, is recognized as legitimate," contends Bourdieu. "The self-representation which describes the court as a separate and bounded space within which conflicts are transformed into specialist dialogues and the trial [is regarded] as an ordered progression toward the truth, accurately evokes one of the dimensions of the symbolic effect of juridical activity as the free and rational application of a universally and scientifically recognized norm" (828–30). Thus, despite a number of contradictory conceptions of race upheld in judicial decisions, and despite the inability of states to come to a definite decision of what constituted blackness and thereby whiteness, American courts routinely worked to "read" and define mulatta bodies and their behaviors in ways that shored up the law's symbolic effectiveness, the very thing the mulatta most threatened by challenging racial distinctions.

The courtroom physical inspections with their disturbing echoes of slave auction blocks, the litany of characteristics taken as evidence of African blood, and the idea that blood carried even the most minute trace of a blackness so powerful it could not be "overcome" by the white blood that may run alongside it in one's veins—all these criteria used to decide race reveal a white American notion of race as "natural" and naturalized in the legal decisions that evoked them. Race was largely defined bodily, through examining and theorizing about "other" bodies from "pure African" to "graduated shades thereof." When white blood was mentioned, it was reified as an agent of purity, as in this judge's instructions to a North Carolina jury in 1857:

> [T]he descendants of negro ancestors become free white persons, not by being removed in generation only, but by that, coupled with purification of blood. . . . [N]o person in the fifth generation from a negro ancestor becomes a free white person, unless one ancestor in each generation was a white person; that is to say, unless there shall be such a purification of negro blood by the admixture of white blood . . . and unless there is such purification it makes no difference how many generations you should have to go back to find a pure negro ancestor; even . . . a hundred, still the person is a free negro. (Catterall 2:209–10)

White physical characteristics were rarely mentioned in cases deciding whether a person who looked white was in fact white; rather, the focus centered on the gradual dissipation of African characteristics like the straightening of hair and lightening of complexion.

Grounding its decisions of identity and definitions of race repeatedly in the body, the courts attempted to naturalize legal disputes over race. This turn to the body's interiors eventually came to outweigh those earlier tensions between "legal" race as biological or social. Legal decisions could be regarded as upholding "natural" differences: the law could be said to "observe" the very racial distinctions it was actively creating. This ability of the law both to appear entirely objective and to be performative in its utterances, to be what Bourdieu calls "the quintessential form of the symbolic power of naming that creates the things named, and creates social groups in particular" because it is "able by its own operations to produce its effects" (838–39), is largely the result of rhetoric. "Juridical language . . . bears all the marks of a rhetoric of impersonality and of neutrality," notes Bourdieu.

"The neutralization-effect is created by a set of syntactic traits such as the predominance of passive and impersonal constructions. These are designed to mark the impersonality of normative utterances and to establish the speaker as universal subject, at once impartial and objective" (819–20). Obvious contradictions within and between states when it came to defining race were not regarded as the fault of inconsistencies in law or in notions of racial difference as "normative utterances," then, but could be explained as differences in interpretations of what governing bodies had actually intended in legislature. However, those contradictions show us that some bodies were clearly difficult to "manage" and that some identities shifted rather than remained stable. In turn, these instabilities threatened constantly to undo a construct that was proving ever more impossible to contain and increasingly difficult to police. That tension between race as biological or as social reputation is one we should keep plainly in sight, for it forestalls easy understandings of the way race circulated in both the popular imagination and courts of law and renders more complex a highly ambivalent social arena in flux. Indeed, the racial imaginary was far from a consensus on how to determine racial identity and what race was. Even when we focus on the human sciences as racialist discourse, we see a narrative that is more discontinuous than "progressivist" in its trajectory. That narrative of turning from unreliable exteriors to the "facts" of the body's inner spaces, particularly its blood, has an even more tenuous hold once we read the sciences and the law against one another.

Clearly, race was a vexed "concept" through the nineteenth and into the twentieth century. Its power rested in its ability to naturalize a social and political order in America that was underpinned by, and had at stake, white power and white identity. The naturalizing power of race began with a recognition of, and stress upon, physical difference that never ceased but shifted and developed as white needs changed. White Americans ushered in scientific schools and racial theories to generate this biologizing of a group's abilities, culture, and behavior, a biologizing that found its greatest power in the blood's transmission of "essence." African American intellectuals, on the other hand, mobilized theories of race that best suited their political aims, invoking a rhetoric to do so that we might expect them to reject. It is hardly surprising that during the nineteenth century and through most of the twentieth, white Americans have been unwilling to conceive of race as a discursive or social construct, despite their obvious suspicion that performing a racial identity might mean one *was* as white or black as one seemed, despite what genealogy or biology might reveal.

It is at this fissure in the color line, where its security gives way to successful traverses and transgressions, that the political work of the mulatta figure becomes important to contemplate. And it is at this fissure that we see African American women rhetors and novelists forwarding a new understanding of "race" and racial difference. The political work of the mulatta, as these women employed the figure, foregrounds race and gender as discursive constructions, undermines the investment of both race and gender in a politics of visibility that relied upon the body as an index to identity and character, and plays on notions of race as a matter of blood and how that blood "tells." As we shall see in the chapters that follow, African American women were using the mulatta to theorize race and womanhood as performable identities in a period in which white Americans expended a great deal of intellectual effort and time to secure inherent and immutable differences between themselves and African Americans. Uncannily picking up on those anxieties over the passing mulatta that the courts registered and were charged to contain, these women played on the visibility and performability of whiteness in unsettling ways.

Chapter 2

"White Slaves" and Tragic Mulattas

The Antislavery Appeals of Ellen Craft and Sarah Parker Remond

The mulatta was not only the anxious obsession of the law and science as these discourses debated and constructed racial identities but was also the fantasy of fiction and theater throughout the nineteenth century. Particularly popular were narratives and dramas of the "tragic mulatta" or "white slave."[1] While depictions of the mulatta varied according to genre, critics generally agree that these contours of the tragic mulatta plot predominated.[2] "[T]he tragic mulatta plot centers on a beautiful fair-skinned young girl whose father is most often her master but who remains ignorant of her slave identity," summarizes Carla Peterson. "Socialized as a young lady, she is courted by a white gentleman. . . . At the moment of narrative crisis, her slave condition is discovered, or remembered, and she is remanded into slavery[,] . . . separated from her lover and most often dies a tragic death" (154). The tragic mulatta is regarded as the creation of white American abolitionist Lydia Maria Child, whose stories, such as "The Quadroons" (1842) and "Slavery's Pleasant Homes" (1843), were printed in the Boston Female Anti-Slavery Society's very popular *Liberty Bell*.[3] Both Jean Fagan Yellin and Karen Sànchez-Eppler have argued that these sentimental narratives, authored by Child and other white American female abolitionists, spoke far more "to the concerns of free white women" in the United States than to the predicament of her "sister slave" (Yellin 73). Circulating in white-authored American antislavery tracts from the 1840s through the Civil War, the mulatta and tragic mulatta also captivated white English audiences in the early to mid-nineteenth century.[4] As Jennifer DeVere Brody documents, in England the mulatta figure, or, as she calls her, the "mulattaroon," becomes "purified, lightened, and whitened," suggesting "that interest in the dark-skinned mulattaroon gradually fades," until by the mid to late 1850s we see a "marked concern with 'white slaves.' . . . The horror of slavery, therefore, was increasingly emblematized by the degradation suffered by 'white' women" (17, 48).

42

The mulatta's Atlantic crossing is significant for our understanding of the political uses to which African American women put this figure. Clearly the mulatta was both popularized and politicized as she registered cultural anxieties regarding race and sexuality in the United States and in England as well. She was also a proxy through whom white American antislavery women "wrestl[ed] with their duty to female slaves" (Yellin 73) and negotiated their conflicting feelings regarding their own sexuality (Sànchez-Eppler 42) and a figure who was "indispensable to the construction of Englishness as a new form of 'white' male subjectivity" (Brody 7). More important for our purposes, the mulatta's, and particularly the tragic mulatta's, transatlantic popularity explains why African American female abolitionists like Ellen Craft and Sarah Parker Remond turned to her as a vehicle who registered, and so could also be used to challenge, a racial imaginary from which abolitionist discourse was far from liberated. On the surface, it appears that Craft and Remond simply turned to a recognizable figure with significant currency who would facilitate their antislavery appeals to British audiences removed from American slavery. Certainly their own popularity and that of other black abolitionists in England at midcentury raise the question of how much farther their appeals went beyond titillating sensation and/or establishing the recognizable for their audiences in order to facilitate British empathy. Yet recent work on this Victorian fad for black Americana, and earlier work on American female abolitionist representations of the female slave and tragic mulatta, inquires little, if at all, into how such tropes may have been managed by African American reformists working in the same period.[5] Abolitionists like Craft and Remond used the trope of the female slave and the tragic mulatta to access existing discourses and forms of representation with a keen sense of both their popularity and their potential risks. Either appearing as "the white slave" or invoking her in lectures, both women worked to elicit their audiences' empathy but also redirected a sensationalistic interest toward their antislavery goals. Perhaps most significantly, Craft and Remond used the mulatta figure, a figure who encodes doubleness and duality (black and white, self and other), in appearances or in double-voiced lectures that play on and seem to capitulate to their audiences' fascination with her only to challenge it.

The White Slave: Slavery's Zero Limit

Before Ellen Craft arrived in Liverpool in early December 1850 she had been circulating in American antislavery publications as slavery's zero limit, a "living proof" of its horrors and extremes. Indeed, Samuel May Jr. brought her to the attention of Bristol Garrisonian John Estlin in just such a fashion, stressing her "whitened" features in a letter dated 2 February 1849:

> E. C. . . . has no trace of African blood discernible in her features . . . but the whole is that of a southern-born white woman. To think of such a woman being held as a piece of property . . . (while it is in reality no worse or wickeder than when done to the blackest woman that ever was) does yet stir a community brought up in prejudice vs. color a thousand times more deeply than could be effected in different circumstances. She was a living proof that Slavery . . . is as ready to enslave the whitest and the fairest as any other provided only the pretext be afforded. (May to Estlin 2 February 1849)

American abolitionists and their audiences were taken as much by the Crafts' "singular and romantic escape" ("William and Ellen Craft") as by Ellen Craft's appearance. Repeatedly, publications would single out her whiteness before proceeding to narrate their journey from Georgia to Philadelphia, as the following excerpt demonstrates: "In a city about nine hundred miles South of Mason and Dixon's line, ELLEN CRAFTS [sic] was held as a slave. Because we find her in this degrading condition, let it not be understood that she is a negro. Ellen Crafts, though a slave, is white . . . and will readily pass in any circle, as a . . . white girl" ("Story").[6]

Ellen and her husband, William, effected a "daring escape" from Macon, Georgia, in December 1848. Ellen, the daughter of her master Major James Smith and his house slave Maria, was light-skinned enough to pass for white. With William posing as her slave, Ellen disguised herself as a rheumatic Southern gentleman en route to Philadelphia for treatment. Traveling by rail car and steamer, the Crafts arrived in Philadelphia four days later. They lived in Boston until the Fugitive Slave Law passed in September 1850 forced them to leave the United States in early November for England, where they remained for nineteen years. Not only were the Crafts well known in the United States where their escape was recounted in both abolitionist and proslavery papers, but their "daring escape . . . [was] widely reported in British newspapers" (Blackett, *Beating* 97). Soon after their arrival in Liverpool, the Crafts accompanied William Wells Brown on a lecture tour of the north and west of England as well as Scotland from January through May 1851, appearing at a score of antislavery meetings (Quarles 137). By 1854, the Crafts would be hailed as having made a "profound and abiding impression" (*Proceedings* 153) on their audiences, who were drawn by the promise of seeing Ellen Craft, "the 'White Slave'" ("Arrival"; "Views"). Ellen's "whiteness" and her status as living proof of the depths to which American slavery would sink elicited both the attention she labored under and a complex circuit of empathy and identification that her fellow African American abolitionist, Sarah Parker Remond, would later come to carefully negotiate.

Though Ellen Craft "reportedly faded from the lecture circuit after her husband gained prominence as a speaker" (Yee 25), his success was arguably indebted to the sensation she caused. Ellen Craft clearly fascinated those who saw her. She very quickly became a silent spectacle presented as bodily evidence of William Wells Brown's sentimental appeals to images of families torn apart by slavery and as the thrilling climax of William Craft's narration of their escape. Addressing an audience said to number 3,000 at the Glasgow Emancipation Society on 6 January 1851, Brown noted a British inconsistency "in denouncing . . . slavery, which separated the husband from his wife, and the mother from her child . . . [and] applaud[ing] the draymen of Barclay and Perkins, for driving General Hayman out of the country," and immediately drew attention to Ellen Craft as a rather violently embodied extreme of the institution: "For was not the individual who could enslave Ellen Craft, and who after she had made her escape, in a manner unparalleled by any man or woman,—could claim her as his property, pursue her to Boston, and then drive her from the land of her birth— was that individual not as mean and contemptible as the man who caused females to be flogged?" ("American Fugitive Slave Bill"). Importantly, while Ellen is not said to have been "flogged" herself, her audience is encouraged to imagine her meeting just such a fate under American slavery. She thus remains both distant enough as fugitive slave to facilitate their imaginings of the peculiar institution's horrors, yet close enough in her "white" appearance to enable their identification. At the close of Brown's address, "Mr. Wm. Craft was then introduced by the Chairman. His wife, in whom the negro blood is scarcely perceptible, accompanied him to the front of the platform. Their appearance was greeted with the utmost enthusiasm" ("American Fugitive Slave Bill"). In what would become an established pattern on this tour, William would narrate their escape, often adding sentimental renderings of families divided and sold separately, while Ellen stood by silently.

Indeed, Ellen's appearances seem to have been part of a well-practiced routine honed in the United States during a lecture tour two years earlier, and this precedent as well as the treatment of these silent appearances by scholars and historians raises the important question of her agency in such "exhibitions."[7] Benjamin Quarles speaks of both William and Ellen Craft as William Wells Brown's "drawing cards." "During the first six months of 1849, Brown toured the antislavery circuit exhibiting William and Ellen Craft. . . . Brown took the couple in his charge and gave them maximum exposure," writes Quarles. "He arranged meetings for them throughout New England, sometimes charging an admission fee, an almost unprecedented practice in abolitionist circles. But the Crafts were drawing cards. They said little, but Ellen's appearance created an instant sympathy in a white audience" (Quarles 62–63).[8]

As a result of such appearances, the Crafts "quickly became an abolitionist *cause célèbre*" (Blackett, *Beating* 90). Barbara McCaskill characterizes these lectures as "tableau vivants" in which the fugitives brought Brown's famous panorama of American slavery to life in a "program . . . [that] silenced and commodified Ellen. At most, it authorized her to respond rather than discuss. At worst, it bounded her response to a cordial and curt coming-out: to a curtsy, to a nod, to a few courteous words of acknowledgment to the crowd" ("Yours" 523).

While Brown certainly introduced the Crafts to the workings of the antislavery lecture circuit, other scholars speculate that William and Ellen were well aware of the attention her appearance garnered, deliberately courting it to advance their cause. R.J.M. Blackett writes of Ellen's silent displays at the close of these lectures as a "pattern" the Crafts had "refined," a "careful orchestration . . . guaranteed to provoke strong antislavery sentiments" in New England and, later, in Britain. During the 1849 American tour, William would heighten Brown's sentimental and domestic appeals by personalizing them: "Using his own experiences, he told how easily families were broken and up and sold separately" (*Beating* 99). Finally, Ellen would take the platform to embody her audiences' worst fears that slavery would not spare even the most womanly and white. Brown and the Crafts' appearances, then, could be said to appeal deliberately to their British audiences' familiarity with representations of slavery as an inhuman system violating domestic bonds and to their interest in a sentimental stress on the violation of feeling or "crimes of the heart." Ellen's appeal as the "white slave," particularly with the female members of her audiences, also intersected with an established and growing rhetoric justifying female petitioning and political work. As Clare Midgley points out, from the 1830s onward British antislavery women cited suffering—bodily suffering as well as moral degradation—as motivation for their growing involvement in political agitation (96). Outrages of the body, feeling, and one's moral sense came to have rhetorical force not only within the abolition movement but also within a developing feminist movement that had since the mid-1830s been likening the position of free white women to slaves, as the popular "woman as slave" trope indicates.[9] In part, Ellen Craft's whiteness may well have been the draw it was because she so emblematized the white "woman as slave" for her audiences, making "real" that more abstract argument that both fueled and justified women's political work and the feminist movement that would be under way by the mid to late 1850s.[10] Seeming to affirm Blackett's reading of Ellen's appearances as deliberately arranged by either Brown, the Crafts themselves, or both—though suggesting Ellen may have been less than comfortable with them—is a letter penned by John Estlin to Eliza Wigham in May 1851. "We have been endeavouring to improve the tone of Brown and Crafts [sic] Exhibition," writes Estlin, "altering their *showman like* handbills, and securing a higher position for Ellen. She fully feels the propriety of all we have said and done and is very thankful to us" (Farrison 186).

Just what Ellen Craft chose as her position on the platform, exactly what she may have agreed to in the name of propriety, or what she may have believed was most effective in advancing the antislavery cause is perhaps unknowable to us. Complicating her response to Estlin's suggestions for "improvement" would be her efforts to navigate the competing British antislavery interests she, William, and Brown were soliciting. In fact, these schisms as well as "bigotry" among British abolitionists were cited by Ellen as a hindrance to their work, as Mary Estlin's letter of 9 May 1851 to Anne Weston reveals: "E[llen] C[raft] says nothing has astonished and pained her here so much as . . . the bigotry of the majority of professed A[nti]-s[lavery] people. . . . She maintains . . . that you are not aware of the manifold difficulties with which we have to contend before we can get up any interest that will produce fruits." Rather than a full knowledge of her intents, motivations, and feelings, we have, instead, press accounts of her silent moments on the platform and their effect upon her audiences. However, we should forestall our too easy assumption that appearances characterized as "embarrassing" for Ellen Craft were ones in which she exercised little, if any, agency or choice. Such assumptions too quickly lead to readings of fugitive slaves in Britain as commodified by audiences whose responses they could little manage, audiences more fascinated with the spectacle of fugitive slaves and more interested in ridiculing America in their nationalist fervor than in assisting in the antislavery effort.[11] Not the least troubling in such readings is the tendency to position fugitive slaves like Ellen Craft as victimized in her very attempt to redress the oppression of those still enslaved. The effect is simply to underscore, rather than read critically, that "staple of abolitionist writing" in the 1850s, "the spectacle of the victimized black woman" (Keetley 6), as though this were a fad the African American lecturer could not manipulate.[12] Women like Ellen Craft effectively become little more than images of suffering, either under slavery or transatlantic abolition, despite our historical and critical remove from that moment. Yet it is possible that fugitive slave lecturers like the Crafts and Brown were well aware of their audiences' predilections, that they played to and capitalized upon what they knew drew a crowd. This is not to say that audience expectation and response little affected the work of fugitive slave lecturers but rather that these men and women were up to the task of managing those interests toward their own ends.

Frequently called upon the platform at the close of such meetings, Ellen Craft was described in British and Scottish papers as visibly embarrassed by her strategic display as slavery's silent and living exhibit. In late January 1851 her appearance at the close of a Perth antislavery meeting was said to be demanded by the audience: "She seemed rather reluctant to ['present herself'] . . . but . . . consented to occupy a standing position on the left side of the [platform]. . . . At first she seemed abashed; but the cheering having continued, she courtesied gracefully, and retired. . . . From her color and contour of features, no one would have thought that she had any African blood in her veins" ("Anti-Slavery Meeting"). Ellen's display as the "white slave" closed meeting after meeting from January through June of that year, but various press accounts depict her as growing no more comfortable with her role as the months passed: "[She] has a complexion very little darker than that of our country-women. She was neatly dressed and exhibited a modest demeanour; indeed, it struck us that she seemed somewhat embarrassed by the marked attentions paid to her" (*American Slavery* 3). Though she was said to be a rather skilled speaker who "kn[ew] how to use her tongue with considerable effect" ("Ellen Craft"), Ellen Craft was described in the press as a "specimen" on display and as slavery's "silent argument" ("American Fugitives"; "American Slavery," rpt. in the *Liberator*).

Ellen's status as specimen and spectacle reached an unusual pitch when American abolitionist Henry Wright wrote to James Haughton of Dublin in early February 1851, suggesting that the Crafts and William Wells Brown be part of London's Great Exhibition at Crystal Palace: "Above all, an American slave-auction block must be there, with William and Ellen Craft on the block, Henry Clay as auctioneer, and the American flag floating over it. . . . Or, if they cannot be admitted *into* the Fair, with other specimens of American ingenuity and skill, they must be exhibited in some place *outside*, but near it, so that they can be seen and examined with convenience" ("American Slavery in the World's Fair"). The Crafts did attend the fair on a crowded Saturday, 21 June, and walked "arm in arm" with British abolitionists "George and Jenny Thompson, Richard and Maria Webb, and William Farmer" (Blackett, *Building* 32). But the abolitionists' representation of their promenade was more sensationalistic than this description would suggest. Farmer wrote William Lloyd Garrison five days later: "Fortunately, we have . . . some specimens of what were once American 'chattels personal,' in the persons of William and Ellen Craft, and Wm. W. Brown; and their friends resolved that they should be exhibited under the world's huge glass case, in order that the world might form its opinion of the alleged mental inferiority of the African race, and their fitness or unfitness for freedom" ("Fugitive Slaves at the Great Exhibition"). How the Crafts and Brown were to prove the African race's intelligence and fitness for freedom by simply touring the exhibitions and becoming one themselves is questionable to say the least; in fact, in Farmer's estimation, their greatest utility is as silent embodiments of, rather than challenges to, a British public's expectations.

Brown and the Crafts, however, had different plans for the Great Exhibition. After this first appearance promenading through the exhibits, they are said to have returned on several occasions to directly confront American spectators. William Still documents one such visit in *The Underground Railroad*: "Brown and the Crafts have paid several other visits to the Great Exhibition, in one of which, Wm. Craft succeeded in getting some Southerners 'out' upon the Fugitive Slave Bill, respecting which a discussion was held between them in the American department. Finding themselves worsted at every point, they were compelled to have recourse to lying" (372). British abolitionists did not comment upon such moments and instead referred to their plans for using the trio solely as exhibits of American slavery who would offer neither comment nor critique.

Robert Reid-Pharr has recently noted that this era's "massive corpus of (liberal racialist) abolitionist [media] . . . that largely defined [William Wells] Brown's" and the Crafts' "ideological and aesthetic universe was marked by what at this distance seems an unquenchable desire for graphic representation of slavery . . . and in particular the slave's body" (38). In particular, Houston Baker has, after Lerone Bennett, referred to the silent exhibition of the fugitive slave as the "Negro exhibit."[13] Central to this display, as Baker describes it, was the slave's "partially naked body" turned to a white abolitionist audience in order to expose his or her "wounds and scars from floggings at the stake of slavery." Baker stresses the fugitive slave's silence during this act, as he or she became a cipher: "His or her body, in all of its marked and visible clarity of wounding, made affective the metaphors of moral suasion propounded by white abolitionists. . . . The silent fugitive slave's body became an erotic sign of servitude in the social, liberational discourses of white abolitionists" (*Workings* 13). While Ellen Craft's silent presence on the platform did not overtly participate in the kind of erotic specularity Baker describes, it did fuel an economy of affect that sought extremes in both a British interest in American slavery and an understanding of the peculiar institution as capable of depths heretofore unimagined. Indeed, that silence was key. Craft's display positioned her as the site of her audience's empathic identification and horror, significantly referred to again and again as so nearly white that her enslavement embodied the lowest to which slavery would sink. Her "whiteness" was elemental in raising an interest in American slavery like never before, as the Reverend R. L. Carpenter noted at a meeting of the Unitarian Association in London on 13 June 1851 attended by Brown and the Crafts: "He made the remark from observing that many persons, when they heard that his friend, Mrs. Craft, was nearly white, expressed more horror than before" ("American Slavery," rpt. in the *Liberator*).

Embodying the Tragic Mulatta

Such a focus on Ellen Craft's whiteness suggests one possible reading of her appearances, her deliberate embodiment of a figure her audiences were familiar with but would soon come to know much better through the enormous popularity of Harriet Beecher Stowe's *Uncle Tom's Cabin*: the tragic mulatta.[14] Becoming well known through Lydia Maria Child's fiction published in the *Liberty Bell* and later anthologized in her *Fact and Fiction* (1846), the tragic mulatta continued to be popular into the 1850s in sentimental fiction like Stowe's and was used by antislavery lecturers such as William Wells Brown and Sarah Parker Remond.[15] Critics examining this figure as white abolitionists put it to use argue that the tragic mulatta functioned as a proxy who would bring distant sufferings and horrors near through the familiarity of her white skin: "[I]t is the white or near-white body that makes the captive's suffering visible and discernible" (Hartman 20). What Saidiya Hartman calls a "racist optics" that refuses to recognize black humanity, Lindon Barrett refers to as a metaphysics in which the African American body signifies an "obdurate materiality" and "exclusion from a privileged presence of mind." While the black body may suffer abuse, the enslaved was believed lacking in "mindfulness" and the ability to reflect upon or be sensible of his or her suffering (Barrett 318). As Hartman puts it, both "the denial of black humanity and the effacement of sentience [were] integral to the wanton use of the captive body," but it was a white abolitionist "optics of morality that . . . in order to recognize suffering . . . substituted the self for the other" (20).

The white skin of the tragic mulatta, then, would register sensibility of suffering, "presence of mind," and also facilitate a degree of identification between the white abolitionist and the enslaved. Moreover, the tragic mulatta keeps such sufferings sufficiently distant to permit the contemplation of their disturbing nature; she is "near white" or white in appearance only, so that her sufferings remain those of the enslaved African American. This figure courts an identification, yet the discomfort she raises prevents that identification or "substitution" from being complete, an ambivalence that arguably lies at the bottom of Craft's popularity and her silent appearances. She does not take the platform to narrate experiences foreign to her audience but rather to embody or become a living representative of their imaginings facilitated by her silence. What Lindon Barrett has argued of their successful escape, we might also say of Ellen's appearances as the tragic mulatta: the Crafts "profit[ed] . . . by training attention on the white body," which is able "to 'direct [its] viewers' gaze' to a narrative with which it is taken as synonymous" (326). In effect, Ellen Craft appeared time and again as a tragic mulatta before English and Scottish audiences who were quite clearly focused on her whiteness and her similarity to them: "Ellen Craft . . . has a complexion very little darker than that of our country-women" ("Anti-Slavery Meeting at Bristol"). The shock, it seemed, was how like yet also how different from her white "sisters" she appeared to be as the "white slave." It seems Brown and the Crafts courted that ambivalent combination of shock, fascination, and identification lecture after lecture, soliciting it immediately after William told of families separated under slavery. Their audiences were thus invited to imagine what they might feel in such situations, lengths they might go to in order to prevent such horrors from happening to people "like" them.

Here, Ellen's decorous reluctance and embarrassment at appearing on the platform become a register through which her audiences would recognize this familiar figure. The tragic mulatta "wants to conform to patriarchal definitions of true womanhood but is prevented from doing so" (Yellin 53) by a sexual economy that fetishizes her, thereby casting her outside true womanhood and its dictates of "piety, purity, submissiveness and domesticity" (Welter 21). Ellen's reluctant submission to repeated demands for her public display encodes both the desire to conform to such standards of womanhood and her inability to do so as the "white slave" on demand. In other words, her womanly submission ensures her unwomanly and fetishistic display; her desire to conform guarantees her inevitable positioning as spectacle. Craft is depicted by the British press as having little chance to circumvent this specularity, despite her evident desire to do so. This repeated characterization may tell us that a number of reporters in various locales accommodated Ellen Craft to popular notions of the tragic mulatta, or its repetition may indicate that Ellen's embarrassment was as much a regular element of the trio's appearances as was Brown's panorama and William's recitation of their escape. Such marked echoes of the tragic mulatta plot may not have been solely an invention of the press. Perhaps Ellen's embarrassment and reluctance were more designed than felt, performed for their affect upon her audiences who would feel that much more sympathy for a woman who, upon escaping slavery, continued to find herself in "compromising" situations. Such a reading is made available by considering Joseph Roach's concept of "performance genealogies" in which Ellen's appearances upon British and Scottish platforms can be seen to echo the slave auction, particularly the fancy-girl markets, themselves a grotesque parody of typical slave auctions, where "a white-appearing body" is symbolically substituted "for a black one" (217). Indeed, white abolitionists evoked just such a genealogy of performance to suit their purposes, notes Roach: "Abolitionist tracts appropriated such spectacles to heighten the pathos of the flesh market, while not coincidentally trading on its erotic titillation" (216). Ellen Craft may have deliberately performed as the tragic mulatta, counting upon both the recognition and response—the "heightened pathos"—that figure could generate in her audiences who had read and heard recounted countless tales of quadroons and mulattas sold into sexual slavery. Significantly, Ellen's platform appearances coincided with "the height" of New Orleans' "spectacular" fancy-girl auctions (Roach 217).

The ambivalent double appeal Ellen's appearances forwarded—an identification interrupted by a near-white skin that is believed to incompletely "mask" an "alien African blackness" (Sànchez-Eppler 40)—is heightened by their performative aspects. We must remember that Ellen performed to effect before she appeared on British platforms, and for her survival as well as her husband's. Frequently, engravings of "Ellen Craft, The Fugitive Slave," in the disguise in which she escaped slavery, were offered for sale at the same lectures in which she appeared as the tragic mulatta embodied (see Figure 1). These engravings were identical to that first published in the *Illustrated London News* on 19 April 1851

Ellen Craft, *The Illustrated London News*, April 19, 1851. Photographs and Prints Division, Schomburg Center for Research in Black Culture, The New York Public Library, Astor, Lenox and Tilden Foundations.

(Weinauer 49) and were also advertised for sale in British antislavery publications, like the Leeds Anti-Slavery Association's 1857 advertisement for both a "youth edition of *Uncle Tom's Cabin* . . . [and] a shilling portrait of Ellen wearing masculine garments" (McCaskill, "Introduction" xvii). Ellen Craft, then, circulated as both tragic mulatta and disguised fugitive on this antislavery lecture tour, calling up for her audiences images of the tragic mulatta as "paragon of virtue . . . [and] a dangerous, potentially treacherous, and undoubtedly chaotic force" (Reid-Pharr 52), even as her engraving referenced her successful masquerade as an elite, albeit sickly, Southern gentleman, Mr. Johnson. Craft was ambivalent in her performances, to be sure, as on the one hand the failed "true woman" whose "taint" of blackness prevents her from attaining the virtue to which she aspires, and on the other Mr. Johnson, whose "masculinity" is produced by "the very signs of his weakness . . . all the markers of disease and invalidity" that read "to his observers

[as] 'white'" (Reid-Pharr 58). In each case, the femininity and masculinity performed are both true to form as well as compromised, debased in unmistakable
ways that in one case is traceable to "blackness" and in the other to "whiteness."

Rather than simply affirming her audiences' expectations and conforming to
a commodifying narrative in which she appeared simply as spectacle on view for
a shilling, Ellen Craft must have been profoundly unsettling at times. The tragic
mulatta's chaos and treachery are also the disguised fugitive's as she transgresses
boundaries of race, class, and gender to cross the Mason-Dixon line. Moreover,
Craft's ambivalent performances raise the question of impossible distinctions
that are at every step interimplicated—whiteness and blackness, feminine and
masculine, "healthy" or virtuous and invalid or debased. Her embodiment of the
tragic mulatta is inextricable in these British appearances from her performance
as Mr. Johnson. The Crafts' narrative underscores this by presenting Ellen as just
as reluctant to assume her disguise as she is said to be to take the stage as the
"white slave": "My wife had no ambition whatever to assume this disguise [as
Mr. Johnson], and would not have done so had it been possible to have obtained
our liberty by more simple means; but we knew it was not customary in the
South for ladies to travel with male servants; and therefore, notwithstanding my
wife's fair complexion, it would have been a very difficult task for her to have
come off as a free white lady" (Craft 24).

Ellen's greater likelihood at successfully passing as Mr. Johnson rather than "a
free white lady" implicitly calls into question the femininity that underwrites the
tragic mulatta narrative and plays on cultural anxieties regarding race, sexuality,
and gender. Simultaneously, her engraving's constant reminder of her successful
escape also undercuts the tragic mulatta's symbolic power. If, as Carla Peterson
argues, the tragic mulatta "reveals the culture's apprehension over what constitutes blackness" but ultimately allays this anxiety with "the sacrifice of the black
woman . . . insidiously . . . privatize[d] and manipulate[d]" by "the white male
gaze and desire" (155), Ellen Craft's escape, rather than sacrifice, would only
heighten the anxieties her performance as tragic mulatta might allay. This double movement—appearing to reaffirm white notions of blackness and femininity through her performance of the tragic mulatta yet challenging racial, class,
and gender distinctions through those engravings of her passing for a white male
elite—is key to understanding the way in which Ellen Craft was far from simply
invoking the mulatta as recognizable fetish and spectacle. Rather, her appearances and performances signified on those racial scripts designed to affirm
"pure" blackness and whiteness and to render any neither/nor position untenable

and doomed to self-destruction. They remind us, as Roach argues, that perform-ance constitutes reinvention not direct repetition, re-creation and transforma-tion rather than recapitulation.

Ellen's engravings constantly reminded her audiences that, unlike the charac-teristically passive tragic mulatta, she undertook the central role in the Crafts' escape from slavery, that she refused to continue a life of enslaved suffering or to pass that life to her children.[16] In several senses, Ellen Craft defied American law that deemed her chattel rather than woman, that would deem her children prop-erty as was "the condition" of their mother, that naturalized her racial identity as "negro" despite her whiteness. In ways those courts that favored the performance of whiteness over its genealogical or biological "proof" surely did not anticipate, Ellen Craft used the law to transgress its central tenets governing racial distinc-tions and the classification and transfer of property. In a "theft" of whiteness, as the Supreme Court would see it by 1896 with *Plessy v. Ferguson*, Ellen Craft was "received into society" as a white man, which American courts would be reluc-tant, to say the least, to concede fulfilled the standard of whiteness so articulated by many of the nation's justices, as we saw in Chapter 1.[17] Consequently, these engravings repeatedly undercut the tragic mulatta's symbolic power. "By defini-tion, the tragic Mulatta is granted her most pronounced symbolic power by virtue of her worldly suffering—her sexual exploitation and the betrayals and abuse she endures usually find physical expression in suicide or fatal illness," contends Nancy Bentley. "For tragic Mulattas . . . the violence they suffer con-firms the value of the soul in a spiritual realm wholly distinct from the body. The problem of racial identity [as a] . . . problem of the body . . . is effaced" (199). Though sexual exploitation is evident in Ellen Craft's genealogy, as the daughter of her master and his slave, and though the Crafts' narrative frequently refers to the sexual exploitation of female slaves, it never once mentions that Ellen found herself under such threat. And even though Ellen's first mistress, the wife of her father and a woman of "incessant cruelty," sold her away from her mother at the age of eleven, Ellen's conditions are said to have improved with a "new mistress . . . decidedly more humane than the majority of her class" (Craft 3, 7). Rather than a figure of worldly suffering, Ellen Craft is said to be "a favourite slave" of her new owners (Craft 21). The Crafts' narrative does not depict Ellen as a tragic mulatta but instead presents their escape as requiring her decisive action on sev-eral occasions, despite crediting the devising of their plan to William. In represent-ing Ellen as decisive, the narrative refuses to position her as that black woman whose suffering and sacrifice allay racial anxieties and foregrounds the "problem of racial identity" as, indeed, a "problem of the body" in its illegibility and performative capabilities. As press accounts of their escape, Ellen's engravings, William's lectures, and eventually their narrative published in 1860 remind their audiences, the mulatta may capitalize upon rather than allay such anxieties; she may not only survive but outwit the slaveholder rather than succumb to his desires.

Yet anxieties were clearly raised by Ellen's performance as less-than-tragic mulatta, evidenced by several retellings of the Crafts' escape. As Barbara McCaskill notes, the Crafts' "romantic" and "singular" escape captured the imagination of notable American abolitionists, such as William Lloyd Garrison, William Wells Brown, Lydia Maria Child, Thomas Wentworth Higginson, and William Still ("Yours" 511–12). Several accounts take pains to highlight Ellen as a stereotypical mulatta, the beautiful and passive product of elicit racial mixing. Henry Ingersoll Bowditch, an abolitionist who helped the couple leave Boston when slave catchers arrived to kidnap the Crafts, describes Ellen as "a delicate, almost white, quadroon girl, with simple ladylike manners. . . . She was evidently tinged with some high blood of the South" (205). Similarly, Lydia Maria Child depicts Ellen in *The Freedmen's Book* (1865) as "a quadroon girl . . . the daughter of her master, but her mother was a slave." Child stresses Ellen's physical features that cause "strangers [to] often mist[ake] her for one of her master's own white family" (180). The mulatta's peculiar family ties are again stressed by the abolitionist *Wisconsin Free Democrat*'s "Story of Ellen Crafts" [*sic*], which, after listing Ellen's "white" features, speculates that when she fled slavery she was "act[ing] as a body servant or slave to another young woman, possibly her sister." While these accounts work to allay any racial anxieties that Ellen's escape passing for white elicits by characterizing her as the familiar tragic mulatta, they, and others, also work to appease those raised by her successful performance as a man. The *Wisconsin Free Democrat* avoids ascribing any element in their escape to Ellen's devising by using the passive voice throughout its account. Child deliberately feminizes Ellen, who she describes as "very modest and timid, at first shr[inking] from" her husband's "bold plan." According to Child, even though she manages to carry it out, Ellen cannot begin the escape without first "trembl[ing] and thr[owing] herself on her husband's breast. There she wept for a few moments, while he tried to comfort her with whispered words of encouragement" (184). And William Still's account in *The Underground Railroad*, though it credits both William and Ellen for conceiving their plan together, concludes by working to recover Ellen's womanliness: "Ellen in her fine suit of black, with her cloak and high-heeled boots, looking in every respect, like a young gentleman; in an hour after having dropped her male attire, and assumed the habiliments of her sex the feminine only was visible in every line and feature of her structure" (370). If this fails to fully restore Ellen's femininity, Still's mention that her "nerves" were so "tried . . . severely, . . . that for days afterwards, she was physically very much prostrated" surely does (370).

Notably, it is William Wells Brown, in his 1853 novel, *Clotel; or, The President's Daughter*, who retains a certain agency for Ellen fictionalized as Clotel. Even though Clotel must fend off the sexual advances of her master before her successful escape and later jumps to her death in the Potomac after having been recaptured in Richmond, Brown's scripting of Clotel as tragic mulatta makes her far less passive than that figure usually appeared. At her urging, her fellow slave William agrees to Clotel's plan to escape, à la the Crafts, to Cincinnati. Upon gaining her freedom, Clotel then determines to return to the slave South to search for her daughter, Mary, in Virginia. The broken tie Clotel cannot accept is not with her master-lover but with her child. And in a clever parody of the child following the condition of the mother, Brown has Mary pose as the rebel slave George Green so that he can escape prison. Like her mother before her, Mary conceives of a plan to enable the freedom of a male slave by dressing as a man. Anticipating his representation of her in *Clotel*, Brown closes an 1849 letter to the *Liberator* announcing the Crafts' escape with an emphasis upon Ellen's part: "Ellen is truly a heroine" ("Singular"). But it is at the pen of Brown's daughter, Josephine, that Ellen is depicted as fully orchestrating the Crafts' escape, despite the anxieties this retelling would have raised rather than quelled. In her *Biography of an American Bondman* (1856), Josephine Brown both emphasizes Ellen's mulattaness—her whiteness, straight hair, and "eyes of a light hazel color"—and has her conceive of the plan that will gain the Crafts' freedom: " 'Now, William,' said the wife, 'listen to me, and take my advice, and we shall be free in less than a month' " (76). She answers William's doubts no less than four times, and at one point chides him, " 'Come, William, . . . don't be a coward!' " (77). While white abolitionists were clearly more comfortable depicting Ellen as a stereotypical mulatta and men like William Still were anxious to show readers the feminine retained under the masculine disguise, writers like William Wells Brown and Josephine Brown pressed upon the anxieties raised by Ellen Craft's escape, her engraving, and her appearances on the antislavery platforms of the United States and Great Britain.

Though it has become something of a critical commonplace to read Ellen Craft as subversively "elud[ing] inscription" in her disguised escape and the engravings that reproduced it (Weinauer 52), her British tour with her husband and William Wells Brown has gained relatively little attention, and her role in it has clearly discomfited critics who see it as "merchandis[ing]" her (McCaskill, "Yours" 523). Even though she caused a sensation and may well have been the drawing spectacle of this lecture tour, the combination of Ellen Craft on stage as the "white slave" so like her British countrywomen, in her audiences' imaginations as the tragic mulatta embodied, and in her engraving as the white Southern gentleman, Mr. Johnson, surely unsettled more than it comforted her audiences with the reassuringly familiar. This forestalling of expectation and a facile identification is significant, for it would enable Brown and the Crafts to direct their audiences' empathy away from the analogous—the white woman as slave, the white British working class as little better than slaves—and toward those who were quite literally enslaved in America. How many may have been drawn to the spectacle but were affected in this way is, of course, difficult to know, yet the Crafts' tour was regarded as "gain[ing them] universal respect" (Estlin to Chapman, 3 April 1852), and they have been lauded as "render[ing] valuable service to [the Garrisonian] movement" with lectures that "made a profound and abiding impression" upon a British public (*Proceedings* 153).

Managing Empathy, Identification, and the "Sister Slave"

A desire for spectacle also complicated the work Sarah Parker Remond would shortly undertake on the British antislavery lecture circuit. On 12 January 1859 Sarah Parker Remond, a free-born African American abolitionist with only two years experience as a traveling lecturer for the American Anti-Slavery Society, arrived in Liverpool to begin a lecture tour of Britain that came to be described as grueling and highly influential (Midgley 143). Remond gave her first lecture at the Tuckerman Institute on the evening of 21 January. In her history of British women's antislavery campaigns, Clare Midgley refers to Remond's lectures between 1859 and 1861 as addresses "of great importance as the first public talks by a woman to mass mixed British audiences on the antislavery question" (143). Remond was evidently in high demand, as she intimated in a letter to Garrisonian abolitionist Maria Weston Chapman in the fall of 1859: "I have lectured very frequently, in fact had more invitations recently than I could fill" (Remond to Weston Chapman, 16 October 1859). Her speaking engagements continued unabated, as did her impact. In December of that year, notes Benjamin

Quarles, "the Leeds Young Men's Antislavery Society hired Miss Remond as an agent and arranged a tight schedule. For three months her life was a whirl of appearances at town halls, chapels and school auditoriums that invariably were crowded to excess" (140). Closing its notice of these lectures delivered throughout Yorkshire, the *Anti-Slavery Advocate* pronounced them "exceedingly interesting. . . . Thousands who have heard her will never forget her visit, and the principles she has advocated . . . will find an abiding place in many hearts" ("Miss Remond in Yorkshire" 306).[18] Far more successful as an abolitionist lecturer in Britain than she would ever come to be in the United States, Remond appeared in cities and towns throughout northern England, Scotland, and Ireland between January 1859 and January 1861.[19]

During this period, Remond delivered several speeches in which she invoked the figures of the female slave and the tragic mulatta, figures that Ellen Craft effectively embodied for her audiences. The 1850s were active years for British women in the antislavery cause and years in which women's rights agitation developed. From this intersection of women's rights and abolition, the woman as slave trope—in use as early as the mid-1820s—had grown popular by the time Craft appeared on British stages and Remond delivered her lectures, as had the tragic mulatta figure and a sentimental and empathic appeal on behalf of the enslaved. These factors worked together to create both the available readings of Ellen Craft's person and the rhetorical situation that necessitated Sarah Remond engage in rather complicated strategies of address. Heard by "crammed" audiences eager to see "a coloured lady—Miss Remond" ("Lecture," *Warrington Standard*), Redmond deliberately solicited, and carefully managed, a sense of "sisterhood" and empathic identification from her British audiences that Ellen Craft's appearances had already established. First, Remond used sentimental and sensational appeals to British empathy through a discourse of domesticity and an invocation of the tragic mulatta figure; second, she drew on rational, impersonal proofs; and finally, she strategically avoided accounts of personal experience. Through her use of the female slave figure in various incarnations, Remond worked in two directions simultaneously and thereby forwarded a "double-voiced" and multi-layered discourse on the lecture platform.

In a broader sense, we may read Remond's lectures within the humanitarian narrative genre as outlined by Thomas Laqueur in "Bodies, Details and the Humanitarian Narrative." She deliberately worked with elements of "a common sensibility and shared sympathy" (Laqueur 202) as registered in the sentimental and domestic. And her citations, what Laqueur would call "the building blocks of the 'reality effect' " (177), accumulated a body of detail that became "the sign of truth" or the "real" of slavery and the suffering it engenders. However, working to evoke "a common sensibility and shared sympathy," establishing what can be acknowledged as fact or the details of slavery's realities, and capitalizing upon the currency of fugitive slave abolitionists with the British public came with certain risks that Remond's audience would either feel too removed from American slavery to act or find it all too easy to identify with the familiar. What bodies her British audiences recognized as enslaved, and the abuses those bodies suffered under, were crucial to Remond's ability to elicit not just her audience's empathy as Ellen Craft's silent appearances had done—an emotional response that could run contrary to these women's abolitionist goals—but also their willingness to act.

Remond delivered a series of lectures in Warrington from 24 January to 2 February 1859. In her second lecture at Warrington on the evening of 31 January, we see her deliberately working to avoid being mistaken for the slave for whom she spoke: "Miss Remond then commenced her lecture. . . . She must present her stand-point, which would be this, that she should endeavor to say for the slave what she would wish that he or she would say for her were she the victim upon the plantations, as they were, in their stead" ("A Second Lecture" 1). Remond begins with this clarification that she is speaking neither for nor as the slave but rather as she would desire to be spoken for "were she the victim." This curious choice of syntax works to delineate a difference in condition between herself and the subjects of her lecture yet also leaves open the possibility that she may yet become slavery's victim if only in the minds of her listeners. Remond needs this potential confusion for several reasons: she must somehow close the gap between enslaved African Americans and free white British in these lectures with only herself, her arguments, and the accounts she reads to rely upon; she must also mark sufficient distance in the empathy she elicits so that it is neither misdirected toward herself nor toward the free "woman as slave"; and she is dependent upon the popularity of fugitive slave lecturers in Britain in order to draw an audience.

As an African American lecturing in Britain at this time, Remond is hardly able, nor may have wanted, to deflect attention from her race. R.J.M. Blackett notes that "blacks [on the antislavery lecture circuit] were aware that their color had become an asset" (*Building* 40). In fact, the success of fugitive slave abolitionists in Britain was reported in the *New York Express* as a fad of no small proportions: "They were . . . so much in vogue that white men and women were 'coloring their faces and hands, and going about London, imitating their sable visitors,' who were reaping a harvest 'bringing off their pockets full of money' " (qtd. in Blackett, *Building* 39). Remond hardly could have avoided being taken as a representative of her race, if not a representative, in the flesh, of those enslaved men and women for whom she spoke. In fact, since the American Fugitive Slave Law of 1850 had turned "the trickle of fugitives" lecturing in Britain into "a flood" (Blackett, *Building* 5), Remond may have been taken as a fugitive slave by audiences not told otherwise.

Two interesting details emerge from local press accounts of her second Warrington lecture. One account notes that a "Mr. William North, a coloured gentleman from Earlestown, late a slave in South Carolina," was also on the platform with Remond, though he does not seem to have addressed the audience ("Miss Remond's Second Lecture," *Warrington Standard*). His presence suggests that perhaps Remond was, at this point, being taken up by her audiences as part of that existing vogue of fugitive slave abolitionists. Moreover, in a brief report of this same speech, the *Warrington Guardian* repeats that turn of phrase that leaves open the possibility of reading Remond as slave: "We *presume she is a free woman*: yet in the land of democracy, under the Fugitive Slave Law, she is liable, if found in the Free States, upon the oath of any brutal fellow, to be carried into a bondage more fearful than that to which the most common negro is subjected" ("Slavery and Democracy"). Significantly, with that phrase, "a bondage more fearful than that to which the most common negro is subjected," Remond is imagined as a potential tragic mulatta and sexual slave. Remond thus becomes a figure whom her audiences can imagine experiencing what they consider to be the most brutal conditions of American slavery. Judging from this report, it seems that Remond's careful though curious choice of syntax, combined with no confirmation and very rarely a mention of her free-born status in either advertisements for, reports of, or introductions to her lectures, was successful in enabling her audience to imagine her own enslavement as a potential, thereby allowing her to capitalize on her audience's expectation that she knew firsthand of what she spoke.[20] Just as Ellen Craft's appearances seemed successful because she was perceived to be both like British white women and titillatingly different as the tragic mulatta, so, too, do Remond's speeches seem to turn on an ambivalent identification. While her womanliness, as noted in repeated references to her "ladylike . . . appearance and address" ("Miss Remond in Bristol" 273), might seem to reach across racial difference to ground an identification with her audience, Remond was nonetheless appealing to an audience largely drawn to these speeches of a "sable visitor" by the double oddity of a black and woman speaker whom they seem to have easily imagined could also be yet a slave.

Attending to the currency of the "woman as slave" trope in both Britain and the United States is also important to understanding Remond's strategies of appeal in this lecture series and the draw of a "white slave" such as Ellen Craft. Jean Fagan Yellin documents the circulation of the "slave woman as sister" image in Britain as early as 1826 and its official adoption as abolitionist emblem by British and American women by 1836:

> Members of the Ladies Negro's Friend Society of Birmingham, England, chose this emblem to decorate the cover of their *First Report*, published in 1826. . . . The female slave image also appeared in . . . the May issue of [the American publication] *The Genius of Universal Emancipation*, facing "The Ladies' Repository", a new feature designed to attract female readers. . . . By 1836, the female supplicant had become the unofficial emblem of the antislavery women. (10–17)

Yellin points out that American antislavery women used the emblem of the female supplicant slave in multiple ways, alternately "addressing and avoiding issues of race, sexual conformity, and patriarchal definitions of true womanhood," but their strategies coalesced around two distinct appeals: "[T]hey recoded and re-recoded the emblem . . . picturing themselves as chain-breaking liberators and as enchained slaves pleading for their own liberty, then asserting it and freeing themselves" (25).

Perhaps the most influential American female abolitionist to position herself as "woman as slave" was Angelina Grimké. In her address to the 1837 Convention of American Women Against Slavery (New York City, 9–12 May), published as *An Appeal to the Women of the Nominally Free States* (1837), Grimké appealed to the moral duty of female abolitionists by likening their condition to enslavement: " 'All moral beings have essentially the same rights and duties, whether they be male or female. . . . The denial of our duty to act, is a bold denial of our right to act; and if we have no right to act, then may we well be termed "the white slaves of the North"—for, like our brethren in bonds, we must seal our lips in silence and despair' " (qtd. in Yellin 35). The affect of Grimké's analogy was also registered in Britain:

> News of these American developments [including Grimké's address to the Massachusetts legislature and her sister Sarah Grimké's publication of *Letters on the Equality of the Sexes, and the Condition of Women* (1838)] reached leading

British women abolitionists through their American contacts, through reports in periodicals, and through Harriet Martineau's descriptions in "The Martyr Age" . . . [and] *Society in America* (1837). . . . Breaking with the dominant tendency among British women abolitionists to contrast their own position with that of enslaved women, Martineau likened the position of "Free" women in North American society to that of slaves. (Midgley 156)

Back in America, analogy had become graphic identification, as is evident in abolitionist lecturer Abby Kelley Foster's letters and speeches from 1838 through the 1840s. "When I . . . become myself the slave," Kelley Foster writes, "I feel the naked cords of my neck shrinking away from the rough edge of the iron collar, when my flesh quivers beneath the lash, till in anguish I feel portions of it cut from my back" (qtd. in Yellin 50).

By the time Ellen Craft appeared on stage with her husband and William Wells Brown in New England in 1849 and Sarah Remond delivered her earliest speeches for the American Anti-Slavery Society in the mid-1850s and attended the New York Women's Rights Convention in 1858, American female abolitionists and women's rights advocates were well versed in the analogy that had become identification—(white) woman as sister slave. Remond must have been quite familiar with this trope and its uses by the time she arrived in Britain in 1859. While she might invoke it in order to narrow the gap between enslaved African American women and free white English women, thereby moving English women to aid the abolitionist cause, she was undoubtedly aware that the "woman as slave" trope also worked to effectively collapse the material differences in the lived experience of these women.

Remond's first speech in Warrington, delivered with no admission charge at the Music Hall the evening of 24 January 1859 to an overflowing crowd, evoked the sufferings of slave mothers as represented in the case of Margaret Garner, by then famous among American abolitionists.[21] Remond's reference to Garner casts her appeal in a familiar form, a domestic drama of threatened motherhood and broken familial bonds.[22] Significantly, Remond marks such "horrors" as unspeakable even while she turns to this widely documented case in order to illustrate them for her audience:

She [Remond] . . . felt almost overpowered and overwhelmed, for what tongue could describe the horrors of American slavery? Who could give the faintest idea of what the slave mother suffered? . . . Miss Remond then touchingly related the case of Margaret Garner, who determined to be free or die in the attempt. She was born a slave, and had *suffered in her own person* the degradation that a woman could not mention. She got as far as Cincinnati with the children. . . . The slaveholder found her; as he appeared at the door she snatched up a knife and slew her first-born child, but before the poor frenzied creature could proceed further in her dread object, the hand of the tyrant was on her, when she called to the grandmother of the children to kill the others, as she preferred to return them to the bosom of God rather than they should be taken back to American slavery. *Above all sufferers in America,* American women who were slaves lived in the most pitiable condition. *They could not protect themselves* from the licentiousness which met them on every hand— *they could not protect their honour* from the tyrant. . . . There were no morals there; no genuine regard for womanhood or manhood. ("Speech by Sarah P. Remond" 437–38, emphasis added)

For Remond to insist upon slavery's horrors as unspeakable is also to insist upon the uniqueness of chattel slavery's material conditions; they are beyond existing or familiar modes of representation.[23] Remond's initial assertion that slavery's horrors cannot be described or conveyed, though brief, is one to which we must attend, for it signals her awareness that enlisting another's empathy through available representations of suffering—sentiment and sensation—risks a collapsing of difference. This collapse upon which empathic identification turns is addressed by Elaine Scarry as "analogical verification," or "analogical substantiation," a concept that has been employed in the study of abolitionist and feminist-abolitionist discourse. Through the process of analogical substantiation, a disembodied discourse evokes and enlists the suffering body in order to appeal to a basis in material reality: "The extreme fact of . . . the body itself . . . is laid edge to edge with . . . a wholly verbal and disembodied assertion. . . . The body tends to be brought forward in its most extreme and absolute form only on behalf of a . . . [discourse] that is without any other basis in material reality: that is, it is only brought forward when there is a crisis of substantiation" (Scarry 126–27). Addressing her audience through generic forms heavily used by abolitionists, Remond must negotiate their use as not mere "translators" of slavery as foreign experience. Rather, the severed family and the pain of an enslaved mother evoked in such discourse work to anchor or substantiate an abolitionist sense of "moral right," while the pain and violations of the enslaved female body provide the material grounding of a feminist symbolization of women's rights. Scarry marks such analogic substantiation as a juxtaposition between extreme, absolute embodiment and disembodied assertion, while the resolution of such a crisis of substantiation is achieved through the elision of this very juxtaposition. In other words, the body and its suffering are not merely *spoken for* by another but are articulated *as* that other's experience or sensibility. Remond must work, then, to intervene in these established figurations of "woman as slave," or slave as the noble sufferer awaiting a moral rescue from slavery's sin, even while she risks their further perpetuation by basing her appeal in the domestic and sentimental.

The Whitened Slave and Tragic Mulatta "in Whose Cheeks the Lily and Rose Vie"

The *Warrington Times* report indicates that in the closing of her second speech delivered the following Monday evening, 31 January 1859, Remond returned to the familiarity of the domestic as indicative of slavery's cruelties, but she chose to cast white victims in the narrative: "Under the Fugitive Slave Law white people . . . were not safe; for instances had been known when white people had been taken away," said Remond. "In fact, she knew of one white girl with not one drop of African blood in her veins, who was dragged away in the open face of day, and only saved from a dreadful life by being recognised. White children, too, were not safe; and many instances were known where they had been taken away" ("Miss Remond's Second Lecture," *Warrington Standard*). The final speaker that evening, Robert Gaskell, kept the image of the white slave before Remond's audiences by invoking the tragic mulatta. Gaskell related a story carried by the *Times* of a Louisville, Kentucky, planter, who at age fifty had never married but whose "house was managed by . . . his daughter by a quadroon, whose complexion was lighter by half than his." Gaskell continued: "She never knew that there was negro blood in her veins, and never dreamed that she was a slave. Last fall a series of misfortunes overtook the planter. . . . [His] attorney . . . advised him to sell off a portion of his negroes . . . and before an hour the transaction [selling his daughter to his attorney] was closed" ("Miss Remond's Second Lecture," *Warrington Standard*).

Such a closing, and Remond's own remarks, risk reducing slavery's "horrors" to melodrama not only by rendering the slave's experiences akin to sentimental domestic plots but also by casting tragic mulattas, white children, and their families as slavery's potential victims. Notably, in her first Warrington speech Remond immediately followed her narration of Margaret Garner's escape and recapture with references to mulatta slaves as concubines: "The more Anglo-Saxon blood that was in them, the more they would bring when exposed for sale at auction. Those that were more white than others were sold for concubines . . . not for plantation slaves" ("Lecture," *Warrington Standard*). Here the mulatta is positioned as a slave woman denied the familial ties routinely violated by slavery and one forced into a perversion of womanhood and affective bonds, valued as a concubine for her "whiteness" and her similarity to her free white American "sister slaves." Such an emphasis upon slavery's violations of affect positioned these kinds of domestic appeals within a discourse of melodrama. "The crime of the trade was seen as a crime of the heart—'the outrages of feelings and affection.' . . . Abolitionist discourse shared melodrama's obsession: virtue, virginity, and the sanctity of the family" (Hartman 27). The abolitionist stress on moral suasion made melodrama particularly appealing for its opposition between good and evil—slavery cast as sin could be opposed to the moral right of its abolition— but this rhetoric, as it intersected with sentimentalism, also implicitly cast the suffering of the enslaved as virtuous (Hartman 26).

However, in what seem like efforts to bring those "horrors" near to her audience rendered in a form and in bodies they would recognize, Remond is also working to retain enough distance to prevent a misidentification. Even as she renders both the general accounts of white children taken from their families, mulattas sold into concubinage, and Margaret Garner's specific case as sentimental domestic dramas with which her audience (and especially its female members) might empathize, Remond is especially careful in her first Music Hall speech to distinguish between the experiences of enslaved women and those of white British women who might cast themselves as "woman as slave." Remond carefully presents Garner's sufferings as those experienced "in her own person," marked in opposition to an analogy of empathy. She further stresses that while "women's condition" might be likened to suffering under the denial of rights, those protections of "regard" that may be extended to white women are denied the enslaved. This is not to say that white women in Britain and the United States did not experience abuses beyond the denial of rights feminist abolitionists addressed but to foreground Remond's work to mark the material conditions of African American bondswomen as distinct from those of free white women. Finally, in her narration of Margaret Garner's case as indicative of American slavery, Remond is also working to prevent her audience from seeing enslaved African

American women as beings without will to self-protection or resistance, who depend entirely upon abolitionists and other interested parties. Even though Remond at times offers her audiences the shock of white children as slavery's victims, making it easier for them to empathize if not somehow identify with the victims of American slavery, she is careful to remind them that the lived conditions of their "sister slaves" are quite different from their own. Moreover, she takes up the significant challenge of asking her audiences to see African American slaves as more than mute and helpless victims but as thinking and feeling men and women who choose resistant and defiant actions.

Her strategy is rather different in that second lecture at Warrington's Music Hall. Here, Remond precedes her account of slavery's domestic drama with an attention to the enslaved body itself, using a stock abolitionist phrase: "When she stated the fact that in the United States of America sixteen hundred million dollars were invested in the bone, blood, and sinews of men and women, was it not a sufficient reason why some advocate should present the claims of these oppressed ones on all and every occasion?" ("A Second Lecture" 1).[24] Remond works to balance a seemingly sensational attention to the body of the slave in that well-worn abolitionist phrase, "bone, blood, and sinews," with what might be called the rational appeal of slavery's "facts," its economics. Arguing that as her lecture tour progressed Remond turned away from a sentimental and toward a rational appeal, Carla Peterson has taken Remond's tendency to quote American accounts of slavery, whether journalistic or fictional, as part of a "rhetorical strategy . . . to convince her public . . . by means of a sheer accumulation of facts" (143).

Certainly that "sheer accumulation of facts" and detail worked to establish "truth" in humanitarian discourse, and I would also argue that Remond's turn to slavery's economics, far from abstracting slave suffering to a matter of sums and figures, works to underscore that these sufferings are lived and for the profit of a few. Laqueur suggests just such a reading when he argues that within humanitarian narratives, such as industrial novels and inquests, "the statistical body becomes the lived body" (195). What is more interesting, however, is the combination of the sentimental, the sensational, and this kind of rational appeal within the same speech and often within the same image of the enslaved, for it marks Remond's handling of audience expectations, desires, and identifications. This Warrington speech is no isolated instance. Months later, on the evening of 24 September 1859 in a lecture at Bolton's Temperance Hall, Remond would mix domestic appeals to enslaved men and women unable to marry with references to the "125 millions worth of cotton" grown by slaves on American plantations, "nine-tenths of which came to England," and the sensation of "eight hundred thousand . . . [slaves] upon the Southern plantations, many of them with complexions as fair as any of her audiences, nine-tenths of whom were the children of white fathers, and these were constantly sold by their parents" ("Lecture," *Bolton Chronicle*). In another version of this description of American slavery, Remond recast those 800,000 slaves as "eight hundred thousand mulattoes . . . in whose cheeks the lily and rose vie for predominance" ("Anti-Slavery in Manchester"). The slave population of the South would become a whitened one in this "densely crowded" lecture at the Manchester Athenaeum from which "hundreds" were turned away ("American Slavery," *Manchester Weekly Times*).

Remond, then, repeatedly negotiated the dangers of empathy in her speeches and what Hartman calls its ambivalence: "The ambivalent . . . [or] repressive effects of empathy . . . can be located in the 'obliteration of otherness' or the facile intimacy that enables identification with the other only as we 'feel ourselves into those we imagine as ourselves.' And as a consequence, empathy fails to expand the space of the other but merely places the self in its stead" (19–20). Remond must take care that by representing the very real material conditions of slavery she also not reduce the enslaved to either spectacle or specter. She risks, however, doing just that with the sensation of that stock phrase "bone, blood, and sinews" in her second Warrington speech. In its connotation of violence, the phrase might have once deflected an easy identification, but its familiarity now risks bringing her audience no closer to witnessing either the slave or slavery's material conditions: "[T]he endeavour to bring pain close exploits the spectacle of the body in pain and oddly confirms the spectral character of suffering and the inability to witness the captive's pain" (Hartman 20). Perhaps this dilemma is insoluble to a degree, and this may be why we see Remond interrupting her lecture's opening—this well-worn reference to the slave's "bone, blood, and sinews"—and its closing domestic note of violated familial bonds with an explication of living conditions North and South. Here Remond is able to pursue a somewhat safer ground for demarcating differences of experience: "She then contrasted the North with the South. In the North, where no slave labour existed, all was intelligence, energy, and industry, and there were free schools in every town and village. . . . But in the South free schools were deemed a nuisance" ("A Second Lecture" 1). At a key point, in the midst of all-too-familiar sentimental and sensational appeals that risk inviting empathic identification, Remond may turn to such contrasts between the American North and South to remind her British audience that the enslaved occupy a contrastive, rather than analogical, position to their own.

Remond's negotiation of empathy and identification further appealed to sentiment and sensation in this speech and her final Warrington lecture at the Red Lion Hotel, raising the stock figure of the tragic mulatta so strategically embodied by Ellen Craft herself. As Remond's lectures in Warrington continued, the image of the enslaved she offered became an increasingly whitened one. On 2 February 1859 at the Red Lion Hotel, Remond detailed the economics of such concubinage in a luncheon lecture "address[ed] . . . chiefly to the ladies":

> Miss Remond['s] . . . remarks chiefly bore on the sufferings and indignities which were perpetrated on her sisters in America, and the fearful amount of licentiousness which everywhere pervaded the Southern States. This fact would be best realized when she stated that there were 800,000 mulattoes in the Southern States of America—the fruits of licentiousness. . . . She then read a graphic description of a young and beautiful girl at a slave sale. The auctioneer was offered 1,000 dollars for her at first. He then expatiated on the superior education she possessed, and 600 dollars more were offered, and lastly he commented on the religious and moral principles she held, when she rose to 2,000 dollars, at which she was knocked down. Thus 1,000 dollars were paid for her blood, bone, and sinew, 600 for her improved intellect, and 400 more for the profession of the religion of Christ! ("Lecture at the Lion Hotel" 1)

This speech offered in economic detail the sale of mulattas into concubinage that she would reference briefly at other times.[25] It also casts in an economic light a familiar narrative Remond would offer as sensational and sentimental elsewhere: "She might possess . . . loveliness . . . be endowed with . . . dignified beauty . . . or have . . . winning grace and charming innocence . . . let her skin be white as alabaster, it has only to be shown that she holds even a remote affinity with the proscribed race . . . that she is the child of a slave and a slave herself, [and] she is liable to the brutality of the vilest wretches, and may be sold at any time" ("Miss Remond's First Lecture" 223).

In this Warrington speech and its echoes in later lectures, Remond draws directly on an image of the fancy-girl auction that William Wells Brown presented in a lecture to the Female Anti-Slavery Society of Salem on 14 November 1847, a lecture Remond undoubtedly attended.[26] Brown later published this description in

"A True Story of Slave Life" in the *Anti-Slavery Advocate* (1852) and enlarged it as the sale of Clotel in his novel *Clotel; or, The President's Daughter* (1853):

> "She enjoys good health, and has a sweet temper. . . . Only five hundred dollars for such a girl as this? . . . Here, gentlemen, I hold in my hand a paper certifying that she has a good moral character." "Seven hundred." . . . "This paper also states that she is very intelligent." "Eight hundred." "She is a devoted Christian, and perfectly trustworthy." "Nine hundred." "Nine fifty." "Ten." "Eleven." "Twelve hundred." . . . "The chastity of this girl is pure; she has never been from under her mother's care; she is a virtuous creature." "Thirteen." "Fourteen." "Fifteen." "Fifteen hundred dollars," cried the auctioneer and the maiden was struck for that sum. This was a Southern auction, at which the bones, muscles, sinews, blood, and nerves of a young lady of sixteen were sold for five hundred dollars; her moral character for two hundred; her improved intellect for one hundred; her Christianity for three hundred; and her chastity and virtue for four hundred dollars more. (63–64)

Remond, then, draws on a scene with which some in her audience may well have been familiar, hearing it rendered in antislavery lectures or reading it in the *Anti-Slavery Advocate* or Brown's novel. While, as John Ernest argues, Brown uses Clotel's sale to critique a "cultural economy" in which "value" is no longer "a carefully produced orchestration of various ideals of human potentiality" and has instead become "a gross transaction" (40), Remond works to confront her audience with the empathic identification that has made the mulatta a proxy for white anxieties.

By using the tragic mulatta figure in these speeches, Remond is both appealing to her audience to recognize the sexual violation of enslaved women as one of slavery's greatest wrongs and confronting them with the limits of what they will acknowledge. This whitened slave woman in Remond's lectures significantly registers that white abolitionist tendency to approach suffering via a proxy. Here, Remond is working with the proxy as facilitating a proximity to, yet not quite an identification with, the suffering of sexual violation. Karen Sànchez-Eppler documents the ways in which white feminist abolitionists negotiated their own embodiment by putting the body of the enslaved to specific rhetorical use in order both to register and disavow their own sexual desire and anxiety:

> [F]eminist abolitionists emphasize the similarities in the condition of women and slaves; nevertheless, their treatment of the figure of the sexually exploited

female slave betrays an opposing desire to deny any share in this vulnerability. Thus in the writings of antislavery women the frequent emphasis on the specifically feminine trial of sexual abuse serves to project the white woman's sexual anxieties onto the sexualized body of the female slave. (33)

Specifically, it was the body and spectacle of the mulatta as concubine that became most adaptable to registering such anxieties: "The polysemous body of the . . . mulatta simultaneously expresses the white woman's desires and protects her from them, by marking them safely alien" (Sànchez-Eppler 44). Remond's invocation of the tragic mulatta might appear to participate in just such an alienating acknowledgment of the white woman's sexual vulnerability, especially if we read her as casting this figure within an economics that seems to echo that of woman commodified within the marriage contract. However, she stresses repeatedly that this is a literal trade in slave women's bodies, marking a difference in the material conditions under which free white and enslaved African American women live. Moreover, while those qualities like education and religious and moral principles mentioned in the Red Lion Hotel lecture seem to close the gap between free white and enslaved women of African descent, Remond is also using them toward a different end. Such qualities convey "traditional notions of female purity," argues Sànchez-Eppler, yet while they might be said to "attach . . . to the body in its vulnerability to rape or enforced concubinage" (42), the body that registers these vulnerabilities remains a white, not "whitened," one. The concubinage of biracial women in Southern states like Louisiana turned on an understanding of the mulatta as a figure of "female purity" rendered sexually available, one whose chastity as a commodity is valued precisely because it is presumed impossible to violate. As Hortense Spillers observes, "the mulatta . . . has value for the dominant other only insofar as she becomes the inaccessible female property that can be rendered, at his behest, instantly accessible" ("Notes" 173).

Interestingly, Remond's double-voiced appeal—offering her audience a "proxy" whose material experience she insists is very different from their own—effected a response in Warrington in which a degree of empathic identification as well as a useful attention to difference is apparent. Remond's "strength failed her" rather early in this luncheon lecture at the Red Lion Hotel, immediately after she read that account of a mulatta's sale. As she concluded, "Mrs. Ashton advanced towards [her, and] . . . said she felt proud to acknowledge her as a sister" ("Lecture at the

Lion Hotel" 1). While Remond expressed her gratitude, Mrs. Gaskell rose to address the women present:

> Miss Remond had been pressing on her the claims which the slave should have upon her consideration . . . [and] said to her with a look she should never forget, "that, whatever might be the claims which their own people's suffering might have upon the English women, there was a depth of suffering in America caused by slavery far surpassing it, and which demanded that they should extend their powers and do something towards its removal." . . . They must do something tangible. ("Lecture at the Lion Hotel" 1)

Even as Remond is received as a "sister," implying her audience of Englishwomen have come to identify with her, we see the demarcation of difference and distance that Remond appears to have successfully channeled into a call for action, "something tangible," rather than mere empathy.

A balance between sensation, sentiment, and "fact" was a highly effective strategy of appeal in these lectures, but Remond's choice to read extracts and reference narratives like Brown's *Clotel* and Stowe's *Uncle Tom's Cabin* is also quite interesting. Remond chose in virtually every lecture, according to press accounts, to read quoted passages from newspaper and fictional accounts of American slavery on the platform. Remond's preference for reading quoted passages rather than offering personal testimony would work to shift her appeal to a more "rational" register: she could be seen to appeal to the "authority" of some third party. In fact, some of Remond's strongest political indictments took the form of quoting accounts of violence against slaves committed by "respected citizens" or religious leaders like "the Rev. Dr. Taylor [who] shot one of his wife's negroes for insubordination" ("Speech by Sarah P. Remond" 439). Nonetheless, her preference for accounts other than those of her own experience would also work to deflect attention from her status as a free-born African American rather than a fugitive slave, as we see in the Red Lion Hotel luncheon lecture, the last of her Warrington addresses: "She preferred, however, giving them unquestionable facts instead of personal statements which she might offer, and to this end read several extracts from books, all proving that the system of slavery and the immorality it engenders are eating out the vitals of the country, and destroying domestic happiness" ("The Lecture at the Lion Hotel" 1). Remond is consequently able to avoid the question of just what "personal statements" of the slave's sufferings she can actually offer as a free-born African American living in New England rather than as a fugitive slave from the South. Repeatedly, Remond is carefully inviting and rechanneling identification through both the figures used in her lectures and the figure she is taken to be as a speaker on the antislavery platform.

As Karen Sànchez-Eppler has noted, the body of the slave and woman was a site of contention at this time. The basis of their "general subjection . . . [and] exclusion from political discourse" as well as "a symbol of that oppression," she argues, "the body becomes within both feminist and abolitionist discourses a means of gaining rhetorical force" (30). Indeed, the "whitened" body, what experiences that figure on stage embodied, and what identifications she enabled are at the center of both Ellen Craft's and Sarah Parker Remond's appearances. Craft's appearances arguably played to and were received as embodiments of the tragic mulatta, her whitened features both a spectacle and the reassuringly familiar that could bridge the gap between the enslaved African American's and free white British woman's experience. Remond, on the other hand, had to carefully negotiate just such an identification so that her audiences did not simply collapse very different material conditions between enslaved and free. Such a collapse would silence the female slave and her particular material condition, a silencing that was used rather differently in Ellen Craft's repeated displays. Remond and Craft seem to have been well aware of the rhetorical force of the slave's body, particularly the force of the abject and abused female slave, the tragic mulatta, and the "white slave." Yet Remond's careful use of such symbols in her Warrington speeches enabled her to accomplish a number of conflictual and complicated rhetorical moves. Remond refrained from accounts of personal experience in favor of the "unquestionable facts" of slavery's horrors, yet also strategically avoided acknowledging her free-born status. Consequently, she was able to shift her address to the level of rational, impersonal proofs even while she relied on the sentimental appeal of domestic plots involving victimized slave mothers and children or the sensationalism of the "white slave" or tragic mulatta sold into a life of concubinage. Remond's turn to the tragic mulatta and an attention to her whitened features allowed her to appeal to her female audience's sense of sisterhood, yet carefully stress that the violence suffered by the bondswoman is very different from the lived experience of English women.

Together, Craft's appearances and Remond's lectures reveal both the risks and success of using the female and "white" slave to embody American slavery for British audiences, audiences for whom slavery had become spectacle and sensation. The Crafts drew audiences numbering in the thousands, and their narrative,

Running a Thousand Miles for Freedom; Or, the Escape of William and Ellen Craft from Slavery, published in Britain in 1860, ran to two printings in its first two years of circulation. Remond's antislavery addresses in Warrington achieved somewhat unprecedented results, beginning a tour described as unforgettable. In addition to raising a donation of $100 for the American Anti-Slavery Society, Warrington residents, politicians, and clergy numbering 3,522 signed an address protesting American slavery. "I may add," wrote William Robson to the editor of the *Anti-Slavery Advocate*, "that no address on any subject has ever been more numerously signed in this town" ("What Miss Remond" 221). In addition to their success at advancing their goals, is Craft's and Remond's importance as African American women mobilizing the mulatta in ways that politicize her, rather than simply reinvoke her as a titillating and sensational figure. Whether they managed their appearances or appeals as double voiced; used the "white slave," bondswoman, or concubine; crossed racial, class, or gender lines to present themselves as tragic mulatta embodied, disguised fugitive, or fugitive slave lecturer, Craft and Remond were adept at both appealing to their white audiences and confronting them with realities they would rather not acknowledge. Both women unsettled distinctions their audiences would have preferred remained unquestioned, and carefully managed their identifications that tended to elide the differences in condition between bond and free. Their attention to the mulatta figure; to audience, reception, and performance; and to the double-voiced techniques these enabled, indeed, demanded, make Ellen Craft and Sarah Parker Remond key figures in our consideration of African American women's political strategies as they center on the mulatta.

Chapter 3

Little Romances and Mulatta Heroines

Passing for a "True Woman" in Frances Harper's Iola Leroy *and Pauline Hopkins's* Contending Forces

While Ellen Craft's and Sarah Parker Remond's "womanliness" was frequently noted in British press reports of their appearances and lectures, it was singled out as a characteristic somehow out of the ordinary and worthy of remark, as unique as seeing a "white slave" or tragic mulatta, or hearing a black woman speak of the concubinage of mulattas in Southern states like Louisiana. Indeed, press accounts of Ellen Craft's appearances often made not only her white skin but also her femininity, as evident in her dress and behavior, the sole focus of their remarks. Time and again, Craft's "delicate," "graceful" ("Anti-Slavery Meeting"), "modest demeanor" ("Anti-Slavery Meeting at Bristol"); her "neat" and "elegant" dress ("Slavery in the United States"); her "intelligent" looks ("American Fugitive Slave Bill"); and her "noble . . . and expressive face" were noted by the press ("Letter"). Abolitionists on both sides of the Atlantic singled out her sense of propriety, comparing it to that of a white woman as American abolitionist Henry Bowditch did in his *Life and Correspondence*: "Ellen Craft [is] . . . a delicate, refined woman, one capable of taking her station by the side of any female in our land, one who, even in her delicacy, performed an act of heroism in her escape from Southern bondage" (210).

Sarah Remond came under similar scrutiny among American female abolitionists before she left for Britain. Anne Warren Weston writes of her impressions of Remond in a letter to her sister-in-law, Deborah Weston, dated 13 July 1842: "Mr. and Miss Remond staid all the next day, leaving just in time . . . for an evening lecture. Nothing can exceed Mr. R's [Charles Lenox Remond] high breeding. . . . Miss R. on the contrary has many of the manners and ways supposed to be peculiar to her race." Such attention paid to Remond's manner continued during her lecture tour in Britain. The *Liverpool Mercury*'s report of her first lecture at the Tuckerman Institute on 21 January 1859 begins by defending the unusual appearance of a woman on the antislavery lecture platform and goes on to report that Remond "dwelt in the most touching manner upon the social degradation of her sisters in slavery . . . and concluded with an earnest appeal for the moral and religious sympathy and influence of free England in the abolition movement." Remond's earnest appeal is attributed to the fact that "she no doubt feels strongly," emotion and evident sentiment that is expressed in "a clear, musical voice" ("A Lady Lecturing"). Later that year, a report of Remond's August lecture in Bristol focuses on her womanliness: "Nothing can be more pleasing or lady-like than her appearance and address—the calmness of her delivery adding no little weight to a statement of wrongs calculated to rouse the indignation of every heart. When . . . such a woman, claim[s] at once our courtesy by her lady-like exterior and our admiration by her mental abilities . . . our regret and sympathy are . . . awakened for the sufferer" ("Miss Remond in Bristol" 273).

In reports like these, Remond's success on the lecture circuit is attributed to her "dignity," "womanly" feeling, and "touching" delivery, while Craft's refined and delicate demeanor seems to have drawn an audience as much as her white skin. Both women, then, gained attention for their similarity to white women in behavior and conduct, something that white American and British abolitionists found unusual, given their rather fixed notions of what "manners and ways" were "peculiar" to African Americans. Craft's and Remond's tours certainly benefited from, if not capitalized upon, their audiences' belief that they were oddities whose manners and conduct seemed more "white" than "black." That "whiteness" could reach across the color line and be used to build a degree of familiarity, empathy, and identification that we have seen Craft and Remond managed rather differently.

Their work, however, also connects with that undertaken by the most prominent nineteenth-century African American women writers some two decades after their lecture tours in ways that combine both the unsettling affect Ellen Craft had upon her audiences and the use of a double-voiced appeal as Sarah Parker Remond forwarded. Craft and Remond are important precursors to the work Frances Harper and Pauline Hopkins undertook in *Iola Leroy* (1892) and *Contending Forces* (1899), respectively, their most well known fiction that centered on mulatta heroines. As in Craft's and Remond's abolitionist work, mulattas in Harper's and Hopkins's novels are ambivalent and politicized rather than simply a familiar stereotype. In these texts the mulatta, far from being tragic, becomes a subversive character who signifies on the color line by effectively passing for a "true woman." While Henry Louis Gates Jr. theorizes "Signifyin(g)" as an African American rhetorical strategy of "indirect communication" that commonly "turn[s] upon repetition and difference . . . [and] functions to redress an imbalance of power, to clear a space, rhetorically" (*Signifying* 79, 124), I want to suggest that we move beyond the rhetorical to include enactments or performances, as well as their representation in narrative form, as acts of signifying in this tradition. Harper and Hopkins signify on nineteenth-century American notions of racialized womanhood by using the mulatta's performance of true womanhood to indirectly subvert the exclusive status of the white woman as "true woman," thereby clearing a space for a noble black womanhood. In this reconstitution of womanhood, their passing as "true women" can be read as performatives in Judith Butler's sense of the performative as constitutive. Arguing that gender is repeatedly constituted by the performance of behaviors that we consider to be masculine or feminine, Butler contends that "there is no gender identity behind the expression of gender; that identity is performatively constituted by the very 'expressions' that are said to be its results" (*Gender Trouble* 25). Moreover, these expressions that repeatedly constitute identity are also productive of what a culture takes to be "intelligible" identities: "Indeed to understand identity as a *practice*, and as signifying practice, is to understand culturally intelligible subjects as the resulting effects of a rule-bound discourse. . . . [W]hen the subject is said to be constituted, that means simply that the subject is a consequence of certain rule-governed discourses that govern the intelligible invocation of identity" (Butler, *Gender Trouble* 145). Butler goes on to consider the question of agency within "culturally intelligible practices of identity," positing that "rules governing signification not only restrict, but enable the assertion of alternative domains of cultural intelligibility. . . . Just as bodily surfaces are enacted *as* the natural, so these surfaces can become the site of a dissonant and denaturalized performance that reveals the performative status of the natural itself" (*Gender Trouble* 145–46). It follows, then, that altering or recontextualizing the performance of a "naturalized" identity can, in turn, subvert the identity that it is believed to express or constitute by both challenging that identity's claim to natural status and working to reconstitute it through an alternative set of expressions.

While Butler's work was initially focused on enacted or material instances of gender performativity, she has since moved in *Bodies That Matter* toward a consideration of how such a theory of gender performativity and the materiality of the body can be productively used in the critical reading of narrative.[1] Her choice of distinctly rhetorical terminology in her phrasing of material performativity invites us to translate it from the register of material acts to that of narrative representation: "[P]erformativity must be understood not as a singular or deliberate 'act,' but, rather, as the reiterative and citational practice by which discourse produces the effects that it names" (Butler, *Bodies* 2). Bringing Butler's notion of identity as performative together with Gates's rhetorical theory of African American signifying, I will argue that Harper and Hopkins represent the mulatta as passing for a "true woman," a performative act that not only challenges the notion that white women have an exclusive and inherent access to *the* intelligible form of womanhood in the nineteenth century but one that also reconstitutes true womanhood as an identity acknowledging the lived experiences of African American women. What is frequently taken to be an individualistic politics pursued in the act of passing is configured in these texts as the communal goal of black feminist politics in this era—debunking dehumanizing stereotypes of African American women as a key component to the "advancement of the race" toward full rights and protections under the law. Yet to represent mulatta heroines as passing for "true women" is to engage in a politics marked by ambivalence, such that we have in Harper's and Hopkins's work complex strategies that are often double voiced rather than easily fixed as either progressive or conservative, oppositional or assimilative.

Noble Black Womanhood and the Black Feminist Politics of the Club Movement

Barbara Welter's work offers us the standard definition of true womanhood, or Victorian womanhood, as a gender identity established through etiquette books, ladies magazines, and religious sermons in America during the 1820s.[2] Domesticity or true womanhood was further disseminated through "the new languages of science and medicine" from 1840 to 1860, culminating in an "insistence that women's biology was women's destiny . . . [which] assumed a far more deterministic form during the 1880s and 1890s" (Smith-Rosenberg 178–80). As Shawn Michelle Smith puts it, "white women were increasingly situated at the center of eugenicist discourse. . . . Specifically, the 'true' white woman's moral suasion was being recodified as the character of a racialized ancestral stock" (137). The "true woman," then, was judged largely by qualities that were increasingly raced white by the late nineteenth century: "piety, purity, submissiveness and domesticity" (Welter 21).

Despite the power of such discourses, many white American women found the dictates of true womanhood in conflict with their condition and desires, and they resisted and revised this ideology to suit their own aims, resistance and revision that were expressed in women's novels throughout the nineteenth century. What Nina Baym refers to as "woman's fiction," Susan K. Harris calls "exploratory" novels, and Mary Kelley names "domestic" fiction are novels that "theorize[d] the middle-class household as a base for newly recognized female power, a space from which women could powerfully influence the world" (Baym xxvii).[3]

Whether the cult of true womanhood, or the cult of domesticity as it is more commonly called, actually provided women with access to power has been the subject of debate, as have the implications of claiming a feminist use for a gender identity that excluded, by definition, the majority of nineteenth-century American women. As Lora Romero has noted, current scholarship on domesticity and women's domestic fiction "seems to have distilled itself into a debate about whether the reign of white middle-class women through their domestic power base either fostered or prevented progressive cultural politics" (14). A similar debate arises in studies of African American women's domestic fiction and the politics of the black women's club movement in the late nineteenth and early twentieth centuries. African American women invoked and revised the ideology of domesticity in their creation of what they called a "noble womanhood" for African American women, yet their use of this discourse has been criticized as an adoption of white bourgeois mores. Wilson J. Moses argues that while the leaders of the late-nineteenth-century black women's club movement were genuinely sympathetic to middle-class, working-class, and poor black women, many clubwomen showed "at the same time a patronizing contempt" for women who occupied a "lower" class position ("Domestic" 969). Similarly, Mary Helen Washington reads Anna Julia Cooper's prototypical black feminist work, *A Voice From the South* (1892), as conceding to the ethics of true womanhood and failing to account for the experience of black women in America: "If there is a serious flaw in this feminist position, it is that it often bears so little relation to the lives of black women of the 1890s, most of whom were sharecroppers, struggling farmers, or domestic servants, few of whom could aspire to anything beyond an elementary education" (xlix). However, clubwomen, black feminists like Cooper, and writers like Frances Harper and Pauline Hopkins—whose novels have been criticized for perpetuating both the myth of the tragic mulatta and colorism—were signifying on nineteenth-century American notions of race and womanhood, rather than simply capitulating to them.

In *Domestic Allegories of Political Desire*, Claudia Tate argues that "repudiating the racist sexual discourse of retrogressionism . . . was crucial to black people's changing their own subjugated social status" (10). While African Americans faced the dehumanizing mythology of turn-of-the-century racialist discourse, African American women at this time also encountered a mythology of sexualized black womanhood. Paula Giddings has documented the short mental leap white moralists made from supposed black female "licentiousness" to the ostensible "immorality of the black race": "[I]t was women who were 'responsible' for moulding the institution of marriage and a wholesome family life which was the 'safeguard against promiscuity.' . . . Black women who saw no 'immorality in doing what nature prompts,' who did not 'foster chastity' among their own daughters, were not only responsible for their own denigration but for that of the *entire race*" (31).[4] As Kevin Gaines notes, African Americans "internalized shame" at such stereotypes, an internalization that produced both ambivalence and anxiety. "African American women bore the brunt" of both. While "elite black women" were defended against such derogatory images, many black elites "scrutiniz[ed] . . . the conduct of black women," particularly working-class and poor women. While they would condemn white male desire for black women, often they "regard[ed] black women as complicitous" in the interracial relationships they would condemn (Gaines 122).[5] Whether it was white Americans, with their "shared social understanding that physical appearance reflected internal qualities of character" (Carby, *Reconstructing* 25) or African Americans who placed their anxieties about "the race's" reputation squarely on black women's shoulders, black women were often seen as "fallen women" in need of "self-control," and interracial relationships were regarded as threatening "moral cleanliness" (Gaines 123).

In the minds of many white Americans, true white womanhood depended upon black fallen womanhood in a dialectical relationship, so that even though constructs of the black female might shift in complex and contradictory ways, black women were consistently called to stand as "other" to true white womanhood.[6] As Hortense Spillers has argued, the black woman as body was central to (white) true womanhood, which relied upon the abjection of the black "other": "[W]e cannot unravel one female's narrative from the other's, cannot decipher one without tripping over the other. . . . [F]emale gender for [the black woman] . . . is the tale writ between the lines and in the not-quite spaces of an American domesticity" ("Mama's Baby" 77). In an attempt both to dispel the myths materializing the black female (as) body and to claim womanhood as a protection and an identity that would gain them access to a voice and a recognized subjectivity, many black women adopted the only other version of "woman" existing at the time—that circulated by the cult of domesticity. At the turn into the twentieth century, while many white women rejected domesticity in favor of "asserting their right to a career, to a public voice, to a visible power" as "New Women," black women sought to acquire the "benefits of . . . [Victorian] womanhood— respect, freedom from constant menial labor, interpretation as a morally pure human being" (Ammons 7–8). Hence Deborah McDowell's well-known asser- tion regarding African American women writers and black women's political cul- ture more generally: "[A] pattern of reticence about black female sexuality tended to dominate novels by black women, particularly in the nineteenth and early twentieth centuries. Like the clubwomen, black women writers responded to the myth of the black woman's sexual licentiousness by insisting fiercely on her chastity" ("That nameless" 141–42).

The national federation of black women's clubs also navigated between con- structs of the black female and the "true woman" and has long been said to have developed, in part, as a response to a direct challenge to black womanhood.[7] With aims such as "moral education," "mental elevation," and proving their "aims and interests are identical with those of all good aspiring women," the National Association of Colored Women seems to have aligned itself with the discourse of domesticity circulated by white Americans (Lerner 441–42).[8] However, African American women used the club movement and domestic discourse to further the politics of a "noble womanhood" grounded in the experiences of African American women. Black feminists and clubwomen like Anna Julia Cooper and Gertrude Mossell argued against limiting women's choices to the roles of wife and mother and were quick to point out that Victorian mores seemed illogical and spoke nei- ther to most American women's experience, whether they were black or white, nor to the financial dependence upon a husband that such a role often entailed.[9] Mossell seems to have coined the phrase "noble womanhood" (47), which Joanne Braxton argues represented an "inclusive vision . . . [that] applied to working- class women as well as to professionals and homemakers. Moreover, it substituted the value of race-conscious activism for the submissiveness of the lady" (xxxiii). Rather than solely attending to Victorian ideals of female morality and virtue, many clubwomen "realized that the realities of black women's lives were in con- flict with the major tenets of the cult of True Womanhood" (Guy-Sheftall 156). Yet despite their goals of "race pride, . . . the defence of the black community and home, and . . . race advancement" (Lerner 437), their apparent endorse- ments of Victorian mores have been interpreted by many twentieth-century readers as attempts to assimilate by adopting a "white is right" policy. Critics charge that many nineteenth-century African American women writers and club leaders perpetuated class divisions in the black community and distanced themselves from working-class blacks, arguing instead for social equality on the basis of their own similarity to leisured, bourgeois whites. However, in her study of black women's clubs in turn-of-the-century Chicago, Anne Meis Knupfer is quick to point out that while club policies might reflect "selectivity, privilege, and cultural capital," they also "illustrated the richness and complexity of the club movement," which needs to be understood as located "within larger socio-political structures"(13).[10] This complexity saw some clubwomen advocating the propriety of domesticity while others were vocal about its limitations.[11]

Many of the assumptions implicit in critiques of the black women's club movement resurface in the negative assessments of turn-of-the-century novels written by black women, novels that must also be understood within the context of black women's political culture and a racial imaginary rife with derogatory images of black women. We may well be misreading the politics of these texts and of the club movement if we continue to reduce their avocation of a noble womanhood—a gender identity that critics have argued reflected the influence of white, genteel standards of behavior—to a simple pursuit of assimilation on white terms. Rather, what appears at times to be a concession to Victorian ideals of domesticity and an adoption of white standards of conduct represented in the mulattas of black domestic fiction like Harper's *Iola Leroy* and Hopkins's *Contending Forces* was a political strategy of parodic imitation aimed at challenging racialized and racist constructions of identity.

The "Passing" Mulatta and a Dual Readership

In the course of her life, Frances Ellen Watkins Harper established an "international reputation as a writer, lecturer, and political activist" (Foster, Introduction to *Iola Leroy* xxviii). Publishing ten collections of poetry between 1846 and 1891; "the first short story by a black woman" in 1851; three recently rediscovered serialized novels in 1859, 1877, and 1887–88 (Boyd 12); and *Iola Leroy* in 1892, "probably the best-selling novel by an Afro-American written prior to the twentieth century," she earned her livelihood by writing and by lecturing throughout the North and South to white and African American audiences (Foster, Introduction to *Iola Leroy* xxvi). Taking up the antislavery cause in the North, Harper was later active in Reconstruction efforts in the South. Pauline Elizabeth Hopkins also lectured, though not on the scale Harper had undertaken, and usually on black history.[12] She began publishing short stories in 1900 in the *Colored American Magazine* for which she would later serve as literary editor from 1903 to 1904.[13] Hopkins was the most prolific African American woman writer at the turn into the twentieth century, publishing four novels, seven short stories, essays, articles, and biographical sketches from 1900 to 1905 (Yarborough, Introduction to *Contending Forces* xxviii). In addition to *Contending Forces* (1899), she published three novels serialized in the *Colored American Magazine*: *Hagar's Daughter. A Story of Southern Caste Prejudice* (1901–2); *Winona. A Tale of Negro Life in the South and Southwest* (1902); and *Of One Blood. Or, The Hidden Self* (1902–3).[14] Hopkins undertook to write fiction as a method of African American self-representation, and in her preface to *Contending Forces* she urged others to counter stereotypes of "blackness" in the popular fiction written by whites: *"No one will do this for us; we must ourselves develop the men and women who will faithfully portray the inmost thoughts and feelings of the Negro with all the fire and romance which lie dormant in our history*, and, as yet, unrecognized by writers of the Anglo-Saxon race" (14). Despite such political commitment, commitment that was praised by their contemporaries, Frances Harper and Pauline Hopkins have been largely ignored or maligned for some time by twentieth-century critics, and even though their work has undergone important critical reevaluation, dismissive misreadings of their fiction persists.[15] Their writing is often misunderstood as aiming to appease a white readership with near-white characters who uphold middle-class values by critics who do not consider that *Iola Leroy* and *Contending Forces* may be deliberately double voiced, addressing in rather different ways the white and black readerships Harper and Hopkins hoped to reach.

While we can only speak generally and in a limited way of the possible effect these texts had on their readerships, Harper and Hopkins undertook to write these novels in order to refute degrading stereotypes of African Americans and to expose the often violent inequities in nineteenth-century American society. In her introduction to the Oxford edition of *Iola Leroy*, Frances Smith Foster details the call Frances Harper answered with her first novel: "Afro-Americans and their friends had been urgently calling for novels that would refute these insidious stereotypes. . . . To fight fire with fire, the call was not just for more facts but for writers who could shape these facts in ways that would appeal to the aesthetics of the late nineteenth century" (xxix). William Still, in his contemporary introduction to the novel, marked it as more than an individual literary effort; rather, Harper and her supporters saw it as a voice for "the race." "I confess when I first learned that Mrs. Harper was about to write 'a story' on some features of the Anglo-African race, growing out of what was once popularly known as the 'peculiar institution,' I had my doubts about the matter," wrote Still in 1892. "Indeed it was far from being easy for me to think that she was as fortunate as she might have been in selecting a subject which would afford her the best opportunity for bringing out a work of merit and lasting worth to the race. . . . [T]his last effort . . . will, in all probability, be the crowning effort of her long and valuable services in the cause of humanity" (Introduction 2–3). Published in both Boston and Philadelphia in 1892, by 1893 *Iola Leroy* had run to five printings and was being reviewed by African American periodicals and the white press, with both black and white reviewers praising the novel. At the time of *Iola Leroy's* publication, Harper was "a national recognized leader" in prominent political organizations like the Woman's Christian Temperance Union and the American Woman Suffrage Association, and her reputation as a poet was well established: "By 1858 [*Poems on Miscellaneous Subjects*] . . . had been enlarged, reprinted eight times, and had sold 12,000 copies. . . . In 1871 . . . *Moses: A Story of the Nile* [1869] was in its third printing, and *Poems on Miscellaneous Subjects* was in its twentieth" (Foster, Introduction to *Iola Leroy* xxix).

Harper's success was not only due to her reputation with reformist circles but also to her writings' deliberate appeal to a diverse audience, an appeal we need to critically consider (Foster, *Witnessing* 93). Both Maryemma Graham and John Ernest have challenged "the conventional view that *Iola Leroy* was written for black Sunday school youth" (Ernest 237, n. 2). They, along with Elizabeth Ammons, note that it was "the first widely distributed novel by a black woman in America" (Ammons 170). Frances Smith Foster has argued that Harper's serialized novels, *Minnie's Sacrifice* (1869), *Sowing and Reaping* (1876–77), and *Trial and Triumph* (1888–89), published in the *Christian Recorder*, require us "to revise our notions that early African American publications were directed to white readers" (Foster, Introduction to *Minnie's Sacrifice* xxv). However, Ernest contends that we should also "recognize . . . that many publications were available for a dual audience, and that many writers had reason to expect a white as well as black readership. One wonders . . . whether the cultural politics of the time made it possible to fully disengage oneself from the white reading eye" (237, n. 2). Unlike her serialized novels, then, *Iola Leroy* widely reached both black and white readers and addressed issues African Americans faced outside their own communities, like employment discrimination. In contrast, *Minnie's Sacrifice*, *Sowing and Reaping*, and *Trial and Triumph* "present[ed] . . . clear moral lesson[s] . . . about the dangers of intemperance, greed and disunion *within* the African-American community" (Ernest 182, emphasis added). *Minnie's Sacrifice* can be seen as a precursor to *Iola Leroy*, with its mulatto characters, Louis and Minnie, choosing Reconstruction uplift efforts like schoolteaching over passing for white; *Sowing and Reaping* carried a strong temperance message; and *Trial and Triumph* posited an affirmation of Christianity as a remedy to the racism and sexism Harper's mulatta heroine experienced. While Harper's serialized novels clearly presented political issues and arguments, *Iola Leroy's* "availability for a dual audience" should not be taken as an indication that it is somehow "a 'safe' novel" or less "bold" than Harper's work in the *Christian Recorder*, as Maryemma Graham and Gina Rossetti have argued (302). Rather, as we shall see, Harper's expectation of a white and a black readership informs the racial politics of *Iola Leroy*.

Pauline Hopkins presented *Contending Forces* as an intervention in African American political life with a preface that began by offering "this little romance" as a "humble way to raise the stigma of degradation from my race," and the novel moved into a forceful critique of white mob rule, the attempts at violent control of African Americans exacted through lynching, and their combined indictment of American democracy:

> In these days of mob violence, when lynch-law is raising its head like a venomous monster, more particularly in the southern portion of the great American republic, the retrospective mind will dwell upon the history of the past, seeking there a solution of these monstrous outbreaks under a government founded upon the greatest and brightest of principles for the elevation of mankind. While we ponder the philosophy of cause and effect, the world is horrified by a fresh outbreak, and the shocked mind wonders that in this—the brightest epoch of the Christian era—*such things are*. . . . I have tried to portray our hard struggles here in the North to obtain a respectable living and a partial education. I have presented both sides of the dark picture—lynching and concubinage—truthfully and without vituperation, pleading for that justice of heart and mind for my people which the Anglo-Saxon in America never withholds from suffering humanity. (Introduction 13–15)

Here we see Hopkins openly affirming that, with this novel, she seeks to reach not only African American readers but also a white audience. In his introduction to the Oxford edition, Richard Yarborough contends that the achievement of

Hopkins's goal "to effect social change" with this novel "depended . . . upon the writer's depiction of Afro-American characters who would be acknowledged by the white reader not only as human beings but also as embodiments of white bourgeois values, manners and tastes" (*CF* xxx–xxxi).

Harper's and Hopkins's appeal to their white and black readerships is, however, decidedly more complex than merely offering "whitened" African American characters for their approval or consumption. In arguing that Harper's and Hopkins's novels and their heroines "pass," I am not suggesting that their heroines were presented as white or passed for white or that these novels were presented to their readerships as written by white women. Rather, both Harper's introduction and Hopkins's preface decidedly call attention to their political projects and to their identification as "black." However, by using fictional elements recognizable to readers of domestic or women's fiction and by representing their female protagonists as possessing many of the traits common to the heroines of this genre, Harper and Hopkins were employing a double-voiced strategy of address that would have appealed rather differently to their white and black readerships. It is in this sense, then, that Harper's and Hopkins's novels "passed," just as we can read their heroines "passing" for "true women" as they signify on that gender identity and the color line that it worked to consolidate.[16]

Perhaps Harper's and Hopkins's novels have "passed" too well. Invariably, the most recurrent criticism of their work centers on their "ladylike," fair-complexioned heroines and what appears to be an uncomplicated capitulation to white audience expectations. Harper's Iola Leroy and Hopkins's Sappho Clark are indeed mulatta heroines whose features would enable them to pass for white should they so choose. Iola's long black hair, blue eyes, and fair skin frequently shock white characters in the novel in ways that echo the shock Ellen Craft elicited: " 'Oh, no,' said Dr. Gresham, starting to his feet, 'it can't be so! A woman as white as she a slave?' " (*IL* 58). Sappho is described in ways that echo Remond's description of "tragic mulatta" slaves, as "tall and fair, with hair of a golden cast, aquiline nose, rosebud mouth, soft brown eyes veiled by long dark lashes which swept her cheek, just now covered with a delicate rose flush . . . a combination of 'queen rose and lily in one' " (*CF* 107). Accompanying their "whitened" beauty is the impeccable conduct that was the hallmark of true womanhood, and that, we should remind ourselves, made Craft and Remond oddities for their audiences and the British press. Sappho's employer in New Orleans considers "himself very fortunate to have a woman of her refinement" to act as governess to his children (*CF* 354), and Iola is referred to as "refined and lady-like . . . a woman of fine culture and good breeding" (*IL* 57). In addition to their "refined" behavior, these heroines possess "womanly" constitutions referenced, much like Ellen Craft's, through the hardships they have survived. Harper represents Iola's "health [as] . . . so undermined by the fearful strain through which she passed" while remanded to slavery that she is forced to resign from her position as a teacher in a black Southern school during Reconstruction (*IL* 200). Sappho, born after the Civil War, is raped by her white uncle and abandoned in "a house of the vilest character in the lowest portion of . . . New Orleans." These experiences ruin Sappho's health: "I could not do housework, because my constitution is naturally weak" (*CF* 260, 127).

Sappho's and Iola's beauty, conduct, and frail health conform both to standards of true womanhood and nineteenth-century novelistic conventions as Barbara Christian documents them: "The nineteenth-century novel promoted a rather fragile beauty as the norm; qualities of helplessness, chastity and refinement rather than, say strength, endurance and intelligence were touted as the essential characteristics of femininity. The nineteenth-century heroine not only had to be beautiful physically, she had to be fragile and well-bred as well" ("Shadows" 199). As "true women," Iola and Sappho conceive of marriage and family life as a woman's highest goal. Iola characterizes her future husband's proposal as "a clarion call to a life of high and holy worth" (*IL* 271), while Sappho speaks of marriage as "the noblest heritage of woman" (*CF* 205). However, they both also survive degrading pasts with "strength, endurance and intelligence": Iola's defiance, inherited from her enslaved grandmother, is self-protective; Sappho's "bold, strong, and ennobling" character (*CF* 114) and determination to think for herself enable her to financially support both herself and her son. Moreover, Iola's and Sappho's labor contradicts the nineteenth-century notion of the "true woman" as helpless and delicate: "Wanness and fragility as virtues reflect an ideology of deliberate uselessness, and thus a visual identity with those who do not have to work" (Green 114). This notion of a "visual identity" with white women of a particular class position, and thus "true women," is significant. At first glance, Harper and Hopkins seem to cast their mulattas as mirror images of bourgeois white women, yet the ways in which they differ are central to understanding the work to which these writers put this figure. Although Iola and Sappho look like "true women," their histories are those of "fallen women"; while Harper and Hopkins "redeem" them from such pasts, their strong characters and ability to survive, albeit with weak constitutions, signal Harper's and Hopkins's ambivalent use of Victorian womanhood. Their redemption paradoxically brings them closer to ideals of true womanhood even as they simultaneously violate others, as Harper and Hopkins seem to fulfill, yet contest and revise, this gender identity.

Such signifying continues as Harper and Hopkins pick up further tenets of the cult of domesticity, only to put them to their own politicized uses. Both novels focus on families torn apart by Southern racial dynamics and the slave system and on the attempts of families to reunite after the Civil War. Infusing the cult of domesticity's stress on home life and motherhood with the very different realities of "home-building" for African American women, Hopkins signifies on this tenet of true womanhood. Sappho initially hides her past, both her rape and the son it produces, but she later "resolve[s] that come what would she would claim the child and do her duty as his mother in love and training. She would devote her life to him" (*CF* 342). Such maternal devotion signals Sappho's true womanhood, for the cult of domesticity reified motherhood, which was believed to add "another dimension to [a woman's] usefulness and her prestige. . . . 'My Friend,' wrote Mrs. Sigourney, 'If in becoming a mother, you have reached the climax of your happiness, you have also taken a higher place in the scale of being' " (Welter 38). When Sappho leaves Boston with her son to begin a new life in New Orleans, she must find employment. However, far from unwomanly, Sappho's position is as angel of the house for a wealthy "man of color," where "she combined the duties of housekeeping with those of teaching, and soon became the moving spirit of the home, warmly loved by her little charges" (*CF* 353).

Hopkins's depiction of her mulatta heroine as "purified" through motherhood is politically charged in the context of the nineteenth-century American decline in Anglo-Saxon birthrates that was interpreted as a weakening of white hegemony: "[F]or white women between fifteen and forty-four years old, the birthrate dropped from 278 live births per 1,000 women in 1800 to 124 live births per 1,000 in 1900," documents Harvey Green. "[T]he drop . . . and the simultaneous immigration of large numbers of allegedly fertile southern and eastern European women threatened the stability of the existing social order of late nineteenth-century America" (30). Read in the light of this growing anxiety over white power, depicting successful and thriving African American families as Harper and Hopkins did signals racial progress toward greater political and economic power. In fact, Hopkins represents Sappho's maternal devotion as a necessary condition for future political action: "The mother-love chased out all the anguish that she had felt over his birth. She wondered how she had lived without him. . . . [I]n the years which followed she learned to value the strong, chastening influence of her present sorrow, and the force of character it developed, fitting her perfectly for the place she was to occupy in carrying comfort and hope to the women of her race" (*CF* 346–47). Within African American women's political culture, Sappho's suitability to comfort other black women is part of a larger discourse that linked racial advancement to "tenets of the Republican motherhood, progressive maternalism, and municipal housekeeping. . . . In their discourse on raising the standards of home, family life, and motherhood, the NACW [National Association of Colored Women] . . . insist[ed] that the future of the race was moored to African American mothers' moral guardianship" (Knupfer 11–12).[17] Finally, as Kate McCullough points out, to redeem Sappho by having her reclaim her son, who Hopkins has also cast as the product of her rape, "transforms unchosen maternity" from a "sign of dispossession" echoing "slavery's model of maternity" into "an assertion of self and kin" (41). On multiple levels, then, Sappho's apparently straightforward conformity to true womanhood is inflected with her "failings" and with the valences of Hopkins's politicized critique—the "fallen woman" as "true woman," the African American mother and family as leading racial progress and challenging white hegemony, the progressive maternalism of a nineteenth-century black feminism, and the recoding of African American maternity from dispossession to self-possession.

With their stress on motherhood and the importance of families reunited, Harper's and Hopkins's novels are part of what Gabrielle Foreman has coined a "black mulatta genealogy," in which "protagonists . . . work to steal away African-American agency by recovering black female motive will and active desire as well as by recuperating an economically, legally viable and racially inflected motherhood" ("Mama?" 507). While "white mulatta genealogies ignore . . . a significant African-American familial politics in slavery and its representation" (Foreman, "Mama?" 506), African American women like Harper, Hopkins, and Ellen Craft before them stage familial bonds as resistant to the institution of slavery and white supremacist politics.[18] By foregrounding a politicized motherhood, *Iola Leroy* and *Contending Forces* are mulatta narratives that differ significantly from their most well known predecessor, William Wells Brown's *Clotel; or, The President's Daughter* (1853).[19] Brown's heroine, Clotel, the daughter of President Jefferson and his slave Currer, enacts a fiercely rebellious maternity by escaping slavery three times and attempting to rescue her daughter, Mary, from a fate that will echo her own. Rather than see her daughter trapped in a sexual slavery like her own, Clotel attempts to challenge the law that "the child follows the condition of the mother" in her failed rescue attempt. However, Brown's characterization of African American womanhood and maternity as resistant is complicated and undercut by Clotel's mother, Currer, who brokers her daughters' *plaçage* at quadroon balls, actively seeking to perpetuate her own condition in her daughters, who she aspires to match with wealthy white gentlemen. While *Clotel* occupies a complicated, if not vexed, position in what Foreman calls a black mulatta genealogy, it clearly is important to consider alongside Harper's and Hopkins's texts, for it throws into relief the political work of a noble black womanhood and politicized motherhood in their novels.

Hopkins's reference to Sappho's teaching both as governess and as "keeper" of her employer's house and that family's morality, as well as Iola's brief occupation as a teacher in a Southern school during Reconstruction, constitutes a further challenge to and revision of racialized gender identities. Nancy Cott has noted that, for white women, schoolteaching was "less a means of essential support for unmarried women than a mode in which daughters of established families enacted their duty to the community" (32). Middle- and upper-class single women took up this occupation because they had access to the required education that working-class women would have found beyond their means. Teaching, then, signaled a privileged class position for white women. Conversely, teaching was one of the few professions open to African American women, for whom it was indeed "a means of essential support." Paula Giddings quotes figures compiled by Booker T. Washington's National Business League at the turn of the century that show a relatively low number of black women in the professions, the majority of whom were teachers: "160 Black female physicians, seven dentists, ten lawyers, 164 ministers, assorted journalists, writers, artists, 1,185 musicians and teachers of music, and 13,525 school instructors" (75). Rather than a dutiful gesture to a community that held their families in high esteem, African Americans saw teaching as a tool of racial advancement and education and literacy as the means to reunite families separated by slavery.

Hopkins's and Harper's readers who were accustomed to the generic conventions of white-authored domestic fiction still very popular in a literary marketplace that had begun to shift its attention to regionalism may well have interpreted their heroines as "true women" employed in a respectable occupation and read their novels as sentimental romances in which love, marriage, and motherhood are the ultimate rewards for proper behavior and pure ideals.[20] However, as Claudia Tate has argued of black domestic fiction generally, African American readers of such texts often recognized themselves in heroines who worked to support themselves and family. Moreover, they tended to see the future of their race in reunited families and close-knit communities pursuing education as a means to economic and political progress. Both Harper's and Hopkins's novels make use of the elements Tate notes. In *Iola Leroy*, Iola is reunited with her mother, brother, uncle, and grandmother following the Civil War, and her schoolteaching is part of the larger Reconstruction efforts of African Americans and Northern whites in the South. The dramatic conclusion of Hopkins's *Contending Forces* not only reconciles Sappho with Will Smith, whom she marries, but also reunites the Smith family with their lost Montefort relatives and a sizeable inheritance, closing with a transatlantic sailing of the entire Smith family to visit their new-found white English relatives. I would hesitate to generalize, and so render monolithic, a white and black readership; however, I find compelling Tate's argument that African Americans read black domestic fiction in distinctive ways and saw themselves or possibilities for themselves in the characters they read about. Similarly, I would argue that a white female reader might tend to note those elements that were highly recognizable to her in such fiction, elements that were shared with the white-authored domestic fiction she was undoubtedly also reading at the time. I am suggesting that writers like Harper and Hopkins, aware that they were addressing a "mixed" readership, created "mixed" texts that may well have spoken quite differently to readers who came to them able to recognize, and indeed looking for, particular representations.

While Tate's focus is largely on the ways in which black women's domestic fiction made possible the imagined realization of African American political desire by offering "the recently emancipated an occasion for exercising political self-definition in fiction" (7), my focus is quite different. In addition to dramatizing the economic success and family unity that would signal the full citizenship of post-Reconstruction blacks as Tate argues, these novels have also "passed" as endorsements of white bourgeois values and standards—perhaps too successfully for a twentieth-century critical readership that has tended to dismiss them—just as their heroines pass as "true women." These acts of passing work to signify on and indict their era's notions of race and womanhood through a strategy of parodic imitation. The sophistication of these novels lies in the ways in which both the texts themselves and their mulatta characters pass, so that subversive critique becomes possible from *within* both the cult of domesticity's ideal of true womanhood and nineteenth-century conventions of the domestic novel or woman's fiction. The differences I have been attending to between the "true woman" and Harper's and Hopkins's mulatta heroines are central to an understanding of the ways in which these authors parody and revise true womanhood, but Harper and Hopkins also worked to signify on true womanhood through female characters who were neither light-skinned nor middle-class. By inscribing the experiences of African American women in the framework of white women's domestic fiction, a framework that simultaneously accesses the tenets of true womanhood, Harper and Hopkins work to indict notions of womanhood that would exclude black women not only because they were strong enough to survive white threat and violence but also because the material conditions of their lives often made it difficult, if not impossible, for them to maintain the family formations or domestic space that was central to the cult of domesticity. Harper and Hopkins— like their black feminist contemporaries—were working to create a noble black womanhood that incorporates African American female experience, rather than silencing that experience in order to capitulate to white American bourgeois ideology.

The Politics of Domesticity and Decorum: Noble Black Women Beyond a "Whitened Ideal"

Claudia Tate observes that African Americans generally "believed they could realize their desire to be full citizens by freely adopting the values of the dominant society" (56). The belief that social equality would accompany acquired refinement culminated in schoolroom classes in decorum and the publication of etiquette manuals.[21] Originally, books outlining manners and etiquette were confined to the schoolhouse, but they later developed a wider readership. Books like Professor and Mrs. John William Gibson's *Golden Thoughts on Chastity and Procreation* (1903) and E. Azalia Hackley's *The Colored Girl Beautiful* (1916) encouraged African Americans to perceive and present themselves as the social equals of white Americans. Just as *Godey's Lady's Book* and *The Young Lady's Friend* instructed young white women in etiquette, Hackley's book addressed motherhood, relationships with men, dress, the home, and manners. Willard Gatewood notes that "one of the book's themes was culture and 'self-control.' . . . Young women were encouraged to 'affect modesty and purity' even if they 'did not feel them'" (184). Like other black writers of her time, Hackley addresses white stereotypes of African Americans; she invokes white notions of black sexuality in order to encourage her black readership to counter such images with exemplary conduct. Writers on etiquette published both manuals and columns in black weekly papers and magazines. The sources may have been diverse and numerous, but the topics addressed were consistent: "The importance of restraint in all matters from emotion and expression to dress[,] . . . the necessity for good manners both in public places and in the privacy of the home[,] . . . [and] a notion that familiarity did indeed breed contempt . . . [were] applied to the proper attitude for young ladies to assume toward the opposite sex" (Gatewood 185).

What may have been an African American presentation of self as "full citizen" has been largely interpreted by twentieth-century readers as a wholesale adoption of white values. Indeed, arguing that "professional attainment, social esteem, intellectual and cultural refinement—in short, the markers of bourgeois class status—were more important than an individual's racial designation" (Tate 62) may have worked to counter the white American assumption that *the* African American community was undifferentiated in its so-called inherent inferiority. But many have contended that the result of such an argument was a widening division among African Americans along class lines, fractures that are often said to be inextricable from the politics of color. Consequently, this attention to conduct and decorum led to "charges that the elite possessed an acute case of 'white fever' and was intent upon transforming itself into a separate caste that would win immunity to the proscription being placed on all Negroes" (Gatewood 154).

However, such charges that bourgeois blacks used their class position to hold themselves aloof from working-class blacks assume that nineteenth-century African Americans adopted the values of white Americans along with the practice of middle-class manners. Instead, decorum and domesticity seem to have signaled very different values for white and black Americans at this time. Nancy Cott observes that the cult of domesticity expressed the dominance of what may be designated a middle-class ideal, a "cultural preference for domestic retirement and conjugal-family intimacy over both the 'vain' and fashionable sociability of the rich and the promiscuous sociability of the poor" (92). Ann Douglas similarly argues that the dress and conduct of bourgeois white women enabled them to differentiate themselves as consumers from the working classes as producers: "Expensively educated, well-treated, and well-dressed, they could . . . advertise male earnings. . . . They did not make homespun; they displayed fine cottons and silks" (61). Yet African Americans did not see domesticity as a sign of individual status; rather, as Carla Peterson argues, nineteenth-century blacks stressed the liberatory and empowering aspects of home life for the community as a whole. "Fundamental to their activities . . . was a conviction that the newly emancipated population must become self-sufficient and achieve community autonomy by means of 'home building,' education, and employment," contends Peterson. "Their emphasis on domesticity . . . must be seen instead as a continuation of those antebellum practices that viewed domestic economy as an instrument of family and community empowerment" (199).

Rather than confining her representation of true womanhood as a performative to which only fair-skinned mulattas had access, and thereby perpetuating colorism, Harper depicts a number of African American women from diverse backgrounds as noble women. In fact, Harper's ideal of true black womanhood does not seem to be Iola but Lucille Delany, a university graduate who establishes a Southern school for African Americans: " '[S]he is of medium height, somewhat slender and well formed, with dark, expressive eyes, full of thought and feeling. Neither hair nor complexion show[s] the least hint of blood admixture. . . . Her manner was a combination of suavity and dignity' " (*IL* 199). Rather than Iola serving as a model of womanhood for "the race," Lucille Delany becomes Iola's "ideal woman. She is grand, brave, intellectual, and religious" (*IL* 242). In addition to depicting "true" black women of the middle class devoted to racial progress, Harper depicts former slaves and working-class women like Aunt Linda as wise "home builders" central to community autonomy. As *Iola Leroy* opens, we see Aunt Linda, the cook on the Johnson plantation, using her enforced domesticity for subversive ends. The slaves on this and the neighboring plantations use a coded "market speech" to communicate recent Civil War events to one another. Domesticity is embedded in this code in such a way that the public sphere of the market is conflated with the private sphere of the kitchen: "[I]f they wished to announce a victory of the Union army, they said the butter was fresh, or that the fish and eggs were in good condition. If defeat befell them, then the butter and other produce were rancid or stale" (*IL* 9). While Harper depicts male slaves like Robert Johnson as able to read and thereby relay the newspaper's latest accounts of the war to the enslaved community, it is Aunt Linda who organizes the slaves on the neighboring plantations and determines their meeting places:

> "Bobby," she said, when he returned, "I thinks we ort ter hab a prayer-meetin' putty soon."
>
> "I am in for that. Where will you have it?"
>
> "Lem me see. Las' Sunday we had it in Gibson's woods; Sunday 'fore las', in de old cypress swamp; an' nex' Sunday we'el hab one in McCullough's woods. Las' Sunday we had a good time. . . . I tell yer, dere was a shout in de camp."
>
> "Well, you had better look out, and not shout too much, and pray and sing too loud, because, 'fore you know, the patrollers will be on your track and break up your meetin' in a mighty big hurry. . . ."

"Oh, we looks out for dat. . . . Now, Bob, you sen' word to Uncle Dan'el, Tom Anderson, an' de rest ob dem, to come to McCullough's woods nex' Sunday night. I want to hab a sin-killin' an' debil-dribin' time." . . .

Although the slaves were denied unrestricted travel, and the holding of meetings without the surveillance of a white man, yet they contrived to meet by stealth and hold gatherings where they could mingle their prayers and tears, and lay plans for escaping to the Union army. (*IL* 12–13)

Aunt Linda galvanizes her community under slavery and fosters its reconstruction after the war. She narrates the community's history to Robert Johnson when he returns to North Carolina with Iola to find their respective mothers, and she later takes them to a revival meeting where Robert is united with his mother and discovers that Iola is her grandchild and his niece. Aunt Linda's influence in her own family is noteworthy as well, for she encourages her husband to buy land, thereby facilitating their transition from chattel to landowners: " 'An' shore 'nough, ole Gundover died, an' his place war all in debt, an' had to be sole. . . . Well, John didn't giv in at fust; didn't want to let on his wife knowed more dan he did. . . . But I kep' naggin at him, till I specs he got tired of my tongue, an' he went and buyed dis piece ole lan'. . . . When we knowed it war our own, warn't my old man proud!' " (*IL* 155)

Aunt Linda is far from being a submissive woman, but her strength is cast in domestic terms such as family and community unity. Lucille Delany is independent, but her independent act is to establish a school for the education of her community, and her independence of mind joins with Iola's to argue that men and women be equally involved in raising children. Iola speaks for a woman's right to work outside the home but bases this on her belief that "'every woman should have some skill or art which would insure her at least comfortable support. I believe there would be less unhappy marriages if labor were more honored among women'" (*IL* 210). Harper's white female readers schooled in the tenets of true womanhood and domesticity may well have seen an African American woman's self-sufficient labor as "unseemly" but may also have accepted it in the name of a happy home and marriage. The novel's "true" black women advocate a woman's role as communal rather than individualistic, and they present their views under the guise of domesticity. Each incorporates a revision of true womanhood that voices rather than silences African American experience: they stress action and independence not submissive obedience, practicality and necessity not refinement.[22] What John Ernest argues of Aunt Linda's "market speech" may well be extended to the novel's signifying play on the cult of domesticity and its icon, the "true woman." Both confront Harper's "white readers with their inability to interpret culturally familiar discourse" (Ernest 187). Those representations that seem the most culturally familiar—domesticity and duty to community and family—are consistently inflected with Harper's political challenges to and revisions of these discourses. We prove ourselves less than capable readers if we do not recognize the double-voiced representations and appeals Harper offers in this novel.

We need to attend to such differences between the "womanly" qualities extolled by the cult of true womanhood and the values Harper and Hopkins ascribe to their noble black women in order to see that they are not simply representing their characters as whitened ideals that elide African American female experience but rather are representing them as engaged in a subversive performance of true womanhood that seeks to unsettle it. The disruption such a performance poses is, for Butler, the power of the performative to expose the notion of a "true," essential, stable gender identity as a "regulatory fiction":

> Gender ought not to be construed as a stable identity or locus of agency from which various acts follow; rather, gender is an identity tenuously constituted . . . through a *stylized repetition of acts*. . . . The possibilities of gender transformation are to be found precisely in the arbitrary relation between such acts, in the possibility of a failure to repeat, a de-formity, or a parodic repetition that exposes the phantasmatic effect of abiding identity as a politically tenuous construction. . . . If gender attributes and acts . . . are performative, then there is no preexisting identity by which an act or attribute might be measured . . . and the postulation of a true gender identity would be revealed as a regulatory fiction. (*Gender Trouble* 141)

Consequently, when Harper and Hopkins work to represent characters who are at once able to be both "true women" and to pursue the values of an African American community whose material conditions and experiences they share, they are not simply translating the tenets of true womanhood and white bourgeois standards into an African American context. Rather, they are working to expose those nineteenth-century dehumanizing constructs of African American identity and true womanhood as contingent.

Similarly, Hopkins's characters perform true womanhood but effectively subvert it by inflecting exclusionary domesticity with race consciousness. A sewing circle organized to raise money for a local African American church "that has been instrumental in . . . helping this race to help itself" becomes the setting for black women's politics (*CF* 142). Talk among the working- and middle-class African American women attending this meeting centers on "[t]he place which the virtuous woman occupies in upbuilding a race" (*CF* 148). As in *Iola Leroy*, communal concerns and domestic activities occupy the foreground in such performances of true womanhood; however, these women also contest constructions of both black female sexuality and racial difference prevalent at the time. Mrs. Willis, clubwoman and lecturer on the "Woman Question," argues that African American women have inherited "'the native African woman['s] . . . impregnable . . . virtue'" (*CF* 149), refuting the construction of the inherently oversexed black female. Hopkins also invokes popular myths regarding mulattas in order to have her female characters contend that arguments against miscegenation are groundless:

> "I shall never forget my feelings," chimed in Anna Stevens . . . "at certain remarks made by the Rev. John Thomas. . . . [H]e touched upon the Negro, and with impressive gesture and lowered voice thanked God that the mulatto race was dying out, because it was a mongrel mixture which combined the worst elements of two races. Lo, the poor mulatto! despised by the blacks of his own race, scorned by the whites! Let him go out and hang himself!". . . Mrs. Willis smiled as she said calmly, . . . "It is an incontrovertible truth that there is no such thing as an unmixed black on the American continent." (*CF* 150–51)[23]

However, even while she clearly sees the liberatory potential of using domesticity and true womanhood as the forms through which to challenge prevailing conceptions of racial difference and to negotiate a space for black women in a society that denied their humanity and womanhood, Hopkins is notably critical of those who would see the wholesale adoption of bourgeois white values as the solution to racism and inequity. Mrs. Willis is characterized as just such an individual. She is introduced as resourceful, self-sufficient, and "shrewd." While driven by necessity to support herself, Mrs. Willis does so by exploiting the current interest in the "Woman Question" and finds herself managed by a white "philanthropist who sought to use her talents as an attraction for a worthy charitable object, the discovery of a rare species of versatility in the Negro character being a sure drawing-card." Mrs. Willis's attempt to exploit early black feminism for her own ends, "[p]lans . . . conceived in selfishness," results in her own exploitation as an "oddity" subjected to the white gaze. She never seems to recognize her compromised position, but Hopkins's indictment of her self-serving aims is unmistakable: "Trivialities are not to be despised . . . love implanted in a woman's heart for a luxurious, aesthetic home life . . . amid flowers, sunshine, books and priceless pamphlets, easy chairs and French gowns, may be the means of . . . freeing a race from servitude. It was amusing to watch" (*CF* 147).

Hopkins, then, makes a clear distinction between African American women performing true womanhood and thereby charging the private sphere and domestic ideology with what were considered radical political concerns at the time—female independence, challenges to racialist discourses, and a championing of African American social and political equality—and a blind faith that bourgeois trappings will uplift a dispossessed race.[24] Mrs. Willis may profess to advocate suffrage and "the *evolution* of true womanhood" (*CF* 146), but she has clearly adopted the Victorian notion of a woman's place: " '*Your* duty is not to be morbid, thinking these thoughts that have puzzled older heads than yours. *Your* duty is, also, to be happy and bright for the good of those about you. Just blossom like the flowers, have faith and *trust*' " (*CF* 157). In contrast to Mrs. Willis who would advocate a submissive and dependent womanhood, Hopkins's black female working-class characters direct their entrepreneurial skills into developing self-sufficient businesses in the African American community. While Richard Yarborough contends that "Hopkins's own elitist views mar her treatment of lower-class black characters like Sarah Ann White and Ophelia Davis" (Introduction to *CF* xli), these characters are, in fact, the site of a significant challenge to "separate spheres" ideology and what power interests it may serve. Ophelia Davis and Sarah Ann White, "raised on neighboring plantations," utilize skills that previously contributed to their masters' capital to form a "partnership in a laundry" (*CF* 104). Like Aunt Linda in *Iola Leroy*, Ophelia and Sarah Ann transform their status from property to propertied, from servitude in the slave economy to self-reliance in the market economy. Moreover, they use the spoils of the Civil War and the profits of their own enforced labor to do so:

> "Yas'm, I've got a silk dress, tow of 'em, an' a lace shawl an' a gold watch and chain. . . . I come by 'em hones', I did. Yas'm, when my ol' mistis left her great big house an' all that good stuff—silver an' things—a-layin' thar fer anyone to pick up thet had sense 'nough to know a good thing an' git it ahead of enybody else. I jes' said to myself: 'Phelia, chile, now's yer time!' Yas'm, I feathered my

nes', I jes' did. Sarah Ann, you 'member that time, honey. . . . You stuffed yerself with greenbacks, but honey, I took clo's, too." (*CF* 105)

Ophelia and Sarah Ann were once relegated to the frontiers of the feminine by their forced circulation as property appraised and sold in public. However, they not only cross these borders to take up the silks and laces of womanhood and the greenbacks of capitalism, but Ophelia and Sarah Ann also conflate these gendered spheres in their boardinghouse laundry. Rather than upholding the social divisions the cult of domesticity worked to police—private versus public, bourgeois versus working class, white versus black—Hopkins's noble black women transgress and blur those boundaries through hybrid performances of "true" black womanhood.

Policing the Social: Performative Identity and Parodic Performances

My contention that Harper's and Hopkins's characters perform true womanhood, rather than imitate or mimetically represent this gender identity, is key to my reading of these novels as contesting, not conceding to, late-nineteenth-century racialist ideology. Mimesis posits a "truthful" relation between model and copy, but Harper and Hopkins deliberately confront their audience with the differences between black and white women's lived experience in America. Moreover, interpreting these characters as engaged in a performative opens a space for seeing such acts as generative rather than parasitic. If, as Butler would argue, "it is only *within* the practices of repetitive signifying that a subversion of identity becomes possible" (*Gender Trouble* 145), what many readers have taken as indices of Harper's and Hopkins's complicity with white bourgeois values can be read as agential acts that seek to subvert, through reinscription, their era's discursive construction of black womanhood as abject.[25] By unseating virtue and purity from the white body and embodying the black woman as a "true woman," Harper and Hopkins not only expose true womanhood as a performative gender identity produced through the often violent abjection of the African American woman but also mobilize the performative in order to reconstitute their era's notions of both womanhood and race. Here it is worth reminding ourselves of Joseph Roach's theory of performance genealogies as "not merely . . . recapitulation but . . . the displacement of . . . cultural forms" (29). Harper and Hopkins employ the performative as part of a political strategy to undermine American ideologies of race and gender that had constructed the "grotesque" black female body. But the timing of such an intervention is also significant to our understanding of its politics. Importantly, Harper and Hopkins undertook to represent African American women as "true women" with the awareness that increasingly in turn-of-the-century America, appearance and behavior were more than indications of character but were taken to *be* an individual's identity.

While rules governing proper behavior, or etiquette, have long worked to construct class and gender identities, race was also read through behavior, as evidenced by those legal decisions examined in Chapter 1 that delimited racial identities according to reputation, conduct, and the society an individual kept. The rapid social change of the late nineteenth century caused by increasing industrialization and urbanization, as well as an influx of immigrants and a migration of African Americans from the South, created a fluid and highly mobile American society in which individuals were able to shift class positions. The instability of social divisions in the late nineteenth century gave rise to a concern among white Americans for what were called the "excesses of democracy" (Kasson 60), excesses that took the form of industrial strikes, middle-class reforms, and the woman's suffrage movement. Moreover, many whites believed that emancipation and Reconstruction epitomized democracy gone too far and increased their attempts to control black Americans, effectively eroding any progress Reconstruction efforts had secured for African Americans.

In addition to segregation and institutionalized racism, bourgeois whites responded to the greater social mobility of the late nineteenth century with an increased regimentation of the social. The production of etiquette manuals surged to an all-time high as the turn of the century approached. However, rather than equipping the bourgeoisie with an ever more elaborate delineation of the "appropriate" with which to police the bounds of class, gender, and racial divisions, these etiquette manuals served to advance the notion that respect and consideration were acquirable commodities. A strict adherence to manners might further segment social roles, but it did little to restrict who took them on. John Kasson observes that while rules of etiquette may have served "as another means of exclusion at the upper ranks of society, for much of urban middle-class life the cultivation of bourgeois manners served as an instrument of inclusion and socialization" (43). American bourgeois culture had come to believe that " 'the *manner* in which a person says or does a thing, furnishes a better index of his character than *what* he does or says' " (qtd. in Kasson 98). Appearance and conduct were not merely indications of character; rather, they had come to constitute identity. The self was largely conceived of as an accretion of behaviors or "a series of dramatic effects" in turn-of-the-century white America (Kasson 94). Paradoxically, the "science" of etiquette and the system of meanings attached to behavior that, in turn, signaled economic and social status as well as a "respectable" upbringing also enabled the performance of "upstanding" character by so-called undesirables. Similarly, white middle-class attempts to reassure themselves that bodies revealed character and essences rather than masked them, as evident in the rise of photographic studies of the criminal body and the phenomenon of "pocket physiologies," could also be "used to create new images and posit new identities, proliferating the possibilities for representing and circulating the self" in performances that "enabled social passing" (S. M. Smith 69, 86, 92).[26]

The stability of "good character" and its attachment to whiteness and the middle and upper classes was eroded by such accessibility. White Americans, clearly disturbed by the idea that African Americans might not "know their place" and keep to it, complained of African American women " 'putting on airs,' desiring 'to play the lady and be supported by their husbands like the white folks' " (qtd. in Sterling 322). Eleanor Tayleur, writing for the *Outlook* in 1904, "recalled" enslaved African American women "copying" their mistress' manners such that " 'many a black woman was a grand dame who would have graced a court.' " Tayleur went on to characterize African American women as "childishly" preoccupied with imitating bourgeois whites: " 'She copies her [the white woman's] extravagance in tawdry finery that is a grotesque exaggeration of fashion, she copies her independence in utter abandon of all restraints, she copies her vices and adds to them frills of her own' " (qtd. in Guy-Sheftall 44). The kind of subversive performance of what were constructed and policed as "white" bourgeois behavior and, therefore, identity in Harper's and Hopkins's fiction was, from these accounts, occurring in society more widely. Notably, as Shawn Michelle Smith points out, "racial surveillance increased even as legally defined racial difference became indeterminate" (92). It should come as no surprise, then, that etiquette manuals and pocket physiologies were the rage around the same time we see legal cases clustering in which one's performance of whiteness, as read in one's behavior and reception in society, began to outweigh a genealogy that included both white and black forbears.

While Tate has encouraged us to re-read nineteenth-century black women's novels as participating in efforts of black communal advancement, arguing that rather than adopting white values African American women put into practice bourgeois conventions to serve their own values and further their own aims, we cannot ignore the ambivalence of a strategy aimed at attaining social and political equality by practicing the very conventions that were meant to ensure the exclusion of African Americans from the dominant culture. Nor should we elide the problematic implications of narratives that seem to argue such parity on the basis of "virtuous" and "near-white" heroines. Instead, in the slippage between true womanhood and its performance by Harper's and Hopkins's heroines—those differences that work to inscribe African American experience and values in a gender identity established to consolidate white hegemony—lies the political import of these writers' works. I am not arguing that any African American who contradicted white stereotypes of blacks was engaging in some form of imitation of white behavior, for to do so would be to invoke and inscribe those very stereotypes at the root of comments like Tayleur's. Rather, Harper and Hopkins used the mulatta figure to challenge the dominant culture's construction and mobilization of race. To do so, these writers exposed true womanhood as a racialized gender identity, constituted and regulated by appearance and behavior, which was performable by the very women it arguably sought most to exclude—biracial women who looked "as *white* as" they did but threatened to "pollute" white American purity with "tainted" African blood. The mulatta figure's very ambivalence is what makes their novels transgressive while appearing to be conciliatory, subversive while engaged in what seem like compromised representations of black womanhood. In addition to the political act of forging a sense of community with their African American readership, as Tate contends, Harper and Hopkins were arguably well aware of the transgressive import of portraying an African American character as a "true woman" in novels read by blacks and whites alike. White readers, who might be interested initially in characters who appear to be as white as themselves, would undoubtedly be unsettled at a deeper level by the boundaries violated in these novels.[27] Indeed, white readers of Hopkins's fiction published in the *Colored American Magazine*—an African American periodical with a circulation of over 15,000—were disturbed by it: "[O]ne white reader cancelled her subscription . . . complaining [of Hopkins's interracial themes], 'The stories of these tragic mixed loves will not commend themselves to your white readers and will not elevate the colored readers'" (Brooks 123).

The Mulatta Heroine: Conflictual Readings of Corporeal Texts

As Hortense Spillers argues, the identity of the mulatta circulates in America as an "overdetermination" to which is attributed "the illicit . . . commingling of bloodlines that a simplified cultural patrimony wishes to deny. But in that very denial, the most dramatic and visible of admissions is evident" ("Notes" 167). The mulatta represents a racial illegitimacy, for she falls outside the American racial fantasy of a binary marking a strict distinction between white and black. In *American Anatomies*, Robyn Wiegman contends that race in America is dependant upon the differential relationship of black to white in what she compellingly argues is a "politics of visibility": "[T]he 'logic' of race in United States culture anchors whiteness in the visible epistemology of black skin. Such an epistemological relationship circumscribes our cultural conception of race, contributing above all to the recurrent and discursively, if not always materially, violent equation between the idea of 'race' and the 'black' body" (21). However, the mulatta is called to function in the production of "race" somewhat differently than the black body of which Wiegman speaks. Albeit a body designated black, the mulatta is frequently illegible in this American politics of visibility but is nevertheless invested with the ability to mark the bounds of blackness and whiteness, as well as signify both the greatest threat to race—its illegibility in certain "unreadable" bodies—and the ultimate assertion of its power. If, as Wiegman argues, "the differential of 'blackness' continues to mark and carry its modern double burden: signifying itself, it also anchors the differential meaning of whiteness by lodging it . . . in the epistemology of black skin" (49), the mulatta carries a "modern" triple burden that never signifies "itself," the mulatta as "neither/nor" but both white and black. Instead, the racial illegibility of the mulatta and the threat she poses to a racial "epistemology of skin" mark the need for racialist discourse to "read" and thereby construct a racialized body if not on its surface then beneath the skin in fractional quantities of "blood." This particular racialized body, as a corporeal racial borderland, comes to "anchor" the meaning of whiteness and blackness even while it threatens to undo notions of racial difference.

The mulatta, as hybrid and illegible body, marks most clearly what Robert Young calls the dialectics of race: "[H]ybridity . . . maps out [racial theory's] most anxious, vulnerable site. . . . The idea of race here shows itself to be profoundly dialectical: it only works when defined against potential intermixture, which also threatens to undo its calculations altogether" (19). Indeed, as Young argues in *Colonial Desire*, "debates about theories of race in the nineteenth century" centered on the question of hybridity, and "as the century progressed, the alleged degeneration of those of mixed race came increasingly both to feed off and to supplement hybridity as the focus of racial and cultural attention and anxiety" (9, 16). In the United States, such cultural anxiety over racial hybridity has focused almost exclusively on distinctions between black and white, again signaling that questions of the mulatta's hybridity and her "blackness" are at the crux of American notions of race. Keeping in sight, then, the fact that Harper and Hopkins were writing in the midst of this cultural anxiety over race and during the rise of attempts to police the social through rigid codes of conduct, we must now recognize that those mulatta heroines conventionally read as appeasing a white audience may have been far more unsettling than we have imagined. Seeming to acquiesce to both white bourgeois standards of civility and the novelistic conventions of white women's domestic fiction, Harper and Hopkins play on, rather than elide, the anxiety surrounding hybridity.

This play on the culturally familiar is not limited to the ways in which Harper's and Hopkins's novels signify on textual forms familiar to their white readers. In the contemporary parlance of Trey Ellis, their texts could be said to be "culturally mulatto," "us[ing] 'white' cultural forms, [while] not . . . desir[ing] to be white or claim that notions of 'race' do not color [the] everyday lives" of their characters (Favor, "Ain't Nothin' " 698), along with "black" cultural forms.[28] Their texts are hybrid or "mixed," just as American culture has long been, but critics have thus far failed to recognize the ways in which both of these writers employ African American cultural expression. Instead, far more critical attention has been paid to the ways in which their texts access "white" cultural and textual forms. One possible explanation for this critical blind spot is that vernacular theories of African American literature that remain popular within the field risk rendering monolithic particular representations of "authentic blackness." Hazel Carby has argued that African American theory is currently "recreating a romantic discourse of a rural black folk in which to situate the source of an Afro-American culture" ("Reinventing" 384). And Ann duCille contends that viewing

> African American expressive culture . . . through the lens of vernacular theories of cultural production and the master narrative of the blues . . . often erase[s] the contexts and complexities of a wide range of African American historical experiences and replace[s] them with a single, monolithic, if valorized, construction: authentic blacks are southern, rural, and sexually uninhibited. Middle-class, when applied to black artists and their subjects becomes a pejorative, a sign of having mortgaged one's black aesthetic to the alien conventions of the dominant culture. ("Blues Notes" 423)

Such dismissal of African American fiction focusing on the black middle class results in "the construction of 'black' as a unified category and the erasure of class as a cultural marker" (duCille, *Coupling* 8).

Yet Harper depicts Iola in a Northern, urban setting of a *conversazione* engaging with her mother, Marie, in the African American vernacular form of call and response:

> "My heart," said Iola, "is full of hope for the future. Pain and suffering are the crucibles out of which come gold more fine than the pavements of heaven. . . ."
>
> "If," said Mrs. Leroy, "pain and suffering are factors in human development, surely we have not been counted too worthless to suffer."
>
> "And is there," continued Iola, "a path which we have trodden in this country . . . into which Jesus Christ has not put His feet? . . . Has our name been a synonym for contempt? 'He shall be called a Nazarene.' Have we been despised and trodden under foot? Christ was despised and rejected of men. Have we been ignorant and unlearned? It was said of Jesus Christ 'How knoweth this man letters, he never having been learned?' " (*IL* 256)

It seems there is a certain "blackness" that texts like Harper's and Hopkins's are not expected to display, given what appears to be their focus on middle-class Northern mulattas and their use of narrative conventions like sentimentality, domesticity, melodrama, and romance. In *Talkin and Testifyin*, Geneva Smitherman defines call and response as a "spontaneous verbal and non-verbal interaction between speaker and listener in which . . . the speaker's statements ('calls') are punctuated by expressions ('responses') from the listener" (104). Iola "preaches" African American suffering and survival, and her mother briefly responds to and extends her call. Iola is engaged in what can be regarded as a sermon in the African American preaching tradition, for she reinterprets the Gospel in terms of African American experience. Hortense Spillers asserts that similar sermons helped enslaved African Americans envision their liberation: "If the captive could make the Gospel 'speak' his or her own state, then the subversion of dominance was entirely possible" ("Moving" 54). Iola's sermon envisions social and political equality for African Americans in the postbellum urban North, rather than freedom in the antebellum rural South, but it is no less a form of sermonic call and response because of this context and because it is "preached" by a middle-class mulatta. In Iola's "sermon," Harper renders the

standard English of a Northern, urban, middle-class character in the form
of African American vernacular expression. We must, then, also attend to self-
expression that lies outside a Southern, rural, "folk" dialect but is, nevertheless,
expression decidedly within an African American vernacular tradition. Significantly, Harper's and Hopkins's subversive strategies turn on those elements in their
narratives that critics have often argued are most complicit with an endorsement
of white bourgeois values and standards. The hybridity of a text like Harper's,
whose "mulatta" or "mixed" status exceeds the backgrounds of her characters,
plays on multiple levels with the ideas of recognizable or "detectable" blackness
and whiteness, challenging readers to consider carefully what such identitarian
categories entail and how they are signaled or performed.

This leads me to return to their representations of the mulatta in order to further complicate her textual and political work in Harper's and Hopkins's fiction.
The mulatta as racial hybrid becomes a figure in Harper's and Hopkins's fiction
for hybridity of another order—true black womanhood as a parodic performative.[29] While the appearance and conduct of these characters seem to stand as an
uncomplicated "approval" of true womanhood and its exclusive tenets, their performances also counter this gender identity at its base—as African American
women, their identity as body was thought to deny them access to a womanhood they corporeally delimited. Harper and Hopkins insist that the violations
African American women experienced because they were seen as publicly accessible bodies—experiences of rape, concubinage, and menial labor that would
disqualify them as "true women"—are part of their characters' lives. Their heroines'
parodic performances play the tenets of true womanhood off against the experiences of nineteenth-century black women in a hybrid construction that contests
and seeks to revise a gender identity that not only excluded black women but
repeatedly defined "true" white women over and against black women as "other."
Those who criticize Harper's and Hopkins's choice of mulatta heroines argue
that they function as inscriptions of colorism and the privilege associated with it
and that they represent a nod to the authors' contemporary white audience, who
would not recognize a black heroine as beautiful or identify with her easily.[30]
However, more recently, critics like P. Gabrielle Foreman have suggested the
complex ways in which nineteenth-century African American texts made their
contemporary moments central to their narratives, at times invoking existing
concerns and debates in white reformist circles in order to argue for attention to
black situations and circumstances. Foreman's reading of *Iola Leroy* documents

the rising concern among white Americans with white slavery in the late nineteenth century, and she argues that Harper used the mulatta to "tap into a central
icon for white activists at that time, the 'white slave,' the abducted girl forced into
prostitution," in order to "connect her own interventions into the debate about
African-American rights to contemporary white reformist rhetoric" (" 'Reading
Aright' " 331). Such a narrative strategy would aim to convince readers that Iola
is "as white as" themselves, her situation akin to those white women forced into
prostitution who had become the focus of what Foreman calls "the white slavery
hysteria" of the late nineteenth century (336). While I agree that Harper and
Hopkins rely on a certain recongizability in their representations, I see this as
only the beginning of a more subversive textual politics. Harper and Hopkins
both work to underscore their heroines' differences from white readers and the
domestic heroines with whom they were familiar, even while proving they are
worthy "true women." Disrupting rather than meeting their audiences' expectations of a beautiful and womanly heroine deserving of their sympathies because
she resembles the white woman trapped by circumstance, these writers foreground the danger that accompanied an African American woman's beauty in
both antebellum and postbellum America. Importantly, as Sarah Remond did
before them, Harper and Hopkins stress that the vulnerabilities black women
experience are not analogous to the specter of the "white slave."

According to the cult of domesticity, a white woman's beauty would signal a
corresponding purity of soul and elicit the protection and respect of white gentlemen, but a mulatta's beauty was a liability that placed her at immediate and
constant risk of sexual violence. The mulatta need not be abducted from her home
and forced into prostitution, for her home was often the site of her legalized
exploitation. White men did not pay for her "services," they owned her. Since
"traditional notions of female purity" attach to a white skin (Sànchez-Eppler 42),
the mulatta's body has been read in two directions simultaneously: her near-
white skin is a sign of whiteness and chaste true womanhood, yet her body is also
believed to be the site of an irresistible lasciviousness. These conflictual readings
cohere in the mulatta, who paradoxically signaled an always already available
and highly eroticized sexuality *and* the promise of a chastity one could violate
with neither reprove nor recrimination. While the white woman was believed to
be inherently virtuous, a virtue violated once she was abducted into the white
slave trade, the chastity of African American women was always under question
and frequently assumed lacking.

Harper represents Iola's body as stripped of protections and sexualized immediately upon the revoking of her manumission along with her identity as a white lady. Upon Eugene Leroy's death, his cousin, Alfred Lorraine, claims the Leroy estate and "property," including Marie Leroy and her children. Lorraine sends his lawyer, Bastine, north to bring Iola home; and upon first seeing her, Bastine speculates upon the price Iola would fetch as a fancy girl: " 'She is a most beautiful creature. . . . She has the proud poise of Leroy, the most splendid eyes I ever saw in a woman's head, lovely complexion, and a glorious wealth of hair. She would bring $2000 any day in a New Orleans market' " (*IL* 99). The very qualities that guarantee her the protection of both respect and privacy as a white woman will attract a Southern aristocrat excited by the paradox of an enslaved courtship with a woman regarded as publicly accessible through the logic of fancy girl markets and quadroon balls. Even before she reaches the South and learns she is not a white woman as she has always been led to believe, Iola is "affronted" and kissed by Bastine, who refers to her as his "lovely tigress" (*IL* 104). Philip Brian Harper, in an argument turning on "private" as denoting "both proprietorship and secrecy or social discretion," reads this scene as the moment in which we see the black woman denied the appeal to a rhetoric of separate spheres that might quite literally protect her:

> Heretofore in the narrative of Iola's life, her identity as a Negro had been almost completely secret—unknown even to her—an almost perversely private affair. With the revelation of that identity—its being made public, as it were—comes Iola's inscription into a literal economy in which her person becomes someone else's private concern: that is to say, she effectively becomes the private property of any white man who conceives an interest in her, and the erotic relation that might develop between her and such a man becomes the expression of that new relation and the sign of the black woman's privatized status. (123)

Paradoxically lacking the protection of privacy in her "privatized status," Iola continues to fend off assaults from white men when she is remanded into slavery, as a fellow slave recalls: " 'One day when he com'd down to breakfas', he chucked her under de chin, an' tried to put his arm roun' her waist. But she jis' frew it off like a chunk ob fire. . . . Her eyes fairly spit fire. Her face got red ez blood, an' den she turned so pale I thought she war gwine to faint, but she didn't, an' I yered her say, 'I'll die fust' " (*IL* 41).

Harper further problematizes a reading of Iola as a privileged mulatta by fore-grounding the complicated dynamics of her parents' relationship. Iola is the daughter of her mother's master. Eugene Leroy falls in love with his "beautiful, faithful, and pure" mulatta slave, Marie—a woman in whose "presence every base and unholy passion died, subdued by the supremacy of her virtue"—edu-cates, manumits, and then marries her (*IL* 66, 70). While Leroy repeatedly attests to his love for Marie, his feelings seem to be inflected with a desire to pos-sess her; he frees her as his slave to take her as his wife: " 'This is the hand that plucked me from the grave, and I am going to retain it as mine; mine to guard with my care until death do us part.' " Marie speaks against slavery in an address to her graduating class, but her former master does not share her views: "Leroy listened attentively. At times a shadow of annoyance would overspread his face" (*IL* 74, 75). Harper represents Marie's marriage to Eugene as an exchange of one form of commodification for another. Moreover, Marie's history and Iola's enslavement are narrated in a series of chapters that follow Dr. Gresham's pro-posal and precede Iola's refusal, thereby characterizing Gresham as yet another white man whose desire for Iola may be inextricably linked to a concomitant desire for power and possession. Here in Harper's aptly titled narrative interrup-tion, "Shadows in the Home" and "The Plague and the Law," we see represented what Lauren Berlant calls "the mulatta's genealogy": "When you are born into a national symbolic order that explicitly marks your person as illegitimate, far beyond the horizon of proper citizenship, and when your body also becomes a site of privileged fantasy property and of sexual contact that the law explicitly proscribes but privately entitles, you inhabit the mulatta's genealogy" (*Queen* 238). Iola and Marie may be so light-skinned they pass as white, but Harper is careful to stress that as mulattas they are denied the protections a white skin offers white women.

While Harper makes it clear that Iola's body will not emerge inviolate from her enslavement, Hopkins stresses that the victimization accompanying an African American woman's beauty continues after slavery ends. Sappho's mother is a "quadroon," and her father is "an educated man, descended from a very wealthy family," who is given an equal share in his white father's fortune. Her family is recognized by their white relatives—her uncle Beaubean, a Louisiana senator, is described as "very warm in his expressions of friendship for the family" (*CF* 258, 259). Sappho attends a Catholic girls' school run by nuns, yet despite her privilege as a member of the black bourgeoisie, her youth, and her very proper education, Uncle Beaubean sees her as sexually available because she is "of mixed blood." He rapes her, abandons her in a house of prostitution at the age of four-teen, and when confronted by Sappho's father believes that he has only to pay for her in order to absolve himself: " '[Y]our child is no better than her mother or her grandmother. What does a woman of mixed blood, or any Negress, for that matter, know of virtue? . . . Now, I am willing to give you a thousand dollars and call it square' " (*CF* 260–61). As a result of her experience, Sappho comes to refer to her beauty as "a curse." Hopkins goes on to represent the stereotype of the "yellow Jezebel" as so powerful it is given currency in the black community. John Pollock Langley, a mulatto himself and a prominent lawyer and politician in Boston, reads sexual availability into Sappho's genealogy and birthplace:

> Her coldness urged him on . . . and made him impatient to force upon her an acceptance of his own devotion, at whatever cost. . . . He had detected in Sappho's personality a coldness more in accordance with the disposition of women of the North than with that of one born . . . of the languorous Southland. Where, with such a face and complexion, had she imbibed a moral character so strong and self-reliant as her conduct had shown her to possess? Not by inheritance, if he read the signs aright. (*CF* 226–27)

Through Sappho's refined behavior and Caucasian features Hopkins ironizes the nineteenth-century belief that "blood tells," or that one's appearance and conduct are the expression of one's biology.

Sappho and Iola are forced to become self-reliant and independent as a result of these experiences. Protected in the privacy of their immediate families, they are endangered and violated when extended family members and their agents view them as sexually accessible because they are African American, not white, women. Harper and Hopkins not only signify on this distinction between the safety of the private sphere and the danger of the public sphere common in fic-tion written by white women of this era, but their African American heroines' development of self-reliance also represents a reversal of that depicted in white domestic novels. Nina Baym notes that in "woman's fiction," a heroine's achieve-ment of "self-dependence is only possible within the boundaries of a peaceful protectorate. She needs protection because she is weaker than a man and cannot fight—more precisely, cannot fight successfully against men—to defend . . . her-self" (xxv–xxvi). This equation of self-dependence with the "private" is, as Gillian Brown and Richard Brodhead have argued, part of the developing char-acterization of the heroine in domestic and sentimental fiction that invested domesticity with the values of interiority and individualism (G. Brown 1–3; Brodhead 18). Rather than attaining "self-dependence" within the protective privacy of the home and family, Iola and Sappho gain self-reliance while defending themselves against the private fantasies of which they are the very public objects.

Iola's and Sappho's experiences in the hands of white men would be enough to deem them tragic mulattas and "fallen women" in the eyes of white Americans heavily influenced by Victorian morality, but as Hazel Carby has argued, their very survival of sexual violence marginalizes them further:

> Measured against the sentimental heroines of domestic novels, the black woman repeatedly failed the test of true womanhood because she survived her institutionalized rape, whereas the true heroine would rather die than be sexually abused. Comparison between these figurations of black versus white womanhood also encouraged readers to conclude that the . . . [black] woman must be less sensitive and spiritually inferior. (*Reconstructing* 34)[31]

A woman lacking in "purity" was considered "unnatural and unfeminine" by the cult of domesticity: "[S]he was, in fact, no woman at all, but a member of some lower order. A 'fallen woman' was a 'fallen angel,' unworthy of the celestial company of her sex. To contemplate the loss of purity brought tears; to be guilty of such a crime . . . brought madness or death" (Welter 23). While Lora Romero notes that middle-class white women used domesticity's rhetoric of submissiveness or powerlessness in order to pursue political activities "not through institutionalized government but instead through informal, irregular, and unofficial avenues" (71), they seem to have stopped short of acknowledging the "fallen woman" as redeemable because powerless to resist either seduction or assault, or as a fitting focus of women's fiction however deserving of sympathy: "Obviously there could be no 'fallen women' among protagonists; not merely unfallen, the protagonist was virtually immune to improper sexual overtures. However they have fallen, women characters whose bodies are marked by sexual passion—whether their own or the man's—have no place in woman's fiction except as occasional recipients of protagonist sympathy or charity" (Baym xxviii). As we have already seen in Chapter 2, one of the ways in which "[w]hite women's unacknowledged feelings of sexual victimization and desire" were represented in the nineteenth century was through the "surrogate" or "proxy" mulatta popular among white women writers of sentimental abolitionist fiction (Sànchez-Eppler 42). Here, with their heroines' allusions to their sexual exploitation, Harper and Hopkins are able to access an established narrative convention—the violated mulatta. Iola and Sappho could be read as tragic mulattas who express "the white woman's desires and protect her from them, by marking them safely alien" (Sànchez-Eppler 44). Simultaneously, however, they also inscribe African American women's survival of rape and brutal assault well after slavery and signal Harper's and Hopkins's representations of black noble womanhood as a gender identity that acknowledges and incorporates this reality.

Unlike the most well known tragic mulatta narrative by an African American, William Wells Brown's *Clotel*, Harper and Hopkins do not sacrifice their mulatta heroines, however heroically, but script them as surviving material and sexual slavery. While Clotel jumps to her death in the Potomac rather than be recaptured and face the sexual exploitation undoubtedly awaiting her, Iola and Sappho endure sexual assaults. Harper and Hopkins deliberately characterize that survival as dignity, making it an element of the noble black womanhood they construct in their novels. Iola makes a distinction between being "tried" or "abased" by those white men who assaulted her while she was enslaved and being "tempted" into a willing compliance or "degradation." Such a distinction furthers Iola's insistence that her pure and chaste character remains inviolate, though her body does not:

> "Tried, but not tempted," said Iola, as a deep flush overspread her face; "I was never tempted. I was sold from State to State as an article of merchandise. I had outrages heaped on me which might well crimson the cheek of honest womanhood with shame, but I never fell into the clutches of an owner for whom I did not feel the utmost loathing and intensest horror. I have heard men talk glibly of the degradation of the negro, but there is a vast difference between abasement of condition and degradation of character. I was abased, but the men who trampled on me were the degraded ones." (*IL* 115)

Hopkins inscribes a similar distinction in *Contending Forces*. Mrs. Willis argues during "The Sewing-Circle" for a conception of virtue that acknowledges the reality of African American women who are offered no protection and are unable to defend themselves against white male brutality: "Our ideas of virtue are too narrow. . . . I believe that we shall not be held responsible for wrongs which we have *unconsciously* committed, or which we have committed under *compulsion*. We are virtuous or non-virtuous only when we have a *choice* under temptation" (*CF* 149). White American society would condemn Iola and Sappho not only for their loss of virtue but also for their ability to survive such assaults. However, African American women put into practice a revised understanding of virtue and womanhood that contested such values and judgments. While Iola and Sappho might be powerless to resist sexual assault, they are far from submissive, and their ability to survive and present themselves as "true women" undercuts a reading of them as either the "fallen woman" absent or marginalized in women's fiction or the "surrogate" for white female desire in sentimental fiction like the tragic mulatta narratives.

Rather than advocating wholesale a gender identity that depended upon their very exclusion for its definition, black women writers like Harper and Hopkins turned its dictates back upon the cult of domesticity. Simultaneously invoking and undercutting white Victorian values in their novels, Harper and Hopkins invite their white readership to follow the conventions of nineteenth-century "woman's fiction" only to violate those conventions in order to inscribe one of the most politically charged experiences of nineteenth-century African American life—the terrorizing of black women through the only too real threat of rape at the hands of white men. Their black female characters refuse to bear the responsibility for white male morality or to keep silent about whose sexuality was indeed uncontrolled. To portray their heroines surviving rape with a virtuous character intact was a highly political undertaking for Harper and Hopkins during the red decade of the 1890s: "[R]apes accompanied riots of the 1890s and the blood baths engendered by the Klan. Regardless of the degree of force and violence involved, such sexual exploitation posited its justification on the myth of the promiscuous black woman" (Campbell 21). Harper and Hopkins not only challenged the myth of "licentious" black female sexuality and signified on Victorian notions of womanhood, but in exposing white men as preying upon defenceless black women, these authors insisted that the root of postbellum lynching and rape was, in fact, a violent physical assertion of white power.[32]

Harper and Hopkins further extended their signifying critique of Victorian womanhood to the hierarchies it upheld, creating characters who in "passing" for "true women" undermined such a regulatory identity. By supplementing the text of physical characteristics with the meanings read through one's deportment, white Americans revealed their anxiety over the growing indiscernibility of racial, class, and gender differences upon which their social order was based. Identities such as whiteness and womanhood, based upon the assurance of the visible, could be adopted by anyone who could play the part. Moreover, as Homi Bhabha argues, we should read such performances as not merely adopting the image of "whiteness" or of "the lady" but functioning to place identity itself and our understanding of it in a state of crisis: "By disrupting the . . . equivalence between image and identity, the secret art of invisibleness . . . changes the very terms of our recognition of the person. . . . What is interrogated is not simply the image of the person, but the discursive and disciplinary place from which questions of identity are strategically and institutionally posed" (46–47). Categories of identity such as race and gender operated in turn-of-the-century America, and continue to do so today, with what Robyn Wiegman calls an "assurance . . . to represent, mimetically, the observable body" (9). But if one's "character"— increasingly read through one's body and behavior near the close of the nineteenth century—is neither a reliable nor even discernible index of one's race or gender, more than the individual's identity is unsettled: the very categories of race and gender become unstable and shifting. By establishing a woman's physical characteristics as the proof of her nature and defining true womanhood by the attributes of piety, purity, submissiveness, and domesticity, the cult enabled its own undercutting. Identities such as whiteness and womanhood, based upon the assurance of the visible, could be adopted by anyone who could play the part. Harper and Hopkins use the mulatta figure as a "true" black woman to unsettle and set in motion a gender identity that supposedly inhered in the white female body. Like Sarah Parker Redmond before them, Harper and Hopkins did not adopt a silence regarding the construction of the black female body and black female sexuality but worked to confront their readers with the violations their characters experienced as a result of these constructions. Mobilizing the myth of the black female body as public in order to foreground their mulatta characters' virtue, Harper and Hopkins worked to claim the African American woman's right to a noble black womanhood.

Chapter 4

Commodified "Blackness" and Performative Possibilities in Jessie Fauset's *The Chinaberry Tree* and Nella Larsen's *Quicksand*

Black women writers in the early decades of the twentieth century challenged racist ideologies that continued to mythologize black womanhood as immoral and negotiated a fraught politics of representation rendered all the more complex by a cult of primitivism in full swing. As part of this larger challenge, Jessie Fauset, the most prolific novelist of the Harlem Renaissance, and Nella Larsen, the first black female novelist to be awarded a Guggenheim fellowship, parodied modern notions of womanhood and racial difference. While Fauset and Larsen used the mulatta figure to parody dominant notions of womanhood and challenge race as it was interimplicated with gender, as had Frances Harper and Pauline Hopkins before them, the empowerment black domestic novels depicted as following from their representations of African Americans is critiqued in Larsen's *Quicksand* (1928) and Fauset's *The Chinaberry Tree* (1931). Fauset and Larsen present the "emancipatory texts" of womanhood and bourgeois individualism represented in late-nineteenth-century African American domestic fiction as displaced from a democratic African American politics by the 1920s and 1930s.[1] Contrary to that liberatory vision, Larsen's and Fauset's novels represent a black middle class that restricts women and pursues a materialism that furthers white economic and social interests and, at times, the commodification of "blackness." The noble black womanhood and the bourgeois individualism depicted in Harper's and Hopkins's novels as challenges to an American racial imaginary and as opportunities for African Americans to imagine their full participation in nineteenth-century American society become problematized in Fauset's and Larsen's fiction.

Harlem: Primitivist Proclivities and a Politics of Respectability

Fauset and Larsen wrote in and of a rapidly changing urban North that commodified "blackness" under the cult of primitivism. In addition to a migration of African Americans within New York City from the middle West Side (Hell's Kitchen, San Juan Hill) to Harlem, the second major migration from the rural South to northern cities like Chicago and New York saw some "[t]hree hundred thousand, and possibly many more, Afro-American farmers, unskilled laborers, and domestics [leave] the South before 1920" (Lewis 20). African Americans migrated from the South to escape white violence and to better their economic possibilities. Drought and the boll weevil disasters of 1915 and 1916, a decrease in European immigrant labor during the First World War, an increase in wartime industrialization that sent northern factory agents South in search of laborers, and later the Great Flood of 1927 in the Mississippi Delta culminated in the largest migration of African Americans northward. Cities like Chicago, and later Harlem, came to be called the promised land.

However much Harlem was touted as a uniquely African American city within a city, it was white Americans who profited economically in Jazz Age Harlem. Whites owned the majority of businesses and saloons in Harlem before 1920, even though many of these businesses displayed the "signs of Negroes and Negro firms" and were managed by African Americans (Anderson 66).[2] By 1915 the National Urban League estimated that "there were ninety-eight saloons and liquor stores in Harlem" (Anderson 66), an area that then stretched east of Eighth Avenue to the Harlem River between 130th and 145th Streets.[3] White gangsters owned the most popular Harlem cabarets and speakeasies through the Jazz Age; many of these establishments, like Connie's Inn and the Cotton Club, served white patrons only and used intimidation tactics to prevent black-owned cabarets from booking top African American musicians.[4] Ann duCille cogently sums up the results of white business interests in Harlem: "From record company, to Broadway theatre, to Harlem speakeasy (the overwhelming majority of which were owned by white racketeers), the 'Negro craze' had made white men and women wealthy, while most of the impoverished black masses who were the putative subjects of the period's so-called authentic black art did not even know they had passed through a renaissance" (*Coupling* 79–80). White America's fascination with the musical, dramatic, and literary output of the "New Negro" was ostensibly new in the Jazz Age. However, this voyeuristic fascination was all too familiar, having been registered nearly a century earlier with the popularity of spirituals, minstrelsy, and the later development of vaudeville.[5] The New Negro was as predictable as the new fad of primitivism, for white Americans sought a well-worn version of blackness—carefree, spontaneous, and physical. *Collier's* magazine described Harlem as " 'a national synonym for naughtiness' " and " 'a jungle of jazz' " (qtd. in Anderson 185). Whites visited Harlem to shed their inhibitions, visit the "jungle," and rejoin "civilization" after last call, as one white New Yorker related in 1926: " 'One by one, the cherished biases are taken off like arctic overcoats. It becomes natural to laugh and shout in the consciousness of an emotional holiday. Then when the last ambiguously worded song is done, one puts on again one's hat, coat, and niceties, and once again is staid, proper, and a community pillar' " (qtd. in Anderson 168–69).

White Americans sought difference in Harlem, but an easily accessible difference. Moreover, they believed they found what they once had, an innocence and vitality that a capitalistic and changing world had robbed them of. However, as Chip Rhodes argues, seeking an escape from capitalism, primitivists only furthered consumerism: "[White Americans] discovered in black culture all those innocent virtues they felt whites no longer possessed due to coerced compromises with modern capitalism. . . . However . . . this ideology informed rather than antagonized corporate capitalism because this human essence found expression . . . in the consumer marketplace" (192–93). Rhodes goes on to observe that the cult of primitivism racialized "socially and economically useful 'instincts' " (197), so that while black artists and performers received the unprecedented interest of white publishing houses, white recording companies, and the Great White Way, this interest was often objectifying to an extreme. Echoing the experiences of fugitive slave lecturers like William Wells Brown and the Crafts some seventy years earlier, Arna Bontemps recalls: " 'When we were not too busy having fun, we were shown off and exhibited and presented in scores of places, to all kinds of people. And we heard their sighs of wonder, amazement, sometimes admiration when it was whispered or announced that here was one of the "New Negroes" ' " (qtd. in Anderson 207). White interest in the New Negro carried with it expectations of "authentic" blackness, expectations shared by publishers that became restrictive for African American writers. In his famous 1926 essay, "The Negro Artist and the Racial Mountain," Langston Hughes characterizes New Negro writers as caught between both an

African American and a white politics of representation that they were beginning to refuse:

> "Oh, be respectable, write about nice people, show how good we are," say the
> Negroes. "Be stereotyped, don't go too far, don't shatter our illusions about
> you, don't amuse us too seriously. We will pay you," say the whites. . . . We
> younger Negro artists who create now intend to express our dark-skinned
> selves without fear or shame. If white people are pleased we are glad. If they
> are not, it doesn't matter. We know we are beautiful. And ugly too. The tom-
> tom cries and the tom-tom laughs. If colored people are pleased we are glad.
> If they are not, their displeasure doesn't matter either. We build our temples
> for tomorrow, strong as we know how, and we stand on top of the mountain,
> free within ourselves. (694)

Hughes's call to New Negro writers to resist both the conservative African
American's and the white primitivist's notions of blackness in order to "express
[their] dark-skinned selves" was intended to defy the commodification of things
black during the Harlem Renaissance. However, Hughes's version of uncom-
modified and "authentic" African American expressivity has perhaps become our
late-twentieth-century vogue, raising the question of what "blackness" sells and
what artistic representations have been marginalized as a result.[6]

Although Jessie Fauset and Nella Larsen approached the primitivism of the
Harlem Renaissance differently, they shared a keen sense of both its workings
and key proponents. Through her position as literary editor of the *Crisis* from
1919 to 1924, the official publication of the National Association for the Advancement of Colored People (NAACP), Jessie Fauset was instrumental in the careers
of writers we have come to see as central to the Harlem Renaissance: Jean Toomer,
Countee Cullen, Langston Hughes, and Claude McKay. While Fauset freely admitted to personally disliking certain aspects of modernist technique and wrote
what has been deemed "conservative" fiction, she did not allow her taste to inter-
fere with the encouragement of young African American writers, as this letter to
Jean Toomer indicates:

> Where did you get a chance to work out your technique? . . . You must have
> studied and practiced to achieve it. I think in some cases it is still a little diffi-
> cult in its form, that is you are a little inclined to achieve style at the expense of
> clearness, but doubtless that will disappear. . . . I think the modern tendency is

toward an involving of ideas,—a sort of immeshing the kernel of thought in envelopes of words. I don't like it and hope that you will not fall too deeply into it. (Fauset to Toomer, 17 February 1922)

In fact, Fauset frequently recognized African American literary talent well before any of her contemporaries. In January 1923 Fauset recommended Toomer's writing to Arthur B. Spingarn, saying he would make a " 'contribution to literature distinctly negroid and without propaganda' " (qtd. in Sylvander 60).[7] Fauset "discovered" Langston Hughes, published his early poetry in the *Crisis*, and introduced him to other writers in Harlem (Sylvander 62), while "[h]er large apartment . . . became, like those of Regina Anderson, Charles Johnson, James Weldon Johnson, and Walter White, a shelter for arriving talent, as well as a forum for cultural activity" (Lewis 123).

Yet while Fauset's apartment was known as a gathering place for New Negroes, she was very reluctant to invite whites interested in the Harlem literary scene, recalls Hughes: "White people were seldom present . . . because Jessie Fauset did not feel like opening her home to mere sightseers, or faddists momentarily in love with Negro life" (*Big Sea* 247). Fauset, as Barbara Christian puts it, "was not fooled by the fad of primitivism" (*Black Women* 43); moreover, she distrusted whites like the by now infamous Carl Van Vechten and their predilection for Harlem. In an undated letter to Hughes sent in the early 1920s, Fauset writes of returning from France to find Harlem a changed place:

> I was interested in your diagnosis of V[an] V[echten]. I don't know what his motives may be for attending and making possible these mixed parties. But I do know that the motives of some of the other pale-faces will not bear inspection. I've been home five weeks and . . . already I've seen such remarkable manifestations of a changing social order that I am ready to retire bewildered. However if I'm going to be a writer I have certainly got to face life, get into it, mix with it. Ideals are not a good forcing-bed for ideas. (Fauset to Hughes, circa 1920–26)

The popular conception of Jessie Fauset is of a woman who decidedly did not "get into it, mix with it." Fauset's focus on the black bourgeoisie in her fiction, her soirees at which no alcohol was served and guests discussed literature, and her preference for avoiding Harlem's primitive vogue quite likely all contributed to her reputation as conservative, a member of the "Rear Guard." Claude McKay, of whom Fauset wrote, "[h]e is a better artist than a man I imagine" (Fauset to Hughes, 6 January 1925), criticized her in *A Long Way From Home* (1937): " 'Miss Fauset is prim and dainty as a primrose, and her novels are quite as fastidious and precious' " (qtd. in Sato 68). If Fauset's response to an era that "exoticized" African Americans was to lead what many regarded a "conservative" life, she seems to have been aware that this was a role like any other. In 1922 Fauset was approached to translate *Batouala* by René Maran, a French West Indian writer and winner of France's Prix Goncourt; she decided against doing so, believing it would be taken as a step out of character: " 'I know my own milieu too well. If I should translate that book over my name, I'd never be considered "respectable" again' " (qtd. in Lewis 123). Here, she reveals herself to be keenly aware of how others perceived her, of the role or character she had taken on in their minds.

Nella Larsen lived and wrote in the same Harlem of speakeasies and literary salons that Fauset did, but she responded quite differently to the American interest in the New Negro. Larsen, it seems, played to rather than eschewed the white fetishization of African Americans. As Thadious Davis's biography of Larsen suggests, Larsen was adept at re-creating herself and appealing to the misperceptions and fabrications that passed for blackness in the 1920s and 1930s.[8] Born Nellie Walker in Chicago, she frequently maintained that she was born in "the Virgin Islands or Danish West Indies not only for whites eager to hear about cultural primitives, but also for blacks curious to learn about an instant celebrity" (T. M. Davis 23). Larsen clearly delighted in the ignorance of those for whom she "performed": "I went to lunch the other day with some people I knew very little (ofays). In the course of our talk it developed that they would have been keenly disappointed had they discovered that I was not born in the jungle of the Virgin Isles. So I entertained them with quite a few stories of my childhood in the bush, and my reaction to the tom-tom undertone in Jazz. It was a *swell* luncheon" (Larsen to Van Vechten, 14 June 1929).[9] Thadious Davis contends that Larsen "welcomed the intense white interest in things Negro as an opportunity for herself and others to achieve" (242).

Larsen obviously turned Carl Van Vechten's interest to her advantage; he gave her *Quicksand* manuscript to Knopf, which published it. Her letters to Van Vechten refer to her attendance at frequent dinners and parties given by him and his wife, Fania Marinoff, and from their correspondence, as well as references to him in letters to her close friend Dorothy Peterson, it seems Larsen cultivated what she considered to be a genuine friendship with him.[10] Yet there are also glimpses in this correspondence of Larsen playing to Van Vechten's penchant for stereotyped blackness. "Carl would adore the Negro streets. They look like stage settings. And the Negroes themselves! I've never seen anything quite so true to what's expected," wrote Larsen to Van Vechten and Marinoff. "Mostly black and good natured and apparently quite shiftless, frightfully clean and decked out in the most appalling colours; but some how just right. Terribly poor" (Larsen to Van Vechten and Marinoff, 22 May 1930). Larsen wrote this letter upon arriving in Nashville, where her husband, Elmer Imes, had taken up a position at Fisk University. Even though Larsen herself had studied at Fisk, Davis notes that Larsen deliberately cultivated an ignorance of working-class black life in Nashville quite likely to "impress Marinoff and Van Vechten with her reportage and her implicit sophistication in contrast to her southern surroundings" (T. M. Davis 356). Whether or not Larsen wanted to appear sophisticated in comparison to southern blacks, she clearly narrates what she knows "Carl would adore," consciously manipulating and mocking Van Vechten's fascination with what he took to be blackness and his preconceptions of southern "Negroes"—"shiftless," "good natured," and dressed in "appalling colours."

Despite the fact that Fauset and Larsen seem to have been keenly aware of, and self-consciously positioned themselves within or against, Harlem's politics of representation, they have been largely judged to be conservative. Similarly, their novels have been historically received as reflections of a small, privileged segment of the African American population.[11] Both writers have been consistently assigned the motivation of attempting to prove that blacks are no different from whites, and, consequently, they have been relegated to the position of cultural mediators.[12] These assessments of Fauset's and Larsen's works reflect an understanding of the Harlem Renaissance as the first sustained collective effort by African American artists to represent themselves and their culture freely and accurately. The accomplishment of the Renaissance has long been located in the period's movement "to gain authority in its portrayal of black life by the attempt to assert, with varying degrees of radicality, a disassociation of sensibility from that enforced by American culture and its institutions" (Kent 27). Such a "disassociation of sensibility" from the white bourgeois "mainstream" has been interpreted almost exclusively as a focus on "the folk," a figure that, in turn, has come to signify "authentic" African American experience.[13]

With few exceptions, however, Harlem's New Negroes did not come from working-class backgrounds, nor did they have strong connections to the rural South. "The black intelligentsia and virtually all of the Renaissance writers came from thoroughly middle-class backgrounds," notes Cary Wintz. "However, a number of writers tried . . . to capture the spontaneity they felt characterized the black lower classes. Many of their most successful novels were set against the life of the lower classes in the urban ghettos" (118–19). We might question along with Wintz and, more recently, J. Martin Favor both the "authenticity" of black life represented in the works of major Harlem Renaissance figures, as well as the degree to which the writing of this period was "disassociated" from white cultural tastes. It is telling that in an era of white fascination with "primitive" cultures and their art, the most successful African American novels of the 1920s and 1930s focused on the rural folk or the urban working classes and that the writers of these novels rarely represented the middle class of which they were a part. Cheryl Wall's observations call into question the veracity of claiming that New Negro writers resisted white influences to connect with a uniquely black artistic tradition. "The peculiar demands of the Jazz Age further complicated matters for the Harlem bourgeoisie. As more and more white New Yorkers, like Americans generally, were drawn to black culture—or at least what they believed to be black culture—the New Negroes felt compelled to increase their own identification with their traditions," writes Wall. "Unfortunately, they were often as ignorant of these traditions as anyone else, and embraced the popular imitations instead" ("Passing" 100). Those writers who represented an African American culture of which they had limited experience and knowledge (but one that clearly interested whites) are not accused of commodifying or betraying their "blackness," while those writing from and of the black middle class have been criticized for adopting white values.

In fact, the black bourgeoisie was so rarely represented that those writers, like Fauset and Larsen, who depicted this class and the experience with which they were most familiar have been accused of distorting and misrepresenting African American life and culture. Ann duCille has argued that this notion of the middle-class black writer as pariah continues to plague our own historical moment, with the term "middle class" becoming "a sign of having mortgaged one's black aesthetic to the alien conventions of the dominant culture" ("Blues Notes" 423). Ironically, such writers are perceived as "selling out," when the market to which they supposedly "mortgaged" their art and themselves was buying elsewhere, getting as much of the uninhibited "real thing" as they could. Moreover, writers we currently hail as faithfully representing African American vernacular culture nevertheless silenced certain aspects of African American lived experience in the 1920s and 1930s. As Hazel Carby has argued, the second migration North of rural African Americans from the South, and with it the growth of an African

American urban working class, made it impossible "to mobilize an undifferentiated address to 'the black people'" (*Reconstructing* 164). Yet we have retrospectively imagined this period as one that accomplished precisely that and, in doing
so, have homogenized a period and culture that were informed by two polarized
visions of African American expressivity as well as a range of positions in between.
Wintz contends that "the Harlem Renaissance blended a somewhat militant
and avowedly independent, bohemian outlook which emphasized freedom of
expression and the quest for black identity with a more moderate attempt at literary success and middle-class respectability" (82). Critics have labeled the latter
an aging "Rear Guard" with diminished influence and have attended to the
former, focusing on writers like Jean Toomer, Langston Hughes, and Zora Neale
Hurston. In fact, both schools of artistic representation were alive, well, and in
dialogue during this period.

It is arguable that racial boundaries and their intersections with notions of
class and gender difference were just as rigidly maintained in the 1920s and 1930s
as they had been during the retrenchment following the failure of Reconstruction, maintained by a Harlem Renaissance politics of respectable representation
and by the existence of the very cult of primitivism that repeatedly traversed
them for artistic inspiration, social entertainment, and psychic gratification. In
many senses, the Jazz Age was not as "free" as it has often been represented, and
certainly it was not free for "the Negro," however new. The "Red Summer" of
1919 and its infamous racial riots in American cities both North and South
opened the decades of the Harlem Renaissance, while "[l]ynchings, having faded
almost into the single digits for three years, went up considerably" in the mid-
1920s (Worth 466). In the early 1920s President Warren G. Harding had promised to enforce civil rights, but in actuality he denounced social equality and
racial amalgamation. Harlem itself was becoming overcrowded by the late 1920s,
which resulted in health problems and the highest infant and general mortality
rates in New York City. By 1930, the mortality rate of African Americans from
tuberculosis in the city was five times higher than that for whites. Job ghettoiza-
tion meant a life lived on the edge of poverty for most black Harlemites. School
district zoning was manipulated to ensure segregated schooling and often
resulted in substandard facilities and resources for blacks, while trade schools
would not train African Americans in fields dominated by whites (Wintz 8–29).
In such a climate of racial segregation, discrimination, and violence, Fauset's and
Larsen's representation of race and gender as performable identities amounted
to a highly political undertaking, making them more radical for their time, one

could argue, than leading African American political figures and canonized Renaissance writers.

The Mulatta's Racial Legitimacy: Stereotypes, Ambivalence, Subversion

The mulatta trope as Fauset and Larsen employ it is ambivalent, signifying on the mulattoes of white American imagination who were believed to be ambivalent beings mentally confused as a result of "blood" intermixture, torn between white and black cultures, and symbols of both taboo and transgression. Judith Butler's observations regarding the construction and use of homosexuality and bisexuality as categories of "abject being" to define heterosexual normativity is applicable to white America's creation of "the mulatta": "This exclusionary matrix by which subjects are formed thus requires the simultaneous production of a domain of abject beings, those who are not yet 'subjects' but who form the constitutive outside to the domain of the subject. . . . This zone of uninhabitability will constitute . . . that site of dreaded identity against which—and by virtue of which—the domain of the subject will circumscribe its own claim to autonomy" (*Bodies* 3). However, this very refusal and attempt to silence the threat the mulatta poses are far more pronounced acknowledgments than America has been willing to admit. Throughout the term's history, "mulatta" has signaled a failure to naturalize what Haryette Mullen calls a "genetically illogical racial system" that reduces "racial identity to a white/non-white binary" (73–74). Yet if the mulatta has been identified as black and assigned to the "other" side of the color line so that whiteness may "remain" ostensibly pure, she has also been labeled "illegitimate" by African Americans. "Yella," "high yella," "all that yellow gone to waste"—the biracial woman has been reminded she is "not black enough" by African Americans. The mulatta's racial identity, then, has been constructed by white Americans as decidedly "blacker" than either biology would indicate or some African Americans have been willing to acknowledge. The mulatta has been overdetermined in American culture from both sides of the color line, but this overdetermination may create the very possibility of a subversion. Stuart Hall argues of black popular culture that the "underlying overdetermination [of] black cultural repertoires constituted from two directions at once"—that is, incorporating European- and African-inflected forms—"may be more subversive than you think. It is to insist that in black popular culture, strictly speaking, ethnographically speaking, there are no pure forms at all" (28). The overdetermination of the mulatta's identity far from silences the threat to race that she poses but rather speaks volumes regarding the impossibility of "pure forms" and stable meanings when it comes to race. The mulatta as "excluded site" not only bounds and constitutes the limits of whiteness and blackness but also "haunt[s] those boundaries as the persistent possibility of their disruption and rearticulation" (Butler, *Bodies* 8).

Race has depended upon the construction and circulation of stereotypes in America, focusing on the "pathology" of blackness and its visible "difference" from a decorporealized whiteness. Homi Bhabha argues that an integral element of colonial discourse is fixity in its constructions of "otherness" and that this fixity is sought through the stereotype. However, as Bhabha goes on to theorize, the power of the stereotype lies not, as we might expect, in that fixity but in ambivalence: "For it is the force of ambivalence that gives the colonial stereotype its currency: ensures its repeatability in changing historical and discursive conjunctures; informs its strategies of individuation and marginalization; produces the effect of . . . truth and predictability which . . . must always be in *excess* of what can be empirically proved or logically construed" (66). To be sure, the mulatta has been constructed selectively as a being superior to "pure blacks" and a potential ally to whites, as well as an effete hybrid in whom a mixture of white and black blood results in a high degree of criminality and viciousness. But if the stereotype's power, as well as the power of race as a "discursive formation" and formative discourse, lies in the ambivalence of overdetermined identities, that very ambivalence may also be the site of a potential subversion.[14] While shifting and selective stereotyping of "the mulatta" has served very effectively to marginalize biracial individuals, such shifts in the stereotype betray the constructedness of "race." Moreover, the ambivalence with which the mulatta herself has been invested proves the impossibility of pure forms—she is at once neither white nor black but both. The ambivalence of the mulatta's constructed identity, then, exposes race as unable to refer to a "pure" body or form without obsessively regulating the formation of that body and its meaning.

In *The Chinaberry Tree* and *Quicksand*, Fauset and Larsen foreground the efforts to fix the mulatta by dramatizing both whites' and the black bourgeoisie's preoccupation with legitimacy. Fauset's novel centers on Sal Strange; her daughter, Laurentine; and niece Melissa Paul. The Stranges find themselves alienated in Red Brook, New Jersey, because of Sal's long-standing relationship with a white man, Colonel Halloway. Halloway publicly recognizes Laurentine as his daughter, providing for her and Sal throughout his life and after his death, but this recognition and their continued relationship even after his marriage cause his white wife to effect the Stranges' "social [and] economic ostracism" (*CT* 22). Fauset plays on notions of Laurentine's illegitimacy as a mulatta and the off-spring of an "unsanctioned" relationship with the surname "Strange" and repeated references to "that Strange blood" (*CT* 25). Laurentine takes on a metaphorical status in Red Brook: "Gradually . . . the case of Sal Strange and her daughter, Laurentine, became confused, the sign was accepted for the thing signified and a coldness and despite toward this unfortunate mother and child became a fetish without any real feeling or indignation on the part of the executioners for the offenses committed. Neglect of these two women became crystallized" (*CT* 49). In white minds, Laurentine is associated with popular conceptions of the mulatta, including a lack of social inhibitions that was believed to culminate in vice and criminal behavior: " 'H'm, well whoever she is, she's like the rest of them . . . you know me, a broad-minded man if ever there was one. But I tell you there's bad, there's vicious blood in that bunch. The town would do well to get rid of 'em' " (*CT* 49). Just as Laurentine's "illegitimacy" is a metaphor for her mother's miscegenous relationship with a white man, Laurentine's "vicious blood" in turn demonizes both her young cousin Melissa and her mother. By extension, Red Brook's blacks see Melissa as not only "high and mighty" but a dishonest "high yaller" like her cousin Laurentine: " 'Who,' fumed Pelasgie, 'does she think she is? Comin there to Mrs. Brown's just as big as any of them real big colored folks from New York. . . . I feels like goin' to her with her fine airs and tellin' her I may not be the high yaller she is, but at least if I'm black I'm honest. My family ain't never been mixed up with white folks yit' " (*CT* 233).

Fauset foregrounds the hypocrisy of whites who label mulattas "vicious" yet institutionalize discrimination that favors light-skinned African Americans. The black bourgeoisie of Red Brook is comprised of professionals and merchants, the majority of whom are biracial and described as "brown" or "bronze" (*CT* 99, 69). Laurentine is shunned by this group as well, not due entirely to her "bad blood" in this case but largely because her mother's behavior has violated their strict moral code. The black middle class is less offended by the fact of Sal's interracial relationship with Halloway than they are by its nature. Neither Sal Strange nor Colonel Halloway attempt to hide their relationship; yet despite the fact that the "black bourgeoisie" or "colored aristocracy" not only acknowledged but were reputed to be proud of their connections to prominent whites, Fauset portrays this class as hypocritically outraged when Sal Strange, a working-class girl, does the same. Even though Sal and Laurentine live a middle-class life supported by Halloway's bequest and Laurentine's dressmaking, they have lived most of their lives alienated from "colored people of [their] own rank and sympathies" (*CT* 87).

The Stranges are also rejected by working-class members of this African American community. Denied the advantages that whites accord fair-skinned blacks, some working-class blacks of Red Brook use reminders of Laurentine's parentage to undermine what they regard as "uppity" behavior on the part of the Stranges, as well as the limited and precarious acceptance they eventually gain with some members of the town's black middle class: "'Take some of the shine outa that high and mighty Melissa Paul, think-so-much-of-hers'ef ever-sence-you-all-tuk-'er up. But ev'y-body 'round yere know that bad Strange blood, yessir-ee'" (*CT* 292). The Stranges are selectively rejected, and their life of seclusion—brought on by Sal's ostracization from the black community as a young woman—is regarded as an act of holding themselves aloof from associations they believe beneath them.

Larsen also focuses on the mulatta's alienation from African American community, despite the white American belief that constructing her identity as "black" renders the racially illegitimate legitimate. Larsen's heroine, Helga Crane, teaches at Naxos, a southern school for blacks where visiting white preachers extol the virtue of students knowing their place and keeping to it: "[I]f all Negroes would only take a leaf out of the book of Naxos and conduct themselves in the manner of the Naxos products, there would be no race problem, because Naxos Negroes knew what was expected of them. They had good sense and they had good taste. They knew enough to stay in their places, and that, said the preacher, showed good taste" (*Q* 3).[15] Larsen ascribes to Helga's white relatives the fear and denial that have been a characteristic white response to the mulatta; her white "stepfather, her step-brothers and sisters, and the numerous cousins, aunts, and other uncles . . . feared and hated her" (*Q* 6). One could read the Crane family's denial of Helga as an historically accurate account of race relations in a society divided by racial segregation. African Americans who had migrated to the North often referred to white northern racism as a fear that "the black will rub off." In Helga's case, this resonates on two levels: a fear of blackness as some sort of contagion but also a fear of the mulatta as more white than the Cranes and other white Americans would care to contemplate. This fear acknowledges Helga's racial liminality and, here, Victor Turner's work to theorize liminality as "a complex phase or condition" proves helpful: "It is often the scene . . . for the emergence of a society's deepest values in the form of sacred dramas and objects. . . . But it may also be the venue and occasion for the most radical skepticism" (22). The mulatta as a liminal figure is a repository for a skepticism that race may be contingent rather than stable; the logical extension of this is the fear that whiteness is also contingent rather than a "pure form." Consequently, the mulatta's liminality must be neutralized by legitimating her identity as "black," keeping her in her place, and consequently legitimating whiteness as "pure."

As a mulatta, Helga not only threatens the fixity of racial boundaries designed to keep the "other" in place, but she also unsettles the black middle class who similarly fear that she may be crossing class borders. Filmmaker and cultural studies scholar Isaac Julien notes that crossing culturally policed lines—in Helga's case, both racial and class lines—"causes anxiety, [and] undermines the binary notions of self/other, black/white, straight/queer" (259). However, Helga does not experience her indeterminacy as a potential ability to undermine constructed identities and thereby redress a power imbalance; instead, she feels a heightened sense of alienation:

> Her own lack of family disconcerted them. No family. That was the crux of the whole matter. For Helga, it accounted for everything, her failure here in Naxos, her former loneliness in Nashville. . . . Negro society, she had learned, was as complicated and as rigid in its ramifications as the highest strata of white society. If you couldn't prove your ancestry and connections, you were tolerated, but you didn't "belong." (Q 8)

Significantly, those who are "disconcerted" by Helga's lack of family are the Vayles, members of the black bourgeoisie. Larsen points out that just as whites banish the mulatta in order to maintain the illusion of whiteness as a "pure" racial identity, the black middle class polices prospective members in order to close ranks against "imposters" and "undesirables." The black bourgeoisie recognizes racial discrimination exercised by whites but willfully blind themselves to their own discriminatory practices along class lines—they may seek social and economic equality with whites but not with all African Americans.

While Helga feels alienated from the black middle class in Nashville and Harlem, she is attracted to black Harlem only when it appears to conform to her notions of the area as exotic and colorful: "Helga caught herself wondering who they were, what they did. . . . What was passing behind those dark molds of flesh. Did they really think at all? Yet, as she stepped out into the moving multi-colored crowd, there came to her a queer feeling of enthusiasm, as if she were tasting some agreeable, exotic food" (*Q* 30). Helga, however, seems more interested in a taste of Harlem than in calling it home, and her palate is very selective. Like the middle-class blacks she criticizes for "proclaiming loudly the undiluted good of all things Negro" while displaying a "disdainful contempt" for African American song, dance, and speech, Helga prefers to distance herself from and avoids identifying with the "black folk" she sees as "other."

Helga's desire to hold herself aloof from Harlem is frequently read as complicated by her own feelings of alienation.[16] She has come to dislike the "Talented Tenth" and their talk of racial uplift while working to distinguish themselves from the very people they profess a desire to help, and she has received a "brief" and final rejection from her white uncle in Chicago accompanied by a $5,000 check. Helga's classism is often as keen as that of her bourgeois friends:

> Here the inscrutability of the dozen or more brown faces, all cast from the same indefinite mold, and so like her own, seemed pressing forward against her. . . . It was as if she were shut up, boxed up, with hundreds of her race, closed up with that something in the racial character which had always been, to her, inexplicable, alien. Why, she demanded in fierce rebellion, should she be yoked to these despised black folk? . . . "They're my own people, my own people," she kept repeating over and over to herself. It was no good. . . . She didn't, in spite of her racial markings, belong to these dark segregated people. She was different. She felt it. It wasn't merely a matter of color. It was something broader, deeper, that made folk kin. (*Q* 54–55)

Helga both rejects blackness and feels alienated by an "inscrutable," "inexplicable, alien . . . racial character" that is simultaneously "so like her own" yet different. Helga's alienation is clearly in part her own creation, in part her rejection of "despised black folk," but it is also seen as complicated and heightened by the rejection she has experienced throughout her life. In pursuing such a reading of the mulatta, we should note its inextricability from, and the way it is limited by, our knowledge of Larsen's own reputed sense of abandonment and by her "fellow feeling" for African Americans in Harlem. In a letter to Dorothy Peterson, Larsen writes, "I'm still looking for a place to move. It's really rather ridiculous I suppose. but——. Right now when I look out over the Harlem streets I feel just like Helga Crane in my novel. Furious at being cooped up with all these niggers" (Larsen to Peterson, undated). Not the least problematic are the ways in which such a reading risks simply invoking and confirming long-held racialist stereotypes of the mulatta as perpetually dissatisfied even as she believes herself superior to "the Negro."

Rather than reading the mulatta figure as a biographical trope in Larsen's novel, I would suggest that Larsen deliberately complicates Helga's alienation from what she protests are her "own people" by her perception of that "packaged blackness" that held a high market value among white Americans as African American life and culture itself. Significantly, Helga's last outing in Harlem before leaving for Copenhagen and her final feelings of being "unhappy, misunderstood" among her middle-class African American friends, are set in a cabaret. Harlem nightclubs were often decorated with tropical plants, imitation African carvings, and "primitive" prints. The infamous and popular Cotton Club, for example, decorated its stage with plantation cabins and cotton bushes, and its shows, as Lena Horne recalls, " 'had a primitive naked quality that was supposed to make a civilized audience lose its inhibitions. The music had an intensive, pervasive rhythm—sometimes loud and brassy, often weird and wild' " (qtd. in Anderson 175). Yet as Jimmy Durante noted in 1929, " '[t]he average colored man you see along the streets in Harlem doesn't know . . . about these dumps' " (qtd. in Lewis 208). It is highly ironic, then, that a white comedian would be more aware of the difference between the blackness sold nightly in clubs and African American lived experience in Harlem than is Helga Crane.

Prefabricated blackness is just one valence of the policing and control of the "other" or the "abject" in the service of preserving whiteness; positioning the mulatta at the boundary between the two is another. The fear Helga incites in her white relatives, her awareness that she does not "belong" to a black middle class that only "tolerates" her, and her repression of a blackness she does not recognize as constructed foreground the established critical reading of the mulatta as a mediator and definer of boundaries between white and black.[17] However, to occupy or embody a borderland is not necessarily to mediate. Even as elements of control and fear remain present in Fauset's and Larsen's representations of the mulatta, these writers also underscore that silence rather than acknowledgment is the key principle in mobilizing the mulatta to define rather than challenge boundaries. In this sense, we might read the mulatta's position as akin to "deviant" sexuality, as Michel Foucault chronicles it in the first volume of *The History of Sexuality*. Documenting both the operation and the results of interdicting nonreproductive sexualities, Foucault argues: "Nothing that was not ordered in terms of generation . . . could expect sanction or protection. Nor did it merit a hearing. It would be driven out, denied, and reduced to silence. Not only did it not exist, it had no right to exist and would be made to disappear upon its least manifestation—whether in acts or in words" (4). More than a parallel, the mulatta as akin to the sexual "deviant" was a deliberate coupling in sexological texts at the turn into the twentieth century, as Siobhan Somerville has documented: "Circulat[ing] within and perhaps depend[ing] on a pervasive climate of eugenicist and antimiscegenist sentiment and legislation . . . the figure of the mulatto was often seen, explicitly or implicitly, as analogous to the [sexual] invert: the mixed-race body evoked the mixed-gender body" (31, 80). Particularly unsettling was the possibility that the racial or sexual "deviant" was difficult to place, indeed refused to stay in place, an anxiety the mulatta embodied, as Somerville argues: "[T]he mulatta's movement between black and white worlds represents sexual mobility as well" (80). Consequently, the "solution" became to fix the mulatta as either black or certainly not white.

Denial, banishment, and silence are central elements in the construction of the mulatta's identity and of her experience as represented in Fauset's and Larsen's novels, and in this way these texts echo many of the juridical pronouncements that defined the biracial individual as "black," particularly those colonial statutes examined in Chapter 1. The Strange house literally marks the boundary between the town of Red Brook and the bordering countryside: "It stood at the end of a street which terminated gracefully in a meadow" (*CT* 1). Laurentine not only lives on the outskirts of town but also outside both black and white communities as a child: "[T]he children at school whether white or colored never included her in their play" (*CT* 7). And the black bourgeoisie continues to hold her at a distance from their society when she reaches adulthood: "The street outside was lined with cars of colored ladies who had driven out . . . from New York, Newark, the Oranges, Trenton, Bordentown. . . . The place was full of . . . well-to-do, well-dressed women. . . . Not even Laurentine had been asked to cross this threshold" (*CT* 33–34).

While Laurentine is driven out and excluded, Helga lives most of her life silenced from within the black middle class. She avoids referring to her family— her West Indian father deserted her Danish mother—but when she does, she is met with silence. "The woman felt that the story, dealing as it did with race intermingling and possibly adultery, was beyond definite discussion. For among black people, as among white people, it is tacitly understood that these things are not mentioned—and therefore they do not exist. Sliding adroitly out from under the precarious subject to a safer, more decent one, Mrs. Hayes-Rore asked

Helga what she was thinking of doing when she got back to Chicago" (*Q* 39). Mrs. Hayes-Rore advises Helga to keep her background to herself, "what others don't know can't hurt you" (*Q* 41). Her white uncle's family in Chicago clearly wishes she would do the same: "[T]his woman, [her uncle's] wife . . . so plainly wished to dissociate herself from the outrage of her very existence. . . . She saw herself for an obscene sore in all their lives, at all costs to be hidden" (*Q* 29). In fact, Helga as mulatta is no more accepted for who she is by her "welcoming" white relatives in Denmark than she was in Chicago. Her aunt may call Helga's belief that "mixed marriages" bring only "trouble" a foolish one, but she also maintains that "we don't think of those things here. Not in connection with individuals, at least" (*Q* 78). As in America, Helga is simultaneously black and "not black enough" in Denmark: "[A]n old countrywoman asked her to what manner of mankind she belonged and at Helga's replying: 'I'm a Negro,' had become indignant, retorting angrily that . . . she knew as well as everyone else that Negroes were black and had woolly hair" (*Q* 76). Larsen dramatizes Helga's asymmetrical racialization in her experiences as Danish "curiosity"; Helga may be scrutinized as both black and not black enough, but the Danes certainly never entertain the notion that she may also be white: "To them this girl, this Helga Crane . . . was not to be reckoned seriously in their scheme of things. True, she was attractive, unusual, in an exotic, almost savage way, but she wasn't one of them. She didn't at all count" (*Q* 70).

As Foucault contends, what cannot be completely silenced from within will be allowed to exist only in "safely insularized forms," referred to only in "clandestine, circumscribed, and coded types of discourse" (4). The mulatta's naming of the taboo threatens, not simply because it voices miscegenation but also because it manifests the failed attempt to fully silence or circumscribe any suggestion that race is not a stable and uniform entity. The "solution" then becomes the mulatta's alienation from, and position bordering, both races. Fauset and Larsen represent their mulatta heroines as corporealized boundaries separating white from black, "good" society from "disreputable." When the mulatta is relegated to, and remains at, the border between whiteness and blackness, she serves to consolidate these racial identities and an entire culture built around them, for, as Stallybrass and White argue, "cultural identity is inseparable from limits; it is always a boundary phenomenon and its order is always constructed around the figures of its territorial edge" (200). As much as white Americans would have the mulatta circulate as "other" and African Americans at times be unwilling to accept her, the mulatta is anything but extraneous to these cultures or to "whiteness" and "blackness." The mulatta is obsessively positioned as "not quite, not white."[18]

The Pathological, Propriety, and Spectacle: "Blackness," Class, and Womanhood

Fauset and Larsen mobilized the mulatta figure to critique what George Hutchinson has called "black and white obsessions with 'racial integrity'" (344). But the Harlem Renaissance politics of representation was not charged exclusively by notions of "authentic" or respectable blackness. Frequently overlooked in chronicles of this movement, gender politics further muddied the aesthetic waters for black women writers and artists. All of the figures promoting the Harlem Renaissance were male, while women like Fauset—who in reality played a crucial role in the workings of the era's literary production—were relegated to supporting roles.[19] Fauset herself has been referred to as a "midwife" of the Harlem Renaissance, attending at and assisting a birth that has not been seen as also her own, despite her prolific literary career. Black women writers also had less access to patronage and support, with the notable exception of Zora Neale Hurston, who impressed Alain Locke, the middleman between Charlotte Osgood Mason's coffers and young African American writers. However, Locke neither promoted nor offered much in the way of encouragement to other black women writers of the 1920s and 1930s.[20] In addition to limited access to financial support, black women writers at times found it difficult to secure suitable publishers for their work. For example, Georgia Douglas Johnson could not find a major press to publish her third and arguably best volume of poetry in 1928, the height of the New Negro vogue.[21] Fauset's first novel, *There Is Confusion*, was rejected by the first publisher to read it because the company believed that "'white readers just don't expect Negroes to be like this'" (qtd. in Starkey 219). Fauset continued to write against such stereotypical notions of blackness and to have her work rejected because of it. In 1931 the Frederick A. Stokes Company, having published *Plum Bun* in 1929, expressed reluctance to publish *The Chinaberry Tree*. Fauset corresponded with white critic and writer Zona Gale, requesting that she write what amounted to a verification that a black middle class did, indeed, exist. The readers at Stokes, Fauset wrote, "'declare plainly that there ain't no such colored people as these who speak decent English, are self-supporting and have a few ideals. . . . If I could find someone much better known than I, speaking with a more *authentic* voice'" (qtd. in Sylvander 74). Stokes Company "used Zona Gale's introduction to *The Chinaberry Tree* prominently, with Gale's name on the cover and referred to her statements in its ads for the novel" (Sylvander 75). The double burden of the demand for "positive" portrayals of "the race" and the voyeuristic interest of white publishers and readers in "exotic primitives" also frequently divided along gender lines, with black female sexuality being the most valued commodity in the period—as the popularity of black women blues singers indicates. On several fronts, then, black women writers negotiated a more problematic politics of representation than did their male counterparts.

Most critics have read Fauset and Larsen as writers adhering to a bourgeois representational politics in their depiction of black female characters.[22] But heeding Deborah McDowell's calls to attend to the ways in which Fauset and Larsen explore the possibilities of representing black female characters as sexual subjects, recent work on these authors has argued that they were far more daring than we have been led to believe.[23] Ann duCille has encouraged us to investigate "the role of ideology in shaping the period [the 1920s and 1930s], its artists, and its attention both to the folk and to black female sexuality," arguing that to champion both the sexually uninhibited lyrics of the blues and the "self-invented" black female blues singer as authentically black is a misreading of this era, as is reading Fauset's and Larsen's novels as sellouts to white ideals a misreading of their work (*Coupling* 69). Instead, duCille argues, we might more productively read Fauset's and Larsen's texts as "unique in their attention to the extremes of their historical moment and the powers of competing ideologies and colliding material conditions" (*Coupling* 70).[24]

Frequently, however, criticism has tended not only to eschew but in fact to react against reading the mulatta in Fauset's and Larsen's texts as a critical trope that may mark "the importance of biracial subjectivity." Instead, as George Hutchinson points out, "[t]he best recent criticism tends to focus on other issues, particularly feminist themes," and to treat the mulatta as a metaphor "for supposedly more important issues, such as black and/or female identity generally" (329).[25] My examination of racialized womanhood and the disruptive possibilities of the mulatta's engagement in gender as a performative is not focused on explicating the feminist themes of *The Chinaberry Tree* and *Quicksand*. Rather, I read the mulatta as a figure through which Fauset and Larsen challenge notions of race and its imbrications with particular class and gender identities that turn on understandings of "acceptable" and "illegitimate" sexuality. The mulatta uniquely enables this rather complex and multifaceted critique that while perhaps enabled by the very gender and racial politics that would seek to contain it, is far from limited to one or the other. In such a reading, we keep in sight, rather than elide for "more important issues," the historical marginalization of the mulatta and thereby the construction of difference in the American racial imaginary through an appeal to these registers. A central way in which Fauset and Larsen engage with the extremes of their moment is through their figuration of womanhood as a racialized, classed, and ultimately performative gender identity. Fauset and Larsen invoke the notion of the black female in two ways: first, as the uninhibited, erotic, and highly sexualized black female who is inscribed in fiction and popular cultural forms like the blues and cabaret dance revues; and second, as the "lady" proscribed by both the black bourgeoisie's and white America's conservative notions of womanhood.

Many early-twentieth-century white women wanted to "share masculine prerogatives . . . wanted the vote, sexual gratification, professional autonomy and economic independence" (Tate 224). Known as the "New Woman phenomenon," such desires, in fact, may have been limited to "a small minority of 'new women'" or to the "legend of the few" women who challenged patriarchal conventions. Instead, "the vast majority of new women 'preserve[d] a large part of their traditional role'" (Tate 278, n. 29). Ideals of womanhood turned on much the same markers as Victorian womanhood—sexual purity, a responsibility to the home, and family morality. Mulattas, too, continued to be sexualized to an even greater degree than "pure black" women generally in the opening decades of the twentieth century: they were said to "prey upon . . . [the men of] the pure-blood native race" and were believed to be "the chief sinners" among Americans of African descent (Reuter 94, 163). Joel Williamson notes that "light mulattoes in Harlem were also . . . associated with pandering to salacious if not criminal tastes," a stereotype that he speculates was, in part, the result of a policy on the part of cabaret owners to hire only fair-skinned African American women for their chorus lines (117). Since the mulatta ostensibly defined both the propriety of white womanhood and the extreme of illicit black female sexuality with her "salacious" behavior, we see the mulatta heroines in Fauset's and Larsen's novels taking on double border duty, defining the poles of womanhood as well as "race." Consequently, Hortense Spillers's contention that black female sexuality is situated "outside the circle of culture . . . defin[ing] the point of passage between inner and outer" resonates on the level of both racial difference and racialized gender difference for the mulatta ("Interstices" 86).

Fauset and Larsen invoke constructions of gender that mobilized the black female as an embodied border separating reified white womanhood from illicit black womanhood and use the mulatta to hold these extremes of womanhood in tension within the same figure. Yet central black feminist critics have read Fauset and Larsen as being far more conservative in their treatment of black female sexuality than may in fact be the case.[26] Even though Hazel Carby contends that Larsen's *Quicksand* offers us "the first explicitly sexual black heroine in black women's fiction," she sees Larsen as part of a larger nineteenth- and early-twentieth-century trend among black women writers to "displace [black female sexuality] onto the terrain of the political responsibility of the black woman" ("It Jus Be's" 748). Deborah McDowell calls Larsen and Fauset "profoundly ambivalent" as they "only hint[ed] at the idea of black women as sexual subjects behind the safe and protective covers of traditional narrative subjects and conventions" ("That nameless" 142). There is an important distinction to be made, however, between Fauset's and Larsen's employment of an ambivalent figure—the mulatta trope— to explore constructions of race, womanhood, and sexuality and what is being taken up as their ambivalent view of feminine cultural scripts. Both Fauset and Larsen represent black female sexuality and, in turn, womanhood and race as dialectical constructs rather than essential identities. The "narrative subjects and conventions" they employ to do so signal a parody and critique of such representational possibilities, rather than a cover. Larsen's and Fauset's novels do, indeed, dramatize a "tension" between the expression and the denial, repression, and displacement of black female desire and sexuality, as Carby argues. Yet far from accepting such representations of black womanhood, Fauset and Larsen critique them as overdetermined performances commodified by both the black bourgeoisie and white primitivists. Continuing to challenge racialized constructs of womanhood, preceded by Frances Harper and Pauline Hopkins in such a performance genealogy, Fauset and Larsen extend their focus to concerns of class, intraracial gender dynamics, and the competing pressures of their own cultural moment. For these writers, the mulatta not only speaks across and transgress the color line as she did in the nineteenth century, but she also unsettles the intramural.

In "Policing the Black Woman's Body in an Urban Context," Hazel Carby traces the development of a white American dis-ease with the migration of large numbers of southern, rural African Americans to urban centers in the North expressed as a fear, and call for control, of a "pathological" black female sexuality: "The movement of black women between rural and urban areas and between southern and northern cities generated a series of moral panics. One serious consequence was that the behavior of black female migrants was characterized as sexually degenerate and, therefore, socially dangerous" (739). Black female sexuality not only came to stand as a metaphor for the black urban condition in white discourses but was also circulated by the African American middle class as a potential social threat. Whites used the myth of black female sexuality along racial lines, while bourgeois blacks used it along class lines:

> The moral panic about the urban presence of apparently uncontrolled black women was symptomatic of and referenced aspects of the more general crisis of social displacement and dislocation that were caused by migration. . . . Thus the migrating black woman could be variously situated as a threat to the progress of the race; as a threat to the establishment of a respectable urban black middle class; as a threat to congenial black and white middle-class relations; and as a threat to the formation of black masculinity in an urban environment. (Carby, "Policing" 741)

Defenders of black women were also effectively engaged in policing the behavior of African American women, whether or not this was their explicit intention. Elsie Johnson McDougald, writing "The Task of Negro Womanhood" in 1925, defends black women against the charge of immorality; yet her defense also contains an implicit call to black women to prove their adherence to a "strict code" of ancestral African morality. "The women of the working class will react, emotionally and sexually, similarly to the working-class women of other races. The Negro woman does not maintain any moral standard which may be assigned chiefly to the qualities of race any more than a white woman does," wrote McDougald. "Yet she has been singled out and advertised as having lower sex standards. . . . Sex irregularities are not a matter of race, but socio-economic conditions. Research shows that most of the African tribes from which the Negro sprang have strict codes for sex relations" (379). McDougald, a teacher, "social investigator and vocational guidance expert" (Locke 419), dissociates the black middle class from "irregular" sexuality, targeting instead the working classes as the repository of immorality and vice.

As our available body of criticism would have it, for black women writers the alternatives to extolling morality and policing the bounds of proper behavior were, as Deborah McDowell has noted, to adopt a reticence to address the issue of black female sexuality; to, as Hazel Carby has argued, "displace sexuality onto another terrain" ("It Jus Be's" 748); or to depict black female characters as sexual subjects and run the risk that audiences would interpret them as "primitive" or immoral. Significantly, as Barbara Christian notes, black women writers rarely chose the latter option: "Not surprisingly, male writers explored the primitive view more intensely than did the women novelists of the day. The garb of uninhibited passion wears better on a male who, after all, does not have to carry the burden of the race's morality or lack of it" (*Black Women* 401). It is worth noting again that these risks were greater for women because primitivism was gendered and thrived on icons. If "no single icon combined the erotic, the exotic, and the innocent to the extent that the new Negro seemed to," the black woman blues singer was believed to go one better. She "became the principal instrument through which the sexually explicit lyrics of the classic blues began to reach the ears of white America . . . in the early 1920s. . . . Under what might be called the cult of true primitivism, sex—the quintessential subject matter of the blues—was precisely what hot-blooded African women were assumed to have always in mind and body" (duCille, *Coupling* 73). Fauset and Larsen chose not to displace, silence, or discipline black female sexuality in their novels; rather, they explored racialized and classed notions of womanhood and sexuality through the effects such constructions had on their characters.

In *Quicksand*, Larsen represents the power of primitivism's "hot-blooded" black female as so insidious that Helga mistakes this construct of black female sexuality for herself. She believes she not only "descend[s] through a furtive, narrow passage, into a vast subterranean" blackness at a Harlem cabaret but that she also enters a "jungle" within herself:

> They danced . . . violently twisting their bodies . . . to a sudden streaming rhythm, or shaking themselves ecstatically to a thumping of unseen tomtoms. For a while, Helga was oblivious to the reek of flesh . . . oblivious of the color, the noise, and the grand distorted childishness of it all. She was drugged, lifted, sustained, by the extraordinary music, blown out, ripped out, beaten out, by the joyous, wild murky orchestra. The essence of life seemed bodily motion. And when suddenly the music died, she dragged herself back to the present with a conscious effort; and a shameful certainty that not only had she been in the jungle, but that she had enjoyed it, began to taunt her. . . . She wasn't, she told herself, a jungle creature. (*Q* 59)

Larsen positions Helga as a corporealized boundary between civilized and primitive in this scene, as she plays on the period's popular belief in atavism—"blood will tell"—through Helga's fear that she has reverted to a primitive state, a state for which whites believed her black blood responsible.

Rather than having their heroines explore the borderland of the mulatta, testing limits and possibilities of transition and transgression, Fauset and Larsen explore the manner in which their heroines' liminality appears to be neutralized. Helga mistakes fabricated blackness for an inherent set of desires and behaviors that she feels she has failed to control in herself. Helga fears what she views as the jungle and believes she can, and has, momentarily crossed a line within herself between civilized and primitive in this Harlem cabaret. However, she has merely mistaken a form of entertainment packaged for white consumption as African American culture and identity itself. Consequently, her belief that only her exterior is civilized while her essence is primitive colludes with white ideology and maintains racist distinctions between white and black. What is more, because Helga mistakes primitivism's "red-hot" black female for the "real thing," she does not recognize this construction as a performable identity. If Helga were to see iconic blackness as provisional, she might also recognize it as an "identity [that] can become a site of contest and revision" (Butler, "Imitation" 19). She does not realize that black female sexuality in the Jazz Age is so overdetermined that it says little, if anything, about her identity or her sexuality. Rather than transgressing gender identities and racial boundaries, Helga consolidates these identities by policing her own behavior and "racial character," both of which she views through the lens of the dominant culture. Laurentine is similarly both drawn to and repelled by what she sees at a Harlem club. "[S]he was also intensely taken by the night-clubs, because she could not puzzle out why people should care for places such as these ... where a dark, sinuous dancer singing a song, whose words she could not catch, and making movements with her supple body, whose meanings she could not fathom, pranced and postured and gestured before a fascinated lad of twenty-one. ... After this she was glad to get out into the air" (*CT* 307–8). Fauset does not fully develop the internalization of such stereotyped versions of blackness in her heroine, as Larsen does in *Quicksand*, but Laurentine's desire "to get out" is clearly a claustrophobic response to an image of black female sexuality she feels thrust upon her. While Helga's response to the iconized uninhibited black female is to suspect its "essence" in her, Laurentine's is to refuse even to attempt a comprehension of the sexually suggestive lyrics and performance of the black female blues singer.

Whether signaled by Helga's "repression" or Laurentine's denial, Fauset and Larsen foreground the powerful effect of white America's icon of primitivism.

While its effect seems to be restrictive, and Fauset's and Larsen's novels seem reticent when it comes to black female sexuality, what appears to be conservative is arguably a quite radical aspect of their work. Ironically, Laurentine's denial and Helga's repression of their so-called illicit black female sexuality parody white sexuality, a crossing of the color line in these texts that has yet to be critically considered. White Americans historically ascribed to the racial "other" what they preferred not to acknowledge in themselves, yet rather than embodying mythic black sexuality, Fauset's and Larsen's heroines enact a version of sexual denial and repression raced "white" from which stereotypes of blackness, in part, arose. Indeed, they perform "white" womanhood in scenes critics have dismissed as examples of Fauset's and Larsen's conservative bourgeois ethos. However, rather than signaling an adoption of white values, such a parody in fact undermines them. Laurentine's and Helga's "illegitimate," though convincing, performance of a controlled sexuality traditionally ascribed to white middle- and upper-class women unsettles the dialectical relation between controlled white sexuality and uninhibited black sexuality by undermining the stability and impenetrability of these racialized gender identities. Laurentine's and Helga's parodic performances, then, not only undermine these gender identities but also the racial distinctions with which they are imbricated. In Fauset's and Larsen's novels, it is their mulatta heroines who aspire to be virtuous, contrary to popular stereotypes of black female sexuality.

While Fauset and Larsen clearly recognize the radical potential to undermine stereotypes of racial hegemony that lies in configuring race and gender as performatives, their characters do not, revealing the fault lines between lived exigencies, the pressures and powers of ideological codes, and the liberatory possibilities of performativity. Throughout *Quicksand*, Helga continues to keep herself at the boundaries of what she takes for "blackness," failing to recognize that what she sees as her forays into its "essence" is a constructed and commodified spectacle feeding white voyeurism and white identity. In Denmark, Helga is disturbed by a vaudeville show she attends. Characteristically, the Danes accompanying her are bored until "out upon the stage pranced two black men, American Negroes undoubtedly, for as they danced and cavorted, they sang in the English of America an old ragtime song." Larsen makes a point of noting that the songs they perform are "old, all of them old, but new and strange to that audience" (*Q* 82). White Europeans and Americans alike sought the "primitive" African, never suspecting a difference or distance between the role African Americans played in such shows and African American identity, experience, and culture; nor does Helga perceive such a distance. The performers are described as moving their exaggerated limbs in excessive gestures: "And how the singers danced, pounding their thighs, slapping their hands together, twisting their legs, waving their abnormally long arms, throwing their bodies about with a loose ease!" (*Q* 83) Their performance takes on a Bakhtinian carnivalesque quality of excess, but it is important to note that Bakhtin also theorizes "disguise" as an "accessory ritual of carnival" (*Problems* 125). The vaudeville performers do not dramatize "something in [Helga] which she had hidden away and wanted to forget"; there is no pure or essential African American character here but rather the excess and disguise of a carnivalesque performance of white notions of "blackness."

This performance, like minstrel and vaudeville acts historically, is the site of a complex interweaving of African American cultural forms and white stereotypes of "blackness." Helga is disturbed both by her fear that this vaudeville performance reflects African American character and identity—her identity—and by the performers' "cavorting" or playing to the voyeuristic pleasure of a white European audience. Helga, who searches for an identity and sense of belonging in one role after another, does not recognize the parodic nature of the performance. Larsen stresses its excess in both the players' gestures and costume, and this excess is invested with what Bakhtin calls "grotesque realism." For Bakhtin, the "grotesque body" is one of "corpulent excess"; it is multiple, oversized, mobile. Minstrelsy and vaudeville acts performed by African Americans in blackface may be interpreted as "grotesque realism," which "is always in process, it is always *becoming*, it is a mobile and hybrid creature, disproportionate, exorbitant, outgrowing all limits . . . a figural and symbolic resource for parodic exaggeration and inversion" (Stallybrass and White 8–9). Rather than a performance in which Helga might see an aspect of herself, her identity, that she prefers stay "hidden," this vaudeville act is a hybrid construction of African American cultural forms and their masking, of parodied stereotypes that are so exaggerated they mock white notions of blackness rather than African Americans themselves. These performances effectively turn the white impulse to commodify blackness back on itself, so that the audience unknowingly laughs at itself as object of the performance's parody.

Vaudeville acts descended from the minstrel shows of the mid-nineteenth century. Eric Lott notes that "the minstrel show's humor, songs, and dances were so culturally mixed as, in effect, to make their 'racial' origins quite undecidable" (94). Vaudeville, like minstrelsy before it, combined a variety of cultural forms that were themselves tailored to suit the expectations and interests of the white audiences in attendance. But they were not solely performances constructed by whites for their pleasure and profit. Lott argues that minstrelsy could be a complex mix of white power expressed through demeaning caricatures and African American control of and profit from the display and sale of roles that masked their own identity and culture.[27] African American performers and their white collaborators performed blackness at the expense of whites who believed they were seeing the "real thing":

> Black performance itself, first of all, was precisely "performative," a cultural invention, not some precious essence installed in black bodies. . . . Black people . . . not only exercised a certain amount of control over such practices but perforce sometimes developed them in tandem with white spectators. . . . In minstrelsy these practices were fed into an exchange system of cultural signifiers that both produced and continually marked the inauthenticity of their blackness; their ridicule asserted the difference between counterfeit and currency even as they disseminated what most audiences believed were black music, dance, and gesture. (Lott 39)

The vaudeville actors in Copenhagen perform an exaggerated and excessive blackness in which social and political interests intersect—white with black, "currency" with "counterfeit," identity with masked role. There is undoubtedly more of "whiteness" and the difference it invests in "blackness" evident in the "cavorting" Helga watches than African American identity. Yet Helga confuses role for reality, not only as a spectator but also when she becomes the spectacle.

Initially, Helga's stay in Copenhagen is "the realization of a dream. . . . Always she had wanted . . . leisure, attention, beautiful surroundings. Things. Things. Things" (Q 67). It soon becomes evident, however, that Helga herself is the "thing," a status symbol drawing attention to Herr and Fru Dahl. In what we might recognize as a performance genealogy linking Ellen Craft's appearances to Helga's "displays," Helga quickly becomes a curiosity. As Joseph Roach contends, "[p]erformance genealogies draw on the idea of expressive movements and mnemonic reserves . . . made and remembered by bodies . . . [and] retained implicitly in images or words" (26). In Larsen's representation of Helga's exoticized display we might read traces of Ellen Craft's appearances as the "white slave" and also the exhibition of black women before her, such as the Hottentot Venus in Paris and London's Piccadilly Circus during the early nineteenth century.[28] Larsen effectively references, and places Helga within, such a genealogy, thereby raising the question of Helga's role, if any, in her appearances and "perform-ances" within her Danish relatives' social circle. Helga's bourgeois materialism and her belief in the white exoticization of the New Negro arguably blind her to, and facilitate her participation in, her own objectification. She is sexualized and objectified in Denmark; Axel Olsen's remarks reflect his own beliefs regarding black women and the manner in which Helga has been displayed and constructed: "You have the warm impulsive nature of the women of Africa, but my lovely, you have, I fear, the soul of a prostitute. You sell yourself to the highest bidder" (*Q* 87). Helga's installation as an exhibit of blackness in Denmark culminates in a portrait that Olsen insists "is, after all, the true Helga Crane" (*Q* 88). She protests that it is not a good likeness, yet Helga must tell herself this repeatedly, ask a maid for confirmation that "it looks bad, wicked" (*Q* 89), and still she seems unconvinced. Larsen establishes a link between representation, commod-ification, and the controlling power of ownership with this portrait of Helga. We are reminded that the tradition of European portraiture began as a vehicle for the bourgeoisie to represent their status through commissioned portraits of their families, mistresses, and themselves set against their residences and grounds, portraits that advertised the bourgeois male's status to others and also served to constantly remind him of his ownership and power. In addition to Helga's par-ticular sexualization through this portrait, Larsen also references the commodi-fication and exoticization of the black female generally in European interpretations of the primitive.

Moreover, Helga's decision to retain the trappings of her exhibition in Denmark upon returning to Harlem signifies both the transatlantic influence and crossings of primitivism as well as the ambivalence of her attempt at self-representation in an era that has thrived on degrading stereotypes of black women. Helga discovers an increased popularity in Harlem: "Her courageous clothes attracted attention, and her deliberate lure—as Olsen had called it—held it. Her life in Copenhagen had taught her to expect and accept admiration as her due. This attitude . . . was as effective in New York as across the sea. It was, in fact, even more so. And it was more amusing too. Perhaps because it was somehow a bit more dangerous" (*Q* 98). Indeed, it is dangerous for Helga, who not only does not control the stereotypes that create her popularity but who also so internal-izes the construction of black female sexuality as lascivious and degenerate that she marries a southern preacher in "the confusion of a seductive repentance" (*Q* 118). Helga moves from the role of upstanding middle-class woman, to exotic black female, to poor and dutiful wife, roles scripted for her and neither allowing her the autonomy to express nor be the subject of her desire. Seeking a redemption from what she sees as her "shameful" sexuality and from an alienation that has dogged her throughout the novel so as to rob her of any sense of self, Helga takes on yet another role. For Helga, salvation takes the form of a sanctioned sexuality in marriage, and while her class position is anything but bourgeois, her aim accords with black bourgeois ideals of womanhood and racial uplift. She becomes what clubwoman Josephine Turpin Washington called the "progressive" black woman as the new "true woman," " 'modest and womanly, with a reverence for the high and holy duties of wife and mother' " (qtd. in Tate 152).

The Mulatta and Double-Voiced Parodies

In addition to exposing the effects of fabricated blackness, the sexualized icon of black womanhood, and the demands the black bourgeoisie made of women, Fauset and Larsen also signified on classed and racialized constructions of womanhood through parodies of the mulatta as she circulated in the popular imagination. It is significant that *Quicksand*'s Helga Crane is a teacher at a black college, for as Barbara Omolade notes, African Americans "encouraged their daughters to become teachers to escape the 'abominations' of the white man. . . . Teaching required of black women an even more rigorous adherence to a sex code enjoining chastity and model womanhood than that guiding other black women" (361). Moreover, teaching continued to be one of the few professions open to black women in the early decades of the twentieth century. Larsen, by representing her mulatta heroine as a teacher like Frances Harper before her, inscribes the experience of African American women in her text, ascribing such experiences to a figure whom the African American community historically rejected as "high yella," or as Helga herself says, "a despised mulatta" (Q 18). Larsen thereby invites her African American readership to identify with a character they may simultaneously regard as "not black enough." Helga as a mulatta schoolteacher may also have been read by a white audience in two directions at once: the schoolteacher as a rigorously chaste "model of womanhood" would "whiten" Helga in this readership's eyes, but at the same time they would also read Helga through their conception of the mulatta as "driven" by sexual impulses beyond her control. Larsen, then, confronts both an African American and a white audience with their essentialist notions of the mulatta through such a representation.

Significantly, Larsen accomplishes this confrontation of essentialism by parodying her audience's beliefs and expectations regarding her heroine's racialized
behavior. Larsen's parody depends upon holding in tension her audience's resistance to, and acceptance of, Helga as a model of both black women's lived experience and ideals of white womanhood. This tension between the parody and a
resistance to its "parodying intentions" is characteristic of the trope's "double-
voicedness," as Bakhtin defines it: "[T]he parodied language offers a living dialogic resistance to the parodying intentions of the other . . . the image becomes
an open, living, mutual interaction between worlds, points of view, accents. This
makes it possible to re-accentuate the image, to adopt various attitudes toward
the argument sounding within the image . . . and, consequently, to vary the
interpretations of the image itself. The image becomes polysemic" (*Dialogic*
409–10). Larsen uses the mulatta figure to parody African American and white
stereotypes of the mulatta as outside black and white womanhood, gender identities that she has Helga access despite the expectation that Helga will police
their borders.

Patricia Hill Collins observes that "in their goal of dispelling the myths about
African-American women and making Black women acceptable to wider society,
some historically Black Colleges may also foster Black women's subordination"
(87). At co-ed Naxos, African American "ladies-in-making" are encouraged to
"at least try to act like ladies and not like savages from the backwoods" (*Q* 12).
Ironically, Helga's affinity with the lived experience of African American women
is set in a school Larsen critiques as working to effectively "whiten" its black students: "This great community . . . was no longer a school. It had grown into a
machine . . . ruthlessly cutting all to a pattern, the white man's pattern. Teachers
as well as students were subjected to the paring process" (*Q* 14). Helga is frustrated by the rigorous discouragement of individuality at Naxos, from behavior
to dress: " 'Bright colors are vulgar'—'Black, gray, brown, and navy blue are the
most becoming colors for colored people'—'Dark complected people shouldn't
wear yellow, or green or red' " (*Q* 17–18). Naxos effectively subjects its female students and faculty to a white notion of black female sexuality as illicit and encourages them to imitate what the dominant culture approves as a bourgeois, ladylike
decorum.

Larsen invites her readers to interpret Helga's dissatisfaction at Naxos as the
expression of an internal confusion. Playing to the stereotype of the "psycholog-
ically . . . unstable" mulatta torn between her white and black blood (Reuter
102), Larsen establishes Helga's "frustration" at the novel's outset and carries it

through the narrative like a refrain: "There was something else, some other more ruthless force, a quality within herself, which was frustrating her, had always frustrated her, kept her from getting the things she had wanted. . . . But just what did she want? . . . She couldn't define it, isolate it, and contemplate it" (*Q* 10–11). Larsen depicts Helga's inculcation into the Naxos cult of the lady as harmful to her. Preferring not to contemplate her sexuality, Helga is shamed by the desire she arouses in her fiancé, James Vayle: "The idea that she was in but one nameless way necessary to him filled her with a sensation amounting almost to shame. And yet his mute helplessness against that ancient appeal by which she held him pleased her and fed her vanity—gave her a feeling of power. At the same time she shrank away from it, subtly aware of possibilities she herself couldn't predict" (*Q* 7–8). She suspects she barely veils a "backwoods" sensuality that can easily be discovered and sees this as a failure on her part. Despite the influence Naxos exerts upon all its "ladies-in-making," Helga perceives in herself "a lack somewhere. . . . She hadn't really wanted to be made over. This thought bred a sense of shame. . . . Evidently there were parts of her she couldn't be proud of" (*Q* 7). Helga, then, resists being labeled a lady because she believes her ancestry defines her and cannot be denied:

> "It's an elusive something," he went on. "Perhaps I can best explain it by the use of that trite phrase, 'You're a lady.' You have dignity and breeding."
>
> At these words turmoil rose again in Helga Crane. . . . "If you're speaking of family, Dr. Anderson, why, I haven't any. I was born in a Chicago slum. . . . My father was a gambler who deserted my mother, a white immigrant. It is even uncertain that they were married. As I said at first, I don't belong here." (*Q* 21)

Helga cannot see that ladyhood is as much a construction as the primitive black sexuality she believes she hides and controls in herself. Larsen, however, under-scores that Helga feels alienated because of, not despite, the Naxos influence and its bourgeois notions of womanhood. Parodying the myth that Helga's frustra-tion and restlessness are essential to her being and the result of her "blood," Larsen represents Helga's dissatisfaction as produced by her discomfort with the limitations to which the black middle class subjects women.

Larsen further extends her use of the mulatta figure to parody not only stereo-types of racialized and classed gender difference but also the sexual mores of the black bourgeoisie. We learn that Helga's conflicted view of sexuality is thoroughly in keeping with black bourgeois mores, rather than either the response of a lady or the result of her "confused" blood. Her refusal to name, much less explore, her desire is represented as a product of her class position and of that class's expectations of women, but it is nevertheless not exclusive to her gender. Robert Anderson, the head of Naxos during Helga's tenure there, represses an attraction to Helga that his new bride, Anne Grey, easily detects: "Anne had perceived that . . . in a more lawless place where she herself never hoped or desired to enter, was . . . a vagrant primitive groping toward something shocking and frightening to the cold asceticism of his reason. Anne knew also that . . . with her he had not to struggle against that nameless and to him shameful impulse, that sheer delight, which ran through his nerves at mere proximity to Helga" (*Q* 94–95). Larsen invokes a ladylike avoidance of the passionate and "lawless" in her characterization of Anne but then dispels any notion of this as an essentially feminine response to sexuality by ascribing an "ascetic protest against the sensuous, the physical" to Robert Anderson (*Q* 94). Such refusals to acknowledge and explore one's sexuality are identified by Hazel Carby as signals of a "secure" bourgeois class position in novels of the Harlem Renaissance.[29]

Larsen's parody of racialized sexuality in this case is multifaceted. On the one hand, she plays to white notions of African Americans as primitives with Helga's suspicion of her "backwoods" sensuality and Robert Anderson's "lawless" sexuality. Yet she undercuts such stereotypes not only with Anne's refusal to acknowledge her sexuality but also with the novel's characters' performances as upstanding ladies and gentlemen. She further parodies constructions of womanhood that would characterize repressed sexuality as essential feminine frigidity, with Anderson's "protest against the sensual." Finally, Larsen parodies the stereotype of the mulatta as an outcast from both races, conflicted and uncertain in every area of her life. Helga is thoroughly middle class in her view of sexuality, and the uncertainty she feels regarding desire and its expression is equally shared by Robert Anderson and other members of the black bourgeoisie, regardless of their genealogy. In every aspect of Larsen's treatment of stereotyped black sexuality and the mulatta, she gestures toward stereotypes only to invest them with a critical difference that undoes their attempt to pass as inherent or natural. Behavior associated with femininity is enacted by male as well as female characters, ostensibly uninhibited African Americans lead highly moral lives, and Helga's confusion regarding her sexuality seems more a product of bourgeois proscriptions than any "crossed signals" resulting from her so-called mixed blood. This is parody as "trans-contextualization" in Linda Hutcheon's theory of the trope as "an integrated . . . modelling process of revising, replaying, inverting, and 'trans-contextualizing' " (11).

As Larsen did in *Quicksand*, Fauset also depicts her mulatta heroine in one of the few professions to which African American women had access in the early twentieth century—Laurentine sews clothing for the white women of Red Brook. Barbara Christian criticizes Fauset's depiction of African American working women as less realistic and decidedly more privileged than those of nineteenth-century black women novelists like Frances Harper, yet Ann duCille argues that representing Laurentine as a seamstress amounts to an arguably Afrocentric inscription on Fauset's part:[30] "Dressmaking . . . is an age-old art for black women traceable to Africa, to the weaving and wrapping of cloth. Before their profit potential as breeders was discovered, their skill at weaving and sewing helped make African women valuable slaves. The fact that Laurentine Strange is a dress designer and seamstress . . . speaks with historical specificity to the limited professional options for African American women in the 1920s" (*Coupling* 88–89). Laurentine's dressmaking may be read as an attempt on Fauset's part to encourage her African American readership to see her mulatta heroine as "blacker" than they may have otherwise, to encourage empathy across the divide of colorism and class. It is interesting to note, however, that she seems to have been unsuccessful with late-twentieth-century readers. Laurentine does lead a privileged middle-class life, but reading her class position and profession as indications that she is "not black enough" only underscores the stereotypical connection between class position and race that readers continue to make today and that continues to homogenize African American lived experience and artistic representation. In the same figure, Fauset both inscribes black women's material conditions during the 1920s and early 1930s and challenges popular conceptions of "authentic" blackness; the parody consequently undercuts stereotypical notions of "the mulatta" and "the Negro."

Fauset plays upon a similar ambivalence that results when white readers' expectations collide with her representation of Laurentine. Laurentine's employment may also have worked to mitigate against the alienation of a white audience, many of whom lived privileged and racially segregated lives. Designing dresses exclusively for the white women of Red Brook despite her desire to do otherwise, Laurentine "knows her place" and keeps to it, which may have appeased the novel's white readers who may well have found her an unsettling figure: " 'I've never had colored customers. . . . You know how Jersey is. I can't afford to trifle with my living' " (*CT* 56). We must remember that Fauset's publisher worried that whites would not favorably receive a novel that countered their stereotypical notions of blacks by portraying African Americans as self-sufficient. Fauset parodies the white American notion that blacks must keep to their subordinate place—Laurentine's dressmaking for an exclusively white clientele is in keeping with segregated life in America and the expectations of Fauset's white audience; yet because this profession enables Laurentine to support herself and her mother, it simultaneously counters these same expectations. Fauset uses the "double-voicedness" of Laurentine's labor as seamstress to parody or "satirize the reception" (Hutcheon 16) of her novel by both white and African American readers alike.

In addition to confronting her readers with their racialization of class that culminates in a monolithic equation of blackness with a subordinate working class, Fauset also indicts the black bourgeoisie for their attention to "good breeding," family connections, and proper behavior, as well as their restrictive ideals of womanhood. Laurentine is "the epitome of all those virtues and restraints which colored men so arrogantly demand in the women they make their wives" (*CT* 124). Her morality and conduct are above reproach: "She personally had been as pure as snow, as chaste as a nun . . . no girl whose mother had been married by a hundred priests before a thousand witnesses could lay claim to a more spotless life than she" (*CT* 59). Yet despite her ladylike decorum, Laurentine is rejected by Red Brook's middle-class African American community because of her "bad blood." Laurentine may "pass" too successfully as a lady to suit critics who read "authentic blackness" as residing primarily in the folk, but she is not successful enough to pass into the black middle class depicted in the text.

Fauset's indictment of middle-class values takes on a gendered slant, for while the bourgeoisie as a whole demand of women certain "virtues and restraints," the black men of Red Brook are attracted to the very qualities in Laurentine for which she has been summarily rejected. Laurentine's physical appearance reflects, and serves as a constant reminder of, her parent's interracial relationship and her own mixed blood. She is both admired and shunned for her appearance and what it signals in "shining rippling hair, [and] the rosy curve of her cheek . . . [that] blended into the smooth lower plane of her apricot-tinted face" (*CT* 100). Yet the basis of her alienation from the African American community also proves to be her greatest attraction for black men, a contradiction that Phil Hackett (a young black professional in Red Brook) cannot resolve: "She knew her beauty stirred him; he liked and yet dreaded the effect of her distinguished appearance. Incomprehensibly, he liked that into which her strange life had transformed her and yet it seemed as though he could never reconcile himself to its sources" (*CT* 20).

Fauset also critiques the black bourgeoisie's hypocrisy when it comes to conduct. Laurentine recognizes that she must play both the lady and the coquette in order to secure a marriage with Phil Hackett: "Laurentine stood before her long mirror putting the finishing touches to her costume. . . . She glanced at herself in the mirror smiling with an unwonted coquetry. As a rule she was distant to the point of haughtiness. No matter what her feeling, she did not . . . dare to exercise any of the 'come-hither' quality employed by most young women. But she was beautiful, she knew it . . . and she would exercise the spell of her beauty on him to its fullest extent" (*CT* 34–35). Fauset invokes the myth of the "low-down yella" in Laurentine's "unwonted coquetry" only to represent her as equally able to pass as a proper lady who dares not exercise a " 'come-hither' quality." Since signifying "turns upon repetition and difference" (Gates, *Signifying* 79), we can read Fauset as signifying on the belief that, as a mulatta, Laurentine is inherently either "high and mighty"—"distant to the point of haughtiness"—or a "low-down yella" coquette.[31] Fauset parodies these stereotypes of the mulatta in a scene that represents Laurentine as haughty and flirtatious yet also fearful of behaving in an improper or unladylike manner.

Like Helga Crane, Laurentine has been so influenced by the double standards of the black middle class that she sees herself as both inferior—"Oh God, you know all I want is a chance to show them how decent I am" (*CT* 36)—and as "some one choice, unique, different," conducting herself with a "real queenliness" (*CT* 20, 56). If Helga's refrain is her "nameless" restlessness, arguably a dissatisfaction with the bourgeoisie's restrictive ideals and a racial imaginary that leaves her "neither/nor," Laurentine's is a fervent desire to comply with those bourgeois ideals in order to belong somewhere: "Perhaps if I am very good, Lord . . . perhaps if I am very generous, I'll meet with generosity,—Lord, Thou knowest. Give me peace and security, a home life like other women, a name, protection" (*CT* 21).[32] Both Helga's and Laurentine's frustrations and aspirations stem from their social isolation. Larsen and Fauset clearly represent their heroines' alienation and conflicted sense of self as the result of reactions to their fabled "blood," not an expression of that blood itself.

While the black bourgeoisie's conservative and restrictive attitudes toward gender roles and women's behavior seem out of step with the Jazz Age, the liberated white flapper, and the New Woman, this may not, in fact, have been the case.[33] Caroll Smith-Rosenberg argues that the second generation of "New Women" repudiated "bourgeois sexual mores" and fought for "absolute equality." "They wished to be as successful, as political, as sexual as men. . . . Not one shred of the Cult of True Womanhood remained to cloak their life style in the symbols of respectability. . . . They, more than any other phenomenon of the 1910s and 1920s, signalled the birth of another era" (177–78). Conversely, Glenda Riley contends that the indices in which many historians read white American women's refusal of traditional gender roles do not accurately reflect their reality in the 1920s: "In a sense, the rising divorce rate was paradoxical, the ultimate object of beauty—sexuality—and consumerism for women was still traditional: to 'catch' men" (87). Popular culture as represented in the "flapper films" of the 1920s also told a different story of women's liberation than did the new "New Woman phenomenon." Leslie Fishbein notes that the heroines of these films were a combination of Victorian and the New Woman. The "flapper's revolt," argues Fishbein, was "a truncated one, her sexuality mostly a tease, her ultimate object no different from that of the Victorian virgin (namely matrimony). . . . [T]he flapper films ultimately upheld the sanctity of the home, with *Motion Picture* magazine in 1920 sanctimoniously branding De Mille 'the apostle of domesticity' " (67).[34] Riley cites a 1929 study of the impact of films on young American women: "[T]he chorus girls and dancing flappers . . . served as a standard of behavior and appearance for a generation of female movie-goers" (86). Our rather stark notions of the New Woman or the flapper may have elided what were rather mixed notions of woman's role and possibilities. Instead, definitions of womanhood were clearly in flux at this time, and "conservative" notions of womanhood were far from outmoded.

One might argue, then, that with definitions of womanhood in flux, an African American woman's ability to "pass" for a "lady" could potentially effect the change that Harper and Hopkins envisioned in their novels and for which black clubwomen agitated with their repeated defense of noble black womanhood. Fauset and Larsen do underscore their mulatta heroines' affinity with the middle-class ideals of a womanhood believed to be exclusive to white women. While white and black citizens of Red Brook see Sal Strange's relationship with Colonel Halloway as so scandalous that it continues to offend them even after Halloway is dead, the white townsfolk are even more outraged that Laurentine not only *looks* like a Halloway but also *behaves* like one: "Aunt Sal had for years been the storm center of the greatest scandal that had ever touched Red Brook. . . . Laurentine, with her beauty and her pride, her independence and above all her faithful reproduction of Colonel Halloway's other two daughters, line for line, feature for feature, had served to increase rather than decrease that scandal" (*CT* 251). But Laurentine fails to see her "faithful reproduction" of bourgeois womanhood as a performance that undermines this ideal as a bastion of whiteness. Nor does she recognize that the myths of bad blood and wanton black female sexuality she has been battling all her life are just as much constructions as the white womanhood they are mobilized to support. Instead, Fauset foregrounds the fact that "true" black womanhood, or "progressive womanhood," as Josephine Turpin Washington called it, furthers the exclusive and elitist ideology of a black middle class that is more interested in attributing exotic and primitive behavior to working-class blacks than in dispelling such notions of black sexuality altogether. Melissa, Laurentine's cousin, learns at a young age that the black bourgeoisie has adopted an ideal of womanhood that Fauset has pointedly characterized as "white": "[S]he might not appear so white, so desirable in her lover's eyes. Malory, she knew, wanted his roses dewy, his woman's reputation, not to say her virtue, unblemished and undiscussed" (*CT* 251–52). Fauset depicts the black middle class as preoccupied with values and standards of behavior that prove exclusive, rather than engaged in an inclusive African American politics. In the black bourgeoisie's notion of what it is to be a lady, there is no place for the nineteenth-century ideal of a noble black womanhood that incorporated African American female experiences of menial labor with ideals of virtue as Frances Harper and Pauline Hopkins represented it.

Both Fauset and Larsen are highly critical of a black middle class they have been judged to collude with. They critique primitivism's iconization of the black female and her commodification in a bourgeois African American economy. Fauset foregrounds the use to which women are put as symbols of black middle-class respectability. Laurentine quickly learns what black men of the middle class seek in a wife: "From some mysterious source she who knew so little of men knew that colored men liked their wives to have straight hair, 'good' hair. They had to have these things for their children . . . their children must surpass them . . . poor colored people, they had so much to attain to in America . . . looks, education, morals, ambition, a blameless family life!" (*CT* 59) Women are commodified by the black bourgeoisie, signs of their husbands' success and the triumph of the middle class in refuting racist stereotypes. Significantly, Laurentine wears red, a color African American mothers traditionally warned their daughters away from, when her hopes to marry Phil Hackett are at their highest: "[S]he thought of the possibility of an engagement ring . . . its safety, its security, its promise! Feverishly she began to dress. . . . The red dress was ravishing, her slippers, her thin smoky stockings. . . . Phil, she thought, her face hot and flushed . . . would be surprised and pleased" (*CT* 58–59). Karla Holloway, recalling her grandmother's view of red, reads her warnings as lessons on the exploitation of black women by a dominant white culture that saw them as sexually accessible. "[T]he ethics my grandmother encouraged in her grandgirls followed her well-considered reflection on the history of gendered ethnic stereotype and abuse in United States history," writes Holloway, "and her determination about what could save us from the abuse that accompanies stereotype. When she warned us away from red, she reinforced the persistent historical reality that black women's bodies are a site of public negotiations and private loss" (21). Fauset indicts the black middle class whose stress on impeccable virtue and conduct leads them to reject Laurentine on suspicion of the immorality carried in her "bad blood"; yet this same class encourages its women to play the vamp to gain a man's attention. Fauset critiques the marriage economy for commodifying women who are taught they must trade on their looks in order to achieve security and respectability.

Helga, like Laurentine, also passes for a lady, despite what behavior whites believed her blood more prone to bring out in her. Her "fastidious" nature characterizes her as even more ladylike than Mrs. Hayes-Rore, a leading speaker in the black women's club movement: "[S]he [Helga] reached out and took her new friend's slightly soiled hand in one of her own fastidious ones" (Q 41). Moreover, the fact that the lady in Helga is more evident than any sensuality she believes she hides is itself a challenge to a gender identity that turns on the "impossibility" of a virtuous black woman. She not only finds it difficult to confront Robert Anderson about their mutual attraction but nearly faints trying: "Helga Crane faced him squarely. . . . She was secretly congratulating herself on her own calm when it failed her. Physical weariness descended on her. Her knees wobbled. Gratefully she slid into the chair which he hastily placed for her. Timidity came over her. She was silent" (Q 106). However, just as Laurentine cannot recognize bourgeois womanhood as a construction or see the ways in which it furthers the interests of both the white and black middle class, so, too, is Helga largely oblivious to and limited by definitions of womanhood.

Helga may successively resist being defined as a lady, respond to situations in "womanly" fashion, and be mistaken for a "scarlet 'oman," but she never seems to see these as constructed and, therefore, performable identities. Instead, she fears others detect either a primitive essence in her or a failure on her part to cover it with a veneer of decorum. It takes only a red dress for the congregation of a storefront church in Harlem to mistake Helga for a "Jezebel":

Without warning the woman at her side . . . in wild, ecstatic fury jumped up and down before Helga clutching at the girl's soaked coat, and screamed: "Come to Jesus, you pore los' sinner!" Alarmed for the fraction of a second, involuntarily Helga had shrunk from her grasp, wriggling out of the wet coat when she could not loosen the crazed creature's hold. At the sight of the bare arms and neck growing out of the clinging red dress, a shudder shook the swaying man at her right. On the face of the dancing woman before her a disapproving frown gathered. She shrieked: "A scarlet 'oman. Come to Jesus, you pore los' Jezebel!" (*Q* 112–14)

In turn, it takes only their call to her as an "errin' sistah" for Helga to marry the Reverend Pleasant Green as a salvation that only proves to trap her.

Larsen foregrounds the limitations Helga faces in attempting self-definition and self-determination through marriage in the final chapters of *Quicksand*. Helga has felt restricted by both poles of womanhood: in Naxos, she resists being defined as a lady; in Copenhagen, she refuses to be taken for a "sensual creature." Helga's "solution" is to marry a southern preacher with whom her "emotional, palpitating, amorous" sexuality can grow "like rank weeds" in the safety and respectability of their matrimonial home (*Q* 122). However, Larsen depicts Helga's marriage as anything but safe for her, as closely spaced pregnancies weaken her body and endanger her health. Helga's respectable sexuality becomes both a prize and the only weapon she wields against her husband: "Helga was lying on her back with one frail, pale hand under her small head, her curly black hair scattered loose on the pillow. . . . The day was hot, her breasts were covered only by a nightgown of filmy *crèpe* . . . which had slipped from one carved shoulder. He flinched. Helga's petulant lip curled, for she well knew that this fresh reminder of her desirability was like the flick of a whip" (*Q* 129). Passing for the exotic stereotype of the black female, performing as a lady, and playing the part of dutiful wife bring Helga no closer to expressing and deriving pleasure from her sexuality. Instead, Helga barters it only to exchange one form of restriction for another.

Helga's and Laurentine's ability to be both ladies and exotics subverts the notion that they are naturally one or the other. Yet these gender identities were defined by the "nature" of those they excluded. Ladyhood was maintained by its dialectical relationship with a black female sexuality that was thought to epitomize the primitive during the Jazz Age. Fauset's and Larsen's novels are notable for their explorations of primitivism, offering its staple exoticism as a counterculture to the black bourgeoisie. Yet their indictment of the effects a patriarchal gender economy has on their characters is further intensified by its similarity to the market primitivism generated—both markets thrive on a definition of the black female that is reductive and restrictive, and both are driven by the iconization of the black female, whether it be as the ultimate symbol of erotic sexuality or of social position. Fauset and Larsen explore these polarized notions of womanhood and sexuality, their points of intersection, and their sites of vulnerability.

Neither Helga nor Laurentine seems able to move beyond the bounds of supposed "essence" to see the liberatory possibilities of performatives that would challenge the hegemony of racialized class and gender identities. However, I would not regard this as a limitation of Fauset's and Larsen's work, a foreclosure of radical possibilities in novels that are hampered by a conservative bourgeois ethos. Rather, I would argue that their characters' failure to see beyond constructions of gender and race is a greater critique of their cultural moment than endowing them with a postmodern sense of identity as provisional would be. Fauset and Larsen speak to the contradictions of the New Negro Renaissance through their heroines' limitations. In an era in which whites and blacks alike marketed images of blackness that were complex mixes of African American cultural expressivity and blatant stereotype, it was, and continues to be, difficult to separate entirely construct from reality, performance from identity. The overdetermination of things black in Harlem proved empowering and limiting, profitable and exploitive for African Americans, a reality that Fauset and Larsen make abundantly clear through their use of the mulatta figure.

Passing Transgressions, Excess, and Authentic Identity in Jessie Fauset's *Plum Bun* and Nella Larsen's *Passing*

Writing on African American drama, Sandra Richards notes that "thanks to feminism, we have apparently come to understand that gender is performative. However, race—or, more properly stated, visible difference in skin color—remains tied to a metaphysics of substance" (47). Currently, race theory speaks of race as power-effect, a metaphor or construct naturalized or grounded through appeals to the body and bodily differences. Just as black British cultural studies theorists like Stuart Hall, Paul Gilroy, and Kobena Mercer call for "de-essentializing" blackness, several African American critics and theorists likewise maintain that "blackness must now be defined as a mediated, socially constructed, and gendered practice" (Wall, "Response" 188).[1] Yet there remains a certain resistance to conceiving of race as performative, as an accretion of behaviors and stylizations on the body's surface that, to quote Judith Butler theorizing gender as performative, produces "the effect of an internal core or substance . . . or identity" (*Gender Trouble* 136). This resistance arguably arises from contested and politicized notions of identity that, despite the waning of identity politics in the academy, continues to have considerable force.[2]

African American performance artist Adrian Piper, in an essay relating her personal experiences of being repeatedly taken for white, maintains that being black in America is "a social condition, more than an identity. . . . Racial classification in this country functions to restrict the distribution of goods, entitlements and status as narrowly as possible, to those whose power is already entrenched" (232). However, while Piper argues that racial categories are too "rigid and oversimplified to fit anyone accurately" (246), she also acknowledges the importance of what Karla Holloway calls "privately authored" identities that invoke race as grounding and binding African American communities together while driving

a variety of politics.[3] African Americans, Piper observes, have taken a "social condition" of rupture and dispossession and made of it privately authored identities
of self- and communal affirmation, yet this is also an identity politics that can
disavow what are perceived to be diminutions and dilutions of "blackness." "[F]or
others, it is the mere idea of blackness as an essentialized source of self-worth and
self-affirmation that forecloses the acknowledgement of mixed ancestry," writes
Piper. "Having struggled so long and hard to carve a sense of wholeness and
value for ourselves out of our ancient connections with Africa after having been
actively denied any in America, many of us are extremely resistant to once again
casting ourselves into the same chaos of ethnic and psychological ambiguity our
diaspora to this country originally inflicted on us" (234). Piper speaks here of
acknowledging biracial and mixed ancestry, but her insights are also applicable
to the idea of race as a performative and the possible limits to conceiving of it as
such. While identity as performance may be rooted in communal and cultural
traditions that inform that performance, it may also be perceived by some to be
a profoundly rootless instability that does not adequately address the lived experience or serve the interests of a good many people.[4] Its very chaotic ambiguity,
to borrow Piper's phrasing, may be liberating for some and lacking in historical
and material specificity for others, thereby proving its very failing. A politics of
identity rooted in the affirmation of African American "community" and a critical
questioning of the performative's political possibilities and efficacy seem to moti-
vate the continued unease with reading racial passing as anything more than an
individual's attempt to better his or her material position.

Rather than reading narratives of passing as making a political intervention in
conceptions of race at a time when racial difference was obsessively policed and
violently asserted, critics have continued to regard them as limited in subversive
potential and impotent in political strategy.[5] Whether guarded on one side of the
color line or the other, "blackness" continues to go carefully policed in American
culture and elsewhere in the West. This kind of border patrol and identity politics has made for one rather long-standing reception of passing narratives as
advocating a rejection of "blackness" for the social access and economic security
gained by passing for white, and of passing itself as a "dishonorable" act that indicates the character's lack of "integrity" or loyalty to their "race" (Wall, "Passing"
109).[6] In fact, passing narratives have been largely understood to be assimilationist in nature and intent: "The narrative trajectories of classic passing texts . . .
depend . . . upon the association of blackness with self-denial and suffering, and
of whiteness with selfishness and material comfort. The combination of these

points—passing as betrayal, blackness as self-denial, whiteness as comfort—has the effect of advocating black accommodationism, since the texts repeatedly punish at least this particular form of upward mobility" (V. Smith 44). We have a rather stark set of available readings firmly established when it comes to narratives of passing, to which recent criticism has added the poststructuralist contention that these narratives expose identity itself as a fiction.[7]

While I will argue in this chapter that Jessie Fauset's *Plum Bun* (1928) and Nella Larsen's *Passing* (1929) offer political critiques of race as it circulated and was interimplicated with gender, class, and sexuality during the Jazz Age, forwarding a constructionist view of identity is not the thrust of their politics. Certainly, given the current favor for "anti-essentialist" views of identity in literary and cultural studies, it would seem that their narratives are most radical when representing identity as performative and unfixed, but that kind of retrospective reading risks eliding central elements of passing as Fauset and Larsen work with it. Rather than enacting an either/or of communal versus individualist politics and practice, of identity as fixed or fluid and understood through essentialist or constructionist paradigms, Fauset's and Larsen's novels instead expose the tensions, ambiguities, and interactions of such oppositions as they compete in a debate over black identity. Contrary to the current critical vogue, I will explore the ways in which Fauset and Larsen use the very stabilizing grounds of identitarian categories—race, gender, class, sexuality—to configure identity as potentially dangerously fluid yet nevertheless circumscribed within policed borders that are consistently and at times violently reasserted.

As we have seen in Chapter 4, despite increased critical attention to their work, Fauset and Larsen have yet to be seen as deeply engaged in interrogating notions of race circulating in the wider culture or engaged in debates over "blackness" and its representations within the Harlem or New Negro Renaissance. Yet through the ambiguous racial identity of the mulatta and the ambivalence of passing itself, Fauset's and Larsen's narratives move between and play on two competing discourses of black identity in the 1920s: an essentialist discourse of "authentic" blackness believed to be embodied in "the folk," the southern, rural, poor African American; and an emerging constructionist discourse refuting notions of essential racial difference, usually identified as a "Talented Tenth" politics and associated with the bourgeoisie, the northern, urban, middle-class African American.[8] For some time, Harlem Renaissance politics have been understood as split along these class lines; however, recent studies like J. Martin Favor's *Authentic Blackness* argue that even the proponent of "Talented Tenth" politics, W.E.B. DuBois, "advocate[d] a wide range of black representations and acknowledge[d] a broad spectrum of black experience" yet also placed "the folk at the center of the discussion of black identity" (12).[9]

Having already discussed the ways that this promotion of "the folk" as embodying authentic blackness held ascendancy during the Harlem Renaissance, and continued to do so in our reimagining of that movement, I turn now to a consideration of the ways in which it did not go uncontested, not the least because it could be used to fuel, rather than counter, what Carla Kaplan calls the "taxonomic fever" of the early twentieth century. "At every turn, this mania was underwritten by hysterical devotion to notions of 'loyalty,' 'pride,' and 'group sense' and racial identity was implicitly understood as an ethics, an obligation to choose one's type, remain constant to it," documents Kaplan. "[E]ven radical black artists and intellectuals could be said to have contributed to this taxonomizing structure of feeling" (152–53).[10] The outcome of such taxonomic fever was "a profound cultural tension between . . . an impulse to stabilize and fix identity and . . . the beginning of our own social constructionist arguments for its destabilization. To make matters even more complicated, celebratory, even if strategic, uses of identity constructions are as likely to inhabit social constructionist terrain as they are to be found among essentialists" (Kaplan 153). We must, then, consider Fauset's and Larsen's passing narratives in this context in which New Negro identity politics centered on questions of "authentic" blackness, while anxieties about miscegenation and race hygiene were fueling racial segregation and an obsession with discerning racial difference in American culture at large. Fauset's and Larsen's intervention in this debate over racial difference and black identity was to explore and play on the cultural tension Kaplan speaks of through the mulatta figure who passes for white. While critics, as we have seen, have read the mulatta almost exclusively as a mediator between white and black, facilitating the exploration of the relationship between the races, Fauset and Larsen make her a much more challenging figure.[11] Far from simply facilitating a rather benign exploration of racial difference and relations across the color line, Fauset's and Larsen's mulattas threaten to call their era's conception of race into crisis.

American Anxieties: Color Lines, Passing, and a "Fundamental Femininity"

In 1921 Hornell Hart published the results of the first study to attempt to estimate the number of "legal Negroes who have . . . permanently passed into the white group," a study considered to be definitive until the mid-1940s (Burma 18).

Hart based his study on census figures of "native whites of native heritage" from ages one to twenty-four years, a group he tracked in consecutive census reports as the individuals aged. This study group would quite likely decrease due to emigration and death but should not increase substantially in number given that it excluded immigrants. He found that between 1910 and 1920, this group of "native-born whites" had in fact increased by 165,000 to 170,000 people and attributed " 'the bulk of the increase . . . [to] the passing of the legal Negro upon reaching maturity' " (qtd. in Burma 19). In 1937 T. T. McKinney estimated that 10,000 African Americans a year pass permanently for white, but by 1946 *Collier's* published an article entitled "Who Is a Negro?" which surmised that 30,000 African Americans passed annually (Eckard 498). These various figures clearly interested and alarmed white sociologists, who investigated the studies supporting them, concluded that the census figures on which they were based were unreliable, and argued that estimates ranging between 2,500 and 2,800 were more accurate (Burma 12; Eckard 500). Of course, the very nature of passing would render estimates such as these unreliable, if not impossible to arrive at. Yet white Americans were obviously concerned with this phenomenon, so much so that many of the studies conducted, and reviews of existing literature, concluded with "reassurances" that permanent passing was far less common than temporary passing (Burma 22); that while the studies estimated the number of African Americans passing for white to be as high as "2,600 per year . . . the number was actually much less" (Eckard 500); and that while some "Negroes" were fair skinned enough to pass for white, there were certain "give-away features" by which concerned whites might detect the passer, "such as everted lips, broad nose, dark eyes, [and] kinky hair" (Kephart 338). The passer's body was believed to be "the repository of evidence negating itself as a refigured 'white' person" (T. M. Davis 316), such that whites could be assured that few who could pass for white would attempt to do so any more than casually, and if they did they would soon be detected. This anxious desire to determine definitively "how many negroes pass" not only fueled sociological studies from the 1920s through the 1940s but was also expressed as a voyeuristic fascination with passing narratives. Judith Berzon has observed that Anglo-American and African American authors focused on passing for white in "mulatta fiction" from 1900 to 1930 but with a distinct difference: "The Negro version of the unhappy passer or the middle-class mulatto who denies his or her people is essentially a Harlem Renaissance phenomenon. In the white version, the mulatto usually dies; in the black version, he is 'summoned back to his people by the spirituals, or their full throated laughter, or their simple sweet ways'" (Berzon 63).[12] Studies like Berzon's positioned fiction as echoing sociological studies: the passer's identity was repeatedly "fixed," and either the passer would be outed by telltale signs of blackness; would die, thereby starkly marking a life passing for white as unviable; or would choose to "return" to blackness.

The mulatta is a key figure through which to consider this taxonomic fever and the fixing of identity and its transgressions on which such anxieties were focused. As Joseph Roach argues, "where bipolar laws and customs attempted to sort out kaleidoscopic tints and hues, mulattoes of any kind might be expected to induce crises of surrogation, but even more so when the marks of mixture were ambiguous or invisible" (182).[13] As we have seen, the mulatta's overdetermination holds in tension both the repeated reassertion of racial difference and the possibility of its subversion. In and through the mulatta, essentialist notions of absolute racial difference are asserted, even as their impossibility is given a "bodily" proof that exposes race as construct. The mulatta's racial overdetermination, in turn, has become imbricated with the overdetermination of both her gender and sexuality in ways that have often gone misrecognized. Considering passing narratives within his larger study of black masculinity, Philip Brian Harper reads the literary conventions of "tragic mulatta" narratives as the highly feminized precursor to the passing novel. Citing conventions like the tragic mulatta's routine position as "the suffering victim of tragic circumstances" and as "the source of moral degradation . . . [resulting from her] failure to be chaste" and her ability to seduce any white man, Harper argues that the mulatta's "illicit sexuality" signals her "fundamental femininity" (*Not Men* 104–8). This fundamental femininity then engenders "the conceptual limits that govern the novel of racial 'passing'" for Harper, its "inevitable" tendency "to support a conservative gender politics . . . with the effect that 'passing' itself appears as a profoundly feminine undertaking" (*Not Men* 112–16). Yet Harper fails to consider that gender and femininity are articulated in racialized forms. However "feminized" Harper might argue the mulatta is, her dangerously illicit sexuality has positioned her outside dominant constructions of womanhood rather than signaled her "fundamental femininity." Far from "feminine" in any dominant sense, the mulatta was excluded from a gender identity she would instead be positioned as defining and policing. Ostensibly marking the limits of both white womanhood's propriety and exotic black female sexuality with her extremely illicit and "salacious" behavior, the mulatta takes on a triple border duty defining the margins of womanhood, race, and acceptable sexuality.

Valerie Smith's reading of passing narratives as gendered takes us in a different direction from Harper's, for rather than arguing that the mulatta makes the genre itself feminized, Smith argues that the trajectories of these narratives differ according to the gender of their protagonists. "Passing male characters can either be re-educated and returned to the bosom of home and community to uplift the race, or they can remain in the white world and be constructed with some measure of condescension, ambivalence, or even approval," contends Smith. "Passing women characters, on the other hand, are either re-educated and returned to the bosom of home and community, or they receive some extreme form of punishment such as death or the sacrifice of a loved one" (V. Smith 45). In many passing narratives, this punishment of the biracial female who chooses to pass for white serves, as Smith observes, to "restrain the options and behavior of black women" (45), but, significantly, in Larsen's and Fauset's novels "punishment" is used to mount a critique of those very restrictions. *Plum Bun* and *Passing* foreground identitarian categories—class, race, gender, and sexuality—representing the borders between them as permeable, their sites of power and authority as shifting.

In both *Plum Bun* and *Passing*, femininity or womanhood is interrogated rather than naively or conservatively inscribed as Harper would argue. Even as a young girl, *Plum Bun*'s Angela Murray actively pursues dominant definitions and attributes of femininity. Though she has approached very few tasks in her life with diligence, Angela applies herself to studying French out of a certain Victorian sense of "ladylike accomplishment": "As for French, . . . languages did not come to her with any great readiness, but there was an element of fine lady-ism about the beautiful, logical tongue that made her in accordance with some secret subconscious ambition resolve to make it her own" (*PB* 37). Moreover, Fauset characterizes Angela as "naturally" chaste. "In the last analysis her purity was a matter not of morals, not of religion, nor of racial pride; it was a matter of fastidiousness" (*PB* 199). In addition to Angela's chaste character and feminine accomplishments, Fauset further invests her with a "womanly" reaction to a period of separation from her "true love": "[T]he strain under which she had been suffering for the past week broke down her defence. Swaying, she caught at his hand" (*PB* 283). Angela may grow faint in periods of emotional crisis like Helga Crane in Larsen's *Quicksand*, but she is calculating in her analysis of conventional "femininity" and her ability to play this role when it profits her: "[S]he wanted to be a beloved woman, dependent, fragile, sought for, feminine . . . she would be 'womanly' to the point of ineptitude" (*PB* 296–97). Fauset invokes the notion of a lady's "natural" propensity to sexual purity and physical weakness under strain in her African American heroine during a period in which black women were still believed to be prone to sexually illicit behavior and in which images of black women as Sapphire—strong-willed, independent, unfeminine, and emasculating matriarchs—that had held ascendancy since slavery continued to be reinforced.

Like Frances Harper and Pauline Hopkins before her, Fauset does not equate American notions of womanhood with either skin color or class position: Angela's darker-skinned sister, Virginia, and their housekeeper, Hetty Daniels, are represented as even more "womanly" than Angela herself. As a young girl, Virginia devotes herself to domestic duties, at the age of "twelve . . . develop[ing] a singular aptitude and liking for the care of the home" (*PB* 20). And with a sentimental show of emotion, Virginia's devotion extends to her faith; Sundays bring her "a sensation of happiness which lay perilously near tears" (*PB* 12). Unlike Angela, whose materialistic motivations are always at the fore, Virginia "envied no one the incident of finer clothes or a larger home. . . . When she grew up she meant to live the same kind of life; she would marry a man exactly like her father and she would conduct her home exactly as did her mother. . . . And on Sundays they would all go to church" (*PB* 22). However naive Virginia's aspirations may be, they nevertheless underscore a certain irony in Fauset's representation of Virginia as more conventionally "womanly" than her fair-skinned sister. Fauset also invokes stereotypes of working-class African Americans as an uneducated and unsophisticated mass leading drab lives when she introduces Hetty Daniels, the Murray's housekeeper, who is characterized as an upstanding woman of "untarnished" virtue: " 'Then young fellars was always 'round me thick ez bees, wasn't any night they wasn't more fellows in my kitchen then you an' Jinny ever has in yore parlour. But I never listened to none of the' talk, jist held out agin 'em and kept my pearl of great price untarnished. I aimed then and I'm continual to aim to be a verjous woman' " (*PB* 66). Even though she uses vernacular speech to mark Hetty's class position, Fauset refutes, rather than inscribes, stereotypes that correlate class position and race to dominant stereotypes of black female sexuality.

While Hetty's and Virginia's behavior is highly moral and their values lie with the interests of family and their community at large, Fauset's characterization of fair-skinned Angela initially approaches the New Woman. Angela shows a somewhat domestic concern for household affairs, but this concern centers on finances rather than housewifery: "[I]t was nice to be independent, to be holding a lady-like, respectable [teaching] position . . . to be able to have pretty clothes and to help with the house, in brief to be drawing an appreciably adequate and steady salary" (*PB* 49). Indeed, Angela's foremost concern is with the salary she earns teaching and the independence it will afford her; she does not enter this career with an altruistic desire to teach and guide future generations, as the heroines of black domestic fiction did, but with the goal of financing and pursuing her artistic talents in a racially segregated society that denies African Americans equal access to educational opportunities.

However much Angela may appear to be a "whitened" New Woman, her necessary labor despite her middle-class position, her equally necessary concern for her personal finances as well as those of her family, and the limitations she experiences reference black female experience in the 1920s.[14] Fauset is partly working, then, in the tradition of Harper, Hopkins, and late-nineteenth-century black feminists and clubwomen who inflected the dominant gender identity of their moment with the material conditions of African American women, using the currency of true womanhood both to contest a racialized gender identity that purported to be "natural" and to establish a noble black womanhood. But Fauset complicates Angela's character further by investing her with interests and aspirations that are a throwback to very conventional notions of womanhood and highly dependent upon a privileged class position that is coded "white." Angela's desire for a largely passive life in which her chief occupations will be exerting a "womanly" influence, entertaining lavishly, and marrying well are achievable through whiteness, as she muses: "Power, greatness, authority, these were fitting and proper for men; but there were sweeter, more beautiful gifts for women, and power of a certain kind too . . . [in] sympathy and magnetism. To accomplish this she must have money and influence . . . she would need even protection; perhaps it would be better to marry . . . a white man" (*PB* 88). Embedded in Angela's traditionally feminine and sentimental aim to marry and exert a "sweet" and "beautiful" influence upon family, friends, and acquaintances are decidedly unladylike aims for power, money, and independence: "[I]t would be . . . great fun to capture power and protection in addition to the freedom and independence which she had so long coveted" (*PB* 88–89). Fauset effectively casts Angela's desires for power and freedom as driving her decision to pass. Angela realizes that in American society, "men had a better time of it than women, coloured men than coloured women, white men than white women" (*PB* 88), and she determines to better her position in a hierarchy that has blocked her access to further artistic training and will limit her social, political, and economic freedoms. Paradoxically, the protection Angela seeks also necessitates a very "womanly" dependence that would effectively limit the freedom she desires. Thus Fauset makes Angela a combination of whitened New Woman, conventionally womanly, and a figure for historicizing the material conditions facing black women in segregated American society. The question of just what Angela is choosing to pass for is a vexed one from the beginning of the narrative.

Not only does Angela pass to gain the protection and privilege denied her as a black woman, but Fauset's text passes as a combination of fairy tale, romance, and novel of manners in order to gain her a publisher and audience. More important, Fauset's novel passes to gain a hearing for her subversive and political contention that racial and gender identities are constructed along, and perpetuate, an imbalance of power in America. Just as Angela's performance of true white womanhood is a hybridization of black female experience and white American notions of femininity, both radically new and somewhat outdated, Fauset's narrative holds in tension both a black feminist subtext that critiques racial and gender hegemony and the sentimental and romantic pretext of a young woman seeking a fairy-tale life of a happy marriage and home.[15] On the surface, then, audiences would likely see *Plum Bun* as rather conventional—a novel in the vein of the romances and novels of manners to which they were accustomed at the time. Angela's search for a handsome, wealthy young man with whom to share a luxurious home and lead a leisured life would seem familiar, even more so since Fauset accesses the well-worn formula of a heroine, often orphaned, on her own in the world—a formula used by women writers since the early nineteenth century.

In addition to these similarities to white-authored novels that a white readership would have found reassuring, however, are the differences they veil, differences that would have conversely forged a connection with African American readers. A white audience may have read Angela's search for freedom and protection in marriage as conventional enough. Further, the idea that a mulatta would consent to a sexual relationship with a wealthy white man would certainly prove titillating but would reaffirm rather than subvert their stereotypical notions that "mixed-blood" women seek exactly these kinds of relations (Reuter 93). An African American readership, on the other hand, may well have identified with Angela's experiences of racial inequity and shared her primary concerns for freedom, economic stability, and some semblance of power to redress their dispossession at the hands of white Americans. The fact that Angela seeks what should rightfully be hers as an American citizen by passing for white would also accord with African American lived experience. Since Reconstruction, African

Americans had come to be only too familiar with a refusal on the part of white Americans to willingly relinquish the power and privilege that were slavery's legacy. Consequently, what white Americans would deny them, some African Americans fair-skinned enough to pass for white determined to gain otherwise. Passing for white was not just the stuff of fiction, and many black Americans knew of people who passed to gain employment, better living conditions, and social freedoms.

Angela's repeated references to attaining "freedom" and "protection" in marriage were, by 1929, standard in both white- and black-authored novels of manners.[16] However, African American readers had a far different experience of "relationships" between white men and black women. Protection was often the last thing an African American woman could reasonably expect from a white man, many of whom saw her as always already sexualized. If white women barter for protection in a gendered economy, Angela must wager her passing in both a gendered and racialized marketplace, one that continues to commodify African American women. These varied readings by two very different audiences center on Angela's performance of bourgeois white womanhood as an act of signifying. Since "Signifyin(g) . . . negotiates the language user through several orders of meaning" (Gates, *Signifying* 79), we might say that Fauset uses the "language" or ideals of bourgeois womanhood and the shared "language" of African American lived experience to negotiate her text between two readerships that attend to several different "orders of meaning" in Angela's performance.

Fauset further develops and extends the polyvalency of her narrative in her exploration of female sexuality in the 1920s. In her introduction to the Beacon edition, Deborah McDowell notes that even though Fauset repeatedly refused throughout her writing career to pander to primitivist tastes, she nonetheless "took pleasure, at least in *Plum Bun*, in teasing commercial expectation. Although there are no explicitly sexual scenes in the novel, it brims with innuendoes" (xxvii). But Fauset "teases" only to disappoint: the white women Angela meets, not Angela or any of Fauset's African American characters, are well versed in the game of "free love" and the use of their bodies in a sexual marketplace. Greenwich Village rather than Harlem, the salons of New York's rich bohemians not a smoky cellar cabaret are the sites of Angela's education in sexuality. Significantly, this education in sexual politics is narrated in the novel's midsections entitled "Market" and "Plum Bun"; moreover, these sections are set in the predominately white area of New York's Greenwich Village, which African Americans had left at the turn of the century for the West Side and eventually Harlem. "The blacks living on the middle West Side in the eighteen-nineties had moved up there from Greenwich Village. . . . By 1900, only a few Negro households remained. . . . Many had been forced out by white immigrant groups" (Anderson 8). When Angela first arrives in New York from Philadelphia, she lives "just at the edge of the Village" (*PB* 92); her geographical positioning parallels her racial positioning—she lives neither inside this once black but now white area nor wholly outside it, but her friendship with Paulette Lister later brings her into the Village and white bohemian life. Angela, whose experience, thoughts, and language are the epitome of propriety, encounters a new lifestyle that Fauset represents as centering on sexuality and the commodification of women.

While living in the Village, Angela's best paintings are of what she calls her "Fourteenth Street 'types,'" portraits of working-class men and women, the homeless, and prostitutes. The primitivist proclivities of the age popularize any and all representations of life outside white bourgeois circles, in turn creating a seller's market for such work, but Angela can barely bring herself to even name her subject: "[T]he smiling despair of a harlot. Even in her own mind she hesitated before the use of that terrible word, but association was teaching her to call a spade a spade" (*PB* 111). Fauset conflates the primitivist marketplace and its sexualized icons with a gender economy; in both markets, the benefits accruing to the seller are fraught and often prove precarious at best. "Free love" is possible for men but becomes an oxymoron for women. Fauset repeatedly underscores the inevitable commodification of women whether they explore and express their sexuality or pursue the traditional goal of marriage. By the novel's end, Angela—with hard-won savvy—comes to regard relationships between men and women as marketplaces in which women have no purchasing power and can only barter their ideals and bodies. Marriage becomes "an effort on our part to make our commerce decent" (*PB* 320). As an artist, Angela refuses to mortgage her talent to patrons she must "flatter," whose "condescension" she must accept along with payment, but as an African American woman she realizes her access to "position, power, wealth" and a name is limited at best in American society and determines to get them through passing for white and marrying a white man: "[M]arriage is the easiest way for a woman to get those things, and white men have them" (*PB* 112).

Even as Fauset seems to suggest that passing for a white woman will be Angela's ticket out, she exposes the ways in which the very attributes of femininity necessary for Angela's successful pass will ultimately restrict her. While passing for white, Angela tries to barter for marriage with Roger Fielding, but

Roger knows too well his value as an eligible bachelor and his parents' expectation that he marry within "his station." Even though Angela realizes, despite denying it, that becoming Roger's lover will cost her the security and upward mobility she has been seeking, she nevertheless agrees to a lifestyle she sees as "promiscuous." Angela's passing—her performance of a conventional femininity and its "virtues"—is represented as most successful, however, when she agrees to Roger's proposition and stakes her body and sexuality on her belief that he is a gentleman and will eventually marry her. Significantly, Fauset describes Angela as conspicuously "los[ing] . . . her colour" (*PB* 179) when she decides to become sexually involved with Roger. An independent young woman who leaves home, family, and friends to pass for white in a strange new city, Angela takes on a ladylike passivity soon after her first sexual encounter with him: "Without him life meant nothing; with him it was everything. . . . Now for the first time she felt possessive; she found herself deeply interested in Roger's welfare. . . . [H]is wishes, his pleasure were the end and aim of her existence; she told herself . . . that the sole excuse for being a woman was to be just that,—a woman. Forgotten were her ideals about her Art; her ambition" (*PB* 203–4). Fauset's tone is unmistakably ironic, with its melodrama and excessive romanticizing of what is effectively Angela's entrapment. In fact, Fauset parodies both the notion of the African American woman as lascivious and the white woman as virtuous through Angela's passing, making her never more believable as a white woman than when in the midst of her illicit affair with Roger. Heightening our awareness of their interimplication, Fauset offers her most severe and incisive critique of gendered and racial constructs in Angela's experiences passing for white. Angela is effectively a "fallen woman" with the most "ladylike" of devotions and motives, at her most "unwomanly" when self-reliant, independent, yet also virtuous.

Fauset parodies this racial dialectic of womanhood through more than the mulatta figure. Paulette, one of Fauset's New (white) Woman characters, speaks of using her sexual attraction as a power to wield over men: " 'I've learned that a woman is a fool who lets her femininity stand in the way of what she wants. . . . I see what I want; I use my wiles as a woman to get it, and I employ the qualities of men, tenacity and ruthlessness, to keep it. And when I'm through with it, I throw it away just as they do' " (*PB* 105). Ironically, in an era that invested African Americans with eroticism, Angela reflects that no African Americans she had known lived a sexually free lifestyle like Paulette's; if they had, "she could not think of one who would thus have discussed it calmly with either friend or stranger" (*PB* 107). Fauset parodies white sexual repression and the projection of untrammeled sexuality onto the racial "other" in her characterization of Paulette as sexually free, while Angela, conversely, can consider sex only under the sanction of marriage. In fact, the white women who befriend Angela all lead unconventional and "liberated" lifestyles. Like Paulette, Martha Burden resists the feminine script of marriage, believing that in marriage "spontaneity is lacking. She wants to give without being obliged to give; to take because she chooses and not because she's supposed to" (*PB* 196). While Fauset's white female characters take up experimentations in "free love," women like Angela, Virginia, and Rachel Salting—Angela's Jewish neighbor—all believe in marriage and true love. Fauset defies the construction of racialized sexuality and gender identities as closed and natural by demonstrating their fluidity in a complex parody; moreover, that same parody confronts her audience with the very stereotypes she, in turn, plays on and subverts.

"Convenient" Passing, Denied Affinities

Both Fauset and Larsen parody racialized and class-inflected gender identities through the act of passing. In her reading of Larsen's *Passing*, Lauren Berlant has argued that "passing for nonblack allows these women [Irene Redfield and Clare Kendry] to wear their gender according to a particular class style" ("National" III). There are, however, significant differences between Irene's passing and Clare's, and they go further than the fact that Irene passes as white only occasionally for convenience, while Clare has "passed over" into the white race. While Irene carefully regulates her life, her behavior, and her appearance in order to solidify her bourgeois class position—an act of passing that, like Angela's, also entails her performance of bourgeois femininity—Clare stages a much more "daring" and "having" performance in which she refuses to keep in her place as either white or black. To note that Irene's passing is not limited to her occasional masquerades as a white woman is hardly a new reading of the text.[17] Like Fauset, Larsen parodies the notion of race and womanhood as natural identities inhering in the body and ideas of the body as governed by a set of essential behaviors that correlate to an individual's class position, race, or gender. Bourgeois values and behaviors once signaled white middle-class hegemony, and notions of "racial character" certainly fueled white racial hegemony, but to represent what were taken to be indices of white identity as performable by African Americans offers a significant challenge to such racializations. Larsen works to undermine the racialization of gender and class identities by representing Irene as mastering and ultimately parodying bourgeois standards of womanhood. Irene does not sleep in the same bedroom as her husband; indeed, only her sons betray Irene's asexuality. She wishes sex to be a silent subject in her home and cannot bring herself even to use the word when she expresses concern over her eldest son to her husband: " 'I'm terribly afraid he's picked up some queer ideas about things—some things—from the older boys, you know.' . . . 'Queer ideas?' he repeated. 'D'you mean ideas about sex, Irene?' " (*P* 189) Predictably, Irene also takes a certain pride in her skilful domesticity: "Pouring tea properly and nicely was an occupation that required a kind of well-balanced attention." Extending her "womanly" skills from the tea table throughout the house in the bourgeois pursuit of a well-appointed home, a home described as "furnished with a sparingness that was almost chaste," Irene is a consummate hostess, arranging "successful" parties as carefully as she arranges a home life for her family (*P* 218–19). As the curator of domestic matters and her family's morality, Irene "wanted only to be tranquil. Only, unmolested, to be allowed to direct for their own best good the lives of her sons and her husband" (*P* 235).

Throughout the novel, Larsen invites her readers to see Irene's domesticity and propriety as a mastery of bourgeois womanhood. To an audience missing Larsen's parody, Irene's performance would be read as mimetic, as an attempt to "ape" the behaviors and values of white bourgeois ideology in an assimilationist maneuver. However, in her representational strategies, there are indications that Larsen was actively engaged in signifying on the reception of *Passing* by her contemporary readership. In a literal reading, Irene's version of womanhood might be seen by some white readers as a thin veneer of civilization "concealing" and "disguising" a "wild" essence to which, like "all Negroes," she risks reverting. Larsen seems to play on such a reading in the scene in which Irene believes she has "discovered" that Clare and her husband are having an affair, representing Irene's preoccupation with the mechanics of hosting a tea party and her sense of proper behavior as the only controls preventing her from indulging in "an almost uncontrollable impulse to laugh, to scream, to hurl things about. She wanted, suddenly, to shock people, to hurt them" (*P* 219). Indeed, *Passing*'s ambiguous ending is an invitation to readers to believe Irene has lost control and has murdered Clare. In such a reading, Irene fulfils rather than challenges white racist expectations and reproduces or re-presents the stereotype of atavistic blackness as an essence she "conceals" or "disguises" beneath her bourgeois propriety. However, readers familiar with the trickster figure that often emerges in African

American literature might recognize Irene as a sort of trickster figure, a "violator of boundaries who . . . eludes banishment" (Baker, *Blues* 183). While many readers see Clare as the more defiantly challenging character in Larsen's novel, she is not allowed to continue to flout the color line.[18] It is Irene who not only survives but preserves her studied pursuit of a bourgeois lifestyle in which she can pass for white occasionally and as a middle-class race woman full time. Irene's "ladylike" values and behavior, combined with her occasional "impulses" to behave in an "uncontrolled" manner, parody and refute both the idea that African American women are naturally and wholly primitive and that ladies are inherently refined and civilized. Irene's combination of "womanly" behavior and "impulsive" desires becomes the parodic "sting" Larsen imparts to a trickster figure who passes across the color line, violates the boundary between racialized forms of womanhood, and is so successful in doing so that she eludes banishment from the black bourgeoisie.

It is Irene's carefully constructed and maintained gender identity that Clare Kendry threatens to disrupt with her insistent presence in Irene's life. Passing for white and married to wealthy John Bellew for twelve years, Clare repeatedly disturbs Irene, who finds her "peculiar caressing smile just a shade too provocative" (*P* 149). Clare is said to behave in "a having way" (*P* 153), at the expense of anything and anyone: " 'Can't you realize that I'm not like you a bit? Why, to get the things I want badly enough, I'd do anything, hurt anybody, throw anything away' " (*P* 210). Irene recognizes that Clare's challenge to the inhibiting prescriptions of propriety threatens the stability of her own carefully constructed middle-class gender identity, as much as Clare seems to threaten the stability of Irene's marriage itself. If Clare turns her provocative smile upon a waiter rather than reserving it for her husband, if she can confess a lack of morality to Irene— " 'It's just that I haven't any proper morals or sense of duty, as you have, that makes me act as I do' "—but still retain her class position, Irene is forced to acknowledge that no amount of prudery will secure her position in the black bourgeoisie (*P* 210).

While Irene fiercely claims an allegiance to "her race," she distinguishes herself from the "disagreeably damp and sticky crowds" of working-class blacks that threaten to "damage . . . her appearance" (*P* 147), and she employs dark-skinned maids to further secure the class divide underscored by colorism. Irene, a consummate "race woman," denies she passes for white "except for the sake of convenience, restaurants, theatre tickets, and things like that" (*P* 184, 227), but the most obvious example of Irene's adoption of class-inflected colorism is the nature of her participation in "racial uplift." Irene, by selling tickets for the Negro Welfare League dance to whites who attend to "get material to turn into shekels . . . to gaze on those great and near great while they gaze on the Negroes," sells blackness as spectacle (*P* 197). And in participating in a commodification of "the race," Irene must distinguish herself as somewhat apart from it, for she would be mortified to be seen as a spectacle herself.

Both Irene and her husband, Brian, undertake what they call racial uplift primarily to further distinguish themselves as members of the middle class and to further distance themselves from working-class blacks in Harlem: " 'Uplifting the brother's no easy job.' . . . And over his face there came a shadow. 'Lord! how I hate sick people, and their stupid, meddling, families, and smelly, dirty rooms, and climbing filthy steps in dark hallways' " (*P* 186). By characterizing Brian as indulging in classist stereotypes of the "ignorant" and "dirty" masses just as Irene does, Larsen indicts elitist versions of uplift that, in the name of elevating the image of African Americans as a whole, often attempted instead to raise the image of bourgeois blacks by arguing for their difference from the urban working classes and poor. Brian would rather live in Brazil, a country reputed to be less racist than America at the time but also one in which, as Carl Degler notes, wealth and color are codeterminants of social acceptance and social position, so that a middle-class income and position can "whiten someone of African descent" like Brian (102). Yet Larsen ironizes Brian's desire to escape Harlem for Brazil; he seems unaware that by the end of the 1920s, Brazil had come to virtually prohibit blacks from entering the country through a series of visa denials to applicants of African descent (Little 182 n. 2).

Brian also fails to recognize that his bourgeois elitism and distaste for his work, which brings him into the homes of Harlem's working class, amount to an act of passing of sorts, but Larsen represents Irene as all too aware of what it takes to maintain her identity. Far from criticizing whites who visit Harlem in such numbers that "pretty soon the coloured people won't be allowed in at all, or will have to sit in Jim Crowed sections" (*P* 198), Irene actively cultivates the shared society and attention of Manhattan's elite, like "*the* Hugh Wentworth." Irene flatters the "too sincere" Hugh as though he were the one exception to the "purely predatory" or merely "curious" white men who frequented Harlem (*P* 207). Moreover, concerned that the whiteness she has adopted remains secure, Irene views passing with disdain in order to deny both the passing she enacts and the danger she is well aware accompanies all forms of it: " 'Tell me, honestly, haven't you ever thought of "passing"?' Irene answered promptly: 'No. Why should I?'

And so disdainful was her voice and manner that Clare's face flushed" (*P* 160). Irene is obsessed with securing both herself and others to the place in which they "belong" (*P* 176) and is frightened by Clare because she can neither place her nor be certain that Clare will keep to her place. Consequently, Irene desperately tries to keep Clare at a distance: "Actually they were strangers. Strangers in their ways and means of living. Strangers in their desires and ambitions. Strangers even in their racial consciousness. Between them the barrier was just as high, just as broad, and just as firm as if in Clare did not run that strain of black blood" (*P* 192). Even though Irene must deny affinity with Clare and her actions in order to deny her own passing, she is unable to "fix" Clare despite warning her that returning to Harlem "isn't safe." Clare refuses to occupy a marginal position, nor does she seem to be willing to continue to choose one racial identity at the expense of another. She comes to threaten Irene's security and the "purity" of whiteness because she views identity as performable and therefore fluid, rather than a fixed essence.

Performativity and "Authentic" Blackness: Transgressing an Epistemological Divide

To this point, it would appear that Fauset and Larsen are focused primarily on the imbrications of gender, race, and class as "fixers" of identity that the passing mulatta can render performable and thereby destabilize. But, as Kaplan points out in her brief reading of *Passing*, "though Clare is a master of performativity, she turns out to be a fervent . . . essentialist," making her a figure "whose racial identity is profoundly torn between essentialism and constructionism" (162, 164). In fact, driving Clare's daring and "having" decision to pass between white and black and making her passing all the more threatening is her reawakened desire to somehow become black again through association: " 'You don't know, you can't realize how I want to see Negroes, to be with them again, to talk with them, to hear them laugh' " (*P* 200). Through her repeated trips uptown to Harlem, Clare hopes to recover that "black" something, "not definite or tangible," that passing for white has cost her (*P* 206). Clare's desire to recover her essential "blackness" and a conversation between Brian, Irene, and Hugh Wentworth at the Negro Welfare League dance foreground various notions of race popular during the early twentieth century. In this conversation, Brian espouses a belief that race is mystical to a certain extent, that passers are almost always drawn back to "the race" for some inexplicable reason: " 'If I knew that, I'd know what race is' " (*P* 185). Irene also expresses a similar view, arguing that African Americans can always determine an individual's race, if "not by looking" then by some almost sixth sense: " 'I'm afraid I can't explain. Not clearly. There are ways. But they're not definite or tangible' " (*P* 206). Whites, on the other hand, cling to the belief that an individual's appearance will always betray his or her race, a notion that Larsen and her African American characters mock and play on. At the novel's outset, Irene fears that she has been found out at the Drayton Hotel in Chicago, but she quickly dismisses the possibility because whites can never "tell": "White people were so stupid about such things for all that they usually asserted that they were able to tell; and by the most ridiculous means, finger-nails, palms of hands, shapes of ears, teeth, and other equally silly rot" (*P* 150). However much Brian and Irene believe race cannot be determined by relying on the body as decipherable text or repository of racial difference, they nonetheless insist that blacks can recognize an individual passing for white, while whites cannot: " 'We know, always have. They don't. Not quite. It has, you will admit, its humorous side, and, sometimes, its conveniences' " (*P* 185). Irene, Brian, and whites like Hugh Wentworth seem equally unwilling to view race as performable and prefer instead to believe that there is a trick by which they can somehow detect an individual's race or who is passing for what. Indeed, Hugh is convinced that if he were to spend some time with Clare, he would know with certainty whether she is as white as she seems.

While Fauset and Larsen saw constructionism as one view of identity alongside essentialism, they were highly aware of the limits of conceiving identity as performative within a racist society. Passing for white may be figured by Fauset and Larsen as a strategy for redressing an imbalance of power in America, but the passer must necessarily access and thereby reinscribe that power imbalance to a certain degree in order to pass successfully. Moreover, this is an act that is limited in scope by the fact that only fair-skinned African Americans can possibly pass for white. Fauset and Larsen dramatize an individual act that few African Americans can choose to perform as potentially subversive of constructions that structure an entire society around racial difference. In passing for white, Fauset's and Larsen's heroines are simultaneously complicit with the racial, class, and gender hierarchies they also subvert. Such ambivalence, it should be noted, is the very nature of parody, as Margaret Rose observes: "[P]arodists may be *both* critical of *and* sympathetic to their 'targets.' . . . In both its general and specific forms, parody . . . is ambivalently dependent upon the object of its criticism for its own reception" (47, 51). And these writers appear to be quite interested in attending to the costs exacted in order to keep the color line firmly in place.

Fauset's *Plum Bun* treats passing with just such ambivalence. While Fauset foregrounds the subversive potential in Angela's decision to pass for both white and black, she seems more critical of Angela's mother's acts of passing. Mattie Murray occasionally passes for convenience, but Fauset is careful to point out that this is a convenience in which the majority of African Americans cannot partake: "Much of this pleasure, harmless and charming though it was, would have been impossible with a dark skin" (*PB* 16). Mattie repeatedly reassures herself that her brief acts of passing violate no "genuine principle" (*PB* 19, 32), but passing ultimately brings about her husband's death by pneumonia contracted on a bitter winter day while waiting outside a whites-only hospital to which Mattie has been rushed after fainting while passing for white. Fauset seems both critical of passing and interested in its subversive potential in *Plum Bun*; yet this is, again, characteristic of parody, as Mikhail Bakhtin maintains: "In vari-directional discourse . . . [there is] inevitably . . . an internal dialogization. . . . [S]uch a discourse . . . loses its composure and confidence, becomes agitated, internally undecided and two-faced. Such a discourse is not only double-voiced but also double-accented" (*Problems* 198). Fauset's ambivalence regarding passing signals the "internal dialogization" of her parody. Far from weakening or undermining Fauset's challenge to race and gender identities, such ambivalence enables a complex rather than simplistic interrogation of the parody's target. Even though she writes the passer's body as an illegible and malleable text through which both whiteness and blackness can be staged, Fauset confronts the limits of particular bodies as they are blocked by a color line that exacts very high costs. Angela's passing hurts no one materially but herself, yet her mother's passing arguably exacts her father's life, thereby raising the question of whether a constructionist view of identity (Angela's passing as performative) risks more than an essentialist view (Mattie's passing as an intermittent dalliance from her "authentic" identity). A performative notion of race might appear to radically undo the logic of racial difference operative in Fauset's time, but can it speak to the material conditions that secure the color line? Fauset interrogates the various possibilities opened up by the epistemological paradigms undergirding passing.

Ultimately, however, Larsen's and Fauset's novels differ from conventional narratives of passing by moving beyond a representation of passing as an act in which the goal is to be mistaken for white. Rather, their novels question the "residual essentialism" operative in the conventional understanding of passing as an act of suppressing a "prepassing identity" in order to perform as the racial "other."[19] Using the mulatta's "genealogy" to hold in tension essentialist and constructionist understandings of passing and race, Fauset and Larsen remind us that the mulatta is no more authentically black before passing than she comes to be white in and through the pass. Offering us passing narratives that refuse to choose a side in such debates over racial difference, Fauset and Larsen can be read as further exploring the implications of those legal cases and statutes that entertained notions of race as biological essence and race as performable. These debates, as we saw in Chapter 1, frequently enabled, rather than foreclosed, the traversing of a color line the courts believed they could secure. What their readers might miss when it comes to this critical understanding of the mulatta, Fauset and Larsen choose to dramatize in Angela's and Clare's determination to pass for both black and white, to move between and within both cultures and communities.

Angela realizes that race is asymmetrically inflected with power in *Plum Bun*'s opening section, "Home," where her experiences teach her not only that whiteness is a "badge of power" but also that for some Americans racial identity is malleable rather than stable: "All the good things were theirs . . . because for the present they had power and the badge of that power was whiteness. . . . She possessed the badge, and unless there was someone *to tell* she could possess the power for which it stood" (*PB* 73–74). Angela also realizes that race is predicated on a belief in the body as a repository of racial "traits" and "instincts" and is thereby rooted in a politics of visibility. Angela chooses to play race against itself by "telling" only her "whiteness": " 'I am both white and Negro and look white. Why shouldn't I declare for the one that will bring me the greatest happiness, prosperity and respect?' " (*PB* 80). Fauset seems to argue for a view of race as neither a self-contained polarization of white and nonwhite nor a stable, reliable text written on the body, yet she also inscribes a rather essentialist view of race in certain scenes. Depicting Angela dressing for her first date with Roger—a man she quickly discovers is a racist, making the credibility of her performance all the more necessary and subversive—Fauset invokes the racialization of gender identities as well as beliefs in the body as an index of "racial character." "There was never very much colour in her cheeks, but her skin was *warm and white*, there was *vitality beneath her pallor*; her hair was *warm*, too, . . . there were little tendrils and wisps and curls in front and about the temples which *no amount of coaxing could subdue*. . . . Her dress was *flame-colour*. . . . The neck was high in back and *girlishly modest* in front" (*PB* 122, emphasis added). Fauset plays on the idea of race read in the body by invoking the notion that blackness—a warm vitality lurking beneath fair skin and in hair that cannot be completely straight-ened—cannot be "subdued" and will betray the passer, even if only in very sub-tle ways, and by representing Angela's whiteness as a "pallor" finding expression in a high-necked and "girlishly modest" dress.

Angela, in an ironic parody of the mulatta as an effete hybrid, is represented as making herself up for a performance that is neither stereotypically white nor black but a hybridization of the two. Theorizing parody as an "intentional sty-listic hybrid," Bakhtin argues: "Every type of intentional stylistic hybrid is more or less dialogized. This means that the languages that are crossed relate to each other . . . there is an argument between languages [and] . . . styles. . . . But it is not a dialogue in the narrative sense, nor in the abstract sense; rather, it is a dia-logue between points of view, each with its own concrete language that cannot be translated into the other" (*Dialogic* 75–76). Going beyond a simple reversal in which passing entails "becoming" white, Fauset represents Angela as undertak-ing a hybridized performance incorporating both stereotyped whiteness and blackness, a parody of racial difference in the Bakhtinian sense. It is important to note Bakhtin's qualification that each dialogized language or style of the intentional hybrid as parody "cannot be translated into" the other. As Sarah Ahmed puts it, "[t]he process of fixation where identities are adopted through dress and manner, also involves the threatening potential of its own unfixabil-ity," so that passing becomes not "passing for" the "other" but "passing through hybridity" or "traversing . . . distinct identities" (100, 98). Rather than "betray-ing her race," these indications that Angela's act of passing is a hybridized per-formance politicize and render subversive what has often solely been regarded as a maneuver complicitous with racial hegemony. Robert Young argues that it is the double-voicedness of hybridity that makes it an effective challenge to race as "pure, fixed, and separate." "[H]ybridity . . . works simultaneously in two ways: 'organically,' hegemonizing, creating new spaces, structures, scenes, and 'inten-tionally,' diasporizing, intervening as a form of subversion, translation, transfor-mation. This doubleness is important both politically and theoretically, [since] it can easily be objected that hybridization assumes . . . the prior existence of pure, fixed and separate antecedents," contends Young. "Hybridization as creolization involves fusion, the creation of a new form, which can then be set against the old form, of which it is partly made up. Hybridization as 'raceless chaos' by contrast, produces no stable new form but rather something closer to . . . a racial hetero-geneity, discontinuity, the permanent revolution of forms" (25).

Angela neither "becomes" white nor "remains" black; rather, Fauset suspends these within the mulatta figure. Angela's performance comprises both identities, and while Roger and the novel's other white characters do "mistake" Angela for white, there is evidently a certain blackness to her performance of whiteness that an African American teacher seems to notice at a party given by Angela's bohemian friends: "The young woman [was] perfectly at ease in her deep chair . . . with a slightly detached, amused objectivity . . . which she had for everyone in the room including Angela at whom she had glanced once rather sharply" (*PB* 115). Amy Robinson's argument that passing is "a triangular theater of identity" enables us to read this scene as yet another instance of Fauset's play on taxonomic fever and "New Negro" identity politics. "In response to the threat of the pass," contends Robinson, "members of the in-group resubstantiate the ground of identity endangered by the passer" ("It Takes One" 721). Suggesting it takes one to know one, Fauset's scene positions the "detached and amused" black schoolteacher as what Robinson calls the "in-group clairvoyant," who along with the passer and her or his white "dupes" form a triangle that "poses the question of the passer's 'real' identity as a function of the lens through which it is viewed. Resituating the question of knowing and telling in the terms of two competing discourses of recognition, the pass emerges as a discursive encounter between two epistemological paradigms" (Robinson, "It Takes One" 723–34). We could say that while the clairvoyant reads race through an essentialist lens—the passer's real identity is knowable, the dupe sees only the performance—the passer is taken to be the white person she or he performs as. Rather than configuring Angela's "real" identity as ultimately detectable by an insider, then, this scene and the conversation in *Passing* where race and its detectability are discussed work to play essentialism and constructionism against one another. Fauset and Larsen refuse to take a position in the identity debates of their day and instead expose their interdependence—the "authentic" or real is inconceivable without, and inextricable from, the performance or construct.

Critics have argued, however, that the ending of *Plum Bun* marks it as a conventional novel of passing because eventually "the passer learns that, regardless of the motivations for passing, such a choice has overwhelming costs" (Little 173).[20] Such assessments have not recognized that Fauset, in fact, violates the convention of returning the repentant passer to the black community and disappoints the expectations aroused by this section's title, "Home Again," by making Angela most at home when on the move between Harlem and Greenwich Village, between black and white, and between America and Europe. Fauset "redeems" Angela's transgression against her family ties and "race loyalty," conventional consequences of choosing to pass for white, in a sentimentalized fashion that paradoxically moves her farther from the return to "home" inscribed in narratives of passing. Angela comes to see her life as a white woman as "pale" and, coupled with the melodrama of her love for Anthony Cross (who is engaged to her sister, Virginia), is represented as fittingly "punished" for her transgressions. Angela contemplates death "more than once" as an escape from her suffering, but her "blackness" is credited with her determination to "set up a dogged fight. . . . She thought then of black people . . . and of all the odds against living which a cruel, relentless fate had called on them to endure. And she saw them as a people powerfully, almost overwhelmingly, endowed with the essence of life" (*PB* 309). In romantic racialist rhetoric, Fauset represents Angela as saved from death by a black "essence of life" and a willingness to endure all cruelty, from which she gains a "newly developed sympathy and under-standing" that makes her think of others in an ideally selfless manner. Angela is certainly "re-educated," but rather than returning home to her family and community, she decides to live "a double life, move among two sets of acquaintances . . . when it seemed best to be coloured she would be coloured; when it was best to be white she would be that" (*PB* 252–53). Fauset represents Angela's life within and passing between white and black as both a performance and the "natural" consequence of her being neither white nor black but both. Yet while Angela's biraciality places her within both races, she also realizes that much of her life will be a performance of both the identity she chooses to adopt in different circumstances and that determined for her by others: "I can't placard myself, and I suppose there will be lots of times when in spite of myself I'll be 'passing'" (*PB* 373). Even in what appears to be a conventional ending, Fauset holds in tension the notion that identity is constructed, and therefore performable, and that it is essential; that identitarian categories can be subverted and played upon at will *and* that they determine our identities. At times when others assume she is white, even though she has not chosen to pass in that moment, Angela will become what Carole-Anne Tyler calls "the object, not the subject, of a desire for white mimicry," or of a desire on the part of whites around her for "the presumptive universal, the unmarked 'same'" undisturbed by difference (215).

Fauset exceeds the confines of conventional narratives of passing, just as Angela exceeds racial boundaries to move not only between white and black, mediating their limits as the mulatta figure has traditionally been read, but also within both racial communities. This inscription of excess is characteristic of mimicry as a political strategy, as Homi Bhabha argues: "[T]he discourse of mimicry is constructed around an *ambivalence*; in order to be effective, mimicry must continually produce its slippage, its excess, its difference . . . . [M]imicry is therefore stricken by an indeterminacy: mimicry emerges as the representation of a difference that is itself a process of disavowal" (86). Fauset's novel disavows the narratives of passing it mimics. Angela's performance repeatedly exceeds the boundaries designed to contain her on one side of the color line or the other, as Fauset represents racial difference as so overdetermined that such distinctions become indeterminate, much like Angela's identity itself. In the end, Angela's racial identity is represented as so ambivalent that it is difficult to determine what is performance and what is "genuine," what is constructed and what is "natural." This exploration of mimicry as parodic excess is a shared aspect of Fauset's *Plum Bun* and Larsen's *Passing*; moreover, mimicry and imitation are also central to African American expressivity. Gates quotes Zora Neale Hurston on imitation in *The Signifying Monkey*: " 'The Negro,' she admits, 'the world over, is famous as a mimic. But this in no way damages his standing as an original.' . . . 'Mimicry,' moreover, 'is an art in itself.' . . . Negroes, she concludes, mimic 'for the love of it,' rather than because they lack originality. Imitation is the Afro-American's central art form" (118). While Hurston notes that mimicry is a pleasurable end in itself for African American artists, it is also an avenue to hybridizing literary traditions to create a uniquely African American tradition combining both ancestral and New World forms, as Gates argues, and a strategy of politicized critique as these writers employ it. Fauset and Larsen, then, participate in an African American expressive tradition of mimicry or "Signifyin(g)" at a generic level, by signifying on narratives of passing and, at a representational level, by signifying on constructions of race- and class-inflected gender identities.

Like Angela Murray, Clare Kendry tests boundaries that she can at times subvert but that are also reasserted in a decidedly forceful way. Clare could be said to pass between white and black so successfully that she renders herself racially ambiguous; her white husband jokingly teases that Clare's complexion is "gettin' darker and darker" and that one day he might "find she's turned into a nigger" (*P* 171), but he never once suspects she has gone the other way and only discovers she's "turned" white when Irene gives her away. Neither Irene's African American nor white friends seem able to tell if Clare is as white as she seems or if she is black. As Irene so accurately perceives, Clare is "some creature utterly strange and apart," determined to live neither wholly within white or black circles (*P* 172). Clare's excessive performance spills over limits in ways Irene finds threatening, but the excesses of Clare's performance also signal Larsen's revision of the narrative of passing. Narratives of passing are largely driven by the fear of detection, a fear that is often expressed through the notion of "atavism"—the belief that blood will tell eventually. Many novels of passing conclude with a return: either the passer discovers her or his "error" and returns, enlightened, to family and the African American community or the passer is discovered (or that discovery imminent) and is forced to resume living as black. Larsen invokes the fear of detection in order to play on it, and Clare, it seems, is in on the game. Irene repeatedly discourages Clare from coming to Harlem under the pretext of concern for her "safety." And while Irene is clearly more concerned with her own safety than Clare's, Clare, conversely, is so unconcerned that she seems to take a certain delight in placing herself in situations of potential jeopardy, "stepping always on the edge of danger. Always aware, but not drawing back or turning aside" (*P* 143). Rather than dressing "inconspicuously" to avoid attracting attention, she chooses to "flaunt" herself: "Clare, exquisite, golden, fragrant, flaunting, in a stately gown of shining black taffeta, whose long, full skirt lay in graceful folds about her slim golden feet; her glistening hair drawn smoothly back into a small twist at the nape of her neck; her eyes sparking like jewels. Irene . . . regretted that she hadn't counselled Clare to wear something ordinary and inconspicuous" (*P* 203). Clare draws attention to herself and to the excesses of her performance, rousing suspicion that she may be "acting" and eventually attracting the speculation that there is something in her that must be "found out" (*P* 205).

Clare's flaunting display not only runs the risk of exposing her passing but also works to expose and transgress the very limits of the identities she performs. While transgressing limits jeopardizes Clare's ability to continue her performance, reading her passing through Homi Bhabha allows us to configure its very power as lying in those self-jeopardizing moments, in their "*performative deformative* structure that does not simply revalue . . . or transpose values 'cross-culturally' . . . [but] introduce[s] another locus of inscription and intervention, another hybrid, 'inappropriate' enunciative site" (241–42). Clare's skin color becomes neither a mark of inclusion nor victimage but "an ivory mask" with which she accesses and challenges notions of race as embodied and fixed in the body (*P* 157). Clare's skin is both "ivory" and "gettin' darker and darker." Rather than concealing a mastery of whiteness, Clare's "ivory face was what it always was . . . *a little masked*" (*P* 220). Clare uses her body and that body's acts—the supposed indices of her identity—as masks that both conceal and display, are both ivory and dark. While Angela's decision to pass as white or black is arguably passive because it is dependent on situations and the perceptions of others that are beyond her control, Clare's daring and flaunting performance seems to be more aggressive and, thereby, more disruptive and subversive. Clare, rather than being satisfied to be who others take her for, or what might be most beneficial in a given situation, seems bent on displaying a difference in her performances that will unsettle categories of identity.

Following Judith Butler's contention that "gender is always a doing . . . performatively constituted by the very 'expressions' that are said to be its results" (*Gender Trouble* 24–25), Clare's performance of both whiteness and blackness refuses a conformity to those identities and, therefore, an affirmation of their stability and a contribution to their regulation. Whiteness and blackness do not preexist in some "original" state that Clare re-presents. Rather, whiteness and blackness are continually reconstituted over time, a reconstitution that can be traced, as we saw in Chapter 1, in legal decisions regarding racial identity and in racial theories advanced by a variety of "sciences," and one we can see being radically "unfixed" in Clare's passing. We might translate Butler's notion of "gender trouble" to a racialized context and argue that Clare transforms whiteness and blackness to include something other that renders them impure and unstable.

Like Angela's, Clare's performative identities also challenge us to rethink our understanding of passing. Passing for white has conventionally been understood as an act of deception taken up by a "black" individual, an act in which the individual conceals or sacrifices his or her "authentic" identity. However, in order to be physically able to pass for white an individual must be of both African American and Anglo-American descent, must "be" both black and white. Clare further places race in a state of crisis by confusing any distinction between original and copy. Clare's copy of "natural" whiteness in passing confuses both the "authenticity" of the whiteness she performs and the blackness she supposedly conceals. Larsen foregrounds this confusion in an exchange between Irene and Clare:

> "What about background? Family, I mean. Surely you can't just drop down on people from nowhere and expect them to receive you with open arms, can you?"
>
> Clare cast a glance of repressed amusement across the table at her. . . . "[I]t wasn't necessary. There were my aunts, you see, respectable and authentic enough for anything or anybody."

"I see. They were 'passing' too."

"No. They weren't. They were white." (*P* 187)

Irene "mistakes" passing, not the supposed original of whiteness it imitates, as "authentic enough for anything or anybody," and the existence of an authentic "natural" is called into question with her "error." Samira Kawash argues that "the passing narrative . . . is about the *failure* of blackness or whiteness to provide the grounds for a stable, coherent identity. Blackness and whiteness as they emerge in the passing narrative belie the possibility of identity or authenticity that would allow one to be unequivocally black or white" (63). However, this is only true of some passing narratives and holds for most only until the drive to "return" the passer to blackness draws the narrative to a close. All narratives of passing do not destabilize the power invested in race as a coherent category of identity; in fact, many simply reassert that power, while some passing narratives, like *Passing* and *Plum Bun*, work to do more than subvert their culture's logic of racial difference.

Just as we can argue that Clare unsettles received understandings of race as natural and fixed by passing between blackness and whiteness, she can also be read as unsettling sexuality as a valence of identity. Clare lives as heterosexual with her white husband, yet she also flirts with homosexuality in a number of "encounters" with Irene that Deborah McDowell has convincingly argued form a homosexual subtext to Larsen's novel.[21] However, reading Clare's sexuality as homosexual passing for heterosexual, as McDowell's reading suggests, elides the possibility that Clare is in fact "passing" between these sexualities, neither of which is more "authentic" than the other, more true to who Clare is. Clare does "caress" Irene with her smile, her touch, and her kiss in flirtations that clearly appeal to Irene, who is repeatedly struck by how "lovely" Clare is. With Irene, our gaze lingers on Clare in what are decidedly sensual descriptions:

[T]hat pale gold hair, which, unsheared still, was drawn loosely back from a broad brow. . . . Her lips, painted a brilliant geranium-red, were sweet and sensitive and a little obstinate. A tempting mouth. The . . . ivory skin had a peculiar soft lustre. And the eyes were magnificent! dark, sometimes absolutely black, always luminous, and set in long, black lashes. Arresting eyes, slow and mesmeric . . . mysterious and concealing. . . . [T]here was about them something exotic. (*P* 161)

However, Larsen is also careful to point out Clare's flirtatious behavior with men; Clare turns "provocative" smiles and her "husky voice" on waiters, her husband, and the husbands of other women as well (*P* 220–21). This act of passing for and between straight and queer is yet another instance of the subversive disruption Clare's performance presents, for it challenges our notions of sexuality as fixed rather than another performative identity.

Still, even as we can read their narratives through theories of identity as performative, Fauset and Larsen do not deny or ignore that such transgression carries with it punishments. Valerie Smith speculates that she finds "discussions of the performativity of race and gender . . . of limited usefulness precisely because . . . I resist the evacuation of historical experience from the construction of raced and gendered bodies" (51). However, texts like Fauset's and Larsen's, like those of Frances Harper and Pauline Hopkins before them, enable readings of race as performative, even as they work throughout to inscribe the historical experience of African American women in their explorations of identity politics.[22] Nor do Fauset and Larsen ignore what has been, historically, the outcome of transgressing the color line in America. However much Angela might continue to pass at her will, she is nevertheless banished from American society with Fauset's decision to relocate her to Paris, where she may appear to be far less threatening. But that removal also acknowledges the realities of racism in America at a time when African Americans were being lynched on the mere suspicion that they had stepped out of place. Fauset suggests that, while seeing identity as construct and radically unfixed has political potential, the potential of passing for both black and white in America is severely limited and imminently dangerous. Clare's "punishment" is realized rather than suggested—she falls to her death from a sixth-floor window. While Larsen leaves the cause of Clare's death ambiguous, inviting readers to imagine that her husband or Irene may have pushed her or that Clare jumped, she clearly underscores the fact that Irene's and John Bellew's identities are resecured with Clare's death. In their endings, then, Fauset's and Larsen's novels acknowledge the very real material effects of passing on the lives of their characters.

In their use of the passing mulatta to challenge notions of essential racial difference and to dramatize the limits and potentials of identity politics in their time, Fauset and Larsen are not only at their most political but also their most relevant to the continuing debates over "blackness" and identity politics. By carefully attending to the complex imbrications of gender, race, class, and sexuality, they suggest that choosing either authentic or performable blackness (and whiteness) will not sufficiently address the investments in and resulting contests over this identity, nor will doing so adequately attend to the highly varied material conditions impinging upon it at particular moments and in specific locations. Fauset and Larsen further develop the mulatta figure as their predecessors mobilized her, making her a trope through which to question the interimplications of identitarian categories kept in place and policed on both sides of the color line. The mulatta's ambiguity and ambivalence make her an ideal figure through which to interrogate the epistemological paradigms undergirding taxonomic fever and its debates over essential, "authentic" identity and identity as constructed and performable, debates that continue to charge the field of African American studies today.

Epilogue

The "Passing Out" of Passing and the Mulatta?

Despite the varied political uses to which African American women have put the mulatta, for some time she has been a vexed figure in African American literary studies. The lack of a concentrated effort to study how this figure might operate in different historical moments for African American writers and the critical dismissal, if not hostility, the mulatta has met with are telling. The mulatta articulates something about race with which many continue to be uncomfortable and is very much at the center, rather than marking or mediating the borders, of an American racial imaginary and its color line. Consequently, this figure continues to have relevance to ongoing debates over race, identity, and a politics of affiliation. And if, as Paul Gilroy has recently noted, "[f]or many racialized populations, 'race' and the hard-won, oppositional identities it supports are not to be lightly or prematurely given up" (12), a figure whose racial "identity" or "loyalty" is ambiguous and one who questions what we understand race to be provokes a good deal of anxiety both for those whom race has empowered and those whom it has historically dispossessed. This may explain why, in their attention to public constructions of racialized identities, the texts of African American women focusing on the mulatta have often been read as eliding those privately authored African American identities that are informed by ancestrally African and uniquely African American cultural forms. However, in attending to publicly authored identities and those lived experiences and cultural forms that, in part, comprise privately authored African American identities, these texts are both points around which the debate over what race means has been pursued and illustrations or enactments of that debate in narrative form.[1] Questions of authenticity and representativeness that have dogged the mulatta since her earliest consideration in African American studies arise from continuing "uncertainty about the limits of particularity and solidarity" inside what Gilroy calls (and questions) "the racial collective" (179).

Rather than mediating or simply exploring and expressing the interracial, then, the mulatta is a highly politicized and significant figure, however uncomfortable she may be to consider. We have much to learn from the way in which she has been developed, toward political ends, in the work of African American women from the mid-nineteenth through the mid-twentieth century, an extended period in which we see her doing rather different work at different moments. While statutes and legal decisions attempted to erase her threatening biraciality and mark what was her frequent physical unreadability, the mulatta has persisted for African American women writers and speakers as a vehicle for challenging the color line. In what we should identify as a performance genealogy that "attend[s] to 'counter-memories' or the disparity between history as discursively transmitted and memory as publicly enacted" (Roach 26), African American women have refused to allow the threat the mulatta poses to be contained either by juridical interdict or the "tragic mulatta" narrative. Even when she seems closest to appearing simply as a "whitened" figure who enables dialogue across the color line in the work of Ellen Craft and Sarah Parker Remond, she is used to signify on and challenge the facile identification and risk-filled empathy she elicited. That empathy and identification were skillfully managed by Craft and Remond, who subtly but repeatedly challenged their audiences to recognize a distinct difference between their own material conditions and those of the enslaved, be it through the engraving of Craft's disguise used to escape slavery or through Remond's references to the sale of mulattas and the bondswoman's sufferings experienced "in her own person." As the mulatta is mobilized by African American women writers and speakers, she variously works to critique political movements and organizations that would elide "race" and collapse the differences it makes in order to advance their own causes; to challenge notions of race as a strict black-white binary, racialized constructs of gender, and intraracial class politics; and to significantly extend debates regarding "authentic" blackness. Far from operating in predictable and limited ways, the mulatta was a figure African American women returned to repeatedly in public appearances, oratory, and fiction as a trope that enabled a rather complex challenge to ideologies and hierarchies opposing or threatening to elide the political concerns of black women. African American women writers and speakers foregrounded public constructions of blackness, whiteness, and womanhood that circulated on both sides of the color line and employed the subversive potential of signifying on supposedly "natural" identities and affinities.

I would not want to suggest, however, that this study's texts comprise the only, or even the most definitive, politicized uses of the mulatta figure in the work of

African American women. Nor would I want to leave the impression that the mulatta ceases to be a viable figure for black women's critique come the 1930s. Consequently, *The Mulatta and the Politics of Race* concludes by looking briefly at two additional texts published by African American women in the 1950s. Dorothy Lee Dickens's *Black on the Rainbow* (1952) and Reba Lee's autobiographical text, *I Passed for White* (1955), center on mulattas passing for white, but rather than exploring racial liminality to the extent that their predecessors Jessie Fauset and Nella Larsen did in *Plum Bun* and *Passing*, these authors return the passer to her community, where she chooses to identify as a black woman. Reba Lee and Dickens's Hilda Ann Parker choose the rootedness of their families and African American communal traditions over the rootlessness they have found passing for white to be. While Lee and Dickens do figure race and womanhood as performative and unstable, they also stress self-affirming identifications that emphasize community and the fixity of a unified racial identity. Like Frances Harper's *Iola Leroy* and Pauline Hopkins's *Contending Forces*, both *Black on the Rainbow* and *I Passed for White* center on mulattas who are born and raised in the South and later travel north seeking greater opportunities. Both Hilda Ann Parker and Reba Lee travel from rural Georgia northward, echoing the three great black migrations: the first saw African Americans in the late 1870s through the 1880s leave Louisiana and Mississippi for the plains of Kansas; during the second, spanning 1916 through the 1930s, African Americans traveled north to the promised lands of cities such as Chicago and New York; the third, between 1940 and 1966, was under way when these works were written and published. A constancy across the fictional texts I have focused on is their publication during one of these three waves of black exodus from the South, a fact that may in part account for their attention to issues of identity and external definitions thrust upon one by whites and African Americans alike. The South has various associations for the mulatta, as we have seen. The scene of slavery, family left behind, and the mulatta's unique sexual exploitation for Ellen Craft and Sarah Remond, the South becomes a site of redemption or commitment to a life dedicated to "the race" for Frances Harper's and Pauline Hopkins's heroines. And while the South is largely absent in Jessie Fauset's *The Chinaberry Tree* and *Plum Bun*, it is problematized as a site of increasing restriction, physical weakening, and impending death for Nella Larsen's Helga Crane. Dickens and Lee return to the notion of African American community and/or the South as redemptive that we encountered in Harper's and Hopkins's novels and look forward to the centrality of the South and communal roots, however problematic, in the late-twentieth-century renaissance of black women novelists.[2]

In works centering on mulatta characters, a common narrative strategy used to mark their "difference" from both Anglo- and African Americans is a childhood education in racial identity through a form of "othering" at the hands of either black or white children. Often called a scene of "racial recognition," Dickens employs this familiar device in *Black on the Rainbow*, with Hilda Ann's schoolmates rejecting her for her color:

> "Who, me . . . respect her? Hell, no! Never in my life will I be found respecting the likes of a dern old mulatto gal. . . . [W]here in the devil did she hail from anyway? Shuh! She certainly don't blend with any of us. Look! Look! She's too doggone pale! And supposed to be colored, too. . . . She ain't nothing but a pink toe, passing as a Negra. . . . God don't own such and Satan wants no part of you. So where is your place . . . ?" (13)

Thus Hilda Ann is confronted with her color, with her schoolmates' opinion that, as a mulatta, she is too white and not black enough to be African American. Hilda Ann's fair skin is proof not only that at least two ancestors in her family's past have not "stayed in their place" but also that she is out of and without place. This childhood accusation that Hilda Ann is "passing as a Negra" in her rural southern African American community foreshadows her later decision to pass for white and foregrounds the mulatta as an outsider from both whiteness and blackness. In *I Passed for White*, Reba moves to a new neighborhood, enrolls at a new school, and is immediately "mistaken" for white by one of her classmates. Shortly after, the class "discovers" she is African American and ridicules her: " 'Oh, you Brownie, is you-all lonesome for your ole Virginia?' . . . Everybody was laughing about the smartie little nigger cutie who had tried to be white. A boy yelled at me, 'Yah, you smoke!' " (43–44). Reba learns that while "whites seemed to have as many shades as the coloreds ever had" (33), many white Americans see race as an absolute distinction between white and black, rather than a matter of degree: "People got tired of talking after the novelty [of Reba's unintentional passing] wore off but I knew I was marked" (46). Both Dickens and Lee foreground race as based on a politics of visibility or "a matter of being able to read a marked body in relation to unmarked bodies, where unmarked bodies constitute the currency of normative whiteness" (Wiegman 170–71). Even though the visible or corporeal may be an unreliable index of race, Dickens and Lee—like Fauset and Larsen before them—represent both white and black Americans as obsessed with marking the mulatta's racially ambiguous body.

Like the other African American women speakers and writers in this study, Dickens and Lee also attend to the historical and material specificity of black lived experience as they explore identity as malleable and multiple. However, the context in which we should place Dickens's and Lee's mulatta figures and narratives also includes the "personal narratives published in the 1950s in popular black periodicals ranging from recognized sources such as *Ebony* and *Jet* to more obscure . . . titles such as *Color* and *Tan*," which Gayle Wald has called "postpassing narratives" (118). Wald characterizes such narratives as part of a larger shift come the 1950s, heralded by these same periodicals as the end of passing, or its "passing out," a change credited to an "eliminat[ion of] the race factor in employment" allowing "the thousands of Negroes who 'passed' . . . [to] 'return' to their race" (119). Consequently, postpassing narratives staged "the obsolescence of racial passing," "expressed heightened optimism regarding the lifting of restraints on African American citizenship," "fail[ed] to represent class . . . [and] minimized the effects of racism and color hierarchy while downplaying class and gender divisions within apparently stable and homogeneous 'black' communities" (Wald 119, 118, 121). Postpassing narratives may well have been less dominant than Wald suggests, however, and were certainly not the only representations of the mulatta and passing read by blacks and whites. Dickens's and Lee's texts are markedly different from this genre, not only in their attention to colorism within their characters' communities but also in their attention to, rather than elision of, class as it intersects with race.

Dickens represents Hilda Ann's family as southern farmers who, apart from Hilda Ann, have had to forgo an education in order to work. Like thousands of southern blacks who migrated North, leaving the back-breaking field work that barely sustained them for the "promised land" of better-paying factory work, Hilda Ann's cousin Elis leaves Georgia for greater opportunities in New York. He has heard he can find work as "a junk man or a bootblack" and eventually earn enough "t' 'stablish a lit'l business of my own . . . an' above all things, learn how t' read an' write my own name" (7–8). Similarly, in the opening chapter of *I Passed for White*, Lee details limited employment opportunities for African Americans in the South, as well as union boycotts and white exploitation of poorly paid African American workers. Reba's adoptive father works as a painter during the 1930s: "Men walked the streets looking for work. Pa . . . said he was lucky that the union didn't take colored men so he could cut union prices and get jobs. . . . Pa talked about the [white] families he worked for, how some . . . [found] fault, making him put on more coats of paint than agreed on because they knew he needed the work and couldn't kick" (6). Her grandmother "went out dressmaking, making five dollars a day," while her mother cooked and served in white homes for "fifty cents an hour . . . never [working] for less than four hours. . . . When she cooked the dinner, she made five dollars" (6–7). While Lee and Dickens go on to interrogate the interimplication of race and gender and identities as constructed, mediated, and performable, they do not elide the ways in which ideologies impinge on the lives and material conditions of African American men and women. Neither text represents the kind of postwar optimism Wald cites as characteristic of postpassing narratives. When Hilda Ann returns to Georgia, she stops first at Columbus's cotton and tobacco exchange, where her Uncle Josh had "traded cotton," but she finds the exchange "practically deserted, except for two robust white men . . . stacking bales of raw cotton in the distance" (207). Later she hears of her friend Jake Simmons's lynching for suspected robbery. When Reba returns to her family in Chicago, she stresses that "they were just the same . . . unchanged" (274), leaving us to wonder where the promise of new "opportunities for upward class mobility . . . [and] social prosperity" characteristic of postpassing narratives is in Lee's 1950s America (Wald 131).

Nor do Lee and Dickens minimize the effects of racism and racial fantasies focused on African American women, as postpassing narratives did. Lee foregrounds the exploitation of African American women by white men, a characteristic her narrative shares with Ellen Craft's appearances, Sarah Parker Remond's antislavery lectures, and Frances Harper's, Pauline Hopkins's, Jessie Fauset's, and Nella Larsen's novels. Lee represents the danger white men represent to African American women both during slavery and well after emancipation. Reba's great-great-grandmother was freed by her master and given a house and a small tract of land; however, she also bore him children in a relationship necessarily fraught with the power imbalance between master and slave. One suspects that the house and land he gave her was as much a measure to keep quiet his "indiscretions" and remove her from the vicinity of his own home, family, and other slaves as it was an effort to provide and care for her and their children: " 'My own grandfather was one of the richest white men in the county—till the war ruined him. He made my grandmother a freedwoman, she and her baby that became my father, and he gave her a nice piece of land with a house to herself. That was in eighteen-fifty-seven,' said Gran precisely" (4). Reba's mother, this slave owner's great-granddaughter, experiences a twentieth-century version of this kind of relationship: while waiting tables at a restaurant near a university, she attracts the attention of a white student from an affluent family and is left pregnant and alone after he learns she is African American. Lee implies that it is quite likely he knew she was not white all along, invoking the exoticization of the African American female in the white mind and its consequences for African American women:

> The boy was a white student . . . from a rich family. . . . The way Gran heard it he didn't know at first that Mom was colored, but I don't see how that could have been because you could spot Mom. . . . She [Gran] never knew whether he was really crazy about my mother and his parents had taken him away or whether he got scared and ran off, or whether he'd been fooling Mom from the start. Anyway, he was gone . . . and Mom didn't know where he lived and if she had known what could they have done about it? (14)

Lee inscribes this history of sexual exploitation in her narrative in a way that both problematizes her own marriage to a white man while passing and affirms African American community as a site of safety and well-being over and against the privilege and so-called protection of life with her white bourgeois husband.

Perhaps the most significant way in which Dickens's and Lee's narratives differ from the postpassing narratives of the 1950s is in their contemplation of identity as performative and, consequently, their questioning of social hierarchies based upon race, class, and gender. While the "social function" of postpassing narratives "was not necessarily to critique existing social structures, but rather to posit the right of 'black' people, as racially-determined subjects, to inhabit those structures" (Wald 130), Dickens's and Lee's narratives, like the work of the other African American women we have examined, are decidedly less optimistic and more critical of both black and white Americans' notions of race. Hilda Ann and Reba perform whiteness so well that those they come to know, work, and live with never suspect them of passing. Dickens and Lee represent passing as an enactment of whiteness and underscore the dramatic or performative aspect of character and identity in different ways. Lee links "being" white with the credibility of its performance, as well as with the meanings produced by and read in both the body's appearance and behavior: "On the beach I wore a big shade hat and rubbed cream into my skin to protect it. I wasn't going to get any brown look. . . . I *was* white. I had a place and a position. I was as thrilled as an actress who sees her name in lights for the first time" (156–57). If identity is both performed by and visible in the body, as Lee represents it here, she must also guard against *being* black. Not only does she stay out of the sun to keep her complexion pale, but she also worries about the authenticity of her performance of propriety, fearing that her husband might detect a blackness in her: "Once he even drew away when I turned to him in bed, saying something about we mustn't overdo—and I realized I'd have to watch myself, that perhaps I was more loving than a white girl would be. I had to watch my words, too. Living so close, so relaxed and intimate, it was hard to be careful" (155). Lee characterizes Reba as internalizing racial fantasies of black female sexuality, a sexuality she must keep in check with a virtue and chasteness she understands as "white." While she passes for a white woman—a performance which in itself unsettles such constructions of racialized womanhood and sexuality and, necessarily, blackness and whiteness—like Fauset's Laurentine Strange and Larsen's Helga Crane, Reba internalizes the very stereotypes her performance subverts. Rather than seeing the erotic black female as an icon of manufactured blackness, Reba polices her behavior hoping to keep hidden a sexualized black essence.

Dickens underscores identity as performative by representing Hilda Ann as a performer in revues and musical comedies staged in New York. Ironically, Hilda Ann's greatest success is landing a part in a musical comedy set in the South, scripted in "Negro dialect," and performed by an "all-white" cast: " 'Harvest' was indeed a gay, spirited play. Many weeks were spent practicing and trying to adapt parts of it to typical Negro dialect. In this regard, Georgiana's kitchen became an auxiliary studio, where we heard Negro dialect in its natural environment. *This was a great help to me*" (119, emphasis added). Hilda Ann passes as a white woman acting the part of a rural southern black woman. In this particular scene, Dickens creates layers of identities all of which are enacted by, not inherent in, her heroine. Rather than fearing her "blackface" performance will betray her "true" racial identity, Hilda Ann's sustained act of passing for a white woman seems to have the effect of erasing any blackness in her. Hilda Ann is raised in the South by her extended family, all of whom are rural African Americans who speak in the vernacular. Yet Hilda Ann needs schooling in "Negro dialect in its natural environment" while passing for white in the North. Unlike Harper, Hopkins, Fauset, and Larsen, who represent passing for a "true woman" and/or white as hybridized performances, Dickens represents her heroine's act of passing across the color line as possibly working more to consolidate, rather than blur, racial identities in her performance. Her passage into whiteness is so complete as to virtually cancel out her experiences as a black child in the South.

On the level of conceptualizing race, such a representation seems decidedly less radical and poses less of a challenge to understandings of race as a unified binary than the ambivalent, ambiguous, and hybrid performances of Fauset's Angela Murray and Larsen's Clare Kendry. However, Dickens's white audience may have been quite disturbed by the thought that her heroine could "become" so white as to forget being raised black. "Negro dialect" was such a powerful marker of blackness to white Americans that Hilda Ann's need to learn it would be tantamount to a near-complete racial transmutation. In fact, white readers may have been far more unsettled by the possibility of Hilda Ann "becoming" white through passing than they were by narratives like Fauset's and Larsen's in which their heroines' blurred performances might be read as proof of a black racial essence that no amount of care could conceal. Those African American readers, on the other hand, who believed passing for white was a betrayal of the race might have read this scene as evidence of Hilda Ann's lost sense of self, her loss of place within African American community, and her loss of access to African American traditions and forms of cultural expressivity. Dickens could very well be working in this scene, then, toward unsettling her white readers' sense of identity and security while questioning whether "blackness" is, in fact, embedded in a strong sense of, and loyalty to, community and its expressive traditions. Dickens's form of address is complicated by the fact that Hilda Ann is characterized as never having spoken in the vernacular. She speaks throughout the novel in standard English, thereby confounding any sense of the vernacular as "authentically" black or of standard English as a marker of whiteness. If the vernacular is a cultural form of expressivity that approaches a "black" essence in some white minds and is regarded as uniquely African American by some blacks, Hilda Ann's race should enable her to access it through more than studied imitation. Her inability to do so works to critique such essentializing notions of blackness. Dickens's strategy of representation may at first seem to consolidate race as a unified binary of white to black, but her form of address complicates and challenges such an understanding of race.

Dickens not only uses complex forms of address as do the other black women writers and speakers in this study, she also signifies on notions of racialized womanhood in such a way that racial distinctions are called into question. When passing for white in Paris, Hilda Ann is propositioned by her show manager and falls into a relationship with him that she characterizes as "illicit." In fact, Mingo Diogenes is reputed to have had many affairs with white women who vie for his attention regardless of Hilda Ann's presence. Contrary to stereotypes of the black female as lascivious, Dickens pointedly characterizes her heroine as "an old-fashioned girl" who maintains her values and morality (if not her chastity), as well as a certain dignity and difference from the white women she calls "painted Jezebels" (181, 188). Hilda Ann "falls," then, as a "white" woman, "a victim of circumstances" and of the passing into whiteness that should improve them (225). Postpassing narratives tended to depict passing as an act that enabled access to greater opportunities and improved social well-being but one that exacted a sense of self and belonging. In contrast, Dickens questions what benefits accrue to whiteness in a gendered economy and refuses to minimize or ignore gender and its interimplication with race and class.

Similarly, during her early and intermittent acts of passing for white, Reba Lee is propositioned while window shopping on Michigan Avenue in Chicago. White men stop and ask her to dinner or coffee in hotels, believing she'll "start with ginger ale and end upstairs":

> At first, when a man tried to pick me up, I was embarrassed and got away from him quickly. But it happened again and again. . . . I'd be looking in a window . . . and a man would stop beside me. Always a white man, it was, never a colored, and that told me what I looked like. Generally he'd say "Pretty hat, isn't it?" . . . or more intimately, "See anything you like?"
>
> Sometimes I'd look startled or haughty, sometimes I'd give him a little smile, but I always moved away. (80)

While Reba always moves away from such men, their persistence indicates that the white women they approach do not always do so. Like Dickens, Lee stresses that not only are black women far from highly sexual and immoral, but the virtue supposedly "inherent" in whiteness is no guarantee that white women will not be exploited by white men. Harper, Hopkins, Fauset, and Larsen may have represented their mulatta heroines as passing for true or bourgeois white women and thereby challenging racialized gender identities, but they stopped short of stating that white women might fail to approach that ideal. Dickens and Lee, in contrast, quite openly critique the reification of white women at the expense of African American women.

These points of continuity and difference signal not only an intertextuality among these texts from the mid-nineteenth through the mid-twentieth century but also the way in which the politics pursued by black women often significantly differed from the larger political climate. Postpassing narratives might have affirmed a changing social and economic situation for African Americans in the United States come the 1950s, indulging in "a faith in postwar economic abundance [and] a faith . . . that such prosperity will . . . promote racial justice" (Wald 148), but African American women writers like Dickens and Lee seem to share more in the challenges their predecessors offered than in the optimism of their contemporaries.

In several ways, Dickens's and Lee's narratives echo Harper's *Iola Leroy* and Hopkins's *Contending Forces* much more than they seem in keeping with the postwar moment Wald describes. We might recall that Hopkins's Sappho Clark returns to New Orleans and takes up a maternal devotion to the son she had kept hidden and to the children she cares for while employed as a governess. Hopkins characterizes these choices as a form of sentimentalized redemption that enables Sappho both to come to terms with her victimized past and to find true love and a home with the Smith family. Sappho's initial "salvation" from rape at the hands of her white uncle and the racial violence that claims the lives of her family is administered by an African American order of nuns; her later redemption is begun in this same nunnery. Similarly, in *Black on the Rainbow*, Hilda Ann's redemption from lost virtue entails being reunited with her lost sister who has become a nun. In a chapter entitled "Bowels of the Deep," Hilda Ann promises her sister that she will " '*seek God* . . . [b]eginning now' " (202). Her sister, Violet, ushers Hilda Ann into punishment and contrition as well as redemption: " 'That scar on your face is the price of extreme folly; although there is happiness which may await you' " (203). But Hilda Ann's punishment for crossing racial lines extends to the loss of her sister in an accident on board a ship returning from Europe to the United States. This rather melodramatic turn is an interesting reversal of Hopkins's conclusion, which saw family reunited through a transatlantic voyage; indeed, both texts redeem their mulatta heroines through rather contrived events.

In *Passing for White*, Reba Lee salvages a disappointing and unfulfilling life as a white woman married to an affluent white man by choosing to identify as African American and return to her family. Like many of the confessional post-passing narratives, Reba chooses her "warm," "kind," and "unfailingly loyal" family in Chicago over the "less genuine, less understanding, less tolerant" whites she has lived among. Dickens, however, not only returns her heroine to her family in the South but marries her to a minister with whom she works on behalf of "the race" promoting a Washingtonian ethic of education and industry. Hilda Ann's marriage echoes those of Harper's Iola Leroy and Fauset's Melissa Paul in this way. Iola Leroy chooses to return to the South and dedicate her life to reconstruction efforts and racial uplift, choices Harper represents as the culmination of Iola's decision to identify as African American after having been raised as white. Significantly, this choice follows Iola's consideration to remain silent on the question of her African American background in order to gain employment in the North. Harper figures the measure of her heroine's decision to affirm an African American identity as a return to the South and life in a rural African American community, and Dickens's ending operates in much the same way. Hilda Ann affirms her pride as a "member of the Negro race" by marrying the Reverend Willy Marshall and "accompany[ing him] . . . on many of his college lecture tours, where lively debates and heated discussions were being thrashed out by prominent Negro Leaders" (227, 232). Together Hilda Ann and Willy attend meetings of the NAACP and conferences at Tuskegee where he delivers "eloquent speech[es]" and she compiles "sheaf[s] of quotations . . . for discussion" (235, 237).

While conclusions that detail redemptions or the punishment racial passing may exact would seem to nullify or retract the challenges Dickens's and Lee's narratives have posed to an American racial imaginary by returning the passer to her place, they are, rather, further explorations of identity and identification. By returning their mulatta heroines to African American communities and families, Dickens and Lee are not simply "putting them in their place," reinscribing publicly constructed identities or affirming postwar prosperity, but are conceptualizing African American identities as a complex interweaving of external and individual determinations of self. These writers question and subvert constructs of blackness and whiteness and explore both the potential of fluid identities and their limitations, much like Fauset and Larsen did before them.

Yet despite the echoes and similarities with their textual predecessors, we must also keep in sight the differences in Dickens's and Lee's texts, for these signal the way in which the mulatta is far from a fixed stereotype in the work of African American women but rather a vehicle for political challenge and debate. For Dickens and Lee, passing, and what can be interrogated through it, has not "passed out" with improving conditions for African Americans come the mid-twentieth century. And even though Hilda Ann and Reba return to their families and communities, black community is not figured as a haven or the site of increased economic opportunity and increased personal freedoms but from the beginning as the site of exclusive notions of blackness that alienate the very figures it would regard as "racially disloyal." Dickens and Lee look to external factors, as did the confessional passing narratives of their contemporaries, but also offer important critiques of intraracial dynamics such narratives tended to silence. Our understanding of passing at the mid-twentieth century, then, must include their work or we risk flattening what is, in fact, another moment in the mulatta's political use by black women writers. Moreover, we risk simply reiterating the claim that passing and passing narratives were dying out, with their last gasps reserved for a repudiation of crossing the color line. Such an end leaves the color line firmly in place, with those who "return" simply recrossing it in narratives that fail to question how it is both kept in place and ultimately contingent.

Notes

Introduction

1. For example, one of the first essay collections to focus on passing, Elaine Ginsberg's *Passing and the Fictions of Identity*, "originated in a call for papers for the annual Modern Language Association convention. The overwhelming number of submissions was evidence that the topic interested a wide range of scholars . . . in the field of literary and cultural studies" (Ginsberg vii). See also, for example, *diacritics* 24.2–3 (1994); Maria Carla Sánchez and Linda Scholssberg, eds., *Passing: Identity and Interpretation in Sexuality, Race, and Religion* (New York: New York University Press, 2001); and studies such as Laura Browder, *Slippery Characters: Ethnic Impersonators and American Identities* (Chapel Hill: University of North Carolina Press, 2000); M. Guilia Fabi, *Passing and the Rise of the African American Novel* (Urbana and Chicago: University of Illinois Press, 2001); Samira Kawash, *Dislocating the Color Line: Identity, Hybridity, and Singularity in African-American Narrative* (Stanford, Calif.: Stanford University Press, 1997); Gayle Wald, *Crossing the Line: Racial Passing in Twentieth-Century U.S. Literature and Culture* (Durham, N.C.: Duke University Press, 2000).

2. The works of Amy Robinson and Gayle Wald are notable exceptions.

3. See, for example, Elizabeth Young, "Confederate Counterfeit: The Case of the Cross-Dressed Civil War Soldier," in Ginsberg, *Passing and the Fictions of Identity*, 181–217; Judith Halberstam, "Brandon Teena, Billy Tipton, and Transgender Biography," in Sánchez and Schlossberg, *Passing*, 13–37.

4. This critical reception will be explored further in chapters that follow.

5. For an important examination of both this vernacular phrase and the critical tendency to construct a black woman's literary tradition that marginalizes those writers whose work falls between the slave narratives and the fiction of Zora Neale Hurston, see P. Gabrielle Foreman, "Looking Back from Zora, or Talking Out Both Sides My Mouth for Those Who Have Two Ears," *Black American Literature Forum* 24 (1990): 649–66.

6. See Chapter 5 of Fabi's *Passing and the Rise of the African American Novel* for a useful historical summary of criticism that has tended to dismiss African American fiction centered on "all-but-white characters" (Fabi 106).

7. I discuss the contours of the "tragic mulatta" plot and Child's creation of this figure in Chapter 2.

8. On the rise of this trope and the mulatta's function as proxy, see Jean Fagan Yellin, *Women and Sisters: The Antislavery Feminists in American Culture* (New Haven, Conn.: Yale University Press, 1989), and Karen Sànchez-Eppler, "Bodily Bonds: The Intersecting Rhetorics of Feminism and Abolitionism," *Representations* 24 (1988): 28–59. I will discuss the circulation of this trope in Chapter 2.

9. See Sterling Brown, *The Negro in American Fiction* (1937; New York: Argosy-Antiquarian, 1969). In the late 1950s Robert Bone used and slightly revised Brown's arguments from the 1930s, contending that black writers used mulatta and mulatto characters to argue the color line be rendered less strict for biracial individuals. See Robert Bone, *The Negro Novel in America* (1958; New Haven, Conn.: Yale University Press, 1968). I will refer to much of this criticism in chapters that follow.

10. For a very useful and extended summary of Brown's critical position on the mulatta, see Werner Sollers, *Neither White Nor Black Yet Both: Thematic Explorations of Interracial Literature* (New York: Oxford University Press, 1997), 223–25.

11. See also Judith Berzon, *Neither White Nor Black: The Mulatto Character in American Fiction* (New York: New York University Press, 1978). The most recent study of the mulatto in American fiction is by Sollers, *Neither White Nor Black Yet Both.*

12. In this sense, my choice of terminology— "the mulatta figure"—is much like Jennifer DeVere Brody's decision to coin the term "mulattaroon" in order to denote the "mixed-race" characters of British Victorian literature and culture upon which she focuses. See Jennifer DeVere Brody, *Impossible Purities: Blackness, Femininity, and Victorian Culture* (Durham, N.C.: Duke University Press, 1998).

13. See Chapter 1, note 14, for a brief etymology of this term's use in the United States.

14. While I'm not sure the texts on which I focus would bear this assertion out, folklorist Roger D. Abrahams contended in *Talking Black* (1976) that "black women . . . and 'to a certain extent children,' utilize 'more indirect methods of signifying'" (19). Gates calls these more indirect forms "mature forms of Signifyin(g)" but insists that "black men and women use indirection . . . to the same degree" (*Signifying* 77). I am uncomfortable with the association of black women and children as distinct from black men; however, the suggestion that black women signify in different ways than men deserves consideration.

15. For a critique of the use of Bakhtin in African American literary theory, including the work of Henderson and Gates, see Dorothy J. Hale, "Bakhtin in African American Literary Theory," *ELH* 61.2 (1994): 445–71.

16. Also, Joseph Roach, *Cities of the Dead: Circum-Atlantic Performance* (New York: Columbia University Press, 1996), connects Gates's "Signifyin(g)" and Margaret Thompson Drewal's examination of Yoruba ritual to notions of performance and the performative as "restored behavior" or behavior repeated "with a difference" (46).

17. See Michael Rogin, *Blackface, White Noise: Jewish Immigrants in the Hollywood Melting Pot* (Berkeley and Los Angeles: University of California Press, 1996); W. T. Lhamon Jr., *Raising Cain: Blackface Performance from Jim Crow to Hip Hop* (Cambridge: Harvard University Press, 1998). See also Susan Gubar, *Race Changes: White Skin, Black Face in American Culture* (New York: Oxford University Press, 1997).

18. James Oliver Horton notes that Election Days or governor elections were more than festive occasions: "The festival might last a week or more . . . and involved the election of a 'governor' or 'king.' . . . Among blacks these were important positions of substantial political power to which only men were elected. Moreover, those who voted for the office holders . . . during the festival days were men" (670).

Chapter 1. Fixing The Color Line

1. Focusing on nineteenth-century Southern cases, Gross argues that "over the course of the antebellum period, law made the 'performance' of whiteness increasingly important to the determination of racial status." She locates the performance of whiteness for men in the performance of citizenship, or "rights and privileges," and for women in the performance of "virtue and honor," or "good conduct and industry" (112, 157, 167). While I find Gross's work instructive, particularly her careful documentation of the Guy case, I disagree with her contention that the performance of whiteness reached a peak in court decisions regarding racial identity in the antebellum period. Rather, we see such decisions clustering later in the nineteenth century and their logic continuing to operate well into the twentieth.

2. In order to underscore my use of "the mulatta" as a figure or construct rather than a naive invocation of terminology at one time operative within a virulent system of racial categorization, I will use "mulatta" throughout, even though we know that the term was gendered under that system, with "mulatta" referring to women and "mulatto" to men.

3. See, for example, Peggy Pascoe, "Race, Gender, and the Privileges of Property: On the Significance of Miscegenation Law in United States History," *New Viewpoints in Women's History: Working Papers from the Schlesinger Library 50th Anniversary Conference*, ed. Susan Ware (Cambridge: Cambridge University Press, 1994), 99–122; Pascoe, "Miscegenation Law, Court Cases, and Ideologies of 'Race' in Twentieth-Century America," *Journal of American History* 83.1 (1996): 44–69; Eva Saks, "Representing Miscegenation Law," *Raritan* 8 (1988): 39–69. Ian F. Haney López's *White By Law*, with its focus on citizenship and naturalization in the early twentieth century, is a notable exception.

4. In *The White Man's Burden*, Winthrop Jordan notes that by 1666, Virginia laws were using the term "mulatto": "[L]aws dealing with Negro slaves began to add 'and mulattos,' presumably to make clear that mixed blood did not confer exemption from slavery" (84).

5. This law reveals the racial classification that held through the pre-Revolutionary era dividing whites from "others," as Joel Williamson documents: "By the middle of the eighteenth century . . . the legal status of mixed bloods was still only loosely defined, though in the white mind they were firmly classed as Negroes and in effect lumped on that side of the race bar. With them was a rather disparate collage of people of Indian and black ancestry, known as mustees, and offspring of Indian and white parents. For the most part, these people grew out of relations with the several hundred Indian slaves taken in each colony in the first few decades of settlement and cast indiscriminately with black slaves and white servants" (13).

6. The laws enslaving all individuals of African descent, and Native Americans taken prisoner in battle and their descendants, account in part for the rapid increase in Virginia's slave population from 1715 through the 1750s. The number of African slaves arriving in the American colonies from Africa had nearly doubled by the mid-1700s compared with those "imported" in the late 1600s (G. W. Williams 544). However, the slave population in Virginia had increased more than four times during this period: "In 1671 they [slaves] were 2,000 strong, and all, up to that date, direct from Africa. In 1715 there were 23,000 slaves against 72,000 whites. By the year 1758, the slave population had increased to the alarming number of over 100,000, which was a little less than the numerical strength of the whites" (G. W. Williams 133).

7. The notion that racial difference was "divinely ordained" was alive and well some 150 years later. By 1842, Ohio courts were still ruling that "all nearer white than black [are] . . . entitled to enjoy every political and social privilege of the white citizens" (Catterall 5:6). However, Justice J. Read of the Ohio State Court of Appeals used similar religious rhetoric to argue against such a definition of whiteness at that time: "The word 'white' means pure white, unmixed. . . . Whether a man is white or black, is a question of fact. . . . The two races are placed as wide apart by the hand of nature as *white from black*; . . . to break . . . the barriers, fixed . . . by the Creator himself, . . . shocks us as something unnatural and wrong" (Catterall 5:6–7).

8. Colonists originally enslaved Native Americans "taken prisoner in war." However, in the late 1600s colonists began limiting their "service": "'*It is resolved* and enacted that all servants not being Christians imported into this colony by shipping shall be slaves for their lives; but what shall come by land shall serve, if boyes or girles, until thirty yeares of age, if men or women twelve yeares and no longer'" (qtd. in G. W. Williams 123).

9. I have chosen to concentrate here on black female sexuality because it appears to be the only spoken way white Americans acknowledged their participation in interracial relationships. It seems to me that black male sexuality operates in an interracial context in a very different way, so that it "exists" as a taboo under the violent threat of excision through white male rituals of lynching that violently refuse acknowledgment of consensual relationships between black men and white women.

10. Eugene D. Genovese documents that at the fancy-girl markets in Louisiana, "girls, young, shapely, and usually light in color, went as house servants with special services required. First-class blacksmiths were being sold for $2,500 and prime field hands for about $1,800, but a particularly beautiful girl or young woman might bring $5,000" (416).

11. Historically, this designation of the mulatta as bastard can be traced to the Victorian fascination with the "Hottentot," or the Khoisan of South Africa. The *OED* defines "bastard" as "[a] person of mixed breed;

a Griqua (*S. Afr.*). . . . 1814; W. Brown, *Hist. Propag. Christianity* II. Ix. 425. 'The term *Bastard* applied to a Hottentot, does not mean that he is illegitimate, but merely that he is of mixed breed' . . . 1900; A. H. Keane, *Boer States*, vi. 85. 'Many are in fact "Bastards," that is to say, Hottentot-Dutch half breeds' " (Simpson and Weiner 1:990).

12. Fredrickson observes that Hoffman's book was "the most influential discussion of the race question to appear in the late nineteenth century" (249). Hoffman's was hardly a lone voice to blame black women for miscegenation. In what purported to be a definitive study of "the mulatto," Edward B. Reuter categorically states that black women, not white men, seek out interracial sexual relationships: "In every case the half-caste races have arisen as the result of illicit relations between the men of the superior and the women of the inferior race . . . . There is no mixed-blood race . . . where the mothers of the half-castes are not of the culturally inferior race. While all the advanced races have . . . mixed with the women of the lower race they have not done so with anything like equal readiness" (88).

13. See also Willard B. Gatewood, *Aristocrats of Color: The Black Elite, 1880–1920* (Bloomington: Indiana University Press, 1990), 9.

14. The polygenists' claim that the world was inhabited by different races that were, in fact, distinct species is reflected in the connotation the term "mulatto" acquired in nineteenth-century America. "Mulatto" existed as a term for biracial individuals as early as 1595, according to the *Oxford English Dictionary*, which notes its derivation from the Spanish for *mule*, the usually sterile offspring of an ass and a mare. However, "mulatto" was originally used "loosely for anyone of mixed race" and did not take on the connotation of a sterile hybrid until the nineteenth century, and then apparently only in America: "1861 Van Evrie *Negroes* 147 The fourth generation of mulattoism is as absolutely sterile as muleism" (Simpson and Weiner 10:68). The polygenist argument for supposed mulatto infertility was circular: biracial individuals must be sterile, it was claimed, *because* they were the offspring of two separate species; yet blacks and whites were "proven" to be distinct species because their mulatto offspring were always infertile, since members of the same species would produce fertile offspring. Nineteenth-century white Americans, then, resorted to a tautological line of thinking to argue for "black inferiority" and against miscegenation.

15. Agassiz's conversion to polygenesis gave this new doctrine a certain authority in the eyes of white Americans, for his reputation was well known before he arrived in the United States to take up a position at Harvard as professor of zoology.

16. Phrenology was developed by Dr. Franz Gall of Vienna in the late eighteenth century and was popularized by Gall and his students Johann Spurzheim and George Coombe.

17. John Blassingame documents a method of sidestepping the New Orleans antimiscegenation law that underscores such a notion of race. Blassingame states that from 1860 to 1880, there were a number of interracial marriages in New Orleans despite their prohibition. While not a common solution to the law's interdiction, some couples avoided violating it by interpreting "blood," its mixture, and the resulting racial definitions quite literally: "The white cashier of a New Orleans bank, for example, married a Negro woman by transferring some of her blood to himself and claiming to be a Negro" (19).

18. Lothrop Stoddard's *The Rising Tide of Color* (1920) foregrounds the dependence of white identity upon received notions of "blackness." Black blood's "prepotency" becomes the cornerstone for his appeal to white racial purity as a prerequisite for continued white power. In Stoddard's estimation, whites are nothing short of all-powerful in their "pure" state, and this power is traceable to a single element: "That element is *blood*. It is clean, virile, genius-bearing blood, streaming down the ages through the unerring action of heredity, which, in anything like a favorable environment, will multiply itself, solve our problems, and sweep us on to other and nobler destinies" (305).

19. Psychologist G. Stanley Hall and sociologist Charles A. Ellwood, noting the influential positions mulattoes held in African American communities, attributed their success to the quality of white blood they inherited. Hall, writing in 1905, stressed that mulattoes had inherited " 'more or less of the best Anglo-Saxon cavalier blood, brain,

and temper.' " A year later, Ellwood contended that " 'good white blood must greatly improve the negroid stock' " (qtd. in Mencke 72). This was a common assertion to make in the 1900s; see Reuter 174, n. 8

20. Appiah is referring here to "the chromosomal structure" of a person as believed to be his or her essence, a refined understanding of "blood" that racial theorists of the period in which I am interested never reached.

21. George Fredrickson notes that plantation romances like "the novels of George Tucker, William Gilmore Simms, James Kirke Paulding, John Pendleton Kennedy, and Nathaniel Beverley Tucker presented slaves who were . . . 'responsive to kindness, loyal, affectionate, and co-operative' " (102).

22. Joseph DeMarco observes that DuBois's conception of "race" in *Dusk of Dawn* "has its greatest emphasis on economic suffering, the sort of suffering that burdens the masses." DuBois moved, then, in both the course of his intellectual career and in his contemplations of "race" away from an emphasis on the "Talented Tenth" and toward an inclusion of "the folk" (37).

23. See Catterall 4:199 (*United States v. West*, District of Columbia, November 1836); Catterall 4:227 (*State v. Dillahunt, negro*, Delaware, April 1840); and Catterall 4:228 (*State v Warrington, negro*, Delaware, October 1840).

24. The 8 March 1856 edition of the *New Orleans Picayune* referred to free persons of color as " 'a plague and a pest in our community, besides containing the elements of mischief to the slave population,' " and called for their removal from Louisiana (qtd. in Williamson 66). Arkansas and Mississippi had already passed laws that prohibited free persons of color from entering the state. The upper South moved earlier to control its "free colored" population: the Virginia constitution of 1850 legalized reenslavement of emancipated slaves if they remained in Virginia longer than a year after gaining their freedom. See Gilbert Thomas Stephenson, *Race Distinctions in American Law* (1910; New York: Negro Universities Press, 1969), 38–39. These laws frequently left free persons of color expelled from one state unable to enter another, and all the while under the threat of reenslavement.

25. I have in mind revolts like Denmark Vesey's in Charleston, South Carolina (1822), and Nat Turner's in Virginia (1831). It is important to note that Vesey was a free person of color, and so the impact of the revolt he led on Southern views of "mulattos" should not be underestimated.

26. See also Stephenson 17, 262. Alabama considered association admissible evidence of race into the 1920s, and Louisiana did so into the 1930s. See Charles S. Mangum Jr., *The Legal Status of the Negro* (1940; New York: Johnson Reprint, 1970), 262.

27. Louisiana abolished its one-thirty-second statute in May 1983 in favor of a "traceable amount rule" in the much publicized Phipps trial, *Jane Doe v. State of Louisiana*. Susie Guillory Phipps, the great-great-great-great-granddaughter of a French planter and his wife's slave, petitioned the Louisiana courts to change her parents' racial classification to white so that she and her siblings could also be classed as white. Phipps had been denied a passport because she looked "white," while her birth certificate listed her race as "colored." And while several of Phipps's relatives testified that they identified themselves as "colored," Phipps claimed that the racial designation on her birth certificate was a shock to her since she had always believed she was white and had "married white." The state's attorneys claimed they were able to prove Phipps was "three-thirty-seconds black"; the district court was convinced, and Phipps and her siblings were legally designated as black. This decision was upheld upon appeal in October 1983, December 1985, and by the U.S. Supreme Court, which refused to hear Phipps's case in December 1986 (F. J. Davis 9–11).

Chapter 2. "White Slaves" and Tragic Mulattas

1. See Berzon, *Neither White Nor Black*, and Sollers, *Neither Black Nor White Yet Both*, on the mulatto and tragic mulatta in American texts; see Brody, *Impossible Purities*, on the "mulattaroon" in British Victorian texts.

2. Brody documents that "sentimental and melodramatic narratives . . . represented her as a youthful, beautiful, obliging, feminine figure . . . [and] comic, gothic, and erotic narratives . . . represent[ed] her as ludicrous,

lurid, or alluring" (*Impossible Purities* 16). Sollers has taken care to point out that, "if one correlated the various 'typical' plot lines that have been offered as constituting *the* Tragic Mulatto, one would be surprised by the differences between one and the next version of the stereotype" (238). See his Chapter 8 for summaries of varied plots.

3. As Sànchez-Eppler notes, sales of the *Liberty Bell* at antislavery fairs were responsible for raising approximately one-fifth of their annual revenue, funding the New England Anti-Slavery Society (34).

4. Sànchez-Eppler maintains that American women involved in antislavery work "wrote virtually all of the sentimental tales that describe the slaves' sufferings" during this period and that women constituted their readership (34).

5. See Brody, *Impossible Purities*; Audrey Fisch, *American Slaves in Victorian England: Abolitionist Politics in Popular Literature and Culture* (Cambridge: Cambridge University Press, 2000). See also Yellin, *Women and Sisters*; Sànchez-Eppler, "Bodily Bonds."

6. See also "Singular Escape," *Liberator*, 12 January 1849; "William and Ellen Craft," *Anti-Slavery Standard*, 8 February 1849.

7. Brown and the Crafts lectured throughout New England in "Norwich, Worcester, Pawtucket, New Bedford, Boston, Kingston, Abington, and Northborough. In late January [1849], Brown introduced the Crafts and Henry 'Box' Brown . . . to the annual meeting of the Massachusetts Anti Slavery Society" (Blackett, *Beating* 90).

8. William Farrison describes the lectures on this tour as follows: Brown began with a lengthy introduction of William Craft; William recounted the Crafts' escape; a persuasive speech by Brown followed and ended with Ellen's introduction. Ellen "sometimes added a few words to what her husband had said" (136–37). Exactly when Ellen's appearances became silent ones is difficult to determine.

9. As Midgley documents, Owenite social feminists made analogies between free white women and slaves between 1835 and 1839; Harriet Martineau did so in *Society in America* (1837) and Marion Reid in *A Plea for Woman* (1843), which ran to several editions in both the United States and Britain (156, 164). I will return to the development of this trope as it pertains to Remond's work in the late 1850s.

10. I have in mind the following markers of an organized Victorian feminist movement under way by the mid to late 1850s: the Married Woman's Property Committee and petitioning campaign (1855), the *Englishwoman's Journal* (1857), and the Association for the Promotion of the Employment of Women (1858). See Midgley 170.

11. In addition to McCaskill's reading of Ellen Craft as "merchandised . . . on the European political marketplace, with the orator's platform replacing the auction block" ("Yours" 523), I would also cite Audrey Fisch's " 'Negrophilism' and British Nationalism: The Spectacle of the Black American Abolitionist," *Victorian Review* 19.2 (1993): 20–47, reprinted as Chapter 4 of her *American Slaves in Victorian England*. Fisch's reading is so focused on what press accounts of Remond's speeches tell us about British nationalism and Victorian anxieties that Remond's strategies receive scant, if any, critical attention.

12. Dawn Keetley documents what she calls "the invasive exposure, literally and rhetorically, of black female bodies" in slave narratives (6).

13. See Lerone Bennett, *Before the Mayflower* (Chicago: Johnson, 1969), 137.

14. Stowe's novel, published in New York in late March 1852 and in Britain in early July of that year, quickly became a best seller and a cultural phenomenon. Audrey Fisch notes the novel's success spawned the production of songbooks, wallpaper, ornaments, dolls, paintings and panoramas, theatrical performances, and products such as coffee, china, and clothing bearing Uncle Tom labels. See Chapter 1 of her *American Slaves in Victorian England*.

15. Brown's abolitionist novel *Clotel; or, The President's Daughter: A Narrative of Slave Life in the United States* was originally published in London (1853); three subsequent novels, which varied its plot, were subsequently published in 1860–61, 1864, and 1867. The narrative culminates with Clotel's tragic death. A fugitive mulatta and the daughter of Thomas Jefferson, she flings herself off a bridge to her death in order to escape recapture. For information on Child's publications, see Yellin, *Women and Sisters*, 53, 72–76.

16. While clearly part of a sentimental rendering of their motivations, it is important to note here that the Crafts' narrative opens by telling the reader they determined to escape because "the fact that another man had the power to tear from our cradle the new-born babe and sell it in the shambles like a brute, and then scourge us if we dared to lift a finger to save it from such a fate, haunted us for years" (Craft 3).

17. See Amy Robinson, "Forms of Appearance of Value: Homer Plessy and the Politics of Privacy," in *Performance and Cultural Politics*, ed. Elin Diamond (New York: Routledge, 1996), 237–61.

18. Under the auspices of the Leeds Young Men's Anti-Slavery Society, Remond made the following appearances: Leed's Music Hall, 22 and 23 December 1859; Wortley, 27 December 1859; Bramley, 29 December 1859; Hunslet Methodist New Connexion Chapel, 4 January 1860; Barnsley Mechanics' Institute, 5 January 1860; Morley, 6 January 1860; and Leeds, 10 January 1860. See "Miss Remond in Yorkshire," *Anti-Slavery Advocate*, 1 February 1860, 306.

19. Remond's lecture tour from 1859 to 1861 included the following, though this list is not comprehensive: Liverpool, Warrington, Dublin, Waterford, Clonmer, Cork, London, Southwark, Bristol, Manchester, York, Edinburgh, Bolton, Bedford, Leeds, Glasgow, Hawick, Dumfries, Carlisle, and Ulverstone.

20. Frequently, Remond opened her lectures identifying herself as the "representative of a race," rather than as the "agent" of an antislavery society. This can be read as an attempt to eschew schisms within the abolitionist community, an "independence" that Blackett identifies as key to the success of African American abolitionists in Britain: "Their independence . . . made them, especially after the split in abolitionist ranks in 1840, the crucial unifying factor among British abolitionists. Generally, their position was straightforward and uncomplicated. Ideological or sectarian issues were secondary to them" (*Building* 42). But this reference clearly also operated to facilitate the imagined possibility of Remond's own enslavement and thus her position as an object of empathy, as is further evident in Rev. Samuel May's closing remarks to her Manchester Athenaeum speech on the evening of 14 September 1859: "[I]f that young lady who has addressed you so eloquently this evening were to travel in our Southern states she would be arrested and most probably sold as a slave" ("American Slavery," *Manchester Weekly Times* 5).

21. For information regarding the popularity of the Garner case among American abolitionists, see Steven Weisenburger, *Modern Medea: A Family Story of Slavery and Child-Murder from the Old South* (New York: Hill and Wang, 1998).

22. Such appeals to violations of the domestic and familial run throughout Remond's speeches on this tour.

23. Remond repeatedly referred to slavery's violences as "unspeakable" and beyond description in speeches through the summer and fall of 1859. I would like to thank Susan Hamilton for her suggestive comments on this point.

24. One might also call Remond's additional references to fugitive slaves in both the 24 and 31 January Warrington lectures sensationalistic: "She related an affecting story of a slave who had secreted himself on board a ship to get out of the land of slavery. He was found out . . . he jumped overboard and was drowned, preferring to be drowned, than to live a life of slavery" ("Lecture," *Warrington Standard*).

25. For example, see Remond's challenge to Lola Montez's depiction of American slavery delivered at London's Music Hall on 15 June 1859 in "Lectures on American Slavery," *Anti-Slavery Reporter*, 1 July 1859, 148–51; "Miss Sarah P. Remond in London," *Anti-Slavery Advocate* 2.31 (1 July 1859): 251–52.

26. Remond was a member of the Female Anti-Slavery Society of Salem. I am indebted to the University Press of Mississippi's anonymous reader for drawing Brown's lecture to my attention.

Chapter 3. Little Romances and Mulatta Heroines

1. In this later work, Butler takes up the texts of both Willa Cather and Nella Larsen, though not to pursue the kind of reading I propose here. I am particularly interested in how we might respond to Butler's challenge "to consider . . . the disjunctive ordering of the human as 'masculine' or 'feminine' as taking place . . . through a complex set of racial injunctions which operate in part through the taboo on miscegenation" (*Bodies* 167).

True womanhood operated as just such a racial injunction against miscegenation by using proscribed attributes of femininity to further secure racial distinctions between black and white.

2. Throughout, I will be using "true womanhood" and "Victorian womanhood" as interchangeable terms to designate the ideal of femininity promoted by the cult of domesticity.

3. See Nina Baym, *Woman's Fiction: A Guide to Novels By and About Women in America, 1820–1870*, 2nd ed. (Urbana and Chicago: University of Illinois Press, 1993); Susan K. Harris, *Nineteenth-Century American Women's Novels: Interpretive Strategies* (Cambridge: Cambridge University Press, 1990); Mary Kelley, *Private Women, Public Stage: Literary Domesticity in Nineteenth-Century America* (Oxford: Oxford University Press, 1984).

4. Turn-of-the-century books and articles written by whites, like "The Negro Problem" and "The Negro Woman: Social and Moral Decadence," argued that black women were failing in their womanly duty to safeguard their race's morality: " '[T]he women, who properly should be bulwarks of sobriety and conservatism . . . are . . . [opening] the floodgates of the corrupting sexual influences that are doing so much to sap and destroy . . . [the black race]. The number of illegitimate children born to unmarried negresses is becoming greater every year' " (qtd. in Guy-Sheftall 42).

5. As James Horton documents, this belief in female responsibility for male morality was also promoted in black newspapers. The *Colored American Magazine* was enjoining the black woman to lead her family by example in moral and economic concerns: "As the popular media demanded of all women, black women were expected to maintain the highest moral standards themselves and to be responsible for the morality of their men. They were instructed to resist all men who indulged in drinking and gambling and 'through your smiles and economical conduct in your domestic pursuits . . . provoke the indolent and improvident husband to active industry and frugality' " (Horton 675).

6. The dialectic of nineteenth-century American womanhood is vividly illustrated in the "topsy-turvy" doll, popular in the nineteenth-century American South and apparently still produced today. Shirley Samuels describes the doll: "[H]eld one way, the doll appears as a white woman with long skirts. Flipping over her skirts does not reveal her legs, but rather exposes another racial identity: the head of a black woman, whose long skirts now cover the head of the white woman" (157).

7. James Jacks, president of the Missouri Press Association, indignant at the picture Ida Wells-Barnett was painting of the South during her antilynching lecture tour of England, wrote an open letter to British antilynching organizations in 1895 denouncing her arguments that blamed whites for creating the specter of the black rapist. This letter, circulated by Josephine St. Pierre Ruffin among black women's organizations, claimed that African Americans were "devoid of morality" and referred to black women as "prostitutes" and all blacks as "natural thieves and liars." Ruffin issued a call to action, citing this letter as the veritable last straw: the first national meeting of African American women's organizations (some of which had been formed as early as the 1830s) was held in Boston in late July 1895. Out of this convention, the National Association of Colored Women (NACW) was formed in 1896, with Mary Church Terrell as its president.

8. The NACW's charter also echoes ideals of racial uplift promoted by African American men since antebellum times. One can trace a widening gender division among African Americans through early-nineteenth-century black newspapers. As Horton documents, these newspapers instructed African American women to be submissive rather than self-assertive: "One anecdote that appeared in an 1827 issue of *Freedom's Journal* related the plight of a woman doomed to a life without a man because she violated one cardinal role of female behavior, she 'could not keep her mouth shut' " (56). Nineteenth-century African American leaders, in accordance with the cult of domesticity's notion of "separate spheres," denied African American women membership in organizations and limited their participation in activist causes to supporting roles. For example, when W.E.B. DuBois, Alexander Crummell, and the Reverend Francis Grimké organized the American Negro Academy in 1897, they drafted a bylaw limiting participation to "men of African Descent" (Giddings 116). In "The Conservation of Races," published that same year, DuBois called for the Academy to "gather about it the talented, unselfish men, [and] the pure and noble-minded women" (824–25). Yet Paula Giddings notes that no

women were ever listed in its membership. As Linda Perkins observes, "it was clear by the end of the nineteenth century that many black men viewed women as their intellectual subordinates and not capable of leadership positions" (24). Frederick Douglass's support for female suffrage was an exception, not the rule, argues Perkins.

9. For example, Cooper argued the following in *A Voice from the South* (1892): "I grant you that intellectual development, with the self-reliance and capacity for earning a livelihood which it gives, renders woman less dependent on the marriage relation for physical support" (68). Two years later, Gertrude Mossell published *The Work of the Afro-American Woman* (1894) and, like Cooper, argued against the "angel of the house" image of woman: "I may not be orthodox, but I venture to assert that keeping a clean house will not keep a man at home. . . . [S]aints are rare and I don't believe that history . . . proves that saintly women . . . *gain men's love oftenest or hold it longest*. . . . I believe that a woman who has a mind and will of her own will become monotonous to a less extent than one so continuously sweet and self-effacing" (119–23).

10. We need to be careful to note that class differences within "the" African American community were, in fact, central to black political culture generally at this time, which is frequently represented as divided between bourgeois DuBoisian and working-class Washingtonian politics.

11. Club leaders like Mary Church Terrell and Josephine St. Pierre Ruffin were ambivalent about the relevance of Victorian womanhood to a political vision that kept in sight the working-class circumstances of the women and families on whom their organization focused its efforts. Terrell believed that women should be politically involved and a strong moral influence in the home; she was also an advocate for working mothers. Ruffin, a middle-class Bostonian, also believed black women were pivotal in the development of a respectable home life that she saw as necessary for racial advancement; yet her experience as editor of *Woman's Era* led her to argue for women's activity in the public sphere. Ruffin founded the *Woman's Era*, the first magazine in America published by and for black women. The earliest extant copy is dated March 1894.

12. See C. K. Doreski, *Writing America Black: Race Rhetoric in the Public Sphere* (Cambridge: Cambridge University Press, 1998), xix, for an examination of Hopkins's "revisionist race history" at the *Colored American Magazine*.

13. Hopkins left the *Colored American Magazine* after it came under the control of Booker T. Washington. Hopkins had been vocal in her opposition to Washington's policies, and even though she moved to New York to continue as editor, she left the magazine a short time later. The *Colored American Magazine* released a statement that attributed her departure to ill health, although Hopkins continued to publish elsewhere during this period of so-called illness that had rendered her unable to work.

14. Hopkins's serialized novels, in contrast to *Contending Forces*, are "situated in a white rather than a black social order," used "more popular fictional formulas," and represented "social and intellectual conflict" through "physical action and confrontation" (Carby, Introduction xxxvi). Her continued attention to existing cultural beliefs and scientific theories of racial difference has made for varied critical readings of her magazine novels, with some critics seeing her as inscribing and others as challenging racialist notions of difference. See, for example: Martin Japtok, "Pauline Hopkins's *Of One Blood*, Africa, and the 'Darwinist Trap,'" *African American Review* 36.3 (2003): 403–16; Fabi, *Passing and the Rise of the African American Novel*; John Nikel, "Eugenics and the Fiction of Pauline Hopkins," *ATQ* 14.1 (2000): 47–63; Debra Bernardi, "Narratives of Domestic Imperialism: The African-American Home in the *Colored American Magazine* and the Novels of Pauline Hopkins, 1900–1903," in *Separate Spheres No More: Gender Convergence in American Literature*, ed. Monika M. Elbert (Tuscaloosa: University of Alabama Press, 200), 202–24; Augusta Rohrbach, "To Be Continued: Double Identity, Multiplicity and Antigenealogy as Narrative Strategies in Pauline Hopkins' Magazine Fiction," *Callaloo* 22.2 (1999): 483–98; Susan Gillman, "Pauline Hopkins and the Occult: African-American Revisions of Nineteenth-Century Sciences," *American Literary History* 8.1 (1996): 57–82; John Cullen Gruesser, ed., *The Unruly Voice: Rediscovering Pauline Elizabeth Hopkins* (Urbana and Chicago: University of Illinois Press, 1996).

15. See the following for arguments that Harper's and/or Hopkins's fiction is apolitical, complacent, assimilationist, or caters to bourgeois white standards: Houston A. Baker Jr., *Workings of the Spirit: The Poetics of*

Afro-American Women's Writing (Chicago: University of Chicago Press, 1991); Dickson D. Bruce Jr., *Black American Writing From the Nadir: The Evolution of a Literary Tradition, 1877–1915* (Baton Rouge: Louisiana State University Press, 1989); Mary Helen Washington, *Invented Lives: Narratives of Black Women 1860–1960* (Garden City, N.Y.: Anchor Press, 1987); Jane Campbell, *Mythic Black Fiction: The Transformation of History* (Knoxville: University of Tennessee Press, 1986); Arlene Elder, *The Hindered Hand: Cultural Implications of Early African-American Fiction* (Westport, Conn.: Greenwood Press, 1978); Bone, *The Negro Novel in America*; Sterling A. Brown et al., *The Negro Caravan: Writings by American Negroes* (New York: Dryden, 1941).

For notable reevaluations of Harper and Hopkins see: Gruesser, *The Unruly Voice*; John Ernest, *Resistance and Reformation in Nineteenth-Century African-American Literature* (Jackson: University Press of Mississippi, 1995); Claudia Tate, *Domestic Allegories of Political Desire: The Black Heroine's Text at the Turn of the Century* (New York: Oxford University Press, 1992). The dismissive misreadings I have in mind include the rather definitive assessments of both Houston Baker and Richard Yarborough. I call these definitive because of Baker's prominent position in the field and the fact that, for many readers, Yarborough's introduction to the Oxford edition is their first, and sometimes only, encounter with Harper criticism. Houston Baker dubs Harper and Hopkins "departed daughters" within an African American women writers' tradition, arguing that they establish a black female "subjecthood . . . [that] finally comes to mean an implicit approval of white patriarchy inscribed in the very features of the mulatto character's face. The nineteenth-century daughters' departure recapitulates, then, the dynamics of the daughters' seduction" (*Workings* 25). Baker's assessment is particularly striking given the way it echoes criticisms leveled at these novels from the 1940s through the 1960s. Likewise, Richard Yarborough's introduction to the Oxford Schomburg Library of Nineteenth-Century Black Women Writers edition of *Contending Forces* is "curious" to critics who read Hopkins as challenging racialist and racist constructions for its argument that Hopkins "endorse[s] contemporary ideas regarding the role of race and ancestry as determinants of physical and psychological development" (xxxiv). He also clearly privileges realist representations over a critical understanding of the work of genres like the sentimental, despite the work of feminist critics like Jane Tompkins in the early to mid-1980s to reassess this genre. See Kate McCullough, "Slavery, Sexuality, and Genre: Pauline Hopkins and the Representation of Female Desire," in *The Unruly Voice: Rediscovering Pauline Elizabeth Hopkins*, ed. John Cullen Gruesser (Urbana and Chicago: University of Illinois Press, 1996), 23.

16. Laura Wexler argues that what she has termed "the expansive, imperial project of sentimentalism" and domestic fiction was "aimed at the subjection of different classes and even races" (15). See also her analysis of bourgeois domestic photography as using visual codes to mark social divisions: "Seeing Sentiment: Photography, Race, and the Innocent Eye," in *Female Subjects in Black and White: Race, Psychoanalysis, Feminism*, ed. Elizabeth Abel et al. (Berkeley and Los Angeles: University of California Press, 1997), 159–86.

17. In fact, Joyce Hope Scott has argued that the rhetoric of domesticity gave African American women a stronger voice and position in black politics during the nineteenth century than they achieved in struggles of the twentieth century: "[W]ithout recourse to the legitimating rhetoric of nineteenth-century domesticity, black women in the Civil Rights era lost their 'earlier vocality and centrality' as a 'phallocentric and patriarchal vision of Black Power relocated the black woman in the margins of the struggle for freedom and equality' " (qtd. in Romero 29).

18. I have in mind both Ellen Craft's refusal to bear and raise children in slavery and her persistence in finding and reuniting with her mother. It bears remembering that Ellen's platform appearances often followed William's narratives of families torn apart by slavery, making the African American family a focus of the Crafts' political appeals.

19. Brown's novel was originally published in London in 1853. The subsequent novels, *Miralda; or the Beautiful Quadroon* (1860–61), *Clotelle: A Tale of the Southern States* (1864), and *Clotelle: or, The Colored Heroine* (1867), drew from the same material as *Clotel*. For a brief mention of *Clotel's* influence on Harper's *Iola Leroy* and Hopkins's *Hagar's Daughter*, see Hazel V. Carby, *Reconstructing Womanhood: The Emergence of the Afro-American Woman Novelist* (New York: Oxford University Press, 1987), 71–72, 146–47. For an examination of Brown's cultural

sources for *Clotel*, including Lydia Maria Child's tragic mulatta narrative "The Quadroons," see Chapter 1 of John Ernest's *Resistance and Reformation*.

20. See Richard Brodhead's *Cultures of Letters: Scenes of Reading and Writing in Nineteenth-Century America* (Chicago: University of Chicago Press, 1993) for an examination of such fiction's continued popularity in the late nineteenth century. Elizabeth Ammons argues that *Iola Leroy* "intermixes a conglomeration of inherited forms—melodrama, journalism, adventure fiction, slave narrative, abolitionist fiction, the realistic novel, oral tradition, the romance" (27). Of course, Hopkins's white and black readers, too, would recognize many of these forms and be schooled in what to expect from them.

21. For example, *On Habits and Manners* was originally written for the students of Hampton Institute. However, this book was published for "general use" in 1888 (Kasson 54). Elias M. Woods's *The Negro in Etiquette: A Novelty* followed in 1899. Woods's etiquette manual began as a lecture "delivered before the Faculty and Students of Lincoln Institute at Jefferson City, [Missouri]." According to the manual's preface, the lecture was then published as a pamphlet entitled "The Gospel of Civility," which sold out; in response to demand, Woods published this longer work (Woods 7).

22. Frances Smith Foster notes that African American women writing autobiographies in the nineteenth century undertook a similar negotiation between the tenets of Victorian womanhood and black female experience. See her "Adding Color and Contour to Early American Self-Portraiture: Autobiographical Writings of Afro-American Women," in *Conjuring: Black Women, Fiction and Literary Tradition*, ed. Marjorie Pryse and Hortense J. Spillers (Bloomington: Indiana University Press, 1985), 25–38.

23. Hopkins's novel problematizes beliefs regarding "blood" popular among whites in her day. Rather than writing blood as determinant of character and destiny, she argues that environment is responsible for an individual's actions and choices. Moreover, the event that sets in motion her narrative of dispersed families is the jealous suspicion that Grace Montefort, the Smith's foremother and wife of a wealthy planter, is of mixed race: " 'Thar's too much cream color in the face and too little blud seen under the skin fer a genooine white 'ooman.' " As a result of this unfounded suspicion, Grace's husband is killed, she is whipped and later commits suicide, and her sons fall into the hands of Anson Pollock. One son, Jesse, escapes his enslavement and takes on the "character of a fugitive slave . . . [and] from the first cast his lot with the colored people of the community" (*CF* 41, 78). Hopkins clearly represents Jesse Montefort as taking on blackness as a subject position, while we never find out whether his mother, Grace Montefort, was biracial or white.

24. Despite such challenges, critics have read Hopkins as subscribing to racialist discourses. Richard Yarborough's introduction in the Oxford edition is one such example: "Hopkins never challenges the basic assumption that races can be ranked qualitatively. . . . [She] suggests not only that physical and, most importantly, psychological characteristics are racially determined and can be inherited, but also that the dominant traits in mixed-blood blacks derive from the white side of their family tree" (xxxvi). Even though Yarborough recognizes that tone is central to this novel, and cites an example of Hopkins's sarcasm, he characterizes the text as having "marked inconsistencies in tone" (xxxvi), rather than reading further for Hopkins's irony and the way in which she may be playing on the very beliefs he ascribes to her.

25. I find particularly helpful here Butler's insistence that we attend to exactly how certain identities are constructed through the attempted, though necessarily incomplete, exclusion of others: "[T]he construction of gender operates through *exclusionary* means, such that the human is not only produced over and against the inhuman, but through a set of foreclosures, radical erasures, that are, strictly speaking, refused the possibility of cultural articulation. Hence, it is not enough to claim that human subjects are constructed, for the construction of the human is a differential operation that produces the more and the less 'human,' the inhuman, the humanly unthinkable. These excluded sites come to bound the 'human' as its constitutive outside, and to haunt those boundaries as the persistent possibility of their disruption and rearticulation" (*Bodies* 8).

26. Pocket physiologies were "thin, pocket-size, paperbound volumes sold on the streets . . . as guidebooks . . . [or] elementary readers for 'respectable citizens' of city life" (S. M. Smith 86).

27. The phrase "as white as" recurs in the writings of nineteenth-century white Americans, voicing an anxiety around the "readability" of bodies. Ray Stannard Baker speaks of meeting "men and women as white as I am, whose assertion that they were really Negroes I accepted in defiance of the evidence of my own senses. . . . Nothing, indeed, is more difficult to define than this curious physical color line in the individual human being. Legislatures have repeatedly attempted to define where black leaves off and white begins" (151). Transcribing the history of Louisa Picquet, an "octoroon," through a series of interviews, the Reverend Mattison repeatedly asks Louisa if her children and any other slaves she knew were "as white as" her. See H. Mattison, "Louisa Picquet, The Octoroon; Or Inside Views of Southern Domestic Life," 1861, in *Collected Black Women's Narratives* in *The Schomburg Library of Nineteenth-Century Black Women Writers*, ed. Henry Louis Gates Jr. (New York: Oxford University Press, 1988). Mary Chesnutt also refers to her slave Martha Adams in her diary as " 'so nearly white' " (qtd. in Carby, *Reconstructing* 31).

28. Ellis defines cultural mulattos as individuals who are regarded as black, "racially," but who "can also navigate . . . the white world" (235).

29. I am drawing on Bakhtin's sense of parody here. In *The Dialogic Imagination*, Bakhtin theorizes parody as an intentional hybrid: "Every type of parody . . . is in a broad sense an intentional hybrid—but a hybrid compounded of two orders: one linguistic (a single language) and one stylistic" (75). For Bakhtin, the intentional hybrid works to unmask the order it seeks to contest in what he calls a "typical double-accented, double styled *hybrid construction*" (*Dialogic* 304–5). As Young notes, Bakhtin's concept of hybridity stresses the idea of a "doubleness that both brings together, fuses, but also maintains separation. For Bakhtin himself, the crucial effect of hybridization comes with the latter, political category, the moment where, within a single discourse, one voice is able to unmask the other. This is the point where authoritative discourse is undone" (22).

30. Considering black domestic novels generally, Tate posits several reasons for a twentieth-century critical rejection of such works as apolitical and accommodationist: "[T]he domestic novels' civility, signs of courtship, and white- or light-skinned heroines appear to undercut racial affirmation, working-class solidarity, and black cultural nationalism. . . . [W]e contemporary readers have largely applauded the representation of freedom found in masculine black protest critiques or an unconsciously male rendition of black cultural nationalism, while we have disparaged domestic stories as narratives of confinement, as narratives of status quo" (80). Tate goes on to argue that we need to attend to the ways in which the mulatta "produced different meanings at the turn of the century": "[T]wentieth-century readers generally use the term *mulatto* as one of exclusion rather than inclusion; that is, to designate black people who claim or appear to claim privilege as a consequence of light skin color. Thus what the black protest writers and the proponents of the Black Arts movement have disparaged as racial ambivalence or denial in the mulatto characters of early black literature, their post-Reconstruction counterparts probably saw as . . . a change that made them distinctly different from their enslaved African predecessors" (80–81). Deborah McDowell argues that Harper's characterization of Iola specifically and the novel's similarity to Harriet Beecher Stowe's *Uncle Tom's Cabin* more generally reflect her attempt to connect with a white Northern readership: "Those northern whites might be more inclined to lend their assistance to this homeless and displaced lot if the images of black life that Harper and her black contemporaries valued and affirmed accorded with that audience's horizon of social and literary expectations" ("Changing Same" 98).

31. Frances Smith Foster makes a similar observation regarding representations of the rape of black women in antebellum slave narratives: "[H]er ability to survive degradation was her downfall. As victim she became the assailant, since her submission to repeated violations was not in line with the values of sentimental heroines who died rather than be abused. Her survival of these ordeals and continued participation in other aspects of slave life seemed to connote, if not outright licentiousness, at least a less sensitive and abused spirit than that of white heroines" (Foster, *Witnessing* 131).

32. In this respect, Boyd's (*Discarded Legacy*) and Foreman's (" 'Reading Aright' ") observations that Harper's heroine is meant to evoke the figure of Ida B. Wells-Barnett and her antilynching crusade through her early journalist signature, "Iola," are particularly salient.

Chapter 4. Commodified "Blackness" and Performative Possibilities in Jessie Fauset's *The Chinaberry Tree* and Nella Larsen's *Quicksand*

1. This phrase is Claudia Tate's. In *Domestic Allegories of Political Desire*, she argues that "black women's post-reconstruction domestic novels used bourgeois gender conventions as an emancipatory text" (97).

2. Jervis Anderson quotes the *Age* reporting in 1916 that of "145 businesses on the Negro stretch of Lenox Avenue, only twenty-three per cent . . . [were] owned and operated by blacks." Even though the figure had increased by 1921—" 'about eighty percent' of the businesses on 135th Street between Lenox and Seventh Avenues were owned by blacks"—African Americans in Harlem often frequented white-owned businesses rather than those owned by members of their own community, citing better selection and a suspicion that black store owners believed their fellow African Americans owed them their business and consequently treated customers poorly (66–67).

3. Lewis notes that by 1923, African Americans "represented no more than 30 percent of the total Harlem population. Whites evacuated Harlem as reluctantly as Afro-Americans flocked to it. Slicing almost the full length of the district, Eighth Avenue cleanly severed black from white" (27). The area west of Eighth Avenue was predominantly white, while black Harlem lay east of Eighth Avenue.

4. In 1930 the *New York Herald Tribune* estimated that "ninety percent of the cabarets in Harlem were owned by whites, ninety-two percent of the speakeasies were operated by white racketeers" (Sylvander 79). Frequently, the black musicians who drew whites to Harlem did not profit economically from the attention. A form of transitional piano playing called "stride" that bridged classical ragtime and jazz was popular between 1914 and 1920, and as one of stride's great innovators, Willie (the Lion) Smith, remembered, black musicians were poorly paid. " 'To the Harlem cabaret owners, to all night-club bosses, the money was on a one-way chute—everything coming in, nothing going out. . . . It was your job to draw in the customers,' " recalled Smith. " 'For all this, they paid you off in uppercuts. That was a saying we got up in those days; it meant you were allowed to keep your tips, but you got no salary. Sometimes they would give us a small weekly amount—like twenty dollars. That was known as a left hook' " (qtd. in Anderson 129).

5. In an essay entitled "Negro Character as Seen by White Authors," Sterling Brown argued that the white writer's "New Negro" was " 'a jazzed-up version' " of the happy, contented slave " 'with cabarets supplanting cabin' " (qtd. in Sylvander 11).

6. Ann duCille ponders, "Are we, in our attempts at cultural criticism, modern-day primitivists? Are our Afrocentric interests and our vernacular theories and our feminist concerns for female agency colluding with primitivist proclivities like those that helped to bring the black 'other' into vogue in the 1920s?" (*Coupling* 85). See also Michele Wallace, "Modernism, Postmodernism and the Problem of the Visual in Afro-American Culture," in *Out There: Marginalization and Contemporary Cultures*, ed. Russell Ferguson et al. (Cambridge: MIT Press, 1990), 39–50.

7. Toomer's *Cane* was published in September 1923.

8. For a critical reading of Davis's text, see George Hutchinson, "Nella Larsen and the Veil of Race," *American Literary History* 9.2 (1997): 329–49.

9. "Ofays" was a derogatory term for whites derived from the pig Latin for "foes." See Geneva Smitherman, *Talkin and Testifyin: The Language of Black America* (Detroit: Wayne State University Press, 1977), 47.

10. For example, Larsen writes: "Sunday night we had dinner at Carl's. . . . Last night we all went to the opening of Ethel Water's show, 'Africana'. *Very* good it was too. Eddie, Carl, Elmer, Harry, Fania, Muriel Draper, Isa and I made a party. Some of it was excruciatingly funny. I thought Harry would have to be carried out" (Larsen to Peterson, 12 July 1927).

11. Addison Gayle groups the fiction of James Weldon Johnson, Fauset, and Larsen together as examples of surrendered African American identity: "The end result of the journey from land, from one's roots, from one's ancestral past, means to sever all relationships with the race. . . . It means too, this journey from race, and thus from self, to surrender one's identity, which once lost is impossible to regain again" (120). Larsen has fared

much better than Fauset, the critical consensus being that she is a superior writer, though nevertheless a member of the "Rear Guard."

12. Mary Dearborn praises Larsen for having "achieved that much-maligned and problematic goal: she showed that black experience was like white experience" (60). Barbara Christian, on the other hand, condemns Fauset for the same reason: "Her novels insist that the upper-middle-class Negro has the same values as the upper-class white. . . . The problem with Fauset's novels is that she gives us this particular Negro exclusively and as the representative of what the race is capable of doing. . . . [B]ecause she was so conscious of being an image maker and because she accepted wholesale American values, except on the issue of race, her novels hardly communicate the intellectual depth that some of her articles do" (*Black Women* 41–43). For accusations that Fauset accepted "white values," see also Hiroko Sato, "Under the Harlem Shadow: A Study of Jessie Fauset and Nella Larsen," in *The Harlem Renaissance Remembered*, ed. Arna Bontemps (New York: Dodd, Mead, 1972), 63–89; for assessments of Fauset as mediating black and white cultures, see also Mary V. Dearborn, *Pocahontas's Daughters: Gender and Ethnicity in American Culture* (New York: Oxford University Press, 1986). Again, it is noteworthy that Fauset is more frequently the object of such critique than Larsen.

13. Several recent studies have begun to read critically the way "the folk" signified "authentic" blackness during the Harlem Renaissance. See, for example, J. Martin Favor, *Authentic Blackness: The Folk in the New Negro Renaissance* (Durham, N.C.: Duke University Press, 1999); Ross Posnock, *Color and Culture: Black Writers and the Making of the Modern Intellectual* (Cambridge: Harvard University Press, 1998). This work to read "the folk" critically is arguably indebted to that of black feminist critics like Hazel V. Carby, "Reinventing History/Imagining the Future," *African American Review* 23 (1989): 381–87; Carby, "The Politics of Fiction, Anthropology, and the Folk: Zora Neale Hurston," in *New Essays on Their Eyes Were Watching God*, ed. Michael Awkward (Cambridge: Cambridge University Press, 1991), 71–93; and Cheryl A. Wall, *Women of the Harlem Renaissance* (Bloomington: Indiana University Press, 1995).

14. Houston Baker refers to race as "an 'old' discursive formation predicated on gross features" ("Caliban's" 387). Of course, we should also identify race as a formative discourse, formative of not only identities but also of bodies and what they come to mean.

15. Several scholars have noted that the school is modeled on Booker T. Washington's Tuskegee Institute and that Naxos is an anagram for Saxon. Larsen clearly indicts Washington's solution to "the race problem" as a sellout to whites who have a decided self-interest in keeping African Americans economically disadvantaged and working as tradespeople, rather than pursuing higher education and employment in the professions.

16. See, for example, Jeffrey Gray, "Essence and the Mulatto Traveler: Europe as Embodiment in Nella Larsen's *Quicksand*," *Novel* 27.3 (1994): 257–71; Thadious M. Davis, *Nella Larsen, Novelist of the Harlem Renaissance: A Woman's Life Unveiled* (Baton Rouge: Louisiana University Press, 1994); George Hutchinson, "Nella Larsen and the Veil of Race," *American Literary History* 9.2 (1997): 341.

17. The mulatta character in fiction has also been read by leading black feminist critics as a mediating figure that facilitates the exploration of cultures and races, as well as the relationship between them. See Carby, *Reconstructing Womanhood*; Carby, " 'On the Threshold of Woman's Era': Lynching, Empire, and Sexuality in Black Feminist Theory," in *"Race," Writing, and Difference*, ed. Henry Louis Gates Jr. (Chicago: University of Chicago Press, 1986), 301–16; Barbara Christian, *Black Women Novelists: The Development of a Tradition 1892–1976* (Westport, Conn.: Greenwood, 1980); Hortense Spillers, "Notes on an Alternative Model— Neither/Nor," in *The Difference Within: Feminism and Critical Theory*, ed. Elizabeth Meese and Alice Parker (Philadelphia: John Benjamins, 1989), 165–87.

18. I borrow Sarah Ahmed's provocative turn of phrase, one she uses to designate the colonized subject as "a mimic subject" (97).

19. In her introduction to *The Sleeper Wakes: Harlem Renaissance Stories by Women*, Marcy Knopf notes that DuBois and Fauset "together . . . published the literature of the 'Talented Tenth.' In fact, Fauset was most responsible for this, although DuBois received most of the credit" (xxi).

20. Locke's reference to "the Negro" and "*his* artistic endowments and cultural contributions" (15, emphasis added) seems not to have been merely a matter of writing style—of thirty-five contributors to the landmark anthology *The New Negro*, including poets, prose writers, essayists, playwrights, folklorists, and artists, he included the work of only six women.

21. See Gloria T. Hull, *Color, Sex and Poetry: Three Women Writers of the Harlem Renaissance* (Bloomington: Indiana University Press, 1987).

22. Brown, *The Negro in American Fiction*; David Littlejohn, *Black on White: A Critical Survey of Writing By American Negroes* (New York: Grossman, 1966); Bone, *The Negro Novel in America*; Sato, "Under the Harlem Shadow; Arthur P. Davis, *From the Dark Tower: Afro-American Writers 1900–1960* (Washington, D.C.: Howard University Press, 1974); Addison Gayle, *The Way of the New World: The Black Novel in America* (New York: Anchor, 1976); Berzon, *Neither White Nor Black*; Christian, *Black Women Novelists*; Dearborn, *Pocahontas's Daughters*; Carby, *Reconstructing Womanhood*; Bruce, *Black American Writing from the Nadir*; Baker, *Workings of the Spirit*; Vashti Crutcher Lewis, "Mulatta Hegemony in the Novels of Jessie Redmon Fauset," *CLA Journal* 35.4 (1992): 375–86.

23. Deborah E. McDowell, "New Directions for Black Feminist Criticism," in *The New Feminist Criticism: Essays on Women, Literature and Theory*, ed. Elaine Showalter, 186–99 (1980; New York: Pantheon, 1985); McDowell, "The Neglected Dimension of Jessie Redmon Fauset," in *Conjuring: Black Women's Fiction, and Literary Tradition*, ed. Marjorie Pryse and Hortense Spillers (1981; Bloomington: Indiana University Press, 1985), 86–104; McDowell, " 'That nameless . . . shameful impulse': Sexuality in Nella Larsen's *Quicksand* and *Passing*," in *Black Feminist Criticism and Critical Theory*, ed. Joe Weixlmann and Houston A. Baker Jr. (Greenwood: Penkevill, 1988), 139–67; McDowell, "Introduction: Regulating Midwives," *Plum Bun; A Novel without a Moral* (1928), in *Black Women Writers Series*, ed. Deborah E. McDowell, ix–xxxiii (Boston: Beacon Press, 1990); Cheryl Wall, "Passing for What? Aspects of Identity in Nella Larsen's Novels," *Black American Literature Forum* 20 (1986):97–111; Carby, *Reconstructing Womanhood*; Ann Hostetler, "The Aesthetic of Race and Gender in Nella Larsen's *Quicksand*," *PMLA* 105.1 (1990): 35–46; Ann duCille, *The Coupling Convention: Sex, Text, and Tradition in Black Women's Fiction* (New York: Oxford University Press, 1993); Deborah Silverman, "Nella Larsen's *Quicksand*: Untangling the Webs of Exoticism," *African American Review* 27.4 (1993): 599–614; Pamela Barnett, " 'My Picture of You Is, After All, the True Helga Crane': Portraiture and Identity in Nella Larsen's *Quicksand*," *Signs* 20.3 (1995): 575–600; Jacquelyn McLendon, *The Politics of Color in the Fiction of Jessie Redmon Fauset and Nella Larsen* (Charlottesville: University Press of Virginia, 1995).

24. See also Hazel Carby, " 'It Jus Be's Dat Way Sometime': The Sexual Politics of Black Women's Blues," in *feminisms: an anthology of literary theory and criticism*, ed. Robyn R. Warhol and Diane Price Herndl (1988; New Brunswick, N.J.: Rutgers University Press, 1991), 746–58.

25. While Hutchinson's remarks are focused on Larsen scholarship, the same is largely true of criticism on Fauset's novels. See Hutchinson for critics who follow this trend (346, n. 1).

26. The same critics who condemn Fauset and Larsen for their concentration on the black bourgeoisie see their treatment of black female sexuality as conservative.

27. The power balance arguably shifted when all-black shows gained a following in the early twentieth century. Out of these shows, the first Broadway productions to feature African American actors and performers developed, which then in turn created a market for drama that was written, staged, performed, and produced by African Americans.

28. On Sara Bartman, or the Hottentot Venus, see Zine Mugubane, "Which Bodies Matter? Feminism, Poststructuralism, Race, and the Curious Theoretical Odyssey of the 'Hottentot Venus,' " *Gender and Society* 15.6 (2001), 816–34; T. Denean Sharpley-Whiting, *Black Venus: Sexualized Savages, Primal Fears, and Primitive Narratives in French* (Durham, N.C.: Duke University Press, 1999); Yvette Abrahams, "Images of Sara Bartman: Sexuality, Race, and Gender in Early-Nineteenth-Century Britain," in *Nation, Empire, Colony: Historicizing Gender and Race*, ed. Ruth Roach Pierson and Nupur Chaudhuri (Bloomington: Indiana

University Press, 1998), 220–36; Elizabeth Alexander, *The Venus Hottentot* (Charlottesville: University Press of Virginia, 1990); Sander Gilman, *Difference and Pathology: Stereotypes of Sexuality, Race and Madness* (Ithaca, N.Y.: Cornell University Press, 1985); Richard Altick, *The Shows of London* (Cambridge, Mass.: Belknap Press, 1978).

29. In "Policing the Black Woman's Body in an Urban Context," Carby analyzes the stereotype of southern African American women who migrated to New York as "sexually degenerate" in Van Vechten's *Nigger Heaven* (1926) and Claude McKay's *Home to Harlem* (1928). Her observation regarding a correlation between the middle class and conservative attitudes toward sexuality is applicable to Fauset's and Larsen's novels as well.

30. Christian writes, "Fauset's heroines tend to be less independent than Iola Leroy, the contemporary pampered young woman. . . . Appropriately Laurentine is a seamstress and a very good dress designer. . . . No teacher of Sunday School or composer of papers on the education of black mothers, the heroine of *The Chinaberry Tree* is touted as the first Negro to introduce fashionable pajamas to her small New Jersey town" (*Black Women* 46).

31. As Barbara Christian documents, the "low-down" mulatta is figured in African American work song lyrics like the following: "Some say, give me a high yaller,/I say, give me a teasin' brown,/ . . . For some folkses say/A yaller is low down,/But teasin' brown/Is what I's crazy about" (32).

32. Although Fauset depicts Laurentine's mother, Sal, as strong enough to defy convention in her relationship with Holloway, Sal subscribes to bourgeois ideals when it comes to her daughter: "[I]f he gave her daughter, her precious baby, a name and protection she would lie down and let him walk over her body" (*CT* 32).

33. Black women were still believed responsible for the race's morality, or lack of it, in the 1920s and 1930s; moreover, their "place" continued to be thought of as the home and their "work" the encouragement of black men in the task of racial uplift. Black newspapers and magazines remained a popular forum for disseminating ideals of conduct for women. One such magazine, the *Messenger*, ran a monthly column entitled "Negro Womanhood's Greatest Needs." Deborah McDowell notes that the majority of the column's contributors "emphasized that a woman's place was in the home," as did one writing in 1927 that it was a woman's duty "to cling to the home [since] great men and women evolve from the environment of the hearthstone" ("New Directions" 192). The *Messenger's* editors, Charles Owen and Asa Randolph, were "the only Afro-Americans to be arrested and tried for violating the Espionage Act" and were considered by J. Edgar Hoover to be "among the most dangerous radicals in America" (Lewis 17). Owen's and Randolph's radicalism evidently did not extend to an enlightened view of women, nor did that of their readership who, presumably, were radical enough in their political views to buy the *Messenger* but remained conservative in their view of gender roles.

34. Fishbein argues that those 1920s films—of the "white slavery genre"—that treated rescued "fallen women" as "the equals or even superiors of true women," as Harper and Hopkins had done in *Iola Leroy* and *Contending Forces*, were more revolutionary and posed a greater challenge to sexual mores than the flapper films but were less popular.

Chapter 5. Passing Transgressions, Excess, and Authentic Identity in Jessie Fauset's *Plum Bun* and Nella Larsen's *Passing*

1. See also the contributions to Gates, *"Race," Writing, and Difference*; Mae Henderson, ed., *Borders, Boundaries, and Frames: Cultural Criticism and Cultural Studies* (New York: Routledge, 1995); Gina Dent, ed., *Black Popular Culture: A Project by Michele Wallace* (Seattle: Bay, 1992); Michael Awkward, *Negotiating Difference: Race, Gender, and the Politics of Positionality* (Chicago: University of Chicago Press, 1995).

2. See Ross Posnock's contention that while "identity politics is at last losing prestige in the academy," the postmodern "rhetoric of anti-essentialism depends on the identity/difference" opposition, keeping essentialism firmly in place (25).

3. In *Codes of Conduct*, Holloway maintains that "in American culture, and in the imaginative representations of that culture in literature, our compromised environments valorize publicly constructed racial and sexual identities, but they do not support privately authored identities that may be at odds with public representations" (60).

4. For an example of stylizations that can reach back to tradition as well as address current political concerns as they stake an identification, see Kobena Mercer, "Black Hair/Style Politics," in *Out There: Marginalization and Contemporary Cultures*, ed. Russell Ferguson et al. (Cambridge: MIT Press, 1990), 247–64.

5. See Harper, "Passing for What?"; Robinson, "Forms of Appearance of Value."

6. Wall distinguishes between Helga Crane of *Quicksand* and Clare Kendry of *Passing*: "Helga is an admirable character because she recognizes early on that 'passing' is not worth the price. Her integrity earns her no victory; her rebellion is as ineffectual as the dishonorable Clare's" ("Passing" 109). Haryette Mullen echoes Wall's contention in her characterization of African American authored passing narratives as a whole (73).

7. See, for example, the essays collected in Ginsberg, *Passing and the Fictions of Identity*, for readings that contend passing narratives render the notion of stable or fixed identity and identity categories like race, gender, and sexuality a fiction.

8. "Talented Tenth" uplift is regarded as stressing differentiation within African American communities through an attention to class in order to counter homogenizing notions of "blackness." As Alain Locke, who first coined the term "New Negro," would put it, by the 1920s it was becoming "ridiculous" to treat African Americans en masse. Even though white Americans found the existence of a black middle class unbelievable, "Talented Tenth" racial uplift argued that it was this segment of "the race" that could best prove its equality with whites and lift the poor and working-class African American along with it. This kind of disbelief in the existence of a black middle class is evident in Fauset's own publishing career, as we saw in Chapter 4. While the "Talented Tenth" could be said to have understood the imbrications of race and class as constructs that bore little relation to African American lived experience, they have been criticized for endorsing white bourgeois norms and regarding the behavior of the black urban working class as impeding their work for social change.

9. Favor renders this stark opposition more complex by noting that not only DuBois but also intellectuals like Alain Locke and Arthur Schomburg saw "the rural folk, who [were] in the process of becoming urban proletariat, [as] the basis of African American experience. . . . [F]olk experience [was regarded as] form[ing] the core of the New Negro's identity" (*Authentic Blackness* 12).

10. Indeed, blood as an image of race loyalty figured prominently in Marcus Garvey's popular "back to Africa" movement of the 1920s. Garvey's Universal Negro Improvement Association agitated for a halt to miscegenation; required its officers to prove that they were "pure African" and forbade them to marry whites; and routinely castigated the NAACP and its "near-white" African American members like DuBois and Walter White for being a " 'bastard aristocracy' " (qtd. in Williamson 160). DuBois also invoked "blood," though his politics differed substantially from Garvey's. See "The Conservation of Races."

11. For example, see Carby, *Reconstructing Womanhood*; Carby, " 'On the Threshold of Woman's Era' "; Christian, *Black Women Novelists*; Spillers, "Notes on an Alternative Model."

12. Berzon is quoting Sterling Brown, who argues that African American authors "urge his unhappiness" until the mulatto reaffirms "a mystical bond" to the black race, while white novelists attribute "the mulatto's unhappiness . . . [to] a divided inheritance. . . . Both are examples of race flattery" (144–45).

13. Here Roach theorizes "surrogation [as] the metamorphosis of one symbolic identity into another" (217).

14. For details regarding segregation, job opportunities, and the labor of black women at this time, see, for example: Paula Giddings, *Where and When I Enter: The Impact of Black Women on Race and Sex in America* (1984; New York: Bantam, 1986); Ann D. Gordon and Bettye Collier-Thomas, eds., *African American Women and the Vote: 1837–1965* (Amherst: University of Massachusetts Press, 1997); Darlene Clark Hine et al., eds. *Black Women in America: An Historical Encyclopedia*, 16 vols. (Bloomington: Indiana University Press, 1994); Hine et al., eds. *"We Specialize in the Wholly Impossible": A Reader in Black Women's History* (Brooklyn, N.Y.: Carlson, 1995); Darlene Clark Hine and Kathleen Thompson, *A Shining Thread of Hope* (New York: Random House, 1999).

15. Several critics have noted that Fauset uses the conventions of the fairy tale, romance, and novel of manners for purposes contrary to their traditional functions. However, this is a largely unexplored dimension of her work that time and space do not permit me to develop fully here, but a dimension that is certainly worthy of

further study. See McDowell, "The Neglected Dimension of Jessie Redmon Fauset"; McDowell, "Introduction: Regulating Midwives"; Foreman, "Looking Back from Zora"; duCille, *The Coupling Convention*, ch. 5; McLendon, *The Politics of Color in the Fiction of Jessie Fauset and Nella Larsen*, 30–49.

16. See, for example, Mary F. Sisney, "The View from the Outside: Black Novels of Manners," in *Reading and Writing Women's Lives: A Study of the Novel of Manners*, ed. Bege K. Bowers and Barbara Brothers (Ann Arbor, Mich.: UMI Research Press, 1990), 171–86.

17. Since the work of Mary Mabel Youmans, virtually every critic working with the novel has made this argument. See Youmans's "Nella Larsen's *Passing*: A Study in Irony," *CLA Journal* 18 (1974): 235–41.

18. Jennifer DeVere Brody also reads Clare as inviting detection: "Clare has never been afraid of being 'found out'—that is Irene's fear. Indeed, Clare might have looked forward to the moment when Bellew would realize that he had been duped by his wife . . . a triumphant trickster" ("Clare" 1064).

19. I borrow the phrases "residual essentialism" and "prepassing identity" from Amy Robinson's "It Takes One to Know One: Passing and Communities of Common Interest," *Critical Inquiry* 20 (1994): 715–36.

20. See also Cheryl A. Wall, "Poets and Versifiers, Singers and Signifiers: Women of the Harlem Renaissance," in *Women, the Arts, and the 1920s in Paris and New York*, ed. Kenneth W. Wheeler and Virginia Lee Lussier, 74–98 (New Brunswick, N.J.: Transaction, 1982); Valerie Smith, "Reading the Intersection of Race and Gender in Narratives of Passing," *diacritics* 24 (1994): 43–57.

21. See her introduction to the *American Women Writers Series* edition. A somewhat different version, entitled " 'That nameless . . . shameless impulse': Sexuality in Nella Larsen's *Quicksand* and *Passing*," appears in *Black Feminist Criticism and Critical Theory*, ed. Joe Weixlmann and Houston A. Baker Jr. (Greenwood: Penkevill, 1988), 139–67. Judith Butler, in a chapter in *Bodies that Matter* entitled "Passing, Queering: Nella Larsen's Psychoanalytic Challenge," also attends to the homosexual subtext of the novel but does not explore the possibility that Clare may be passing between sexualities. Similarly, David Blackmore argues for a reading of Brian as closeted and of Irene's desire for Clare as sexual longing she cannot bring herself to acknowledge, yet he does not explore this possibility of passing for and between queer and straight.

22. Fauset characterizes the Murrays as part of the black middle class and attends to the ways in which their class position still cannot afford Angela the access to further education and artistic training that she desires during a period in which segregation limited educational and employment opportunities for African Americans. Larsen positions Clare as the working-class outsider in her largely middle-class circle of schoolgirl friends and traces her passing back to her desire to have the kind of security and acceptance she lacked then.

Epilogue

1. Here I am invoking Karla Holloway's phrasing of "publicly" and "privately" authored identities. See Holloway, *Codes of Conduct: Race, Ethics and the Color of Our Character* (New Brunswick, N.J.: Rutgers University Press, 1995).

2. Among others, see, for example: Toni Morrison's *Sula, Song of Solomon, Beloved*, and *Paradise*; Alice Walker's *The Third Life of Grange Copeland, Meridian*, and *The Color Purple*; Gloria Naylor's *Mama Day*; Octavia Butler's *Kindred*.

Works Cited

Abrahams, Roger D. *Talking Black*. Rowley, Mass.: Newbury House, 1976.

Ahmed, Sarah. " 'She'll Wake Up One of These Days and Find She's Turned into a Nigger': Passing Through Hybridity." *Theory, Culture and Society* 16.2 (1999):87–106.

"American Fugitives in England." Rpt. in the *Liberator*, 30 May 1851.

"American Fugitive Slave Bill." *Glasgow Herald*, 10 January 1851.

"American Slavery." *Manchester Weekly Times*, 17 September 1859.

American Slavery. Report of the Great Anti-Slavery Meeting, Held April 9, 1851, in the Public Room, Broadmead, Bristol, To Receive the Fugitive Slaves, William and Ellen Craft. Bristol: James Ackland, 1851.

"American Slavery." Rpt. in the *Liberator*, 25 July 1851.

"American Slavery." *Warrington Guardian*, 5 February 1859.

"American Slavery in the World's Fair in London." Rpt. in the *Liberator*, 28 February 1851.

Ammons, Elizabeth. *Conflicting Stories: American Women Writers at the Turn into the Twentieth Century*. New York: Oxford University Press, 1991.

Anderson, Jervis. *This Was Harlem: A Cultural Portrait, 1900–1950*. New York: Farrar, Straus & Giroux, 1982.

"Anti-Slavery in Manchester, England." *National Anti-Slavery Standard*, 15 October 1859.

"Anti-Slavery Meeting." *Dundee and Perth Advertiser*. Rpt. in the *Liberator*, 7 March 1851.

"Anti-Slavery Meeting at Bristol." *Inquirer*, 19 April 1851.

Appiah, Kwame Anthony. *In My Father's House: Africa in the Philosophy of Culture*. New York: Oxford University Press, 1992.

———. " 'But Would that Still Be Me?' Notes on Gender, 'Race,' Ethnicity, As Sources of 'Identity.' " *Journal of Philosophy* 87 (1990):493–99.

"Arrival of Three American Fugitive Slaves." *Glasgow Chronicle*, 1 January 1851.

Awkward, Michael. *Negotiating Difference: Race, Gender, and the Politics of Positionality*. Chicago: University of Chicago Press, 1995.

Baker, Houston A., Jr. *Workings of the Spirit: The Poetics of Afro-American Women's Writing*. Chicago: University of Chicago Press, 1991.

———. "Caliban's Triple Play." In *"Race," Writing, and Difference*, ed. Henry Louis Gates Jr., 381–95. Chicago: University of Chicago Press, 1986.

———. *Blues, Ideology, and Afro-American Literature: A Vernacular Theory*. Chicago: University of Chicago Press, 1984.

Baker, Ray Stannard. *Following the Color Line: American Negro Citizenship in the Progressive Era*. 1908. New York: Harper & Row, 1964.

Bakhtin, M. M. *Problems of Dostoevsky's Poetics*. Ed. and Trans. Caryl Emerson. 1929. Minneapolis: University of Minnesota Press, 1984.

———. *The Dialogic Imagination: Four Essays*. Trans. Caryl Emerson and Michael Holquist. Ed. Michael Holquist. 1975. Austin: University of Texas Press, 1981.

Banton, Michael, and Jonathan Harwood. *The Race Concept*. London: David & Charles, 1975.

Barrett, Lindon. "Hand-writing: Legibility and the White Body in *Running a Thousand Miles for Freedom*." *American Literature* 69.2 (1997):315–36.

Bay, Mia. *The White Image in the Black Mind: African-American Ideas about White People, 1830–1925*. New York: Oxford University Press, 2000.

Baym, Nina. *Woman's Fiction: A Guide to Novels By and About Women in America, 1820–1870*. 2nd ed. Urbana and Chicago: University of Illinois Press, 1993.

Bentley, Nancy. "White Slaves: The Mulatto Hero in Antebellum Fiction." In *Subjects and Citizens: Nation, Race, and Gender from Oroonoko to Anita Hill*, ed. Michael Moon and Cathy N. Davidson, 195–216. Durham, N.C.: Duke University Press, 1995.

Berlant, Lauren. *The Queen of America Goes to Washington City: Essays on Sex and Citizenship*. Durham, N.C.: Duke University Press, 1997.

———. "National Brands/National Body: *Imitation of Life*." In *Comparative American Identities: Race, Sex, and Nationality in the Modern Text*, ed. Hortense Spillers, 110–40. New York: Routledge, 1991.

Berzon, Judith R. *Neither White Nor Black: The Mulatto Character in American Fiction*. New York: New York University Press, 1978.

Bhabha, Homi K. *The Location of Culture*. New York: Routledge, 1994.

Blackett, R.J.M. *Beating Against the Barriers: Biographical Essays in Nineteenth-Century Afro-American History*. Baton Rouge: Louisiana State University Press, 1986.

———. *Building an Antislavery Wall: Black Americans in the Atlantic Abolitionist Movement, 1830–1860*. Baton Rouge: Louisiana State University Press, 1983.

Blackmore, David. " 'That Unreasonable Restless Feeling': The Homosexual Subtext of Nella Larsen's *Passing*." *African American Review* 26.3 (1992):475–84.

Blassingame, John W. *Black New Orleans 1860–1880*. Chicago: University of Chicago Press, 1973.

Bontemps, Arna, ed. *The Harlem Renaissance Remembered*. New York: Dodd, Mead, 1972.

Bourdieu, Pierre. "The Force of Law: Toward a Sociology of the Juridical Field." Trans. Richard Terdiman. *Hastings Law Journal* 38 (1987):805–53.

Bowditch, Vincent Y. *Life and Correspondence of Henry Ingersoll Bowditch*. Vol. 1. Boston and New York: Riverside Press, 1902.

Boyd, Melba Joyce. *Discarded Legacy: Politics and Poetics in the Life of Frances E. W. Harper 1825–1911*. Detroit: Wayne State University Press, 1994.

Braxton, Joanne. Introduction to *The Work of the Afro-American Woman*, by Mrs. N. F. Mossell. 1894. In Gates, *The Schomburg Library of Nineteenth-Century Black Women Writers*, xxvii–xlii.

Brodhead, Richard. *Cultures of Letters: Scenes of Reading and Writing in Nineteenth-Century America*. Chicago: University of Chicago Press, 1993.

Brody, Jennifer DeVere. *Impossible Purities: Blackness, Femininity, and Victorian Culture*. Durham, N.C.: Duke University Press, 1998.

———. "Clare Kendry's 'True' Colors: Race and Class Conflict in Nella Larsen's *Passing*." *Callaloo* 15.4 (1992):1053–65.

Brooks, Kristina. "Mammies, Bucks, and Wenches: Minstrelsy, Racial Pornography, and Racial Politics in Pauline Hopkins's *Hagar's Daughter*." In Gruesser, *The Unruly Voice*, 119–57.

Brown, Gillian. *Domestic Individualism: Imagining Self in Nineteenth-Century America*. Berkeley: University of California Press, 1990.

Brown, Josephine. *Biography of an American Bondman, by His Daughter*. 1856. Digital Schomburg African American Women Writers of the 19th Century, http://digilib.nypl.org:80/dynaweb/digs/wwm975/@Generic__BookView.

Brown, Sterling. *The Negro in American Fiction*. 1937. New York: Argosy-Antiquarian, 1969.

Brown, William Wells. *Clotel; or, The President's Daughter*. 1853. New York: Arno Press, 1969.

Burma, John H. "The Measurement of Negro 'Passing.'" *American Journal of Sociology* 52 (1946):18–22.

Butler, Judith. *Bodies That Matter: On the Discursive Limits of Sex.* New York: Routledge, 1994.

———. "Imitation and Gender Insubordination." In *Inside/Out: Lesbian Theories, Gay Theories,* ed. Diana Fuss, 13–31. New York: Routledge, 1991.

———. *Gender Trouble: Feminism and the Subversion of Identity.* New York: Routledge, 1990.

Campbell, Jane. *Mythic Black Fiction: The Transformation of History.* Knoxville: University of Tennessee Press, 1986.

Carby, Hazel V. "Policing the Black Woman's Body in an Urban Context." *Critical Inquiry* 18 (1992):738–55.

———. "It Jus Be's Dat Way Sometime: The Sexual Politics of Black Women's Blues." In *feminisms: an anthology of literary theory and criticism,* ed. Robyn R. Warhol and Diane Price Herndl, 746–58. 1988. New Brunswick, N.J.: Rutgers University Press, 1991.

———. "Reinventing History/Imagining the Future." *African American Review* 23 (1989):381–87.

———. Introduction to *The Magazine Novels of Pauline Hopkins,* xxix–xlx. New York: Oxford University Press, 1988.

———. *Reconstructing Womanhood: The Emergence of the Afro-American Woman Novelist.* New York: Oxford University Press, 1987.

Catterall, Helen T., ed. *Judicial Cases Concerning American Slavery and the Negro.* 1936. 5 vols. Shannon: Irish University Press, 1968.

Child, Lydia Maria. *The Freedmen's Book.* Boston: Ticknor & Fields, 1865.

Christian, Barbara. "Shadows Uplifted." In *Feminist Criticism and Social Change: Sex, Class and Race in Literature and Culture,* ed. Judith Newton and Deborah Rosenfelt, 181–215. New York: Methuen, 1985.

———. *Black Women Novelists: The Development of a Tradition 1892–1976.* Westport, Conn.: Greenwood, 1980.

Collins, Patricia Hill. *Black Feminist Thought: Knowledge, Consciousness, and the Politics of Empowerment.* New York: Routledge, 1991.

Cooper, Anna Julia. *A Voice from the South, by a Black Woman of the South.* 1892. In Gates, *The Schomburg Library of Nineteenth-Century Black Women Writers.*

Cott, Nancy F. *The Bonds of Womanhood: "Woman's Sphere" in New England, 1780–1835.* New Haven, Conn.: Yale University Press, 1977.

Craft, William, and Ellen Craft. *Running a Thousand Miles for Freedom: The Escape of William and Ellen Craft from Slavery, by William Craft and Ellen Craft.* Ed. Barbara McCaskill. Athens: University of Georgia Press, 1999.

Crummell, Alexander. *Africa and America: Addresses and Discourses by Reverend Alexander Crummell.* 1891. New York: Negro University Press, 1969.

Davis, F. James. *Who is Black? One Nation's Definition.* University Park: Pennsylvania State University Press, 1991.

Davis, Thadious M. *Nella Larsen, Novelist of the Harlem Renaissance: A Woman's Life Unveiled.* Baton Rouge: Louisiana University Press, 1994.

Dearborn, Mary V. *Pocahontas's Daughters: Gender and Ethnicity in American Culture.* New York: Oxford University Press, 1986.

Degler, Carl N. *Neither Black Nor White: Slavery and Race Relations in Brazil and the U.S.* New York: Macmillan, 1971.

Delany, Martin R. *The Condition, Elevation, Emigration, and Destiny of the Colored People of the United States.* 1852. New York: Arno Press, 1968.

DeMarco, Joseph P. *The Social Thought of W.E.B. DuBois.* Lanham, Md.: University Press of America, 1983.

Dent, Gina, ed. *Black Popular Culture: A Project by Michele Wallace.* Seattle: Bay, 1992.

Dickens, Dorothy Lee. *Black on the Rainbow.* New York: Pageant, 1952.

Dominguez, Virginia R. *White By Definition: Social Classification in Creole Louisiana.* New Brunswick, N.J.: Rutgers University Press, 1986.

Doreski, C. K. *Writing America Black: Race Rhetoric in the Public Sphere*. Cambridge: Cambridge University Press, 1998.

Douglas, Ann. *The Feminization of American Culture*. New York: Doubleday, 1977.

DuBois, W. E. B. "The Conservation of Races." 1897. In Huggins, *W.E.B. DuBois*, 815–26.

———. *Dusk of Dawn: An Essay Toward an Autobiography of a Race Concept*. 1940. In Huggins, *W.E.B. DuBois*, 551–802

duCille, Ann. "The Occult of True Black Womanhood: Critical Demeanor and Black Feminist Studies." *Signs* 19.3 (1994):591–629.

———. "Blues Notes on Black Sexuality: Sex and the Texts of Jessie Fauset and Nella Larsen." *Journal of the History of Sexuality* 3 (1993):418–44.

———. *The Coupling Convention: Sex, Text, and Tradition in Black Women's Fiction*. New York: Oxford University Press, 1993.

Echeruo, Michael J. C. "Edward W. Blyden, W.E.B. DuBois, and the 'Color Complex.'" *Journal of Modern African Studies* 30 (1992):669–84.

Eckard, E. W. "How Many Negroes 'Pass'?" *American Journal of Sociology* 52 (1947):498–503.

"Ellen Craft." *New National Era*, 14 December 1871.

Ellis, Trey. "The New Black Aesthetic." *Callaloo* 12.1 (1989):233–46.

Ellison, Ralph. "Change the Joke and Slip the Yoke." In *Shadow and Act*, 45–59. 1958. New York: Random House, 1964.

Ernest, John. *Resistance and Reformation in Nineteenth-Century African-American Literature*. Jackson: University Press of Mississippi, 1995.

Estlin, J. B., to Maria Chapman. 3 April 1852. Bayswater. MS A.912.v26no.23. Weston Papers, Boston Public Library.

Estlin, Mary, to Anne Weston. 9 May 1851. Bristol. MS A.92v25no.87. Weston Papers, Boston Public Library.

Fabi, M. Giulia. *Passing and the Rise of the African American Novel*. Urbana and Chicago: University of Illinois Press, 2001.

Farrison, William. *William Wells Brown: Author and Reformer*. Chicago: University of Chicago Press, 1969.

Fauset, Jessie Redmon. *The Chinaberry Tree*. 1931. In *The Northeastern Library of Black Literature*, ed. Richard Yarborough. Boston: Northeastern University Press, 1995.

———. *Plum Bun; A Novel without a Moral*. 1928. In *Black Women Writers Series*, ed. Deborah E. McDowell. Boston: Beacon Press, 1990.

Fauset, Jessie Redmon, to Langston Hughes. Circa 1920–26. James Weldon Johnson MSS Hughes Papers (Correspondence). Bienecke Library, Yale University.

———, to Jean Toomer. 17 February 1922. James Weldon Johnson Small Collections. Bienecke Library, Yale University.

———, to Langston Hughes. 6 January 1925. James Weldon Johnson MSS Hughes Papers (Correspondence). Bienecke Library, Yale University.

Favor, J. Martin. *Authentic Blackness: The Folk in the New Negro Renaissance*. Durham, N.C.: Duke University Press, 1999.

———. "'Ain't Nothin' Like the Real Thing, Baby': Trey Ellis' Search for New Black Voices." *Callaloo* 16.3 (1993):694–705.

Fishbein, Leslie. "The Demise of the Cult of True Womanhood in Early American Film, 1900–1930." *Journal of Popular Film and Television* 12 (1984):66–72.

Foreman, P. Gabrielle. "Who's Your Mama? 'White' Mulatta Genealogies, Early Photography, and Anti-Passing Narratives of Slavery and Freedom." *American Literary History* 14.3 (2002):505–39.

———. "'Reading Aright': White Slavery, Black Referents, and the Strategies of Histotextuality in *Iola Leroy*." *Yale Journal of Criticism* 10.2 (1997):327–54.

Foster, Frances Smith. Introduction to *"Minnie's Sacrifice," "Sowing and Reaping," "Trial and Triumph": Three Rediscovered Novels by Frances E. W. Harper*, ed. Frances Smith Foster, xi–xxxvii. Boston: Beacon Press, 1994.

———. Introduction to *Iola Leroy, or Shadows Uplifted*, xxvii–xxxix. 1892. New York: Oxford University Press, 1988.

———. *Witnessing Slavery: The Development of the Ante-bellum Slave Narratives*. Westport, Conn.: Greenwood Press, 1979.

Foucault, Michel. *The History of Sexuality*, Vol. 1, *An Introduction*. Trans. Robert Hurley. 1976. New York: Random House, 1980.

Frazier, E. Franklin. *The Negro Family in Chicago*. Chicago: University of Chicago Press, 1932.

Fredrickson, George M. *The Black Image in the White Mind: The Debate on Afro-American Character and Destiny, 1817–1914*. New York: Harper & Row, 1971.

"Fugitive Slaves at the Great Exhibition." Rpt. in the *Liberator*, 18 July 1851.

Gaines, Kevin K. *Uplifting the Race: Black Leadership, Politics, and Culture in the Twentieth Century*. Chapel Hill: University of North Carolina Press, 1996.

Gates, Henry Louis, Jr. "Criticism in the Jungle." In *Black Literature and Literary Theory*, ed. Henry Louis Gates Jr., 1–24. New York: Routledge, 1990.

———. *The Signifying Monkey: A Theory of African-American Literary Criticism*. New York: Oxford University Press, 1988.

———, ed. *Reading Black, Reading Feminist: A Critical Anthology*. New York: Penguin, 1990.

———, ed. *The Schomburg Library of Nineteenth-Century Black Women Writers*. New York: Oxford University Press, 1988.

Gatewood, Willard B. *Aristocrats of Color: The Black Elite, 1880–1920*. Bloomington: Indiana University Press, 1990.

Gayle, Addison. *The Way of the New World: The Black Novel in America*. New York: Anchor, 1976.

Genovese, Eugene D. *Roll, Jordan, Roll: The World the Slaves Made*. New York: Random House, 1972.

Giddings, Paula. *When and Where I Enter: The Impact of Black Women on Race and Sex in America*. 1984. New York: Bantam, 1986.

Gillman, Susan. "The Mulatto, Tragic or Triumphant? The Nineteenth-Century American Race Melodrama." In Samuels, *The Culture of Sentiment*, 221–43.

Gilroy, Paul. *Against Race: Imagining Political Culture Beyond the Color Line*. Cambridge: Belknap Press of Harvard University Press, 2001.

Ginsberg, Elaine. "Introduction: The Politics of Passing." In Ginsberg, *Passing and the Fictions of Identity*, 1–18.

———, ed. *Passing and the Fictions of Identity*. Durham, N.C: Duke University Press, 1996.

Goldberg, David Theo. *Racist Culture: Philosophy and the Politics of Meaning*. Oxford: Blackwell, 1993.

Gossett, Thomas F. *Race: The History of an Idea in America*. Dallas: Southern Methodist University Press, 1963.

Graham, Maryemma, and Gina M. Rossetti. *"Minnie's Sacrifice. Review." African American Review* 30.2 (1996):302–5.

Green, Harvey. *The Light of the Home: An Intimate View of the Lives of Women in Victorian America*. New York: Pantheon, 1988.

Gross, Ariela J. "Litigating Whiteness: Trials of Racial Determination in the Nineteenth-Century South." *Yale Law Journal* 108 (1998):111–88.

Gruesser, John Cullen, ed. *The Unruly Voice: Rediscovering Pauline Elizabeth Hopkins*. Urbana and Chicago: University of Illinois Press, 1996.

Guillaumin, Colette. "Race and Nature: The System of Marks." Trans. Mary Jo Lakeland. *Feminist Issues* 8 (1988):25–43.

Guillory, Monique. "Under One Roof: The Sins and Sanctity of the New Orleans Quadroon Balls." In *Race Consciousness: African-American Studies for the New Century*, ed. Judith Jackson Fossett and Jeffrey A. Tucker, 67–92. New York: New York University Press, 1997.

Guy-Sheftall, Beverly. *Daughters of Sorrow: Attitudes Towards Black Women, 1880–1920*. Brooklyn, N.Y.: Carlson, 1990.

Hale, Grace Elizabeth. *Making Whiteness: The Culture of Segregation in the South, 1890–1940*. New York: Pantheon, 1998.

Hall, Stuart. "What Is This 'Black' in Black Popular Culture?" In Dent, *Black Popular Culture*, 21–33.

Harper, Frances E. W. *Iola Leroy, or Shadows Uplifted*. 1892. In Gates, *The Schomburg Library of Nineteenth-Century Black Women Writers*.

Harper, Philip Brian. *Are We Not Men? Masculine Anxiety and the Problem of African-American Identity*. New York: Oxford University Press, 1996.

———. "Private Affairs: Race, Sex, Property and Persons." *GLQ: A Journal of Lesbian and Gay Studies* 1.2 (1994):111–33.

Harris, Cheryl. "Whiteness as Property." *Harvard Law Review* 106.8 (June 1993):1707–91.

Hartman, Saidiya V. *Scenes of Subjection: Terror, Slavery and Self-Making in Nineteenth-Century America*. New York: Oxford University Press, 1997.

Henderson, Mae G. "Speaking in Tongues: Dialogics, Dialectics, and the Black Woman Writer's Literary Tradition." In Gates, *Reading Black, Reading Feminist*, 116–42.

———. Introduction to *Borders, Boundaries, and Frames: Cultural Criticism and Cultural Studies*, ed. Mae G. Henderson, 1–30. New York: Routledge, 1995.

Higginbotham, A. Leon. *In the Matter of Color: Race and the American Legal Process, the Colonial Period*. New York: Oxford University Press, 1978.

Hine, Darlene, ed. *Black Women in United States History*. Vol. 2. Brooklyn, N.Y.: Carlson, 1990.

Hirsch, Jay. "Behavior-Genetic Analysis and the Study of Man." In *Science and the Concept of Race*, ed. Margaret Mead et al., 37–48. New York: Columbia University Press, 1968.

Hoffman, Frederick L. *Race Traits and Tendencies of the American Negro*. New York: Macmillan, 1896.

Holloway, Karla F. C. *Codes of Conduct: Race, Ethics and the Color of Our Character*. New Brunswick, N.J.: Rutgers University Press, 1995.

Hopkins, Pauline E. *Contending Forces: A Romance Illustrative of Negro Life North and South*. 1899. In Gates, *The Schomburg Library of Nineteenth-Century Black Women Writers*.

Horton, James. "Freedom's Yoke: Gender Conventions Among Antebellum Free Blacks." In Hine, *Black Women in United States History*, 667–92.

Huggins, Nathan, ed. *W.E.B. DuBois: Writings*. New York: Library of America, 1986.

Hughes, Langston. *The Big Sea*. New York: Hill & Wang, 1940.

———. "The Negro Artist and the Racial Mountain." *Nation*, 23 June 1926, 692–96.

Hutcheon, Linda. *A Theory of Parody: The Teachings of Twentieth-Century Art Forms*. 1985. New York: Routledge, 1991.

Hutchinson, George. "Nella Larsen and the Veil of Race." *American Literary History* 9.2 (1997):329–49.

Jacobs, Harriet. *Incidents in the Life of a Slave Girl*. 1861. In Gates, *The Schomburg Library of Nineteenth-Century Black Women Writers*.

Johnston, James H. *Race Relations in Virginia and Miscegenation in the South 1776–1860*. Amherst: University of Massachusetts Press, 1970.

Jordan, Winthrop D. *The White Man's Burden: Historical Origins of Racism in the United States*. New York: Oxford University Press, 1974.

Julien, Isaac. " 'Black Is, Black Ain't': Notes on De-Essentializing Black Identities." In Dent, *Black Popular Culture*, 255–63.

Kaplan, Carla. "Undesirable Desire: Citizenship and Romance in Modern American Fiction." *Modern Fiction Studies* 43.1 (1997):144–69.

Kasson, John F. *Rudeness and Civility: Manners in Nineteenth-Century Urban America.* New York: Farrar, Straus & Giroux, 1990.

Kawash, Samira. "*The Autobiography of an Ex-Coloured Man*: (Passing for) Black Passing for White." In Ginsberg, *Passing and the Fictions of Identity*, 59–74.

Keetley, Dawn. "Racial Conviction, Racial Confusion: Indeterminate Identities in Women's Slave Narratives and Southern Courts." *a/b: Auto/Biography Studies* 10 (1995):1–20.

Kent, George. "Patterns of the Harlem Renaissance." In Bontemps, *The Harlem Renaissance Remembered*, 27–50.

Kephart, William M. "The 'Passing' Question." *Phylon* 9 (1948):336–40.

Knopf, Marcy. Introduction to *The Sleeper Wakes: Harlem Renaissance Stories by Women*, ed. Marcy Knopf, xix–xxxvi. New Brunswick, N.J.: Rutgers University Press, 1993.

Knupfer, Anne Meis. *Toward a Tenderer Humanity and a Nobler Womanhood: African American Women's Clubs in Turn-of-the-Century Chicago.* New York: New York University Press, 1996.

Krasner, David. "Parody and Double Consciousness in the Language of Early Black Musical Theatre." *African American Review* 29 (1995):317–23.

Kronik, John W. "Editor's Note." *PMLA* 107 (1992):425.

"A Lady Lecturing on American Slavery." *Liverpool Mercury*, 22 January 1859.

Laqueur, Thomas. "Bodies, Details and the Humanitarian Narrative." In *The New Cultural History*, ed. Lynn Hunt, 176–204. Berkeley: University of California Press, 1989.

Larsen, Nella. *Passing.* 1929. In *American Women Writers Series*, ed. Deborah E. McDowell. New Brunswick, N.J.: Rutgers University Press, 1994.

———. *Quicksand.* 1928. In *American Women Writers Series*, ed. Deborah E. McDowell. New Brunswick, N.J.: Rutgers University Press, 1994.

Larsen, Nella, to Dorothy Peterson. Undated. James Weldon Johnson Collection. Bienecke Library, Yale University.

———, to Carl Van Vechten and Fania Marinoff. 22 May 1930. James Weldon Johnson Collection. Bienecke Library, Yale University.

———, to Carl Van Vechten. 14 June 1929. James Weldon Johnson Collection. Bienecke Library, Yale University.

———, to Dorothy Peterson. 12 July 1927. James Weldon Johnson Small Collections. Bienecke Library, Yale University.

"The Lecture at the Lion Hotel." *Warrington Times.* Rpt. in the *Liberator*, 11 March 1859.

"Lecture on American Slavery by a Lady of Colour." *Bolton Chronicle*, 1 October 1859.

"Lecture on American Slavery by a Lady of Colour." *Warrington Standard*, 29 January 1859.

Lee, Reba. *I Passed For White, as told to Mary Hastings Bradley.* New York and London: Longmans Green, 1955.

"Leeds Young Men's Anti-Slavery Society." *Leeds and West Riding Express*, 24 December 1859.

Lerner, Gerda, ed. *Black Women in White America: A Documentary History.* New York: Random House, 1972.

"Letter from Francis Bishop, Liverpool, 28 December 1850." *Liberator*, 28 February 1851.

Lewis, David Levering. *When Harlem Was in Vogue.* New York: Knopf, 1981.

Lhamon, W. T., Jr. *Raising Cain: Blackface Performance from Jim Crow to Hip Hop.* Cambridge: Harvard University Press, 1998.

Little, Jonathan. "Nella Larsen's *Passing*: Irony and the Critics." *African American Review* 26 (1992):173–82.

Locke, Alain, ed. *The New Negro: An Interpretation.* 1925. New York: Arno Press, 1968.

López, Ian F. Haney. *White By Law: The Legal Construction of Race.* New York: New York University Press, 1996.

Lott, Eric. *Love and Theft: Blackface Minstrelsy and the American Working Class.* New York: Oxford University Press, 1994.

Mangum, Charles S., Jr. *The Legal Status of the Negro.* 1940. New York: Johnson Reprint, 1970.

May, Samuel, Jr., to J. B. Estlin. 2 February 1849. MSB 1.6 Boston Public Library.

McCaskill, Barbara. "Introduction: William and Ellen Craft in Transatlantic Literature and Life." In *Running a Thousand Miles for Freedom: The Escape of William and Ellen Craft from Slavery*, by William Craft and Ellen Craft, ed. Barbara McCaskill, vii–xxv. Athens: University of Georgia Press, 1999.

———. "'Yours Very Truly': Ellen Craft—The Fugitive as Text and Artifact." *African American Review* 28.4 (1994):509–29.

McCullough, Kate. "Slavery, Sexuality, and Genre: Pauline Hopkins and the Representation of Female Desire." In Gruesser, *The Unruly Voice*, 21–49.

McDougald, Elsie Johnson. "The Task of Negro Womanhood." In Locke, *The New Negro*, 369–82.

McDowell, Deborah E. "'The Changing Same': Generational Connections and Black Women Novelists." In Gates, *Reading Black, Reading Feminist*, 91–115.

———. "Introduction: Regulating Midwives." *Plum Bun; A Novel without a Moral*. 1928. In *Black Women Writers Series*, ed. Deborah E. McDowell, ix–xxxiii. Boston: Beacon Press, 1990.

———. "'That nameless . . . shameful impulse': Sexuality in Nella Larsen's *Quicksand* and *Passing*." In *Black Feminist Criticism and Critical Theory*, ed. Joe Weixlmann and Houston A. Baker Jr., 139–67. Greenwood, Fla.: Penkevill, 1988.

———. "New Directions for Black Feminist Criticism." In *The New Feminist Criticism: Essays on Women, Literature and Theory*, ed. Elaine Showalter, 186–99. 1980. New York: Pantheon, 1985.

McLendon, Jacquelyn Y. *The Politics of Color in the Fiction of Jessie Fauset and Nella Larsen*. Charlottesville: University Press of Virginia, 1995.

Mencke, John G. *Mulattoes and Race Mixture: American Attitudes and Images, 1865–1918*. Ann Arbor, Mich.: UMI Research Press, 1979.

Midgley, Clare. *Women Against Slavery: The British Campaigns 1780–1870*. New York: Routledge, 1992.

"Miss Remond in Bristol." *Anti-Slavery Advocate*, 1 October 1859.

"Miss Remond in Yorkshire." *Anti-Slavery Advocate*, 1 February 1860.

"Miss Remond's First Lecture in Dublin." *Anti-Slavery Advocate*, 1 April 1859.

"Miss Remond's Second Lecture on Slavery." *Warrington Standard*, 5 February 1859.

"Miss Remond's Second Lecture on Slavery." *Warrington Times*. Rpt. in the *Liberator*, 11 March 1859.

Moses, Wilson J. "Domestic Feminism Conservatism, Sex Roles, and Black Women's Clubs 1893–1896." In Hine, *Black Women in United States History*, 959–70.

———. *The Golden Age of Black Nationalism 1850–1925*. Hamden, Conn.: Shoe String Press, 1978.

Mossell, Mrs. N. F. *The Work of the Afro-American Woman*. 1894. In Gates, *The Schomburg Library of Nineteenth-Century Black Women Writers*.

Mullen, Hareyette. "Optic White: Blackness and the Production of Whiteness." *diacritics* 24.2–3 (1994):71–89.

Myrdal, Gunnar. *An American Dilemma: The Negro Problem and Modern Democracy*. 1944. New York: Harper & Row, 1962.

Omolade, Barbara. "Hearts of Darkness." In *Powers of Desire: The Politics of Sexuality*, ed. Ann Snitow et al., 350–67. New York: Monthly Review, 1983.

Parker, Andrew, and Eve Kosofsky Sedgwick. "Introduction: Performativity and Performance." In Parker and Sedgwick, *Performativity and Performance*, 1–18.

———, eds. *Performativity and Performance*. New York and London: Routledge, 1995.

Pascoe, Peggy. "Miscegenation Law, Court Cases, and Ideologies of 'Race' in Twentieth-Century America." *Journal of American History* 83.1 (1996):44–69.

Perkins, Linda M. "The Impact of the 'Cult of True Womanhood' on the Education of Black Women." *Journal of Social Issues* 39.3 (1983):17–28.

Peterson, Carla L. *"Doers of the Word": African-American Women Speakers and Writers in the North (1830–1880)*. New York: Oxford University Press, 1995.

Piper, Adrian. "Passing for White, Passing for Black." In *New Feminist Criticism: Art, Identity, Action*, ed. Joanna Frueh et al., 216–47. New York: Harper Collins, 1994.

Posnock, Ross. *Color and Culture: Black Writers and the Making of the Modern Intellectual.* Cambridge: Harvard University Press, 1998.

Proceedings of the American Anti-Slavery Society at Its Second Decade, Held in the City of Philadelphia, Dec 3d, 4th and 5th, 1853. New York: American Anti-Slavery Society, 1854.

Quarles, Benjamin. *Black Abolitionists.* New York: Oxford University Press, 1969.

Reid-Pharr, Robert. *Conjugal Union: The Body, the House, and the Black American.* New York: Oxford University Press, 1999.

Remond, Sarah Parker, to Maria Weston Chapman. 16 October 1859. Warrington. MS A.9.2.29.71. Weston Papers, Boston Public Library.

Reuter, Edward B. *The Mulatto in the United States.* 1918. New York: Johnson Reprint, 1970.

Rhodes, Chip. "*Writing up the New Negro*: The Construction of Consumer Desire in the Twenties." *Journal of American Studies* 28 (1994):191–207.

Richards, Sandra L. "Caught in the Act of Social Definition: *On the Road* with Anna Deavere Smith." In *Acting Out: Feminist Performances*, ed. Lynda Hart and Peggy Phelan, 35–53. Ann Arbor: University of Michigan Press, 1993.

Riley, Glenda. *Inventing the American Woman: A Perspective on Women's History, 1865 to the Present.* Arlington Heights, Ill: Harland Davidson, 1986.

Roach, Joseph. *Cities of the Dead: Circum-Atlantic Performance.* New York: Columbia University Press, 1996.

Robinson, Amy. "Forms of Appearance of Value: Homer Plessy and the Politics of Privacy." In *Performance and Cultural Politics*, ed. Elin Diamond, 237–61. New York: Routledge, 1996.

———. "It Takes One to Know One: Passing and Communities of Common Interest." *Critical Inquiry* 20 (1994):715–36.

Romero, Lora. *Home Fronts: Domesticity and Its Critics in the Antebellum United States.* Durham, N.C.: Duke University Press, 1997.

Rose, Margaret A. *Parody: Ancient, Modern, and Postmodern.* Cambridge: Cambridge University Press, 1993.

Rothenberg, Molly Anne, and Joseph Valente. "Performative Chic: The Fantasy of a Performative Politics." *College Literature* 24.1 (1997):295–305.

Samuels, Shirley. "The Identity of Slavery." In Samuels, *The Culture of Sentiment*, 157–71.

———, ed. *The Culture of Sentiment: Race, Gender, and Sentimentality in Nineteenth-Century America.* New York: Oxford University Press, 1992.

Sánchez, Maria Carla, and Linda Scholssberg, eds. *Passing: Identity and Interpretation in Sexuality, Race, and Religion.* New York: New York University Press, 2001.

Sànchez-Eppler, Karen. "Bodily Bonds: The Intersecting Rhetorics of Feminism and Abolitionism." *Representations* 24 (1988):28–59.

Sato, Hiroko. "Under the Harlem Shadow: A Study of Jessie Fauset and Nella Larsen." In Bontemps, *The Harlem Renaissance Remembered*, 63–89.

Scarry, Elaine. *The Body in Pain: The Making and Unmaking of the World.* New York: Oxford University Press, 1985.

Scholssberg, Linda. "Introduction: Rites of Passing." In Sànchez and Scholssberg, *Passing: Identity and Interpretation in Sexuality, Race, and Religion*, 1–12.

"A Second Lecture by Miss Remond." *Warrington Times*. Rpt. in the *Liberator*, 11 March 1859.

Simpson, J. A., and E.S.C. Weiner, eds. *The Oxford English Dictionary*, 2nd ed. Oxford: Clarendon Press, 1989.

"Singular Escape." *Liberator*, 12 January 1849.

"Slavery and Democracy." *Warrington Guardian*, 5 February 1859. Supplement.

"Slavery in the United States." *Bridgewater Times*, 15 May 1851.

Smith, Shawn Michelle. *American Archives: Gender, Race, and Class in Visual Culture*. Princeton, N.J.: Princeton University Press, 1999.

Smith, Valerie. "Reading the Intersection of Race and Gender in Narratives of Passing." *diacritics* 24 (1994):43–57.

Smitherman, Geneva. *Talkin and Testifyin: The Language of Black America*. Detroit: Wayne State University Press, 1977.

Smith-Rosenberg, Caroll. *Disorderly Conduct: Visions of Gender in Victorian America*. New York: Knopf, 1985.

Sollers, Werner. *Neither Black Nor White Yet Both: Thematic Explorations of Interracial Literature*. New York: Oxford University Press, 1997.

Somerville, Siobhan B. *Queering the Color Line: Race and the Invention of Homosexuality in American Culture*. Durham, N.C.: Duke University Press, 2000.

"Speech by Sarah P. Remond Delivered at the Music Hall, Warrington, England, 24 January 1859." Document 73. In *The Black Abolitionist Papers*, ed. C. Peter Ripley et al. Vol. 1, 435–44. Chapel Hill: University of North Carolina Press, 1985.

Spillers, Hortense J. "Moving on Down the Line: Variations on the African-American Sermon." In *The Bounds of Race: Perspectives on Hegemony and Resistance*, ed. Dominick LaCapra, 39–71. Ithaca, N.Y.: Cornell University Press, 1990.

———. "Notes on an Alternative Model—Neither/Nor." In *The Difference Within: Feminism and Critical Theory*, ed. Elizabeth Meese and Alice Parker, 165–87. Philadelphia: John Benjamins, 1989.

———. "Mama's Baby, Papa's Maybe: An American Grammar Book." *diacritics* 17 (1987):65–81.

———. "Interstices: A Small Drama of Words." In *Pleasure and Danger: Exploring Female Sexuality*, ed. Carole S. Vance, 73–100. Boston: Routledge and Kegan Paul, 1984.

Spurlin, William J. "Theorizing Signifyin(g) and the Role of the Reader: Possible Directions for African-American Literary Criticism." *College English* 52.7 (1990):732–42.

Stallybrass, Peter, and Allon White. *The Politics and Poetics of Transgression*. Ithaca, N.Y.: Cornell University Press, 1986.

Stanton, William. *The Leopard's Spots: Scientific Attitudes Toward Race in America 1815–1859*. Chicago: University of Chicago Press, 1960.

Starkey, Marion. "Jessie Fauset." *Southern Workman* 61 (May 1932):217–20.

Stephenson, Gilbert Thomas. *Race Distinctions in American Law*. 1910. New York: Negro Universities Press, 1969.

Sterling, Dorothy, ed. *We Are Your Sisters: Black Women in the Nineteenth Century*. New York: W. W. Norton, 1984.

Still, William. Introduction to *Iola Leroy or Shadows Uplifted*. 1892. London: Oxford University Press, 1988.

———. *The Underground Railroad*. 1872. New York, Arno Press, 1968.

Stoddard, Lothrop. *The Rising Tide of Color Against White World-Supremacy*. New York: Scribner's, 1920.

Stoler, Ann Laura. "Racial Histories and Their Regimes of Truth." *Political Power and Social Theory* 11 (1997):183–255.

"Story of Ellen Crafts." *Wisconsin Free Democrat*, 11 July 1849.

Sylvander, Carolyn Wedin. *Jessie Redmon Fauset, Black American Writer*. Troy: Whitston, 1981.

Tate, Claudia. *Domestic Allegories of Political Desire: The Black Heroine's Text at the Turn of the Century*. New York: Oxford University Press, 1992.

Toll, William. *The Resurgence of Race: Black Social Theory from Reconstruction to the Pan-African Conferences*. Philadelphia: Temple University Press, 1979.

Turner, Victor. "Liminality and the Performative Genres." In *Rite, Drama, Festival, Spectacle: Rehearsals Toward a Theory of Cultural Performance*, ed. John J. MacAloon, 19–40. Philadelphia: Institute for the Study of Human Issues, 1984.

Tyler, Carole-Anne "Passing: Narcissism, Identity, and Difference." *differences: A Journal of Feminist Cultural Studies* 6.2&3 (1994):212–48.

"Views of American Slavery." *Aberdeen Journal*, 12 February 1851.

Wald, Gayle. *Crossing the Line: Racial Passing in Twentieth-Century U.S. Literature and Culture*. Durham, N.C.: Duke University Press, 2000.

Wall, Cheryl A. "Response to 'Performing Blackness: Re/Placing Afro-American Poetry'" by Kimberly W. Benston. In *Afro-American Literary Study in the 1990s*, ed. Houston A. Baker Jr. and Patricia Redmond, 185–90. Chicago: University of Chicago Press, 1989.

———. "Passing for What? Aspects of Identity in Nella Larsen's Novels." *Black American Literature Forum* 20 (1986):97–111.

Washington, Mary Helen. Introduction to *A Voice From the South, by a Black Woman of the South*, by Anna Julia Cooper. 1892. In Gates, *The Schomburg Library of Nineteenth-Century Black Women Writers*, xxvii–liv.

Weinauer, Ellen M. "'A Most Respectable Looking Gentleman': Passing, Possession, and Transgression in *Running a Thousand Miles for Freedom*." In Ginsberg, *Passing and the Fictions of Identity*, 37–56.

Welter, Barbara. "The Cult of True Womanhood 1820–1860." In *Dimity Convictions: The American Woman in the Nineteenth Century*, 21–41. Athens: Ohio University Press, 1976.

Weston, Anne Warren, to Deborah Weston. 13 July 1842. Gorton. MS A.9.2.17.82. Weston Papers, Boston Public Library.

Wexler, Laura. "Tender Violence: Literary Eavesdropping, Domestic Fiction, and Educational Reform." In Samuels, *The Culture of Sentiment*, 9–38.

"What Miss Remond Has Effected in Warrington." *Anti-Slavery Advocate*, 1 April 1859.

Wiegman, Robyn. *American Anatomies: Theorizing Race and Gender*. Durham, N.C.: Duke University Press, 1995.

"William and Ellen Craft." *Anti-Slavery Standard*, 8 February 1849.

Williams, George W. *History of the Negro Race in America, 1619–1880*. 2 vols. New York: Arno Press, 1968.

Williams, Patricia J. *The Alchemy of Race and Rights*. Cambridge: Harvard University Press, 1991.

Williamson, Joel. *New People: Miscegenation and Mulattoes in the United States*. New York: Free Press, 1980.

Wintz, Cary D. *Culture and the Harlem Renaissance*. Houston: Rice University Press, 1988.

Wirth, Louis, and Herbert Goldhamer. "The Hybrid and the Problem of Miscegenation." In *Characteristics of the American Negro*, ed. Otto Klineberg, 249–369. New York: Harper & Row, 1944.

Woods, E. M. *The Negro in Etiquette: A Novelty*. St. Louis: Buxton & Skinner, 1899.

Worth, Robert F. "*Nigger Heaven* and the Harlem Renaissance." *African American Review* 29 (1995):461–73.

Yarborough, Richard. Introduction to *Contending Forces: A Romance Illustrative of Negro Life North and South*. 1899. In Gates, *The Schomburg Library of Nineteenth-Century Black Women Writers*, xxvii–xlviii.

Yee, Shirley J. *Black Women Abolitionists: A Study in Activism, 1828–1860*. Knoxville: University of Tennessee Press, 1992.

Yellin, Jean Fagan. *Women and Sisters: The Antislavery Feminists in American Culture*. New Haven, Conn.: Yale University Press, 1989.

Young, Robert J. C. *Colonial Desire: Hybridity in Theory, Culture and Race*. New York: Routledge, 1995.

Index

CPSIA information can be obtained at www.ICGtesting.com
Printed in the USA
LVOW11s1811171214

419284LV00003B/715/P